Real Law@Virtual Space

Communication Regulation in Cyberspace

Second Edition

The Hampton Press Communication Series
Communication and Law

Susan J. Drucker, Supervisory Editor

Free Expression in Five Democratic Publics:
  Support for Individual and Media Rights
    Julie L. Andsager, Robert O. Wyatt, and *Ernest L. Martin*

Freedom, Democracy, and Responsibility:
  The Selected Works of Franklyn S. Haiman
    Franklyn S. Haiman

Outsiders Looking In:
  A Communication Perspective on the Hill/Thomas Hearings
    Paul Siegel (ed.)

Real Law@Virtual Space:
  Communication Regulation in Cyberspace
  Second Edition
    Susan J. Drucker and *Gary Gumpert (eds.)*

forthcoming

Emerging Law on the Electronic Frontier
    Anne Wells Branscomb (ed.)

The First Amendment: Theoretical Perspectives
    Joseph J. Hemmer

RealLaw@Virtual Space

Communication Regulation in Cyberspace

Second Edition

Susan J. Drucker
Hofstra University

Gary Gumpert
Communication Landscapers

HAMPTON PRESS, INC.
CRESSKILL, NEW JERSEY

Printed in the United States of America

Library of Congress Cataloging-in-Publication Data

Real law@virtual space : communication regulation in cyberspace /
  [edited by] Susan J. Drucker, Gary Gumpert. --2nd ed.
        p. cm. -- (The Hampton Press communication series.
        Communication and law)
      Includes bibliographic references and index.
      ISBN 1-57273-551-1 (cl) -- ISBN 1-57273-552-X (p)
      1. Information superhighway--Law and legislation. 2. Computer
networks--Law and legislation. 3. Internet. 4. Cyberspace. I. Title: Real
law at virtual space. II. Drucker, Susan J. III. Gumpert, Gary. IV. Series

K564.C6R43 2004
343.09'944--dc22

                                                          2004060605

Hampton Press, Inc.
23 Broadway
Cresskill, NJ 07626

Contents

Preface

Most volumes have a preface, because the authors or editors have some preliminary remarks to make outside the scope of the body of the book. The first preface for a volume is much easier to write than one for a second edition, but in the case of *Real Law@Virtual Space: Communication Regulation in Cyberspace* there are comments that need to be made beyond those stated in the previous volume.

There are two points that need to be made: one stating the obvious and the other reflecting a moral and ethical position. Cyberspace continues to evolve at a furious rate in terms of adoption and technological developments. In the 5 years since the first edition of this volume was published there has been an ever-growing migration of users to cyberspace. From toddlers to seniors, the World Wide Web ensnares more and more people. Daily activities and social engagements are being reconfigured or moved online. Children rattle off their favorite URL addresses. Businesses seem to require a Web site to attain legitimacy. Banking, diplomacy, commerce, education, government, medicine, and shopping all continue to gravitate toward cyberspace. The distinctions between life online and off blur. The pace is rapid and regulators, legislators, lawyers, and law enforcement officers struggle to keep up with that pace.

The second point is an expression of concern written from the perspective of Americans who are Constitutional zealots. The impact of 9/11 and the Iraq war on the regulation of the Internet and cyberspace is almost impossible to assess, because of the convoluted and fragmented nature of the U.S.A. Patriot Act, the Homeland Security Act, and subsequent executive branch actions. It is, however, clear that U.S. action is linked to the current media landscape. Law enforcement initiatives and regulations reveal a full understanding and appreciation of the power of Internet if not full respect for rights of communicators in cyberspace.

We thank the authors for their thought-provoking and timely contributions. To a person they have been a pleasure to work with. We thank our publisher for support and understanding. Our special appreciation goes to our families who once again prove what it means to say "without whom not." Most of all, we wish to acknowledge the U.S. Constitution, and even those who seek to violate it; the communication technological inventions that continually confound it; the judges, lawyers and netizens who are building a body of new law and keep communication scholars off the street.

SJD   GG

Great Neck, New York

October 2004

Preface to the First Edition

One scenario suggests that the technology of the internet was developed in order to keep legislators, judges, and lawyers busy for the next several decades. The impact of a new communication technology provides the opportunity for old regulations to be reshaped and revitalized in their impact upon the future. There is something about the process of communication that attracts administrative and regulatory zealots. Make no mistake about it, communication is the compelling factor and pressure which magnifies the efforts to regulate, restrain, and shape the accelerating technology of the Internet. The problems and social and ethical concerns of any new technology can be immense, but those of the Internet are almost incomprehensive-because of the uniquely converging and pervasive nature of the medium. Within the medium you will discover one medium enclosed within another enclosed within another. We listen to the radio, read the newspaper, order books, wine, and groceries, shop for homes, administer our bank accounts, pay our bills, watch television and films, send e-mail, manuscripts, and pictures to one another, and we globally connect and send musical greeting cards to those we love.

But how does one write and publish *Real Law@Virtual Space* quickly enough to avoid the calamity of publishing a tome that could be outmoded, out-of-touch, out-of-date the moment it appears in print? The cases, attempts at regulation, and philosophical debates about such control and oversight or the denial of restraint and restrictions, erupt with daily certainty. The *New York Times* on June 28, 1998 proclaimed that the "Internet is New Pet Issue of Congress." More than 300 bills were being considered by the 105th Congress In 1998.

The Internet with its influence on everything from commerce and national security to privacy and crime, has become an issue as politically alluring to many lawmakers as cutting taxes, educating children and locking up criminals. It seems that not a week goes by on Capital Hill without a hearing, a meeting or a gathering about one of a bevy of Internet-related issues confronting Congress. (Alvarez, 1998)

In the short time between the completion of this volume and putting finishing touches to the galley proofs, the Internet Tax Freedom Act and the Digital Millennium Copyright Act were signed into law as was the Child On Line Protection Act. We confess to having the television on in the background while writing this preface and as we wrote, CNN reported that the Federal Communications had just announced that it was considering a regulation which would alter the rate that could be charged for online access to the Internet, allowing telephone companies to charge more than for local calls. The reporter warns-stay tuned.

The topics and subject proliferate: online marketing practices, privacy gambling on the Internet, encryption, pornography, Fair Trade, Pedophilia, junk-E-Mail, anti-trust action, violation of civil rights, copyright infringement, media mergers, filtering software-the list is endless. And the complexity is compounded by global attempts to regulate the Internet. Thus the development and impact of the European Union Is grossly underestimated by most Americans. The imposition by the European Union of a new basically laissez-Faire privacy law contrasts sharply with the approach taken by the U.S. administration.

We have inherited a judicial heritage rooted in the quest for equality, justice, and constitutionality. It is a bequest that Is not to be taken lightly or ever to be taken for granted. Therefore, the editors wish to thank not only our immediate family members, collaborators, mentors, and our publisher, but also a system of justice that we have inherited and to which we hope *Real Law@Virtual Space* contributes in some small degree to that tradition.

SJD   GG
Great Neck, New York
June, 1999

REFERENCES

Alvarez. L. (1998, June 28). Internet is new pet issue in Congress. *The New York Times* web site: archives.nytimes.comarchives/search/ fastweb?search.

1

Legal Geography

The Borders of Cyberlaw
Introduction

Susan J. Drucker
Hofstra University

Gary Gumpert
Communication Landscapers

It cannot be helped, it is as it should be, that the law is behind the times.

— Oliver Wendell Holmes

The one constant discovered when exploring the evolution of media law is that technologies develop more rapidly than the concomitant legal framework. So, governments around the world are faced with challenges to existing laws and for some, perceived threats from new electronic sources and the need to "protect children, thwart terrorists and silence racists and hate mongers" ("Silencing the Net," 1996, p. 1). This is the way the first edition of *Real Law@Virtual Space* began in 1999. A great deal has happened in the world and in the regulatory landscape of cyberspace since then, but the statement remains a true reflection of the realities of today. The first edition was written about a nascent medium and the body of law beginning to emerge from it. It explored the regulatory developments of cyberspace during its formative period in which we emphasized the widening gap between new technologies and old laws. This second edition reflects the maturation of the new media environment brought on by the Internet. A body of legislative measures and case law can now be traced to reveal patterns of jurisprudential wisdom. The first edition provided an introduction to approaches to regulation, particularly from the perspective of initiatives and reactions within the legal system of the United States. Specifically, it addressed the earliest forays into the unique legal challenges raised by traditional areas of civil and criminal law brought into cyberspace. Libel, copyright, intellectual property, obscenity, pornography, sexual harassment, privacy, criminality and jurisdictional issues were considered. In the intervening years more people have migrated to live, in part, lives in cyberspace. Simultaneously, the Internet has been at the heart of the convergence of communication media. Convergence has come to be associated with the super-imposition of one medium on the platform of another medium. Digitalization is at the heart of convergence with the Internet being the primary transmission medium or platform. The convergence of technology has led to the need for regulatory convergence. Although some questions have been addressed, many others, perhaps more complex, emerge daily as a result of convergence. This second edition also reflects the new reality of a post September 11th world. Where security in cyberspace was identified as a key concern underlying much early policy and regulation, today, it assumes an ever more elevated place on the regulatory agenda particularly as it is embedded within legislation responding to the threats of global terrorism (i.e., USA Patriot Act, Homeland Security Act, etc.).

Today there are many "cyberlawyers" who have hung out their shingles, and growing precedent through which to anticipate and view judicial decision making. Subspecialties of cyberlaw have developed in internet service provider (ISP) law, digital copyright law, and cybercrime. Yet fundamental questions remain raised in the first volume remain:

- If the uses (the informational and social substance) of communication have not changed, are *new* legal *rules* and *procedures* called for by the transmission of such substance by convergent technologies of communication?
- Do technological advances require rethinking *legal principles* that have existed for previous modalities?
- What is the relationship of self-regulation and the new regulatory schema that may at times transcend traditional jurisdictions?

- Does the global nature of the Internet form a separate legal jurisdiction?

This volume addresses public and private regulations and restrictions of computer-mediated communication (CMC) in the realm of online communication and the Internet. For purposes of this volume, we use the popular term *cyberspace* to encompass a variety of forms of CMC ranging from mass communication to interpersonal interaction. The term is attributed to science fiction author William Gibson who coined it in the 1980s. *Cyberspace* was described in Gibson's *Neuromancer* "where it names a 21st century virtual dimension, entered into via a neuro-electronic interface, in which the world's data networks unfold before the user as a sensually vivid geography" (Gibson, 1984, p. 5). As traditional media distinctions crumble, converging technologies challenge established laws and policies. "The digitization of information enables online transmission of services that can substitute for newspapers, books, magazines, catalogs, records, film, audio and videotape, radio, television and telephone" (Stuckey, 1996, p. ix) as well as written memoranda and personal notes. Lance Rose (personal communication, March 6, 1996), an attorney specializing in high-tech and information law noted, "there is no one coherent thing known as 'cyberspace.' It's a whole bunch of different shared communication realms, each with its own sense of space and its own structure. The term 'cyberspace,' ultimately, is no more than a convenient way of saying 'everything on the other side of the screen of a net connected electronic device'" (Rose, 1996).

Each form of communication often raises troubling and unresolved legal and ethical dilemmas. Among the forms of communication that are encompassed in various conceptualizations of cyberspace are the following:

- *Internet*—Called the "network of networks" (Stuckey, 1996, p. xvi), the Internet is often erroneously used as a synonym with the term *cyberspace*. The Internet began in 1969 as a US Defense Department network called the Advanced Research Project Agency (ARPnet). It was opened to academic use at the same time as commercial services were introduced sometime between 1979-81 (Stuckey, 1996) and slowly, corporations, universities and information providers phased and dovetailed their networks into the system agreeing on compatible connecting software or a set of standard network protocols called "TCP/IP," which led to the expansion of the Internet. TCP/IP is the Transport Control Protocol/Internet Protocol that takes any data and converts it into packets. The standard programming language, hypertext markup language (HTML), arrived in 1994 laying the foundation for the Internet application known as the "World Wide Web." The Internet is an Internet Provider

(IP) network providing diverse services. E-mail is an IP service (simple message transfer protocol [SMTP]) that utilizes the Internet as its transport, as is Instant Messaging or Internet Relay Chat (IRC).

- *Cyberspace*—Cyberspace is the aspatial construct, the psychological space visited by users of the Internet. The amorphous nature of cyberspace makes regulation improbable if not impossible. Distinguishable from cyberspace is the Internet, which is the infrastructure consisting of nodes, routers, gateways, paths, and so on. This distinction, often neglected when considering regulatory challenges, makes the Internet more definable and therefore more regulable than cyberspace.
- *The Web*: The "Web" refers to the thousands of host computers and servers interconnected through the Internet, featuring graphical sites called "home pages," which feature graphics, HTML or highlighted text, and "hot links" that provide ease in interlocking sites globally, allowing one to browse or "surf" many sites. Web browsers operating on a "point-and-click" basis have fueled the enormous growth of the Internet. The Web allows for the display of text, images, sound and video. *Commercial online services* such as America Online (AOL), CompuServe, and Prodigy provide content and organization and now incorporate Web browsers. The number of Internet users is growing at rates difficult to keep to date. According to Netree Internet Statistics (1997), an online statistics generator, there were 99,264,180 people on the Internet as of January 1997. There are more than 160 countries reported to have links to the Internet, more than 100 nations with full access and some through E-mail ("Silencing the Net," 1996). The "Web" is another IP service (HTTP) that uses the Internet as its transport.

A distinction is made between open and closed systems (Stuckey, 1996). When introduced in 1979, online services were completely closed—consisting of consumer time sharing, using applications that users could access, managed by a single provider. Then gateways were established that provided access to information and applications residing on third-party systems. The shift to open online services using the Internet emerged and grew.

One of the distinctive characteristics common to cyberspace is the interactive nature of communication. *Interactivity* and *nonlinearity* mean that the end user may determine the sequence, timing, and repetitions of the work and may include the option to "talk back" or submit information or comments. Access to data and interaction come on an "on-demand" basis and "enables a customized experience for users that is interactive. Users can control what information they see, and direct their communications to specific individuals or groups of any size, In this way, this technology is characterized as offering "'mass customization' or a 'de-massifying' media and potentially, the economy in general" (Stuckey, 1996, p. x). It has been said to be a truly "mass medium" more threatening than earlier media given that a personal computer and modem offer fairly inexpensive, accessible means of reaching enormous international audiences. Online technology provides opportunities for the disenfranchised to voice their political arguments, for example, as no medium ever before. Yet, one-to-one global interpersonal communication opportunities are also available. In some situations, even real-time interaction is possible.

The Internet has become a medium that increasingly serves as a platform for other media, carrying not only its own connection and content, but facilitating the connections of other media (e.g., the telephone) and carrying the content of print and electronic mass media. This convergence is manifested in so many different ways that it is becoming transparent with users becoming desensitized to it and regulators remaining confounded by it. Convergence raises many issues with regard to regulation ranging from "can there be regulation?" to "should there even be regulation?" Debates rage over the amount of regulation and user control and choice. The Internet is a global communications medium. Decentralized, flexible, and user-controlled, it is particularly suitable to the promotion of pluralism, freedom of expression, and access to public information but convergence is also characterized by the coming together of previously unrelated technologies, leading to a scramble for market leadership and to further media concentration. The industry trend toward vertical integration and concentration of media ownership, in the United States and throughout the world, is fueled by the transition to digital format of virtually all media and forms of communication.

SOURCES OF CYBERLAW

Whether at the forefront of cyberspace connection or faced with establishing initial e-mail connection, governments around the globe are faced with considering appropriate policies and applying or drafting laws and regulations addressing fundamental economic, political, social, and religious/moral issues.

Sources of law range from the formal to the informal, from action taken between individuals and private concerns to regulatory actions taken by state authorities, from action taken by local governments, to legislative action taken by nation-states, to international accords to the creation of a separate and distinct cyberspace jurisdiction. In a special issue of the *Journal of Computer Mediated Communication*, Oberdiny and Norderhaug (1996) argued that one way in which cyberspace will be regulated is through the creation and enforcement of community norms. Oberding and Norderhaug noted that bulletin board (BB) operators often oversee postings and may disconnect or unsubscribe "troublemakers" (p. 12). They find self-regulation emerging from the cybercommunities forming online.

> Online communities clearly maintain community norms and have the ability to create and enforce rights and responsibilities. Offenders are censored if they breach commonly accepted rules. The Internet contains a high number of communities that make and enforce individual rules and obligation. (n. p.)

Norms and rules of conduct in the cybercommunity simply reflect that laws embody the norms of a society and make enforceable the principles of morality on which a community organizes (see Chapter 16, this volume). Through the law, values become the final, authoritative, and enforceable disposition of conflict (Katsch, 1988).[1]

Contracts between parties provide another source of enforceable behavioral norms, restrictions, and restraints. For example, Internet service providers, those providing access to the Internet, Intranet, or E-mail, often provide explicit service agreements to be entered into or, in the employment or university setting, may distribute guidelines for use of systems seen as a revocable opportunity for access. Private service providers including Prodigy, Compuserve, and AOL, which under the contract with customers to deliver service, make specific reference to appropriate behaviors and delineate rights of providers and users. For instance, Codes of Conduct included in the AOL Terms of Service Agreement states:

> some common violations of the Terms of Service. This list is not exhaustive. AOL Inc. reserves the right, but does not assume the responsibility, to restrict communication which AOL Inc. deems in its discretion to be harmful to individual Members, damaging to the communities which make up the AOL Service, or in violation of AOL Inc.'s or any third-party rights. Please be aware, however, that communication over the AOL Service often occurs in real-time, or is posted on one of the AOL Service's thousands of message boards or libraries, and AOL Inc. cannot, and does not intend to, screen communication in advance.

> If you witness chat in a public chat room that violates AOL's Terms of Service, you may contact an AOL Service Guide by using the keyword

"Guide Pager." You may also contact AOL's Terms of Service Staff about any violation by using the "Write to the Terms of Service Staff" icon located in the Terms of Service area of the Member's Online Support department.

C. Online Conduct.

(a) Any conduct by you that in AOL Inc.'s discretion restricts or inhibits any other Member from using or enjoying AOL will not be permitted and may result in termination of Membership. You agree to use AOL only for lawful purposes. You may not post or use AOL to:

(1) harass, threaten, embarrass or cause distress, unwanted attention or discomfort on another Member or user of AOL or other person or entity, (2) post or transmit sexually explicit images or other content which is deemed by AOL Inc. to be offensive, (3) transmit any unlawful, harmful, threatening, abusive, harassing, defamatory, vulgar, obscene, hateful, racially, ethnically or otherwise objectionable Content, (4) cause the screen to "scroll" faster than other Members or users are able to type to it or any action to a similar disruptive effect, (5) impersonate any person, including but not limited to, an AOL Inc. official or an information provider, forum leader, guide or host, or communicate under a false name or a name that you are not entitled or authorized to use, (6) disrupt the normal flow of dialogue in a chat room or otherwise act in a manner that negatively affects other Members, users, individuals or entities, (7) post or transmit chain letters or pyramid schemes, (8) post or transmit any unsolicited advertising, promotional materials, or other forms of solicitation to other Members, individuals or entities, except in those areas (e.g., the classified areas) that are designated for such a purpose, (9) violate any operating rule, policy or guideline of any other interactive service, including but not limited to the operating policies of the International Areas, or (10) intentionally or unintentionally violate any applicable local, state, national or international law, including but not limited to any regulations having the force of law. . . . (for an extended listing of rules of conduct see endnote 5.[2]

Under such a contract, the service provider may claim the right to monitor not only publicly posted BB messages but person-to-person messages.[3,4,5]

Monitoring assumes not only potential loss of privacy but also presumably some sanctions for inappropriate behavior. CompuServe has expelled a number of users. "Users tend to feel quite territorial about the CompuServe forums . . . so our members are very much self-policing" (Wald, 1995, p. 4). At one time, Prodigy screened every message that members wanted to post on its BBs causing long delays in posting. As such, they began using a program called "The George Carlin Scanner" and the service has only "bounced a handful over the years" (Wald, 1995). Most services have warnings and some send warning copies directly to parents if children are found to violate appropriate behavior. In its "Terms of Service," AOL reserves the right to terminate service, leading to discontinuation for violation of these terms. Thus, a father reports having his service cut off when his child reportedly typed in inappropriate words on a made-for-children chatroom, an act noted and reported by a watchful AOL monitor.

The validity and enforcability for such so-called "shrink-wrap/point-and-click agreements" is being considered by legal experts and courts alike. Such agreements are generally standardized written agreements used to create and structure relationships between companies and customers with standard terms and conditions promulgated, appearing online in the customer's initial session. These predetermined contract terms and conditions, which are not negotiated by parties are sometimes marketed as "self-executing" when there is no direct contact between contracting parties and the vendor or service provider attempts to impose standard terms on the product.[6]

A distinction must be made between regulation via community standards, express or implied contract terms, and the standards imposed by governmental entities. Regulatory action has been taken or explored by states and nations and internationally negotiated accords. Most attempts to define new rules for the development of cyberspace ultimately rely on weakening or disintegrating concepts of territory while ignoring the new network and technological borders that transcend state and national boundaries The global information infrastructure potentially undermines substantive legal sovereignty.

JURISDICTION

One of the fundamental and troubling questions that impacts on individual rights is simply "which laws govern behavior in an aspatial world of connection rather than a environment characterized by propinquity?"[5] Jurisdiction, the power and authority of a court to hear and adjudicate a given case, is a fundamental concept of law, which has historically been based on geographic area (*Black's Law Dictionary*, 1979, p. 766).

Information flow has long been on the international agenda but never with more complexities than in the age of convergence. The Internet, perhaps more than any other medium, has been said to render traditional terrestrial borders meaningless. It is generally accepted that some degree of regulation is required if the Internet is to operate and grow. Although rationale, areas of regulation, and the form those regulations take are debatable, nondebatable is that the responsibility and legal parameters of jurisdiction are shifting from the proximate local to any site removed from spatial constraints. Does site of transmission or site of reception determine jurisdiction? Jurisdiction, geographically/territorially based terms, is undermined when borders become transparent, easily permeable and often imperceptible. Jurisdiction claimed by nation-states has been called into question. The earliest phase of exploring regulatory approaches to the Internet was characterized by efforts to govern the "new frontier," "the chaotic," "and the ungovernable." The claim was made that governments could not regulate cyberspace and therefore cyberspace was unavoidably free. We are now in a subsequent or second phase of regulation characterized by the search for pragmatic approaches to regulation. Stanford law Professor Lawrence Lessig sees this phase of Internet regulation emerging from an alliance of commerce and government. Lessig (1999) argued that, rather than direct content-based regulation, it will be through the regulation of the architecture of software and hardware that a system will develop.

It has been suggested that various ways to implement rules (choice of law rules) to the Internet would include the following:

- Creation of a forum selection agreement clause between contracting parties;
- No-Man's Land, where no applicable law of any land would apply in cyberspace, therefore the applicable law would be the law of the forum where a suit is brought;
- Law merchant—rules evolving from the customs and practice of merchants applicable to all countries meaning a system of self-regulation on the Internet would be created.

Diverse suggestions with regard to regulation have led some legal thinkers to advocate that cyberspace be conceptualized as a "place" rather than a medium with its own constitution on which to base a developing body of applicable law.[7]

A SEPARATE CYBER-JURISDICTION?

The meaning of jurisdiction is complex when the legal significance of borders is blurred, when the victim may be located in different countries or states and the threshold question of personal jurisdiction that, whether the person would anticipate being brought into the specific court for a lawsuit, is so difficult to answer. Some leading thinkers advocate that cyberspace be considered a "place," rather than a medium, with its own constitution on which to base a developing body of applicable law and self-regulatory systems (Stuckey, 1996, p. xxiii). One reaction to efforts to regulate cyberspace came in the form of a Declaration of Independence "from a political body holding no jurisdiction or authority over transactions occurring throughout Cyberspace" (Cyberspace Declaration, 1996). The Cyberspace Declaration of Independence declares cyberspace an autonomous zone and begins:

> We have no elected government, nor are we likely to have one, so I address you with no greater authority than that with which liberty itself always speaks. I declare the global social space we are building to be naturally independent of the tyrannies you seek to impose on us. You have no moral right to rule us nor do you possess any methods of enforcement we have true reason to fear. Governments derive their just powers from the consent of the governed. You have neither solicited nor received ours. We did not invite you. You do not know us, nor do you know our world. Cyberspace does not lie within your borders. Do not think that you can build it, as though it were a public construction project. You cannot. It is an act of nature and it grows itself through our collective actions. (Cyberspace Declaration, 1996)

Another approach to surmounting the issues of border-based jurisdiction has been via the regulation of the architecture of the Internet rather than content or access.[8] Whatever the approach, the past 5 years have seen worldwide consideration and action, from formal to informal, from governmental to private enterprise, from individual to multinational, from multinational governmental to multinational nongovernmental, from global to local. Rulers and legislators, nation-states, promulgate rules; issue ordinances that attempt to carve out cyberlaws as they would telecommunication laws.

Undeterred by the daunting issues of jurisdiction, governments around the world have jumped into the regulatory arena, attempting to address diverse issues arising in and from cyberspace and the Internet, whereas just a few have addressed the complexities of true convergent technologies and industries in their policies and regulations. Censorship, firewalls, filtering, and restrictive access policies have been approaches used to regulate Internet growth in the Middle East and North Africa, China, Singapore, and other nations. The State Council in China issued a draft set of rules to regulate use of the Internet; subscribers were ordered to provide a written guarantee that they would not use the Internet for purposes "harmful to the state." It has been said that China is trying to erect boundaries between "China's cyberspace" and "foreign cyberspaces" and between online political communication and apolitical discussions. The government has blocked popular search engines such as Google and prevailed on Western companies such as Yahoo! to voluntarily restrict their Web content in China. In one U.S. study, China was found to be blocking 19,000 Web sites including those providing news, health information, political coverage, and entertainment (Festa, 2003). In Singapore, there have been protests against restrictive government Internet policies (Ang, 1997; Rodan, 1998). Protests have occurred against the Indonesian government's arrests related to online communication (Hill & Sen, 2000). Because the Internet dramatically empowers people to exercise their right to seek, receive, or impart information regardless of frontiers, some governments have chosen from a variety of techniques to restrict the flow of information online. Saudi Arabia, Yemen, and the United Arab Emirates impose censorship via proxy servers, devices that are interposed between the end-user and the Internet in order to filter and block specified content. In many countries, including Jordan, taxation and telecommunications policies keep Internet accounts quite costly and thus beyond the means of many (Kalathil & Boas, 2001; Study of Media Laws and Polices in the Middle East & Maghreb, 2003).

Tunisia has enacted the region's most detailed Internet-specific legislation, which is in large part designed to ensure that online speech does not escape the government's tough controls on critical speech in other media. In the majority of countries where Internet-specific laws have not been enacted, legal or de facto constraints on freedom of speech and of the press have a chilling effect on what is expressed online, especially in public forums like open BBs and chatrooms (online discussions where participants communicate in real time). And in a region where many governments routinely tap the phones of dissidents, Internet users in many countries, including Bahrain and Tunisia, suspect that the right to privacy of correspondence is being violated by government surveillance of E-mail. One Bahraini spent more than a year in jail on suspicion of E-mailing "political" information to dissidents abroad ("Freedom of Expression," 2003).

According to Henry H. Perritt, Jr., dean of Chicago-Kent College of Law, "If a Web site is accessible to all, and is subject to jurisdiction by every nation on earth, then the law of the lowest common denominator nation will govern the Internet. . . . On the other hand if we say that the only important law is the one where the content provider resides, then local values of foreign nations will not be enforced. We also run the risk of creating havens for shyster practices" (Kaplan, 2000). The vexing questions of jurisdiction are illustrated by a case heard in French courts in 2000 involving French authorities seeking to require Yahoo Inc., an American company, to limit French citizens from accessing Nazi artifacts on an auction site available throughout the world. Yahoo! was sued by the International League Against Racism and Anti-Semitism and the French Union of Jewish Students. A French judge issued a ruling that was effectively a prior restraint against a foreign Internet company. French law forbids the display in France of Nazi souvenirs for the purpose of sale. Furthermore, Judge Jean-Jacques Gomez of the Superior Court of Paris noted the online expo-

sition of Nazi artifacts in France is "an offense against the collective memory of a country profoundly wounded by the atrocities committed by and in
the name of the Nazi criminal enterprise" (Kaplan, 2000). Yahoo! asked the
California court for relief from a restrictive French court order that would
have limited Yahoo!'s ability to publish on the global Internet. The French
court ordered Yahoo! to limit the display of Nazi memorabilia and images
on Yahoo!-hosted sites in the United States—displays that are illegal in
France, but are protected by the First Amendment in America. On
November 8, 2001, the California court's judgment affirmed Yahoo!'s right
to publish online, and it was argued that this set an important precedent for
online speech worldwide and the openness of the Internet. Some critics feel
this was not a major victory because the California court would not have
enforced a foreign judgment anyway. This was not the first, or only occa-
sion when the question of extra-territorial jurisdiction over Web content
has been at issue.

Not surprisingly, the two major players in the regulation of the new
telecommunications and cyber-environments are the United States and the
European Union (EU). Given the two distinct regulatory and market environments from which these two approach the task, it is not surprising that
there has been much disagreement. U.S. regulatory policies are influenced
by Constitutional guarantees of free speech and press that shape the
requirements and limitations placed on government regulation and policies.
Emerging policies are molded by the dictates of the First Amendment to
the U.S. Constitution. Regulation has been framed as a matter of public
policy with individual freedoms and the concept of "the public interest"
influencing public intervention. This is not to suggest that the United States
has ignored the economic sector addressing taxation and customs, intellectual property protection, privacy, security, content, a Uniform Commercial
Code for Electronic Commerce and Internet governance (Wasserman,
1998).

In the EU, media law reform is "traditionally presented as a shift from
Regulation to Competition (law)" (Nihoul 1998/1999, p. 2). Emphasis has
been placed on the convergence of not only technology but of economic
sectors of broadcasting, information, and telecommunications (Blackman &
Nihoul, 1998). The EU has alleged that the notion of "public interest" is
vague and overbroad (Aragón, 1999). The EU places market issues in the
foreground of regulatory analysis and activity (Gumpert & Drucker, 2001).

The array of legislation from the EU to police the setting up, transmission, content, and advertising of online services risks deterring potential
operators. They also have to consider what technical norms to use for payments and threats from holders of copyright material. U.S. policy under the
Clinton administration was ultimately altered to provide for trade with the
EU[9] (see Chapter 14, this volume). Content regulation reveals tensions in

approaches between regulatory leaders. Under interpretation of the U.S. Constitution, protection of noncommercial free speech is afforded the greatest protection from government regulation, so the United States has advocated a system of self-regulation in terms of content, promoting the importance and effectiveness of parental controls and other filtering devices to block some Internet sites. "Here the United States is protecting its very broad principles of freedom of speech that are protected by the First Amendment. Especially, if the Internet is regarded as a public forum rather than as a forum for commercial speech" (Aragón 1999). Constitutional requirements will continue to significantly influence all future regulations. Throughout the world, emphasis has been placed on rudimentary and pragmatic concerns including privacy, taxation, intellectual property rights, pornography/morality, secured transactions, harassment, defamation, and access.

Other Approaches to Regulation

Increasingly, regulatory activity has come in the form of international agreements, and the work of nongovernmental organizations (NGOs). International agreements to facilitate developments in communication media are not new. Since the early 19th century, governments have tried to establish an international regulatory regime for the trans-border flow of communication. In 1815, after the defeat of Napoleon, the powers of the Holly Alliance started negotiations toward a treaty that regulated the transport of printed materials across borders and gave governments the right to confiscate unwanted books and journals (Carlsbad Treaty). On May 17, 1865, following the invention of the telegraph, participating countries signed the first International Telegraph Convention and the International Telegraph Union was established. The motivation to forge an international agreement and standards remain today alongside new trends of globalization, deregulation, industry restructuring, and convergence (of services and technologies; International Telecommunication Union Overview, 2003;[10] Kleinwachter 1999). International agreements between nation-states have been an arena of increased activity focusing on specific areas such as copyright (i.e., 1996 agreement between 160 countries on an extension of international copyright law).

International organizations purporting to govern the Internet have received much attention. The Internet Corporation for Assigned Names and Numbers (ICANN), a nonprofit corporation formed under California law, was selected in 1998 by the U.S. Commerce Department to "take over administration of the Internet" from U.S. domination (Kleinwachter, 1999). ICANN was formed to assume responsibility for the IP address space allocation, protocol parameter assignment, domain name system management, and root server system management functions previously performed under U.S. government. It has been called the "Internet's new governing body" (Clausing, 1999, p. C17), but this has really referred to the very limited authority over the Internet domain name system and Internet standards.[11] It has been argued that ICANN has a technological rather than a political mandate, but the political, social, and economic implications cannot and should not be overlooked (Kleinwachter, 2000). The structure of ICANN as a private corporate entity is composed of 19 members of the board, 3 councils, and 2 advisory committees. The governmental role is an advisory one *through* the Government Advisory Committee *(GAC)* in which government representatives lobby ICANN members. By 2002, the president of ICANN, M. Stuart Lynn, called for a radical reconceptualization of ICANN, which would include a much-increased level of government involvement in ICANN, including raising the possibility of having national governments appoint to the ICANN Board of Trustees (ICANN, 2003).

Recognizing that with the global information infrastructure (GII), "territorial borders and substantive borders as key paradigms for regulatory governance disintegrate" (Reidenberg, 1996, p. 45), we see the need for fundamental and long-accepted concepts having to be reconsidered. Given the global nature of the Internet, the challenges to territorially based regulatory approaches, it is difficult to do justice to the legal landscape taking shape with regard to cyberspace by focusing on the laws of one nation. However, this volume is limited in its scope to the body of law developing in the United States.

The chapters to follow have been gathered to offer historical perspective, the current state of the law, and the principles and yardsticks that will shape future laws and judicial interpretations in the development of a body of "cyberlaw." Some of the authors cope with the lessons of history and existing regulatory approaches that lend themselves to application in CMC contexts (see Chapters 2, 3, 16) other authors examine the need for developing new rules (Chapters 1, 6, 7). Others evaluate situations in which existing laws are being applied to new developments and evolving medium resulting in a somewhat imperfect fit (see Chapters 4, 5, 9 – 12, 14, 15). The scope of this volume encompasses governmental and nongovernmental, commercial and personal, public and private sources of rights and limitations on those rights.

Part I provides an overview outlining the existing regulatory approaches currently being applied to the increasingly complex and frequent issues raised by emerging computer mediated options and activities. In Chapter 2, Jassem provides the historical context for the extension and/or creation of legal rules to new modes of distribution and interaction. He considers how emerging patterns of regulatory policy reflect significant changes in both policy and the media. He traces the results of the 1996 Telecommunications

Act identifying the operative regulatory philosophy prior to and since 1996. He explores how the U.S. regulatory/legal policy has been significantly affected as a result of economic, technological, and legislative changes.

Chapter 3 is reprinted from the original edition with an addendum provided re-evaluating guiding regulatory metaphors in light of the increasingly convergent nature of content transported via the Internet. We examine the dilemmas raised by the transition to postmodern media and the growing role of cyberspace in civic life. This chapter examines the application of the use of metaphors in the regulation of free speech laws and judicial decision. We examine the spatial terminology being applied to the aspatial realm of cyberspace and implications of those place-based metaphors emphasizing the need to re-evaluate appropriate metaphors given the fact that in part, cyberspace has become a locale for interaction vital to a democratic society and an alternative public forum.

Part II is devoted to an analysis of the regulation of indecency in cyberspace. History reveals that inevitably, new technologies raise concern over their use in the transmission of "indecent" materials, particularly to minors. From the printing press to photography, from musical recordings to movies, from telephone services to video games, sexually explicit content in diverse technological innovations have been the target of censorship and regulation so comes as no surprise that such material available via computer systems is a natural target. Attempts to regulate have, therefore, commonly sparked argument, debate, and deliberation of the legal issues and policy dimensions inherent in limiting sexually oriented materials. This section focuses on the repeated efforts to legislate a policy in the United States on a federal level beginning with the first *Communications Decency Act* (CDA) signed into law by President Clinton in February 1996 through the June 2003 decision supporting the filtering of Internet access in public libraries. It addresses the landmark ruling in *ACLU et al. V. Reno* and *American Library Association et al. v. Dept. of Justice,* in which the high court noted that the Internet is a unique medium entitled to the highest protection under the free speech protections of the First Amendment to the US Constitution, traces the Child Online Protection Act (COPA) known as CDA II, the more narrowly drafted law containing many of the same elements that ultimately led to the Supreme Court's ruling that the CDA was unconstitutional and the Children's Internet Protection Act (CHIPA), which requires public schools and libraries to install filtering systems on Internet computers to block objectionable Web sites.

The five chapters in this section examine these laws, legal challenges, and judicial decisions not only for what they suggest about the regulation of sexually oriented material, but for the larger lessons to be learned from direct attempts to regulate Internet communication. The section begins with Fraleigh's examination (Chapter 4) of different standards by which restrictions on the content of expression in cyberspace could be judged. This discussion is followed by Tuman's (Chapter 5) comparison of the CDA and COPA, examining how the legitimate governmental interest in shielding children from material "harmful to minors" considers what parental and governmental responsibilities toward children should be in cyberspace.

In Chapter 6, Freedman's argument against the "inside–outside" or "protected–unprotected" approach to diverse categories of speech is provided and then applied to the context of the CDA. Freedman's analysis of the general approach to communication freedoms within U.S. constitutional analysis places the CDA, the Child Pornography Protection Act of 1996 and the COPA of 1998 into an important conceptual framework applied even in times when the technologies of communication may be outrunning the legal mechanisms of control. Docter (Chapter 7) critiques the rationale for regulating indecent speech across various media. She examines policy alternatives concerning the regulation of indecent speech communicated via electronic communications. The section is rounded out by Hunter's analysis of the Internet filters and the First Amendment implications of mandated filtering in public libraries.

Part III deals with the property and ownership interests inherent in CMC. When approaching electronic reproduction, the legal implication, which emerges most prominently, is that of intellectual property. In an era in which Napster has become a household word, downloading a controversial but frequent activity, Fishman (Chapter 9) examines the implications of digitalization of images for copyright holders. Although much in this realm is undecided, the principle that copyrights apply to cyberspace (i.e., electronic digitalized media) has been established but troubling issues remain with regard to display rights and what constitutes copying. Fishman addresses questions such as the following: Does saving or using a file constitute copying? Does downloading a file result in a copy under copyright law? When is a work "fixed" in a tangible medium of expression meeting a U.S. standard for creative works eligible for copyright protections? This discussion is followed Colfin and Jacobson's (Chapter 10) examination of the copyright issues associated with music on the Internet. Considered are issues such as music licensing, the Digital Millennium Copyright Act, reproduction and distribution of music, public performance and recording of music, and what constitutes piracy. O'Connell (Chapter 11) and Dee (Chapter 13) both consider the legal implications of a fundamental feature of the Internet—linking. In Chapter 11, O'Connell considers how interactivity at the heart of the Internet raises legal issues from virtual trespass to unfair competition.

Personal liberties and interests are the subject of concern in the five chapters comprising Part IV. The right to one's good name is the subject of

Dale Herbeck's contribution (Chapter 12). Herbeck provides an analysis of Web sites and computer BB systems and the controversies surrounding prescreening and censorship in online postings. Herbeck focuses on the question of whether ISPs are legally responsible for third-party speech. In Chapter 13, Dee explores how linking potentially effects defamation online, exacerbating damages, and bringing to the fore issues of source liability.

In Chapter 14, we consider the personal right most associated with the conception of the protecting the individual—the right of privacy. Privacy is often conceptualized as "the right of the individual" to decide for him or herself how much he or she wishes to share with others in terms of thoughts, feelings, and facts of personal life. This chapter considers issues ranging from expectations of privacy in E-mail to anonymity in electronic communication, from associational privacy to encryption and electronic signatures. Online privacy in a post September 11th environment is examined as the U.S. Patriot Act, Terror Information Awareness program, and other security-driven initiatives are critically examined. This section is rounded out by an examination of penal law in cyberspace. In Chapter 15, Drucker traces four distinct types of criminal conduct making use of the Internet from those utilizing the Internet in the commission of a crime to virtual crimes indigenous to a computer environment like cyber-harassment. Substantive and procedural areas of criminal law are strained by terrorism, espionage, software piracy, fraud, forgery, illegal gambling, and even cyberstalking.

The volume concludes with a thought-provoking alternative to traditional regulatory approaches emanating from the legal system. Flynn and Chase (Chapter 16) trace the debate on approaches to regulation. They trace the arguments made by legal theorists who posit that the Internet is capable of self-regulation and the promise of "community-based regulation" given the nature of cyberspace. The authors then contrast this approach to the "code-based regulation" proposed by Lessig.

This volume addresses public and private regulations and restrictions, government regulations, and industry self-regulation. The chapters approach this subject of growing significance from multiple perspectives including legal, economic, social, and ethical approaches. The rights and restrictions governing CMC, particularly in the realm of online communication, Internet, or what is commonly referred to as cyberspace, are at a critical period. There is a growing literature concerning cyberlaw, a much richer field than when our first edition was published. We hope that this second edition of *Real Law@Virtual Space: Communication Regulation in Cyberspace* keeps pace and continues to contribute to the debate, understanding, and evolution of this exiting field of communication law.

NOTES

1. Laws provide the standards by which society may judge right and wrong and resolve disputes in a final and enforceable manner. According to legal philosopher Karl Llewellyn (1960), the prevention and settlement of conflict and dispute both appeal to law and make up the business of law.

2. The following extended information appears in the service provider's agreement posted online:

> (i) Offensive Communication. AOL is a community-oriented service composed of many different communities of people. Our goal is to provide an interesting, stimulating and fun place for all Members. Using vulgar, abusive or hateful language undermines this goal and is not allowed. Please use your best judgment and be respectful of other Members. Remember, there may be children online. If you use vulgar, or abusive language online, even if masked by symbols or other characters, you may either receive an "on-screen-warning" by a Guide or Room Host, or in some cases be terminated immediately. A warning indicates that your language is not in compliance with the TOS [terms of service] or ROR [Rules of the Road]. Should you receive such a warning, take the time to read the AOL Rules again, comprising the TOS and these ROR which you will find posted in the Members Services area.
>
> (ii) Harassment. When a Member targets another individual or entity to cause distress, embarrassment, unwanted attention, or other discomfort, this is harassment. AOL Inc. does not condone harassment in any form and may suspend or terminate the accounts of any Member who harasses others. You may have a disagreement with someone's point of view — we encourage lively discussion in our chat rooms and message boards — but personal attacks, or attacks based on a persons race, national origin, ethnicity, religion, gender, sexual orientation, disablement or other such affiliation, are prohibited. If you have a disagreement with someone's point of view, address the subject, not the person.
>
> (iii) Graphic Files. AOL Inc. prohibits the transfer or posting on AOL of sexually explicit images or other content deemed offensive by AOL Inc.
>
> (iv) Scrolling. "Scrolling" means repeatedly causing the screen to roll faster than Members are able to type to it. It is caused by a user entering a set of random characters or by repeatedly entering a carriage return or any such action to a similar disruptive effect. Scrolling is an expressly prohibited form of disruption.
>
> (v) Impersonation. This can involve the portrayal of another person or entity, such as the impersonation of AOL Inc. staff or an information provider, authorized Guide or Host, or communication under a false name or a name that you are not authorized to use.

Members must avoid the portrayal of AOL Inc. personnel or others persons in all forms of online communication, including, but not limited to, screen names, member profiles, chat dialogue and message postings.

(vi) Room Disruption. This includes purposefully interfering with the normal flow of dialogue in a chat room. Room disruption may occur by repeatedly interrupting conversation between Members, or by acting in such a way as to antagonize, harass or create hostility in a chat room . . .

(viii) Advertising and Solicitation. You may not use AOL to send unsolicited advertising, promotional material, or other forms of solicitation to other Members except in those specified areas that are designated for such a purpose (e.g., the classified area).

If you witness chat in a public chat room that violates the AOL Rules, you may contact an AOL Service Guide by using the keyword "Guide Pager." You may also contact AOL Inc.'s Terms of Service Staff about any violation by using the "Write to Terms of Service Staff" icon located in the TOS area of the Members Services area.

3. America Online Service Membership Subscriber Agreement, 1995.

4. The realm of electronic communication raises issues with regard to some of the most fundamental acts and within legal systems such as contract. Many service agreements are made online, thus raising issues of validity due to questions such as lack of traditional signatures to indicate intent to be bound, authentication of signatures, rules regarding offer and acceptance, authority to bind, legal capacity and the Statue of Frauds, which indicates which contracts must be set out in writing. For a full discussion of these issues see Stuckey (1996).

5. The AOL service agreement (Section 4.1) goes on to reserve the right to remove "any content that it deems in its sole discretion to be unacceptable, undesirable or in violation of the Rules of the Road. AOL Inc. May terminate immediately any Member who misuses or fails to abide by the applicable AOL rules. AOL Inc. May terminate without notice Member's access to and use of the AOL Service and America Online Software on a breach of the AOL rules, including without limitation, misuse of the software libraries, discussion boards, E-mail, or public conference areas (AOL Service Agreement, 1995).

6. In a related case, the U.S. Court of Appeals for the Third Circuit considered several issues related to shrink-wrap agreements in *Step-Saver Data Systems v. Wyse Technology*, 939 F.2d 91 (3d Cir. 1991).

7. Nicholas K. Blomley (1994), provided a historical geography of the law. He argued that there has been a process of disembedding of local legal life and legal autonomy marked by a "pervasive judicial suspicion of the vagaries and contextuality of place."

8. One reaction to attempts to regulate cyberspace came in the form of a Declaration of Independence (1996), which declares cyberspace to be an autonomous zone and states:

You have no moral right to rule us nor do you possess any methods of enforcement we have true reason to fear.

> Governments derive their just powers from the consent of the
> governed. . . . Cyberspace does not lie within your borders.

9. Legislative action has been taken to develop a U.S. policy on electronic signatures in order to encourage international electronic commerce. On June 9, 2000
a bipartisan bill was agreed on in the U.S. Senate. The bill was called The
"Electronic Signatures in Global and National Commerce Act." Although this
bill did not become law, it represents an effort within the U.S. government to
provide legal protections to bolster confidence in electronic commerce
(Statement By Secretary Daley Regarding the Filing on Conference Report ON
S. 761 2000).
10. In another historical example of international cooperation, there was the
International Radio Convention in 1906, Geneva Broadcasting Convention
1936, drafts for UN Treaties for the International Flow of Information (1948),
drafts or a convention for satellite broadcasting (1972) and the discussion on the
New World Information and Communication Order (until 1990)
(Kleinwachter, 1999).
11. At one time, domain names were assigned by one person, John Postel in southern California, USC, with technical standards set by the Association of
Engineers; then IAB served a coordination/management function run by Vint
Cerf, called the father of the Internet and Internet governance. Under the
authority of the U.S. Dept. of Defense. Internet was going global but under
United States jurisdiction. ICANN is concerned with the following issues: the
guaranteed stability of the NET, the promotion of competition, bottom-up
competition and global representation (Kleinwachter, 1999).

REFERENCES

AOL Terms and Conditions of Use. (2003). Site visited June 15, 2003.
  http://www.aol.com/copyright.adp
Ang, P.H. (1997, June). *How countries are regulating Internet content.* Paper presented at the 1997 annual meeting of the Internet Society, Kuala Lumpur.
Aragón, A.R. (1999, Summer). Competing telecommunications and cyber regulation: Is there a need for transatlantic regulatory framework? *International
  Journal of Communications Law and Policy,* http://www.digital-
  law.net/IJCLP/1_1999/ijclp_webdoc_6_1_1998.html.
Black's Law Dictionary (5th ed.). (1979). St. Paul, MN: West.
Blackman, C., & Nihoul, P. (Eds.). (1998). Convergence between telecommunica-
  tion and other media: Telecommunications and other media: How should regu-
  lation adapt? *Telecommunication Policy, 22*(3), 163-170.
Blomley, N.K. (1994). *Space and the geographies of power.* New York: Guilford
  Press.
Clausing, J. (1999, August 25). Internet's governing body debates domain names.
  Cybertimes. Site visited September 26, 1999. http://archives.nytimes.
  com/plweb-Cyberspace Declaration of Independence. (1996). Http://
  www.eff.org/~barlow.

Festa, P. (2003, April 16). Software rams great firewall of China. *Cnet News.com.* Site visited June 3, 2003. http://news.com.com/2100-1028-997101.html?tag =mainstry

Gumpert, G., & Drucker, S. (2001, Fall). Commercial marketplace and the market-place of ideas. *Inter/Media*, pp. 19-25.

Gibson, W. (1984). *Neuromancer.* New York: Ace Books.

Hill, D.T., & Sen, K. (2000). The Internet in Indonesia's new democracy. *Democratization, 7*(1), 119, 136.

Freedom of Expression on the Internet. (2003). *Human Rights Watch Report.* Site visited June 12, 2003. http://www.hrw.org/wr2k/Issues-04.htm

ICANN website. (2003). Site visited June 12, 2003. http://www.icann.org/

International Telecommunication Union Overview (2003). Site visited November 12, 2001. http://www.itu.int/aboutitu/index.html.

Kalathil, S., & Boas, T.C. (2001). The Internet and state control in authoritative regimes: China, Cuba and the counterrevolution. First Monday, Site visited, June 13, 2003. http://www. firstmonday.dk/issues/issue6_8/kalathil.

Kaplan, C.S. (2000, Aug. 11). French Nazi memorabilia case presents jurisdiction dilemma. *Cyber Times, New York Times.* Site visited August 12, 2000. http://emoglen.law.columbia.edu/CPC/archive/hatespeech/11law.html; http://archive.nytimes.com/library/tech/00/08/cyber/cyberlaw/11/law.html.

Katsch, M. E. (1988). *The electronic media and the transformation of law.* New York: Oxford University Press.

Kleinwachter, W. (1999, July 30). *200 Years of international communication regula-tion*: From the *"Carlsbad Treaty" (1815) to the bylaws of the ICANN* (2000). Conference paper, International Association of Media Communication Researchers, Leipzig, Germany.

Lessig, L. (1999). *Code and other laws of cyberspace.* New York: Basic Books.

Llewellyn, K.N. (1960). *The common law tradition: Deciding appeals.* Boston: Little, Brown.

Netree Internet Statistics. (1997). http://www.netree.com/netbin/internetstats.

Nihoul, P. (1998/1999, Winter). Convergence in European telecommunication: A case study on the relationship between regulation and competition (law). *International Journal of Communications Law and Policy, 2*, 1-33.

Oberdiny, J., & Norderhaug, T. (1996). A separate jurisdiction for cyberspace? *Journal of Computer Mediated Communication, 2*(1).

Reidenberg, J.R. (1996). Governing networks and cyberspace rule-making. *Emory Law Journal,* 45.

Rodan, G. (1998). The Internet and political control in Singapore. *Political Science Quarterly, 113*(1), 63-89.

Silencing the Net—The threat to freedom of expression on-line. *Human Rights Watch, 96.* gopher://gopher.igc.apc.org:5000/00/int/hrw/expression/7.

Stuckey, K. (1996). *Internet and online law.* New York: Law Journal Seminars-Press.

Study of Media Laws and Policies in the Middle East and Maghreb. (2003). Site vis-ited June 13, 2003.http://www.internews.org/arab_media_research/jordan.pdf

Wald, M.L. (1995, February 26). A child's Internet sins visited on the parent. *The New York Times*, p. S4.

Wasserman, E. (1998, November 30). White House unveils e-commerce plan. *TechWorld*. Site visited June 19, 2000. http://www.thestandard.com/article/0,1902,2687,00.html

2

The Turning Tide

Electronic Media Regulatory Principles Then and Now

Harvey Jassem
Loyola University Chicago

Harvey Jassem traces the historical approach taken in regulating emerging media beginning with the 1927 Federal Radio Act. The lessons learned from the challenge of regulating cable television provide a roadmap for his consideration of newer technologies. He examines changes in policy that have resulted from the 1996 Telecommunications Act. He argues that the patterns of regulation may reveal the values of regulatory policy and the philosophy behind them. In the U.S. those have traditionally been grounded in a balancing between the public interest and the protection of media economic viability.

In the first edition of this book, I noted that the world of telecommunication policy was coming to an end, or just beginning (Jassem, 1999). There had been a trend toward deregulation of existing media and awkwardness in dealing with new media. The dominance of the so-called deregulatory philosophy, if taken to its logical extreme, portended an end to telecommunication regulation. I argued that there was a discontinuity of fit between the mechanisms of policy and emerging media, resulting in awkward attempts to fit new media into old media models. Like attempting to place square pegs in round holes, policymakers were trying to limit the shape and development of new media so that they would fit into old regulatory models. This sort of approach necessarily limited the scope of change. The existing situations were protected or modified gradually, and new entrants were permitted to exist as long as they behaved as any proper guest would. Of course, new entrants were anxious for more. The loudest voices were calling for deregulation, suggesting that something approximating the end of media regulation was the next logical step. Another view of policymaking suggested that the very emergence of new media called for a brand new set of regulatory assumptions and mechanisms, rather than the abandonment of regulation.

Shortly after that chapter was written, the 1996 Telecommunications Act was enacted, ostensibly to more adequately deal with emerging media and the potentials they offered. The round holes/square peg problem would be less intrusive if policymakers weren't shackled to the dictates of the 1934 Communications Act, the reasoning suggested. Indeed, since the 1996 Act and its regulatory aftermath, we have witnessed ever more rapid changes in the structure and defining qualities of media. Many of those changes were hastened by the post-1996 regulatory climate. All of them continue to pressure the ongoing regulatory environment.

In this chapter, I look at the historical patterns of regulating emerging media, particularly as they speak to the values of media regulatory policy, major changes in both policy and the media themselves resulting from the 1996 Telecommunications Act, the challenges these changes present, and identify operative regulatory philosophy since 1996.

THE OLD PROBLEM OF NEW MEDIA

The regulation of electronic media has always been something of a tortuous affair. At the very inception of telegraphy, telephone, and radio services, it was unclear what role government should play. Some countries nationalized these services. The United States generally developed a system of privately owned telecommunication systems, operating under a regulatory framework. That framework itself embodied sets of values. Should there be private ownership, open markets, local or national monopolies, rate/price regulation, content regulation, or the like? Policymakers had to decide the goals of the regulatory system they were building. How important was a diversity of voices, localism, regional service equity, and so forth? Beyond all of that, policymakers had to legally justify their regulatory system. In a nation where the economy is based on capitalism and private ownership, regulation of business must always be carefully crafted. When that business is the business of information, which is guaranteed special freedom and protection by the First Amendment to the Constitution, regulations must be crafted all the more carefully.

The 1927 Radio Act and later the 1934 Communications Act established the Federal Communications Commission (FCC) to establish, shape, and protect a viable nationwide telecommunication system. The FCC was designed to oversee common carriers (initially telegraph and telephone) and broadcasters (initially radio). Each form was regulated completely differently. Common carriers were generally given local monopolies, had their rates and technical aspects regulated, and were prohibited from being more than channels of communication. They themselves could not be content providers. Broadcasters, on the other hand, were not permitted to be local or national monopolies. Indeed, diversity of ownership was key. And broadcasters were to be content providers operating in the "public interest." Their rates were not regulated.

Those structures resulted in remarkably stable and robust media development. To the extent that they were static, however, they may not have been well equipped to deal with change. Critics have long argued that although the principles of regulation can withstand technological change, the specifics of regulation lag behind technological development, and as such hinder progress. Furthermore, once the regulators create stakeholders, they tend to protect those stakeholders.

Regulation involves the allocation of resources and enforcing public policy. It is very much a political process, where interested parties work to affect the shape of the regulations, (see Kim, 1992; Krasnow & Longley, 1973; Krasnow, Longley, & Terry, 1982). The players are those who are directly regulated, those who wish to enter into the regulated industries, and those who have a potential interest in or are affected by what those industries do. The system is a rational one. Entities tend to favor protecting their own interests, be those interests financial, power, or political. The most powerful are the most influential. And because they tend to want to maintain their power, there is pressure toward inertia. Change comes slowly. Braybrooke and Lindbloom (1963) called the safe baby steps that are typically taken by regulators *incremental politics*. When changes are small they pose the smallest threats, garner little opposition, and if mistaken can be rectified easily. Also contributing to the inherent conservatism of regulation is the structure of the regulatory agencies themselves. Experts are hired in bureaus or divisions. They see the world through those categories of expertise. The individuals in those roles have self-interests in maintaining those categories, after all, they have developed expertise in them. Hence, when new media that do not fit those categories present themselves, there is a tendency to either force them into the pre-existing categories, think about them in terms of how they might impact those categories, or stifle them because they are somehow different. Many such media technologies faced that problem, but the one that provides the richest examples is cable television.

THE REGULATION OF CABLE TELEVISION

Today we think of cable television as a service that delivers hundreds of channels of television programming, most of which come from nonbroadcast outlets. It wasn't always this way. Its infancy, when it was known as community antenna television (CATV), mirrored the development of broadcast television. At its simplest, it was little more than a shared antenna that allowed residents to receive weak or distant broadcast television stations. It served a purpose, it carried television, but it wasn't broadcast television and it wasn't regulated. None of that mattered until CATV entered markets that had some local television stations that did not like the competition CATV brought in.

Acting rationally, concerned television stations and program syndicators who feared losing markets for their syndicated programs demanded that CATV be stopped. Acting as an expert agency, the FCC declined, noting that CATV was neither a common carrier nor a broadcaster, and hence fell outside the purview of the commission. As CATV's capabilities grew and as it garnered more and larger enemies by entering more and larger markets, there was a great deal of political pressure to regulate it (see FCC, 1959; Jassem, 1972, 1973; LeDuc, 1973). In the mid-1960s, the FCC finally asserted its authority to directly regulate cable television. In justifying its decision to regulate *and restrict* cable television, the FCC noted the following:

> we have decided that a serious question is presented whether CATV operations in the major markets may be of such a nature or significance as to have an adverse economic impact on the establishment or maintenance of UHF stations or to require these stations to face substantial competition of a patently unfair nature. (FCC, 1966, ¶ 139)

Through its 1965 and 1966 rulings (FCC, 1965, 1966) and various other proposed and "interim" rules throughout the remainder of the 1960s, the FCC very much restricted cable television's ability to develop, all in the name of protecting the broadcast system that was of such value to the viewing public. This anti-cable regulatory attitude changed in the early 1970s as a result of a coalescence of new political forces (the new Nixon administration), more effective and powerful lobbying by the growing cable television industry, stronger and more positive public discussion of the communication revolution that cable television would afford the public, and the resultant public/political pressure to let cable grow (Jassem, 1972). During this modern period of cable television, the FCC was restructured to include a Cable Services Bureau that "develops, recommends and administers policies and programs with respect to the regulation of services, facilities, rates and practices of cable television systems and with respect to the creation of competition to cable systems" (47 Code of Federal Regulations § 0.101).

In 1972, new cable rules required cable operations to have a multitude of channels, access channels, two-way communication capabilities, local franchise review, and so on. These requirements reflected a new philosophy for media regulation. This new medium was being shaped by the regulators to be more democratic than broadcasting had been. The government would push toward the television of abundance. Micro-localism in program sources, content, and even operation and oversight would be fomented. Small communities would be served and would have more outlets through which they could themselves be heard. Protection of existing broadcasters would not be the guiding principle by which cable television would be shaped. This was a bold step away from the previous model of CATV regulation, and from then-existent models of broadcast, common carrier, or newspaper regulation.

But bold steps can be tripped up. And that is precisely what happened to most of these and later cable television regulations. One after another they were rescinded by the courts and or abandoned by the ever-changing FCC. They did not, after all, fit the broader models of media regulation. The problems experienced in attempting to regulate cable television, by now an old electronic medium, pointed to the need for broader regulatory reform.

THE 1996 SEA OF CHANGE

The 1996 Telecommunications Act was the most comprehensive attempt to redirect media regulatory philosophy since 1934. Its supporters claimed that particularly with the digitization of "information," old definitions of media were irrelevant and a new regulatory framework needed to be developed. That framework was intended to "provide for a pro-competitive, de-regulatory national policy framework designed to accelerate rapidly private sector deployment of advanced telecommunications and information technologies and services to all Americans by opening all telecommunications markets to competition, . . ." (H.R. Conf. Rept. 1996). The purported aim of the legislation may be gleaned from its title: "S. 652. An act to promote competition and reduce regulation in order to secure lower price and higher quality services for American telecommunications consumers and encourage the rapid deployment of new telecommunications technologies." Deregulate and the market will provide plenty and inexpensive media.

The 1996 act was ushered in on the wings of such democratic promises. Yet, these changes were not the result of a sudden populist upsurge in democratic values. Rather, the act was crafted because communication media were merging technologically. Digitization was blurring the definition of media at the same time many media companies, caught up in the worldwide booming economy, were changing the nature of their businesses. Media firms measured much of their success on reports of cash flow or potential synergies that could result from the acquisition of other firms (and their cash flows or synergistic potentials). As a result, there was heightened pressure for a rewrite of the rules that would permit these new entities to profit from their investments. For rhetorical purposes, the language that was used stressed the democratic values and the potential for greater service to the public arising from revised rules. One might imagine that a rational policymaking system responding to pressures of and for converging media would enact new rules that might enable such convergence.

Despite its bulk and groundbreaking promises, the 1996 act continued to promulgate regulations and policy in ways that attempted to recognize, establish, or maintain the differences between telecommunication common carriers, broadcast services, cable services, and video programming services provided by telephone companies. Indeed, the act has titles and parts devoted to each of these separate categories, whether or not they truly needed to be dealt with separately. That left many of the same "square hole round peg" kinds of notions that had plagued policymakers prior to the act. Steve Kelly, a member of the Minnesota legislature, noted that the act's definitions of these types of services failed to recognize the ways in which telecommunications operated even in 1996, and hindered the very competition that was supposed to be at the heart of the act (Kelly, 2001).

The 1996 act, although maintaining the differences between technologies, made major changes in a number of respects. Perhaps most significantly, it dramatically deregulated ownership limitations. For example, it says "The Commission shall modify section 73.3555 of its regulations (47 C.F.R. 73.3555) by eliminating any provisions limiting the number of AM or FM broadcast stations which may be owned or controlled by one entity nationally" (Telecom. Act, 1996, Sec. 202). The act did not totally remove ownership restrictions on radio or any other medium, but it loosened them enormously. Shortly prior to 1996, a single owner could not own more than 36 radio stations in the United States. In 2002, Clear Channel Radio owned approximately 1,200 radio stations in the United States, as well as hundreds in other countries (Clear Channel, 2002). Clear Channel also owned television stations, Internet communication outlets, outdoor media, advertising operations, and other entertainment enterprises. In many ways, Clear Channel represents the aftermath of the 1996 Telecommunications Act: a huge horizontally and vertically integrated multimedia operation that operates internationally and controls vast empires of content providers, media outlets/distributors, and multistream advertising channels. The consolidation of owners of television stations has not been quite as dramatic as it has been in radio, but it has been significant enough to prompt the demise of the Association for Local Television Stations. That organization, which started out as the Association of Independent Television Stations but changed its name and focus when the FCC changed some programming and station ownership regulations, had as its primary constituents relatively small group owners and small "networks." With the post-1996 rules, these groups had almost all been bought or merged with a small number of large media conglomerates. The organization lost nearly all of its members, reflecting the new organization and ownership patterns in American television (Albiniak, 2002).

By some notions of competition, when a marketplace is transformed from one in which there are a vast number of often similarly sized competitors to one in which there are fewer competitors, and in which market participants are dominated by a small number of Goliaths, it might seem that there is a diminution of competition. Those who are disappointed in the telecommunications marketplace that has developed since 1996 make that contention. They suggest that the effect of the act, which called itself "pro-competitive," has been ultimately anticompetitive.

THE STRUCTURE OF THE ELECTRONIC MEDIA IN THE UNITED STATES

A description of the structure of U.S. media is important because it demonstrates the effect policy and economics have had on the media, and because the structure describes incentives as well as some of the participants in the policymaking stew. There has long existed some vertical and horizontal integration of media in the United States, and such integration has been the subject of scrutiny. The principle concern has been that excessive concentration of ownership reduces the very protections and advantages a free marketplace is supposed to afford. When a few large studios dominated the production, distribution and exhibition of movies, the U.S. Supreme Court broke up the industry in an effort to protect the market and possibility of competition from other producers, distributors, and exhibitors (*US v. Paramount Pictures,* 1948). AT&T was similarly broken up when the government decided that the nation would likely see improved services and lower prices if the telephone industry was opened to competition (*US v. AT&T,* 1982) In both of these situations, it was relatively easy to analyze the degree of existing ownership concentration. The motion picture industry was highly focused on making films to be shown in theaters, distributing those films, and showing them in the theaters. The telephone industry was a wired, voice-based method of telecommunication. It owned terminal equipment, transmission lines, switching equipment, and oversaw the sale of point-to-point communication over its network. Telephony was developed as a regulated monopoly, and it was relatively easy to define its parameters.

When considering more recent notions of media markets, the waters are murkier. Those old telephone lines are used by competing companies doing exactly the same as well as vastly different things. And those movie studios are still making movies to be shown in theaters, but now most of their revenues from those films come from nontheatrical releases. Additionally, making "movies" constitutes just a portion of their business. A company such as Disney makes films, owns and operates major broadcast and "cable" television networks, radio stations, and a radio network, publishes books and magazines, has an impressive Internet presence, produces and sells music, television programs, runs live theatrical productions, operates huge amusement/theme parks, runs a cruise line, and has a huge international presence. It is clearly in more businesses than any single market description could cover. And being in so many related businesses gives the firm synergy. That is, it gives the firm ample opportunities to develop multiple revenue streams from its products and gives it ample opportunities to cross promote its products while, at the same time, denying access to potential competitors. Existing methods designed to measure market concentration are unusable if one cannot define the parameters of the market being examined. This is not a new problem, but it is a rapidly growing one.

Once again, cable television seems to have led the way in raising the awareness of this complication. When regulators regulated cable rates, they justified their intervention on the basis of cable's local monopoly. In almost every part of the United States, consumers had but one choice of a cable television provider. Those opposed to such rate regulation pointed out that cable was far from a monopoly. They pointed to functional alternatives available to consumers. For television programming, consumers could turn to local television stations, satellite television providers, and videotape distributors. If the product were defined more broadly, as video entertainment, one could add local movie theaters to the list of competitors. If cable television were defined even more broadly, radio stations might be considered part of the competition. And as cable *and its competitors* expand into more services and products, the market definition gets ever more fluid and confused. Cable now offers telephone service, high-speed Internet connection, Internet portals and content, television program directory services, time-shifting capabilities, interactive information and purchasing services, and so on. So they are competing with wired phone services, wireless phone services, other Internet services of all types, newspapers, magazines, retail outlets, telemarketers, video recorder manufacturers, and so on.

The 1992 Cable Act amended the Communications Act of 1934 (§628 [g], 47 U.S.C. 548 [g]) to require the FCC to report annually to Congress on the status of competition in the market for the delivery of video programming. In its Eighth Annual Report (FCC, 2001), the FCC looked at, in addition to cable television, direct broadcast satellite, home satellite services, wireless cable systems using frequencies in the multichannel multipoint service ("MMDS"), private cable or satellite master antenna television ("SMATV") systems as well as broadcast television service. "We also consider other existing and potential distribution technologies for video programming, including the Internet, home video sales and rentals, local exchange carriers ("LECs"), and electric and gas utilities. In addition, for the first time this year, we address broadband service providers ("BSPs"), a new category of entrant into the video marketplace" (¶ 3). The report also looked at horizontal and vertical integration throughout the industry. Pointing to how important and how difficult market description is in any consideration of policy, Commissioner Martin released a separate statement decrying the report's exclusion of broadcast television from the analysis of horizontal concentration. "I question whether the relevant product market is properly defined," he wrote. Only *multichannel* services were considered in that analysis (Martin, 2001). Other participants in the inquiry, notably AT&T, the largest cable operator, also asked that the market be defined more broadly to include broadcast television (FCC, 2001, ¶ 138). The point here is not that the FCC described the market correctly or incorrectly, rather that the nature of that description is arbitrary and affects the findings.

The bulk of the FCC's report on video programming concentration focuses on the concerns of the businesses involved more than it does on the market facing the end users (people watching television). For example, the FCC employs the Herfindahl-Hirschman Index (HHI) to calculate how competitive the market is for the purchase of programming by the various multichannel services (it finds that market to be "unconcentrated"), but does not use the HHI to assess how competitive the market is for the distribution of video programming to the home. Perhaps this is due to the fact that most areas have but a single multichannel distributor, making use of the somewhat sophisticated HHI unnecessary. Or perhaps the FCC is simply less concerned with this issue. Nevertheless, it finds "the market for the delivery of video programming to households continues to be highly concentrated and characterized by substantial barriers to entry" (FCC, 2001, ¶ 118). Almost every one of the comments and "reply" comments in this proceeding were representing telecommunication companies or their professional associations. The public added almost nothing to the record under consideration.

It is something of a conundrum that at once many conglomerates are growing larger and more powerful than ever, entering new businesses, with one result being an increase in many functional alternatives and a diminishing ability to compare round pegs to round pegs. As conglomerates take on increasingly more roles, relationships that once existed between independent but interdependent players are changed. Where once television stations might have been concerned if programmers became too concentrated, thus forcing increased programming prices, if the programmers and the television stations are increasingly part of the same organization, which also owns cable systems and networks, those same television stations play a strategic role in the overall function of the larger owner. The prices a station pays its parent or sibling company for programming matter less than the overall corporate strategy. This results in changed political dynamics of the media players. Predictably, the pressures on policymakers reflect those changed dynamics.

THE PHILOSOPHY OF MEDIA REGULATION

Guiding principles for the regulation of electronic media in the United States have traditionally been grounded in a mix of maximizing the public interest, protecting the economic viability of existing media (either because regulators have been "captured" by the industry or because they really believe in the importance of the existence of the system they helped create), and permitting entry of competing media forms in an incremental fashion such that primary interests of incumbent media and their owners wouldn't be dramatically threatened. There has been a balancing act where compromise seemed to steer the policymakers. New technological advances have generally been adopted using standards that did not maximize their potential, but instead took advantage of some improvements while making sure they were backward-compatible and did not pose serious threats to existing media. For example, color television has never been as good as it could have been because of the demand that it be compatible with the older "black-

and-white" form of TV. Also slowing the introduction of new media has been the regulatory system itself with its built in conservatism and almost endless opportunities for appeals. FM radio took 30 years longer than necessary to develop as a direct result of the FCC's policies toward it. Telephone and wireless phone competition and innovation have been slowed by the FCC. Digital high-definition television is arriving late in the United States due to the regulators. These delays are often couched in technological terms, wherein the commission notes it has to be sure of how to best handle the new media before unleashing them, and those slow introductions always work in the interest of existing media which thereby avoid competition for extended periods. Regardless of the explanation, the result has been regulatory barriers to entry for new media.

Compromise has also characterized ownership regulation. Traditionally, in the name of diversity, the FCC has limited the number of broadcast stations an entity might own. Those restrictions grew gradually, whereas the number of actual stations on the air grew dramatically. Stability and incumbents were protected. There has long been a tendency to protect the viability of incumbents. Perhaps that's because regulators do what they know how to do, and they don't wish to squander their expertise. Perhaps it is because regulators believe in the system they helped shape. Perhaps it is because the incumbents have more power and resources than new entrants and are better able to make their case for protectionism.

Regulatory philosophy has also long held dear the notion that basing regulations on the channel of communication was appropriate. And the courts have upheld the viability of different regulatory approaches for different media. Content and ownership regulations that have been upheld in the broadcast arena have been deemed unconstitutional in the print media, for example.

Regulators had long espoused the belief that telecommunication regulation was necessary to protect the public good. Some believed it to be a necessary evil, others had a more positive view. But the necessity of regulating telecommunication media went largely unchallenged since it began in the early 20th century.

POST-1996 CHANGES

Recently, however, the situations and philosophies began to change. On the philosophical end, regulators who believe in the so-called deregulation movement now hold senior positions, or new regulators intent on dismantling the traditional regulatory system are more likely to be nominated and confirmed than might have been the case 30 years earlier. A case in point is FCC Chair Michael Powell. He proclaims that "My religion is the market."

"We want to see competition create new and innovative services rather than five regulators in Washington." "Which state-central plan is the one that made life so good for the citizens of their country?" he asks. "Was it the Soviet social model? Was it the Chinese social model?" (Davidson, 2002a, p. B1). Regarding the value of or purported goodness of regulations fostering diversity of ownership, he opines: "This is some sort of *Citizen Kane* idea that our thoughts will be directed to particular viewpoints [if there is concentration of ownership]. But the overwhelming amount of programming we watch is entertainment, and I don't know what it means for the owner to have a political bias. When I'm watching *Temptation Island*, do I see the little hallmarks of Rupert Murdoch?" (Davidson, 2002b, p. B2).

Although Powell clearly believes the economic marketplace is the proper arbiter of good, one may argue that he is wrong on at least four accounts. First, assuming one accepts the notion that the marketplace is the best forum, Powell's notion of deregulation is not synonymous with a free and open marketplace. The marketplace is supposed to work best when there is free and relatively easy entry into that marketplace so that competitors might effectively address any deficiencies that exist in the market. Yet, as the FCC's report on competition for video programming notes, as the size and breadth of the surviving firms in the field grow, the barriers to entry for new firms grow as well. Barriers to entry can be erected by government regulations or by industry structure. Simply taking down the government barriers does not assure or even heighten the likelihood of reduced barriers to market entry. And as long as barriers are high, the marketplace cannot be relied on to do whatever magic the faithful believe it does. Second, there has never been a pure marketplace model in U.S. telecommunication. Government has underwritten research and development of every form of electronic media, and has played a huge role in selecting the players and distributing resources. It is impossible to undo that. It is a government-created, subsidized, and shaped resource. A third argument against the marketplace-as-savior model asserts that only some interests are represented in the marketplace, and to the extent that others may not be, reliance on a pure marketplace model inherently disenfranchises those interests. In broadcasting, for example, one could make a case that the real participants in an economic marketplace are the programmers, broadcasters, and advertisers. Viewers have about as much influence in the television market as any other product being sold might have. That is, just as a box of breakfast cereal does not impact the grocery store, viewers, whose attention is what is being sold to advertisers, don't directly affect the television market. And fourth, the physical nature of electronic media requires some forms of regulation/control/structure. The electronic chaos that ensues without such control is what led to government regulation in the first place. And although there are numerous alternatives for how to structure a differently regulated electronic media marketplace, any of those structures entail regulations and policies that create winners, losers, and barriers to entry. There simply cannot exist a truly free and open market for telecommunication.

The situation and structure of media are also changing, and those changes come with regulatory consequences. Convergence of form, function, and ownership have palpable impacts on the regulatory system. Regulators respond to the requests and pressures they face. Prior to 1996, there was a greater number of competing owners, and there was much less cross ownership of media outlets. One result was that owners had a vested interest in maintaining those differences. With the great consolidations that have occurred since 1996, owners' incentives have changed. *The New York Times* or the *Chicago Tribune* or the *Washington Post* or the *Los Angeles Times* ownership must feel more sympathetic to regulations permitting cross media ownership and media empire building now that they are all doing it. Profits come more readily from "repurposing" content across platforms. Hence, to the extent that regulation is a political system responsive to the forces pushing it, it is being influenced by large multimedia and even multinational firms who are more interested in adding the newest form of media outlet to their mix than they might be in protecting the old forms of media. Predictably, one result is a more hospitable regulatory environment for new media that might once have been seen as threats needing to be slowed down. This is a tremendous attitude change.

There have been some accommodations to opening the market to new entrants, even when such opening has been opposed by entrenched interests. For example, the FM radio spectrum has been opened a crack with the introduction of a new class of low power FM licenses. These licenses permit very low power noncommercial stations to exist along side of their full power commercial peers. Existing broadcasters generally opposed this, worrying that new stations might degrade the signals of existing ones. In this case, the powerful dominant broadcasters did not win the regulatory fight. Yet, the very existence of many low power noncommercial stations helps those large conglomerates more than it hurts them. Surely, those low power stations have very little impact on the audience listening to the full-powered stations. And the very existence of thousands of low power stations makes the radio market seem much more robust. Hence, with the addition of these low power nonthreatening stations, the FCC has made it even easier for conglomerates to "demonstrate" that the market can withstand additional concentration of ownership. Similarly, the addition of satellite-delivered radio and television, although partially reflecting the interests of the owners who also have terrestrial interests (and are in better positions to reposition content), also help others who wish to further grow through consolidation.

Globalization and digitization are going to further affect media policy. With the globalization of the media businesses and the ease with which communication crosses borders, there are growing tensions between domestic-based regulation and the international sphere of telecommunication. Increasingly, there are observations such as:

> "Cyberspace" is most easily characterized by reference to the Internet: it is the virtual, non-physical, space between computer terminals, across which most communication now flows. The telephone is now also a digital device which conveys information by the same technical means, as will be the television and radio. Because the space is not "real" in a physical space, it raises novel issues of regulation. . . . This territory is international, indeed, transnational, because anyone can connect to anyone else who has access to cyberspace.
> Cyberspace is built on software code. It is a space based on information and communication exchange. (Marsden, 2001, p. 368)

The goal of some sort of global regulation seems a bit far-fetched. Governments are not likely to want to cede a great deal of control, but a growing number of international "free trade" treaties may hasten international "regulation" of telecommunication, both by example and by the very fact that communication itself is an important and growing part of the global economy. Additionally, we know from the American experience that the media have a history of driving government regulation of media. Just as international business interests were the primary forces behind global trade agreements, so too might global media interests seek protection from conflicting national media rules that treat their products differently depending on some presence the firm may have much or little control over. If mergers that might have been approved in one nation are outlawed by others, as has been the case recently, look for industry support for an internationalization of the regulatory playing field.

To the extent that media policy may be examined domestically, it is significantly different than it was prior to 1996. This is a result of the 1996 Telecommunications Act, and technological and economic shifts and

- The vastly different interests of the vested parties (the media owners) who increasingly define themselves as comprehensive vertically and horizontally integrated operations that defy medium-based distinctions.
- A changed regulatory philosophy.
- Changes in the ways in which media form and content and production and reception interact, now that almost anyone can be

some level of producer and audiences have at least seemingly more choices.

On its face, it appears that traditional regulation of media has undergone a major change such that it is no longer even pretending to be the arbiter of the public's interest. Given the enormity of the media mogul players and the political regulatory system that is responsive to the players, and given the so-called deregulatory philosophy, it seems as if the public cannot turn to government for the redress of grievances. If that is indeed the case, the public is not without recourse. Because the Internet and converging media are so pervasive, it is possible that those who feel underserved or even angry can address their needs and anger through some forms of the very communication media they are upset about. Regulatory systems are always influenced by political pressure and dominant cultural values. It may be that the discussion takes on a very different form. Perhaps, using the Internet or wireless based forms of communication, the public will call for subsidized access to the production, distribution, and storage of information, a modern functional extension of the library. Perhaps pressure will be applied to transfer public funds from the building and maintenance of public highways to the building and maintenance of information highways. As we are increasingly an information society, there are a myriad of ways to reconceptualize our needs and functions, and to share those very same reconceptualizations. As these ideas are shaped and developed across cyber communities, movements may coalesce around these issues. If/as they do, these coalitions can enter and affect the political economic policymaking system. Remote as they might seem, there are opportunities to transform the system.

REFERENCES

Albiniak, P. (2002, February 4). It's all over for ALTV: Consolidation has swallowed indies the organization served. *Broadcasting &Cable,* p. 11.

Braybrooke, D., & Lindblom, C.E. (1963). *A strategy of decision: Policy evaluation as a social process* New York: The Free Press.

Clear Channel. (2002) http://www.clearchannel.com.

Davidson, P. (2002a, February 6). FCC chief Powell takes hands-off approach. *USA Today,* p. B1.

Davidson, P. (2002b, February 6). FCC could alter rules affecting TV, telephone. *USA Today,* p. B2.

Federal Communications Commission. (1959). First Report and Order. 26 FCC 428.

Federal Communications Commission. (1965). First Report and Order. Docket Nos. 14895, 15233, 38 FCC 683.

Federal Communications Commission. (1966). Second Report and Order. Docket
    No. 14895, 2 FCC 2d 750.
Federal Communications Commission. (2001, December 27). Annual assessment of
    the status of competition in the market for the delivery of video programming.
    CS Docket No. 01-129, FCC 01-389.
H.R. Conference Rep. (1996, January 31). 104 th Cong., 2d Session #104 458,
    (ftp://ftp.loc.gov/pub/thomas/cp104/hr458.txt).
Jassem, H.C. (1972). *The selling of the compromise—1971—or—Cable television
    goes to the city.* Unpublished master's thesis, Ohio State University, Columbus,
    OH.
Jassem, H.C. (1973). The selling of the cable TV compromise. *Journal of
    Broadcasting. 17*(4), 427.
Jassem, H. (1999). Different strokes for different folks: The intersection of regulato-
    ry principles and technology. In S.J. Drucker & G. Gumpert (Eds.), *Real
    law@virtual space: Communication regulation in cyberspace* (pp. 31-49).
    Cresskill, NJ: Hampton Press.
Kelly, S. (2001). Telecommunications in the 21st century: Liberating our digital
    future: How the 1996 telecommunications act definitions are hobbling change.
    Wm. Mitchell L. Rev., 27, 2137.
Kim, H. (1992, Spring). Theorizing deregulation: An exploration of the utility of
    the "Broadcast Policy-Making System" model. *Journal of Broadcasting and
    Electronic Media*, 153.
Krasnow, E.G., & Longley, L.D. (1973). *The politics of broadcast regulation.* New
    York: St. Martin's Press.
Krasnow, E.G., Longley, L.D., & Terry, H.A. (1982). *The politics of broadcast regu-
    lation* (3rd ed.). New York: St. Martin's Press.
LeDuc, D.R. (1973). *Cable television and the FCC.* Philadelphia: Temple
    University Press.
Marsden, C.T. (2001, Summer). Cyberlaw and international political economy:
    Toward regulation of the global information society, *Law Review of Michigan
    State University—Detroit College of Law Det. C.L. Rev.* 355.
Martin, K.J. (2001). Separate Statement of Commissioner Kevin J. Martin Re:
    Annual Assessment of the Status of Competition in the Market for the
    Delivery of Video Programming, CS Docket No. 01-129, FCC 01-389.
US v. Paramount Pictures, Inc. (1948). 334 U.S. 131.
US v. AT&T. (1982). 552 F. Supp. 131 (D.D.C.)

3

Freedom and Liability in Cyberspace

Media, Metaphors, and Paths of Regulation

Susan J. Drucker
Hofstra University

Gary Gumpert
Communication Landscapers

At the earliest phase in the developments in "cyberlaw," innovations in "cyberspace" resulted in legal issues, which were handled through the application of preexisting legal doctrines, and laws, the application of which have been justified through metaphors. The authors examine the existing metaphors being used and focus upon the free speech and privacy implications of developing a distinct area of "cyberlaw." In this chapter, the legal metaphors and directions that emerged to describe computer-mediated communication are explored. The addendum added to this chapter closes with a consideration of the emergence of convergence fueled by the Internet. The authors conclude that the Internet remains a medium in search of a much needed guiding regulatory metaphor.

We have walked or keyboarded ourselves into a critical and formative period for the new communication frontier of cyberspace, a period of growth in both the phenomenon and the regulatory schema governing it. The one constant discovered when exploring the evolution of the media law is that technologies develop more rapidly than can new legal approaches. This fact is being faced by courts attempting to grapple with the liability and free expression implications of the technological developments that are producing the emerging principles of "cyberlaw" (Stuckey, 1994).

The relationship of outside to inside, public to private, has been transformed by our mediated capability. Relationships are neither delineated by the circumstances of place or the conditions of time. The circumstance of communication requires description if one is to understand the context of relationship and interaction. Thus, communication is a functional phenomenon requiring qualitative description and assessment. Currently, communication may or may not be interactional, one-way, face-to-face, oral, written, permanent, impermanent, electronic, nonelectronic, human, nonhuman, monosensory or multisensory, public, private, semi-public, functioning in real or delayed time.

Communication laws are found in a web of regulatory, statutory, and judicial statements aimed at human interaction and information dissemination that have been face to face or facilitated via telecommunication or mass media technologies. Yet, laws designed primarily to regulate noncommunicative activities may function to promote or limit communication. The law of property and land use is one such area of regulation. Land-use regulations are also particularly interesting with regard to not only physical space but to the electronic realm as well as the nomenclature of space, urban planning, and architecture have been transformed into metaphors of cyberspace. Thus, the user is linked to bulletin boards, malls, rooms through ports, highways, exits, gateways, bridges, and routers. The vocabulary surrounding new technologies, new uses for old technologies, and the joinder of multiple media is significant as it not only allows us to talk about a phenomenon but shapes the perception of the reality being named. In fact, the words created and metaphors employed function persuasively. Burke argued that "naming" is an interpretive act that functions as a guide to action toward that which is named. Thus, "the command that one act one way rather than another is 'implicit' in the name" (Blankenship, 1980).

The language of the law has been a topic of study (Bosmajian, 1992; Strauber, 1987), particularly the ways in which metaphors have functioned. For example, recently Bosmajian (1992), in *Metaphor and Reason in Judicial Opinions*, focused on the role of tropes, particularly metaphors in judicial opinions in free speech cases. He argued that metaphor shaped the substance of laws having become institutionalized and relied on as principles and standards in arriving at legal judgments (Bosmajian, 1992). The significance of metaphors such as the "marketplace of ideas," and the "chilling effect" were cited in support of this argument.

The metaphors of free expression are being expanded to encompass the ever-changing landscape of cyberspace. The adoption of spatial terminology may appear a ready and useful mechanism for making the revolutionary changes of the information age less strange, intimidating, and boundless. At the same time, the technology of communications challenge developments in applicable laws governing rights of privacy, free expression, liability in such areas as libel,[1] hate speech[2] and obscenity[3] as well as sexual harassment,[4] and jurisdictional issues. In attempting to keep pace with technological growth, developments in cyberlaw have been handled through the application of pre-existing legal doctrines. Media are explored through descriptive terms leading to a comparison between an existing medium and a newly emerging medium. Descriptive terms are ways of depicting or representing the characteristics of a medium of communication or form of dissemination. The descriptive terms chosen have been selected to mirror those characterizations relevant in prior unrelated free speech cases and doctrines. This is evidenced by legal doctrines that have emerged from the notion of publication (that is to say, newspaper, book, magazine publication) that may be applied to electronic publication and transmission. So, for example, in the realm of defamation law, the standards and concepts of libel rather than slander have been applied to broadcasting as the descriptive terms of libel have been viewed as most similar to the dissemination of broadcast information.[5] Therefore, the descriptive terms of libel (focusing on some permanence in written or printed form), have been stretched to apply to the once ephemeral signals of radio and television also characterized by large audiences. The *Restatement of Torts (Second)* (1976) contends broadcasting should be treated as libel rather than slander because broadcasts may reach more homes than printed publications and may damage reputations just as easily as print. Similarly, broadcasting (such as by radio and television) descriptive terms have been applied to the cable industry and established principles of intellectual property rights and copyright established in the realm of print have been stretched to apply to motion pictures, visual, or multimedia works. A metaphor is then created comparing a body of regulatory approaches, legal principles, doctrines, and case law developed with regard to the older medium. In this way the regulatory schema of cyberspace today reflects a patchwork of regulations inherited by the application of mixed metaphors. To date, the laws of cyberspace have not developed beyond the inherited regulatory metaphor stage.

The descriptive terms applied to a medium have been linked to the regulatory approaches taken to create applicable law. The descriptive terms and regulatory approaches taken from other media are explored in this chapter as are the descriptive terms (spatial in nature) used with regard to electronic networking. We focus on the free speech and privacy implications of developing a distinct area of cyberlaw emerging from the descriptive spatial (real property) terms unique to that medium.

PHASES OF MEDIA DEVELOPMENT AND THEIR REGULATORY APPROACHES

Communication occurs in a flexible, malleable, nonrestricted environment—one that co-exists with, influences and is shaped by the environment of the built form. It is absolutely essential to grasp the symbiotic link between the environments of place and nonplace. Although some form of mediation, and some form of social control, has always been a part of humankind, we can perhaps divide the question into three developmental periods:

Nonmediated Period

The nonmediated period is the time in which public communication was essentially restricted to one time and place without aid of a medium to preserve or disseminate the social event. The regulatory approach was based on political or religious security as well as concerns for orderly and peaceful conduct.

Media Period

The media period consists of several major periods in which social interaction is extended in time and beyond place.

a) Thus, the initial period has as its chief characteristic "chirographic distancing"—the reliance on handwriting as the primary means of communication between two or more individuals not located in the same time and place essentially altering the nature of public talk by disrupting and elongating interaction once occurring in the same time and place, now occurring at different times.

b) The "Mass Media" period was introduced with Gutenberg's invention of print in the 15th century, thereby allowing for relatively efficient and quick preservation and replication of interaction, but also interrupted in time.

c) The addition of electronics allows for the almost instant replication of data, but with a separation of place. Electronic communication is further divided into two variations: "media" that are/were essentially considered telecommunication "common carriers," thus defined as quasi-monopoly point-to-point public utilities such as the telephone companies and "mass media," which, although licensed by the government, transfer content to a large simultaneously attending audience generally without immediate feedback.

The regulatory approach of this period is marked by a shift to concerns not only of the communicative message but of the messenger as an institution. "The media" as synonymous with press as an entity or medium as carrier of messages created external to the utility carrying the message formed the backbone of the body of law commonly known as Media Law.

Postmodern Media Period

The time of the electronic network characterized by the introduction of cable and computer communication and in which the distinction between mass media and telecommunications become ambiguous is the postmodern period. "Unlike the traditional media, [mass media] which generally disseminate their own message, or mail and telephone services, which typically act as common carriers for messages of others, information service providers both serve as a conduit for information created by others and may deliver information of their own devising—they are both medium and messenger" (Stuckey, 1994, p. 413). Postmodern media thus challenge the existing body of communication law based on media distinctions.

There are numerous variations in online services including E-mail (immediate delivery of written messages), electronic bulletin boards (BBs) and newsgroups (in which messages are posted for system users), file transferring systems, libraries and databases (with information often created by third parties), electronic publication, conferencing (of two or more users in real-time interaction), and listservs (which allow topics to be "broadcast" via E-mail messages). Many of these options are available through the Internet, "an ad hoc 'network of networks' that spans the globe" (Stuckey, 1994, p. 415). The Internet is a dense global matrix of 46,000 computer networks, 3.2 million host computers, woven together by telephone lines, undersea cables, microwave links, and gigabit fiber-optic pipes. Touching down in 146 countries, the Internet links 25 to 30 million people and is growing by 1 million users each month, doubling in size each year (Internet Society, 1994; P. Lewis, 1994a). It's a super data highway that carries the freight of the information age—electronic mail, digital video and sound, computer viruses, and more (Markoff, 1993).[6]

The evolution and development of media technology is simply a change in the way information is moved from one space to another. Ong

(1977) said that "each of the so-called 'media' . . . makes possible thought processes inconceivable before" (p. 46). Similarly, the very nature of public interaction and the way it is regulated and governed is fundamentally altered by the technology. The developing models being applied to the protection and regulation of freedom of expression and privacy in the postmodern media period dominated by communication in cyberspace is the subject of the following discussion.

STRETCHING REGULATORY SCHEMA

> Technological advances must continually be evaluated and their relation to legal rules determined so that antiquated rules are not misapplied in modern settings. . . . Yet, if the substance of a transaction has not changed, new technology does not require a new legal rule merely because of its novelty. (*Daniel v. Dow Jones & Co.,* 1987)

Each new medium challenges the existing regulatory structure, a truism that is clearly evidenced by postmodern media. In an effort to provide a solid foundation to clarify overriding First Amendment rights with regard to postmodern media, such as computer networks, Professor Laurence Tribe proposed a constitutional amendment protecting information and expression without regard for the medium through which they are transmitted or stored (Resnick, 1991). Tribe's proposal states:

> This Constitution's protections for the freedoms of speech, press, petition and assembly, and its protections against unreasonable searches and seizures and the deprivation of life, liberty or property without due process of law, shall be construed as fully applicable without regard to the technological method or medium through which information content is generated, stored altered, transmitted or controlled. (p. 1, 19)

In the event this is not accepted as a constitutional amendment, Tribe recommended this proposal be accepted gradually as a principle of interpretation.

Yet another regulatory approach taken in the past and presently being applied with regard to postmodern media has been that of "mapping electronic data communications onto existing legal metaphors." In a *1993 Villanova Law Review* article by that title, Johnson and Marks explored this approach noting "existing metaphors can serve as shorthand 'signals' of the types of relationships and ground rules the parties intend to adopt." They note, "There is substantial utility in asking ourselves how particular online environments are similar to or different from other environments where the rights and duties of participants have been analyzed more fully in the past." (p. 488)

A wide variety of legal metaphors have been brought from the non-mediated and the media periods to grapple with the postmodern media period. Selection of appropriate legal metaphors "presuppose[s] that there is some 'best fit,' some metaphor that will accurately characterize all the activities involved in these systems" (Johnson & Marks, 1993, p. 487). Of these, many from the media period have been explored.

Publishing

From the mass media period, the metaphor of publishing has been brought to postmodern media. The term *publisher,* as defined in the Restatement of Torts (Second) (1976), includes all those who communicate statements to third persons. A publisher is presumed to have control over content and has thus been held liable for any harmful results, including the torts of defamation, false light invasion of privacy, public disclosure of private facts, and intentional infliction of emotional harm (Becker, 1989). The standard of liability for publication torts has depended on the degree of editorial control and sponsorship assumed in the publication, which formed the basis for a claim. A publisher once strictly liable for publication of false or obscene material under common law (a doctrine now abolished) can escape liability under some circumstances including those times not considered the primary creator of a publication. The "wire service" privilege for defamation thus absolves the publisher from liability for the mere reiteration of an actually false but apparently authentic news dispatch received by a recognized reliable source of news from reputable news service agencies (*Layne v. Tribune Co.,* 1993).

Prodigy, one of several information service providers (ISP), chose to embrace this publisher metaphor when it canceled accounts of subscribers based on the content of messages in October 1990. The ISP announced it had decided to curtail public postings about such topics as suicide, crime, sex or pregnancy. Critics argued this policy was part of a larger effort to suppress a consumer protest by subscribers that began when Prodigy announced an increase in the cost of E-mail service. Subscribers posted public messages on the Prodigy BB which led the company to announce it would no longer allow public postings concerning fee policy. Prodigy eventually revoked subscribers' memberships without notice. Applying the publisher metaphor, the nature of private ownership presumes that publishers may exclude any content (*Miami Herald Publishing Co. v. Tornillo,* 1974). According to Johnson and Marks, the publisher metaphor fails to account for the lack of direct control over content.

Common Carrier

From the electronic communication media period, telecommunication regulatory approaches have been borrowed. Common carriers have a duty to carry all content, without discrimination (47 U.S.C. Section 202(a), 1988) and are therefore immune from liability based on content. Statutory regulation of common carriers as defined by section 153 (h) of the Communications Act have been clarified through court interpretations from which a three-part test (*National Assn. of Regulatory Comm'rs v. FCC*, 1976) has been fashioned to determine the existence of a common carrier. The carrier must be of a "quasi-public" character, must have uniform business practices, and must not operate where "individualized decisions determine terms and must allow the user to determine what is transmitted or carried (Johnson & Marks, 1993, p. 496). Common carriers avoid liability when they simply made equipment available (Restatement of Torts (Second) Section 581 comment b). Here again Johnson and Marks noted the implications of applying the common carrier metaphor to regulations of such post-modern media as electronic BBs noting the operators would impose an affirmative duty to make facilities available to all (47 U.S.C. Section 202 (a), 1988) and would also require prior FCC approval before start up.

Distributor

Another metaphor, distribution, has been applied to cyberspace (Stuckey, 1994). The distributor metaphor raises issues of control or knowledge of content. Generally, the distributor such as a bookseller, news vendor, or library is not liable for harmful information created by others (Restatement of Torts (Second) Section 578, 1976). Thus, in cases dating back to 1959, the Supreme Court adopted a First Amendment rationale to prevent the imposition of strict liability for distributors such as bookstore owners stocking obscene writing (*Smith v. California*, 1959) or television stations providing air time for political candidates exercising right to reply time (*Farmers Educational and Cooperative Union of America v. WDAY, Inc.*, 1959). Additionally, the Electronic Communications Privacy Act (Title 18) and related state statutes limit and may prohibit providers from reviewing communications made through their facilities, again supporting the distributor metaphor (*Cubby v. CompuServe Inc.*, 1991). Yet, this metaphor is strained in that most service provider agreements retain the right to review and control content (America OnLine Subscriber Agreement). Prodigy censors messages that directly attack other subscribers and uses what it calls "George Carlin" software. The software searches for and deletes messages containing objectionable words (P. Lewis, 1994b).

Contract Law

From the nonmediated perspective, contract law has been favored as a regulatory approach to the postmodern media, which it is argued would forestall direct government regulation while promoting growth of the medium (Johnson & Marks, 1993, p. 497). The traditional concepts of public forum, in which rights and limitations on nonmediated discourse are regulated with regard to communication contexts, provide a particularly significant avenue of thought in search of a regulatory schemata for postmodern media.

Spatial Metaphors, Communication, and the Laws of Electronic Space

Words are what we make them, but they change and transform their origins. The landscape orientation of cyberspace is significant in that space has traditionally served as media of face-to-face communication (so called nonmediated communication). Now a prior spatial identity has been applied to a nonterritorially defined medium. In this way, metaphors from the laws governing free speech and privacy in physical space (i.e., real property in legal terms) appears a logical extension of a body of well-established law. When the International Standards Organization adopted an Open System Interconnect reference model (somehow also linked with IBM's Systems Network Architecture) in order to assure compatibility among users, the language of architecture and urban planning had already provided a metaphorical lexicon to guide future development, usage, and regulation.

With the power of the spatial metaphor in mind, this portion of the chapter surveys the land-use regulations that apply to the extension of the laws of physical public space to the ever growing vistas of electronic space.

Public Space/Public Forum

On a very fundamental level, the interaction of individuals in public space, without reference or presence of any other media of communication, involves regulation. Communication, particularly, political communication, requires two types of sites: public fora and public places. The public forum is the platform for rhetoric and protest, the type of space traditionally devoted to programmed public expression. It is the forum of the designated site, the display piece of government, the stage for performance, the potential media event. Public oration and symbolic confrontation of demonstration is seldom, if ever, a spontaneous event. Rather, it is the climax of intricate development of communication relationships. It ideally represents a prior process of thought, deliberation, debate, discussion, dialogue, and talk circumscribed by culture and tradition that once occurred in the public place. The character of public streets, parks, and sidewalks have historically lent themselves to being considered natural sites for the public activity of dialogue. In the United States, access to both the public forum and the public space has been viewed as a corollary to the right to free speech, enjoying special status in the law as court decisions have consistently recognized the "vital role for people who lack access to more elaborate (and more costly) channels of communication" (Tribe, 1978, p. 689.)

Public places provide the site for interpersonal interaction as well. The public place is an environment such as a plaza, promenade, street, mall, park, cafès, pubs, coffeehouses, and community centers, which serves as a site for potential interaction. The public place is the catalyst for expression in the public forum, it is the backstage area for unstructured, informal social gatherings. These sites have become, according to Ray Oldenburg (1989, p. 67), vital to the personal and political life of a society. "Public places for social interaction run counter to the type of political control exercised in totalitarian societies, so they are essential to the political processes of a democracy" (1989). The public forum without public place represents potential danger to a peaceful orderly democratic process. The public place offers a site where ideas may be exchanged and the blueprints for revolt designed.

Each is protected, defined, and limited, by law. Public space is a far more difficult concept to legally define because so many jurisdictional issues are involved and because public space may or may not be both public or private with public access agreed to each component. So municipal regulations in the form of zoning laws will determine the kind of activities permitted (Drucker & Gumpert, 1991). Further Board of Health restrictions, drinking laws, smoking laws, building permits, political activity in shopping centers and malls, regulate communicative activity. A whole series of "newsstand cases" have gone through the court in which a municipality refused permission for publishers to place coin-operated newspaper dispensers on public property (*City of Lakewood v. Plain Dealer Publishing Co.*, 1988). In recent years, in cases including *City of Lakewood v. Plain Dealer Publishing Co.*, the high court has attempted to balance a municipality's legitimate interest in limiting the size, appearance, and placement of newspaper boxes on streets and pedestrian paths against the First Amendment rights to distribute and citizen rights to receive newspapers. These cases have ruled it an unconstitutional content regulation to ban newsracks in residential areas. So one of the interesting questions that arises is whether a publisher is engaged in a constitutionally protected speech activity when seeking to put a newspaper vending machine on a street corner.

Recently, several members of Congress were arrested by the District of Columbia police for protesting without a permit in front of the White House (*The New York Times*, 1994). Licensing, within constitutional limits (those that do not vest "unbridled discretion in the hands of a government official or agency") is a permissible prior restraint (*City of Lakewood v. Plain Dealer Publishing, Co.*, p. 750).

The Federal Courts have established characteristics "that a public space must possess if it is to be considered a public forum" (Naughton, 1993):

> First, the property must have as a principal purpose the free exchange of ideas, and this purpose must be evidenced by a long-standing historical practice of permitting speech. Second, a public forum is not creation by inaction; a public forum is created only when the property is intentionally open[ed] . . . for public discourse. (p. 429)

With more and more activity once held to be a traditional function of the public space and/or forum domain being shifted over to an electronic form, what protection is afforded such functions as the shift occurs? That is to say, when a function is assumed by the newer medium, what legal protection is afforded the coopted activity? To some extent, the implementation of the Fairness Doctrine, Equal Time, and Section 315 as developed by the Federal Communications Commission (FCC), responded to a shift in which public activities had to be protected because the spectrum limitation of the medium required such protection. Because, in a pre-cable world, stations and channels were limited by the availability of space on the electromagnetic spectrum, the concept of public access to the channel was written into the law. It must be noted that, theoretically, at least, broadcasters had their license renewal applications evaluated on the basis of whether they served "the public interest, convenience, and necessity."

But it is the postmodern media period, a time in which the audiovisual landscape is being reshaped and reformulated, in which computers, fiber-optics, satellites, cellular phones, CD-ROMs, and facsimiles coalesce and converge, that the shift in functions of public interaction has accelerated and radicalized how we deal with each other in the public domain. It is in the postmodern media period that electronic space becomes a functional equivalent of public space, but where such electronic space is primarily a construction rather than a reality confirmable in any kind of physical reality.

In many countries around the world, the kiosk has been a primary focal point for social interaction; the multifunctional stands where tobacco can be purchased, telephone calls made, where multiple newspapers are conveniently hung so that the strolling individuals can peruse the headlines and possibly engage others in conversation and discuss the state of the world or the problems of the community. Such public places play an important social and cultural role. In urban Greece, for example, such kiosks, known as *peripiteros*, are found on most major street corners and serve as a kind of community bulletin board. And to some extent, similar kind of bulletin boards have existed in American life—with the village green and barber shop, soda fountain, pot-bellied stove—serving such a function.

So it is interesting to note that a legal issue has emerged regarding computer BBs in relationship to First Amendment rights.

> Advocates of a right of access to bulletin boards contend that the public message areas of computer bulletin boards are the modern day equivalents of the streets, parks and commons of the eighteenth century town, and just as the First Amendment guarantees access to those fora, it guarantees access to computer bulletin boards.

The board operators respond by arguing that bulletin boards are not public fora, but rather the electronic equivalent of the press, and the operators may, in their editorial discretion, refuse to publish messages they deem inappropriate (Naughton, 1993).

Real Property and Cyber Property

From a legal perspective real property—physical space—is distinguished by possession, use, and enjoyment. The laws of real property and access to that property in order to communicate produce distinct issues determined by whether the public space is publically or privately owned. Although title to real property is easily identifiable, who owns cyberspace? Cyberspace is described by CompuServe as "that nowhere space [electronic space] in the telephone line between you and where all things online happen, but it's also the 'room' or other expanse you're not really in when you're visiting any form of virtual reality" (*CompuServe*, 1994, 12). Bulletin boards have been called the computer-age equivalent of a public forum (Naughton, 1993) but approximately 90% are operated by private individuals or organizations on privately owned computers (Feder, 1991, D5).

Public Forum, Public Space, and Property Rights

The public forum doctrine first developed in *Hague v. Committee for Industrial Organization* (1939), a plurality, held that the right to assemble and discuss national issues was a privilege of national citizenship secured by the Fourteenth Amendment. Justice Robert's dictum laid the foundation for the doctrine:

> Wherever the title of streets and parks may rest, they have immemorially been held in trust for the use of the public and, time out of mind, have been used for the purposes of assembly, communicating thoughts between citizens, and discussing public questions. Such use of the streets and public places has, from ancient times been a part of the privileges, immunities, rights and liberties of citizens. (p. 515)

This public forum doctrine developed to limit the legitimate power of the state to prohibit expression on publically owned property. *Marsh v. Alabama* (1946) began the expansion of this doctrine to some privately owned sites that were the functional equivalents of public property. The Supreme Court held that the fact that title may belong to a private corporation or individual is constitutionally insignificant with regard to the public forum doctrine as whether publically or privately owned there may be an identical interest in the functioning of the community in such manner that the channels of communication remain free. Justice Black's opinion noted:

> Ownership does not always mean absolute dominion. The more an owner, for his advantage, opens up his property for use by the public in general, the more do his rights become circumscribed by the statutory and constitutional rights of those who use it. (p. 506)

Private property was opened further to communicative activities in *Amalgamated Food Employees Union Local 590 v. Logan Valley Plaza, Inc.* (1968) when members of a union having been enjoined from picketing a supermarket in a private shopping center successfully appealed the injunction with the Court finding that shopping centers had become the functional equivalent of the "business block," particularly with the migration to the suburbs. The Court decision, limited to those situations where the private property was open to the public, made clear that states can constitutionally regulate the exercise of First Amendment rights if the exercise interfered with the use to which the property was put (*Amalgamated Food Employees v. Logan Valley*, 1968, pp. 317-318). Ultimately, in *Hudgens v. NLRB* (1976), the Court held that if a shopping center is in fact the functional equivalent of a municipality, the First and Fourteenth Amendment would not permit content-based restrictions on speech (520) but that they are not automatically considered the functional equivalent of a municipality.

Cyberspace becomes cyber property when it is privately owned and operated. In attempting to extend the law of real property to access in cyber property, the concept of *municipality* enunciated in Marsh would have to be redefined in that although

> a computer network has many of the attributes of a traditional public forum . . . the network is analogous to a very large public place. This space is truly a marketplace of ideas and a public forum for the communication of ideas and information. Like city streets and parks, which have immemorially been . . . used for purposes of assembly . . . and discussing public question, computer networks since their inception have been used as a means of communication. Like a city street, a computer network is continually open, often uncongested, and . . . a place where people may enjoy the company of friends . . . in relaxed environment. (Naughton, 1993, pp. 429-430)

Bulletin boards are designed to be opened for the purpose of communication whereas sidewalks, streets, parks, and other traditional public fora were created for a variety of other public purposes as well. "For a substantial population, the electronic arenas of computer networks have displaced the nation's streets and parks as the quintessential public fora. Like streets and parks, computer bulletin boards provide individuals with a low-cost yet extremely effective means of communication" (Naughton, 1993, p. 431), a forum far larger than the real property counterpart. Yet, in *The Georgetown Law Journal* article entitled "Is Cyberspace a Public Forum?" Naughton noted that despite the similarities between computer networks and traditional physical space public fora, the analogy is strained in that the bulletin boards have not "immemorially been held in trust for the use of the public and, time out of mind, . . . been used for purposes of assembly . . . and discussing public questions" (p. 431), thus lacking the special status afforded the traditional historical concept of public forum. Furthermore, many BBs (particularly commercial ventures) are governed by subscription agreement that generally expressly reserve the right to reject messages deemed inappropriate or to terminate the user's privilege to use the board. For example, America OnLine "reserves the right, at its sole discretion, to immediately, without Notice, suspend or terminate a Member's access to and use of America Online on any breach of the Terms of Service" (America OnLine Terms of Service, 1994).

The public space arguments and spatial legal metaphors surrounding electronic BBs were tested in the fall of 1990 when, as previously noted, Prodigy banned discussion of rate increases in public areas and canceled the accounts of 13 dissident users (Edelman, 1990). Prodigy later stated they conceived of the network as a newspaper publisher that would reject "grossly repugnant" messages and use editorial discretion to determine which posting fell into this category. This position was soundly criticized by groups such as the American Civil Liberties Union (Berman & Rotenberg, 1991).

Commercial BBs are only open to a public able to pay fees, not to the public at large. The contractual nature of the access strains the analogy to spatial access. Yet, the majority of BBs are open to the general public without limitations based in contract (Naughton, 1992). The status with regard to public access and use of this area of cyber property remains without a clear legal status or regulatory policy and is unregulated to date.

Nonpossessory Rights to Space

The nature of the relationship of parties interacting in electronic space includes not only cyber property or space but telephone connection as well. These relationships may be clarified through an analogy to legal concepts governing these relationships in physical space.

In the law of torts, the legal status of one who enters the land of another has been divided roughly into three categories: trespasser, licensee, and invitee. As the legal status changes, the obligations of protection owed the visitor by the possessor of the land increase, in other words, the categories have been used in determining liability for negligence. A *trespasser*, lowest on the scale, is defined as "a person who enters or remains on land in possession of another without a privilege to do so, created by the possessor's consent or otherwise" (Prosser, 1971, p. 357) and generally no one has the right to enter without consent. Intruders have no right to demand protection from harm. In electronic space, the unwanted e-mail message or the obscene or harassing phone call made for social purposes would be akin to the trespasser. Thus, the relationship of the sender of the obscene message may be viewed this way. A *licensee* includes anyone who has a privilege to enter the land, including those who enter for social visits or personal business dealings, tourists visiting at their own request, salesmen canvassing at the door of private homes, and those soliciting money for charity (Prosser, 1971). The licensee takes the premises as the occupier does, which suggests that at most, the licensee is entitled to a warning of dangers on the land. Unsolicited commercial messages soliciting for charity or selling everything from investment opportunities to magazine subscriptions thus fall under this category. *Invitees* have been defined as those who "enter premises on business which concerns the occupier, and on his invitation express or implied" thus creating an affirmative duty to protect the invitee from all dangers known or discoverable (Prosser, 1971, p. 385). This category is also called the business invitee and includes customers entering a store, patrons of restaurants, theaters, and other commercial places open to the public. A social guest, "however cordially he may have been invited and urged to come, is not in law an invitee . . . the guest is legally nothing more than a

licensee" (Prosser, 1971, p. 378) meaning that the possessor owes no affirmative duty of care for safety. If applied to electronic space, the relationship created by a social or business contact made when one has given out an
E-mail address or has an address posted on the directory would be considered that of invitee/possessor of land. In attempting to unravel the nature of
the interpersonal-mediated relationship formed in commercial telephone
interaction we return to the issue of power and control, which has been significantly altered in the unique context of the 900 number. In a traditional,
noncommercial telephone interaction, the caller (akin to a licensee status) is
in a relationship in which he or she exercises some control vis-à-vis determining time and duration of the "visit," but the parties are essentially equal
unless the underlying relationship dictates otherwise. But the
consumer/caller of the 900 number has been invited for business purposes
and the guaranteed economic benefit of the party called (in other words,
the possessor of electronic space) and is therefore similar to the higher status invitee who enjoys a different position during the interaction rooted in
the commercial nature of the customer/merchant relationship. The merchant is obligated to interact when and for how long the caller (able to pay)
so wishes.

Nuisance Laws and Other Regulations of Real Property

Nuisance laws provide an alternative means of regulating land use and
thereby interaction. Before the beginning of this century, common law nuisance was a principle means of regulating use of real property. Private nuisance provides a tort action (civil liability) on which to litigate, focusing on
the reasonableness of conduct while enjoying one's property as compared
to the inconvenience and harm inflicted on others for activities such as
excessive noise (Prosser, 1971). Private nuisance applies to the interest of a
possessor of land in freedom from any unreasonable, nontrespassory interference with use and enjoyment of land, whereas public nuisance involves
the public interest in freedom from activity that endangers health, safety,
property, comfort convenience or offends public morals. Public nuisance
provides criminal liability and has been directly linked with communicative
activity in such circumstances as enjoining the operation of adult movie
houses as public nuisances because of past exhibition of obscene films
(*Vance v. Universal Amusement Co.*, 1980). Public profanity has also been
found to create a public nuisance (*Wilson v. Parent*, 1961). Under these
interpretations, providing opportunities for interaction or open spaces for
public gatherings could expose one to criminal liability if the interaction
goes beyond controlled limits. Nuisances exist in cyberspace. Hate speech
may be found on computer BBs (Leroux, 1991). Prodigy has been criticized
for allowing users to post anti-Semitic slurs in public area BBs (Miller,

1991). Obscene and pornographic material may appear on BBs. Once again issues of culpability may well rest in the determination of public versus private ownership — of whether a nuisance may be said to exist in public cyberspace or privately owned and operated cyber property.

Covenants are promises involving reality (*Black's Law Dictionary*, 1979). Restrictive covenants provide another alternative real property regulation which may have bearing on communication. Covenants are provisions in a deed limiting the use of property and prohibiting certain uses, which may limit interaction by prohibiting certain activities on premises (*Black's Law Dictionary*, 1979). Restaurants, pubs, meeting halls, and other businesses that are open to the general public may be prohibited or the hours the property is open to the public could be restricted, thus affecting the opportunity for public interaction. Covenants may be personal between parties or may be said to "run with the land." Covenants that run with the land

> are not merely personal between the immediate parties, but are also intended to benefit and/or bind others in the future and cannot be separated from the [estate] [land], nor can the land be transferred without the covenant binding. These promises may directly circumscribe the communicative activities taking place on privately owned real property, functioning to limit activities of possessors and their guests. (*Black's Law Dictionary*, 1979, p. 329)

Restrictive covenants may provide a useful metaphor for privately owned and operated electronic space so that operators of not only more public arenas like BBs, but those concerned with E-mail content and telephonic communication may find a mechanism for control. Such covenants might be extended to deal with cybersex or dial-a-porn if they are seen as a hazard.

Expectations of Privacy on Real Property and Cyber Property

The laws of privacy an area of law that has advanced much further in addressing electronic, nonphysical spaces of interaction. The evolution of right to be let alone, or the right to privacy, and reasonable expectations of privacy often emerges from nature of a particular geography location. Fourth and Fifth Amendment rights are implicated when considering search and seizure and freedom from self-incrimination associated with places in which there is a reasonable expectation of privacy. Courts have explored these expectations in physical spaces ranging from cars to school lockers and of course, homes, and offices (Kamisar, LaFave, & Israel, 1986). Reasonable expectations of privacy are no longer restricted to the physical spatial realm. In 1967, in *Katz v. United States* (1967) the Supreme Court found "the emphasis on the nature of a particular targeted area deflected attention from the issue of Fourth Amendment infringement" (p. 351). Justice Steward wrote the following:

> For the Fourth Amendment protects people not places. What a person knowingly exposes to the public, even in his own home or office, is not a subject of Fourth Amendment protection. . . . But what he seeks to preserve as private even in an area accessible to the public, may be constitutionally protected. (p. 351)

Congressional regulation of electronic surveillance of electronic spaces (originally wiretapping in particular) was addressed in a comprehensive federal legislative action in 1968 entitled Title III of the Omnibus Crime Control and Safe Streets Act (18 U.S.C. Sections 2510-2520, 1982). This act addressed both *wire communication* and *oral communication*, requiring government authorities to obtain a court-ordered warrant in order to conduct a surveillance. With the proliferation of methods of nonvoice communications including E-mail, cellular and cordless telephones, fax machines, video teleconferencing, paging devices, and digitized information networks, Congress was confronted with the need to revise Title III protections (Cutrera, 1991). Person-to-person interaction was subject to disparate legal treatment depending on the medium utilized. In 1986, Congress responded with the passage of the Electronic Communications Privacy Act (ECPA), which amended Title III to include electronic communications as a protected form of communications (18 U.S.C. Section 2510 (12), 1988). Although the act clearly encompasses communication of the mediated period such as telecommunications, the amount of protection afforded computer messages is in doubt. ECPA does recognize protection of electronic communication storage such as the storage of BB or E-mail messages (18 U.S.C. Section 2703, 1988). However, in *United States v. Miller* (1976), which involved bank records, information kept by a third party was not given Fourth Amendment protection because records were out of the possession of the originator producing no legitimate expectation of privacy concerning the information (Cutrera, 1991). This would indicate that stored electronic communication may not require a warrant in order to be seized and admitted in criminal court proceedings.

Since the early 1980s, more than half a dozen cases have ruled that private citizens do not have an expectation of privacy when conversing on a cordless phone (Marcus, 1989). Courts have emphasized the broadcast nature of the communication and thus the decreased expectation of privacy. In *Tyler v. Berodt* (1989), the Eighth Circuit Court of Appeals held that users of cordless phones did not have a reasonable expectation of privacy that would apply to those participants in ordinary line telephone communication (1989, cert. denied 1990). Those aware that their conversations were being transmitted by cordless telephone were presumed to have no expectation of privacy when the conversation would be "broadcast by radio in all directions to be overheard by countless people" (*Edwards v. Bardwell*, 1986). Instruction manuals (packaged with the phones) alert owners to the fact that conversations could be transmitted to others and thus there is no expectation of privacy (*State v. DeLaurier*, 1985). The remote scanning of private computer activity using CRT (Cathode ray tube) microspy devices are becoming available as an electronic surveillance technique. Computer monitors include an FCC warning notifying users that there are unintentional radiators. "The government, in an effort to conduct such scans without warrants, could analogize between computer monitors and cordless telephone receivers" (Cutrera, 1991, p. 163) finding no reasonable expectation of privacy so that remote scans could be conducted without warrants.

CONCLUSIONS

Cyberlaw pushes the envelope on existing legal doctrines, particularly those protecting First Amendment rights. Many legal metaphors and fields of extant law have been suggested as approaches for gaining a foothold on managing emerging questions of liability and rights. From treating postmodern media as akin to publications, common carriers, and distributors, to simply coping with the contractual nature of relationships, approaches that do not quite fit have been put forward. A state of confusion and gaps in the law have resulted from mixing legal metaphors to grapple with the legal issues emerging by the developments in cyberspace. We suggest that yet another metaphor, one that emphasizes the spatial dimension of the communicative event, may well be emerging as a favored regulatory metaphor as it is the one most closely linked to the descriptive language being used about the medium to be regulated. The evolutionary process by which the laws governing the nonmediated and media periods have followed this path by which the descriptive terms used about the characteristics of a medium have been linked to the applicable law developed, suggesting the spatial terms and laws may well provide a useful source during a time marked by uncertainty.

This discussion of the application of the laws of real property to cyberspace should not be read as a recommendation but rather as a reflection not only of a seemingly logical approach, but one in which the symbiotic relationship between the use of physical space (used for face-to-face interaction) and electronic space (offering options for mediated communication) is acknowledged.

If a regulatory approach borrowed from a noncommunicative orientation toward rights and liabilities forms the basis of cyberlaw, the future of free speech and privacy rights may be threatened. One may easily envision the need for a period of legal skirmishes and battles to re-establish the primacy of First Amendment rights in cyberspace.

It is significant that at a time when we seek refuge from the street, when the highway has been reduced to a connection between hostile zones, as we continue down the path of interiorizing and privatization, that the nomenclature of urban planning and architecture has been transformed into metaphors of cyberspace. The significance of the landscape orientation of cyberspace and the regulations being brought to regulate this new frontier is not only that a prior spatial identity has been applied to a nonterritorially defined medium, but that the very process of naming redefines the earlier application. Developments in the law of electronic space are not only significant in and of themselves as a symbiotic relationship exists between physical and electronic space. As the law develops and focuses on communicative rights and liabilities in the mediated realm of cyberspace, the significance of the physical realm of social interaction will be de-emphasize portending serious implications for traditional expressive rights in that realm. Precedents being set in electronic space may well reflect and shape attitudes and rights with regard to physical space as well.

ADDENDUM

We remain in Phase 3, the postmodern media period, a period in which media convergence is both a technologically and commercially dominant force. Broadcasting, satellite, and computing traditionally operated independently with associated industries independently regulated along the same lines. Convergence toward a single multimedia market in which the Internet is delivering both basic voice telephony and radio and television retransmission has been rapid. Increasingly, functionality is placed in the foreground, whereas the specific medium is relegated to the background in the minds of end users. Due consideration to the nature of the media/medium to be regulated is key to the development of a manageable new regulatory framework but it is difficult to fix the nature of the medium when considering a technological picture that includes the Internet. The Internet defies traditional categorization because of its convergent character which joins various media, each with its unique grammar, syntax, and convention—the letter, the telegraph, radio, television, recorded sound, film, the telephone, facsimile, and so on. Multipurpose networks have replaced the single-purpose medium. On the Internet, every node is literally both a transmitter and a receiver. Issues and inquires are less media-specific with regard to regulation reflecting the need for a new "digital media framework" of regulation.

Vertical regulatory models of broadcasting, telecommunications, and computer services are challenged by technological convergence. When radio and television programming is transmitted over the Internet, does the concept of broadcasting apply? Internet telephony now accounts for more than 10% of international calling traffic. Is that a telephone call or computer-mediated form of communication? Does convergence create a new medium . . . a new user or audience or both? Can the content of an older medium be transmitted over a new platform without altering the old medium or without creating a new medium? For example, when a book or article traditionally transmitted through a print medium is digitalized and made available via downloading, is that the same as a book? If a book is downloaded in a format that has not been protected and could easily be altered, is that the same medium as a book? If the book is encrypted to preserve content and limit possible alteration of content, is that more like the printed book? If the manuscript is read on a computer screen is that a different medium than if the downloaded manuscript is printed and then read? What is being regulated—a public act or private act? Broadcasting once was a public act thereby justifying regulation. It was a local act whose reach could be extended to reach a mass of individuals. Telephonic communication was a private act. Is watching a live webcast a public or private act . . . when it is essentially a closed-circuit form requested on demand? What is listening to an archived radio program—demand via the Internet—public or private? Is a message posted to a listserv a public act? The answer to these questions is not always clear and the applicable metaphors become murkier with the rapid maturation of the Internet. We are faced with a series of questions plaguing regulators around the globe.

The complex realities of convergence suggest that no one metaphor, not publishing, common carrier, distributor or spatial—reflects the permutations of the modern media landscape. Each traditional metaphor of media regulation emphasized the platform or the mode of transmission rather than the end user's experience. To understand the medium in a context of convergence it is necessary to distinguish between "technological" and "qualitative dimensions" of that medium, suggesting an emphasis on user experience rather than technology in making the selection of guiding legal metaphor. In this regard, spatial metaphors retain their appeal. As it stands, the Internet is a medium in search of a guiding metaphor because there can be no reasoned regulation without an applicable legal metaphor.

Acknowledgment

This chapter originally appeared in the *Free Speech Yearbook* in 1995. It is reprinted with permission. The addendum has been added for this edition.

NOTES

1. *Cubby v. CompuServe Incorporated* (1991) is the sole case to date in which a libel action was reportedly brought against an information service provider. In this case, a plaintiff sued CompuServe on the basis of allegedly false and defamatory statements contained in an electronic newsletter available in CompuServe's Journalism Forum. The newsletter was published by a third party (not CompuServe). The court granted CompuServe's motion for summary judgment relying on CompuServe's actions as distributor, exercising no editorial control and acting as an electronic library.

    Note: Subsequently, Congress provided immunity to service providers in Section 230 of the Communications Decency Act, which stipulates that "No provider or user of an interactive computer service shall be treated as the publisher or speaker of any information provided by another information content provider" (Section 230 (c)(1)). In addition, there is a "Good Smaritan" clause that exempts service providers from liability for "any action voluntarily taken in good faith to restrict access to or availability of material that the provider or users considers to be obscene, lewd . . . or otherwise objectionable" (Section 230 (c)(2)(A)). For additional information, see Chapter 12, in this volume.

2. Hate speech has become an issue faced by information providers. The Anti-Defamation League of B'nai B'rith cited anti-Semitic notes sent via E-mail but rejected for public posting by Prodigy as an example of electronically networked hate speech (Miller, 1991). For a further discussion see Leroux (1991).

3. Obscenity has received a good deal of attention within the context of cyberspace (Jackson, 1994). In one prominent case, the operators of "Amateur Action" electronic BB service were convicted under the federal law criminalizing transmitting obscene images electronically from California to Tennessee (Landis, 1994).

4. Three students at Santa Rosa Junior College in California were offended by sexual comments on a computer BB run through the school. In this case, separate male and female BBs were operated and the students alleged sexual discrimination bringing charges under Title IX of the Civil Rights Act prohibiting sexual discrimination in schools. Furthermore, it was found that one female student, Jennifer Branham, had been subjected to sexual harassment in that a hostile educational environment had been created with regard to the posting of the messages. A settlement was reached between the students and the college in the amount of $15,000. The case against the Education Department under Title IX remains open (P. Lewis, 1994).

5. The libel/slander distinction in law is particularly significant as damages for libel are generally larger than those for slander and the elements required to be

proven are generally less burdensome than those for slander as slander suits require plaintiffs prove actual monetary damages (Restatement of Torts (Second), 1976).

6. The Internet began in the 1970s as a U.S. Defense Department network called ARPnet. Slowly, corporations, universities, and information providers phased and dovetailed their networks into the system agreeing on compatible connecting software (McNichol, 1994). And it is the Internet that is a focal point of the electronic data highway featured as a high priority in the Clinton–Gore administration. Such a system includes digital libraries (making libraries accessible to everyone), database publishing, E-mail, electronic communities (virtual or non-place communities that link people with similar interests), software access, weather information, entertainment, and data exchange (Markoff, 1993).

REFERENCES

Amalgamated Food Employees Union Local 590 v. Logan Valley Plaza, Inc. 391 U.S. 308. (1968).
America OnLine Subscriber Agreement: Terms of Service. (1994).
Becker, L. (1989). The liability of computer bulletin board operators for defamation posted by others. *Connecticut Law Review*, 203-238
Berman, J., & Rotenberg, M. (1991, January 6). Free speech in an electronic age, *The New York Times*, p. C:13.
Black's Law Dictionary (5th ed.). (1979). St. Paul, MN: West Publishing.
Blankenship, J. (1980). The search for the 1972 Democratic nomination: A metaphorical perspective. In B. Brock & R. Scott, (Eds.), *Method of rhetorical criticism: A twentieth century perspective* (2nd ed.). Detroit, MI: Wayne State University Press.
Bosmajian, H. (1992). *Metaphor and reason in judicial opinion.* Carbondale: Southern Illinois University Press.
Bosmajian, H. (1982). Fire, snakes and poisons: Metaphors and analogues in some landmark free speech cases. *Free Speech Yearbook*, 20, 16-22.
City of Lakewood v. Plain Dealer Publishing Co., 108 S. Ct. 2138. (1988).
Compuserve Magazine. (1994, March 12).
Cubby v. CompuServe Incorporate, 776 F. Supp. 135 (S.D.N.Y). (1991).
Cutrera, T.A. (1991). The constitution in cyberspace: The fundamental rights of computer users. *University of Missouri—Kansas City Law Review*, 60(1), 139-167.
Daniel v. Dow Jones & Co., 520 N.Y.S. 2d 334. (1987).
Drucker, S.J., & Gumpert, G. (1991). Public space and communication: The zoning of public interaction. *Communication Theory*, 1(4), 296-310.
Edelman, L. (1990, November 20). Is this man invading your privacy? *Boston Globe*, p. 25.
Edwards v. Bardwell, 632 F. Supp. 584. (1986).
Farmers Educational and Cooperative Union of America v. WDAY, Inc. 360 U.S. 525. (1959).

Feder, B.J. (1991, November 3). Toward defining free speech in the computer age. *The New York Times*, p. D5.

Greenhouse, S. (1994, April 22). U.S. says later that it will pressure his foes: Six lawmakers arrested during protest. *The New York Times*, p. A1.

Hague v. Committee for Industrial Organization, 307 U.S. 496. (1939).

Hudgens v. NLRB, 424 U.S. 507. (1976).

Internet Society. (1994). Latest Internet measurements reveal dramatic growth in 1994. Press release August 4.

Jackson, D.S. (1994, July 25). Battle for the soul of Internet. *Time*, pp. 50, 56.

Johnson, D.R., & Marks, D.A. (1993). Mapping electronic data communications onto existing legal metaphors: Should we let our conscience (and our contracts) be our guide? *Villanova Law Review, 81*(2), 487-516.

Kamisar, Y., LaFave, W.R., & Israel, J.H. (1986). *Modern criminal procedure* (6th ed.). St. Paul, MN: West Publishing.

Katz v. United States, 389 U.S. 347. (1967).

Landis, D. (1994, August 9). Regulating porn: Does it compute? *USA Today*, p. D1.

Layne v. Tribune Co., 146 So. 234. (1993).

Leroux, C. (1991, October 27). Hate speech enters computer age. *Chicago Tribune*, p. C4.

Lewis, P. (1994a, June 19). Getting down to business on the Net. *The New York Times*, p. C.1.

Lewis, P. (1994b, June 29). No more "anything goes": Cyberspace gets censors. *The New York Times*, p. A1.

Marcus, A.D. (1989, November 29). Callers on cordless phones surrender privacy rights. *The Wall Street Journal*, p. B4.

Markoff, J. (1993, September 5). The Internet. *The New York Times*, Styles, p. 11.

Marsh v. Alabama, 326 U.S. 501. (1946).

McNichol, T. (1994, January 21). Fellow travelers on the Info Highway. *USA Weekend*, p. 4.

Miami Herald Publishing Co. v. Tornillo, 418 U.S. 241. (1974).

Miller, M.W. (1991, October 22). Prodigy network defends display of anti-semitic notes. *The Wall Street Journal*, p. B1.

National Association of Regulatory Commissioners v. FCC, 525 F. 2d. 630. (1976).

Naughton, E.J. (1993). Is cyberspace a public forum? Computer bulletin boards, free speech, and state action. *The Georgetown Law Journal, 81*, 409-441.

The New York Times, (April 22, 1994). p. 1.

Oldenburg, R. (1993). *The great good place: Cafes, coffee shops, community centers, beauty parlors, general stores, bars, hangouts, and how they get you through the day*. New York: Pergamon Press.

Ong, W. (1977). *Interfaces of the word: Studies in the evolution of consciousness and culture*. Ithaca, NY: Cornell University Press.

Prosser, W.L. (1971). *Handbook of the law of torts* (4th ed.). St. Paul, MN: West Publishing.

Resnick, R. (1991, September 16). The outer limits. *National Law Journal*, pp. 1, 19.

Restatement of Torts (Second). (1976). St. Paul, MN: West Publishing.

Smith v. California, 361 U.S. 147. (1959).

State v. DeLaurier, 488 A. 2d 688. (R.I. 1985).

Strauber, I.L. (1987). The rhetorical structure of freedom of speech. *Polity, 19,* 507-528.

Stuckey, K.D. (1994). Rights and responsibilities of information service providers. In E. Kirsh, L. Rose, & S. Steele, *Business and legal aspects of the internet and online services* (pp. 407-450). New York: Law Journal Seminars-Press.

Tribe, L. (1978). *Constitutional law.* Mineola, NY: Foundation Press.

Tyler v. Berodt, 877 F. 3d 705. 8th Cir. 1989, cert. denied.110 S.Sct. Rptr. (1990).

United States v. Miller, 425 U.S. 435. (1976).

Vance v. Universal Amusement Co. 445 U.S. 308. (1980).

Wilson v. Parent, 365 P. 2d 72. (1961).

18 U.S.C. Sections 2510-2520. (1988).

47 U.S.C. Section 202. (1982).

4

First Amendment Challenges to Content-Based Restrictions on Internet Expression

The Importance of the Standard of Review

Douglas Fraleigh
California State University,
Fresno

The evaluation of the constitutionality of a law is based upon the standard of review or legal criteria applied. When deciding a First Amendment case, the standard of review is particularly critical. In this chapter Douglas Fraleigh traces the selection and application of the standard for reviewing government restrictions on the content of Internet expression. Typically, if a challenged restriction impacts a fundamental right, a rigorous form of analysis known as the strict scrutiny test is applied. The standard in a broadcast context is not as exacting. Specifically, in this chapter the author considers how the standard of review was at issue in the Supreme Court's consideration of Reno v. ACLU, *the first federal law passed to significantly regulate Internet communication. He then considers how the standard of review has been considered with regard to Internet regulation since that decision.*

Sports fans are well aware of how the results in sports such as ice skating, snow boarding, or gymnastics can vary greatly, depending on the standards used to judge the competitors. Civil libertarians are more concerned with the judicial standards for review of legislation that imposes on individual rights.

In freedom of expression cases, the standard of judicial review is often pivotal. The criteria that a court uses to evaluate the government's justification for restricting communication will greatly influence whether the restriction will be upheld or found unconstitutional.

The growth of the Internet in the 1990s created a new context for debating the appropriate standard of review. Although the Internet was relatively unknown at the beginning of the 1990s, there were 10 million users by 1994 (Markoff, 1994). There were 104 million adult users (and 30 million children) in the United States by the year 2000 (*Pediatrics*, 2001). Worldwide, there were 332 million people connected to the Internet in 2000 (Numbers, 2000).

Rapid expansion of Internet communication was accompanied by the looming threat of government restriction. Volkoh (1995) forecast attempts to limit extremist speakers and regulate "inaccurate" news and information. Senator Dianne Feinstein argued that hate speech and bomb-making manuals should be banned from the Internet (O'Connor, 1995). The Communications Decency Act (CDA) was the first federal law to impose significant constraints on Internet communications. The CDA banned the online transmission of indecent communications to minors, and imposed criminal penalties on violators.[1]

Shortly after the president signed the CDA, 20 plaintiffs, including the American Civil Liberties Union (ACLU), filed a lawsuit challenging the constitutionality of the act. A federal district court entered a preliminary injunction against enforcement of the statute (*ACLU v. Reno*, 1996) and the government appealed that decision to the Supreme Court.

The stakes were high when the Supreme Court considered *Reno v. ACLU* (1997), the case that would ultimately resolve the ACLU's challenge. The choice of a standard for reviewing Internet restrictions would be likely to have a pivotal effect on the ACLU's challenge to the CDA, and also on the constitutionality of future government efforts to regulate the content of Internet expression. This is because the burden of justification placed on the government varies greatly, depending on the standard of review that is chosen. When analyzing First Amendment rights for new communication technologies as they developed in the 20th century, the Court had treated each new medium as a law unto itself (Greenhouse, 1997) and had applied different standards of review.

This chapter traces the selection and application of the standard for reviewing government restrictions on the content of Internet expression.

First, three potential standards of review are contrasted, to demonstrate the stakes involved in *Reno*. Next, the selection and application of a standard in *Reno* are explained. Finally, the impact of the standard chosen is analyzed.

POTENTIAL STANDARDS OF REVIEW

Historically, the Supreme Court has determined the standard of review for restrictions on new technology by asking which existing technology was most analogous to the new. When Reno was argued before the Supreme Court, one of the major subtexts was which analogy to Internet communication was most appropriate (Greenhouse, 1997). The primary candidates were telephone services, radio and television broadcasting, and cable television, and each would have a different implication for restrictions on Internet expression.

Strict Scrutiny of Restrictions on Expression

Strict scrutiny is the most difficult standard of review for the government to meet. This level of scrutiny applies to content-based restrictions on traditional modes of communication such as newspapers, pamphlets, and speeches. It was also applied to restrictions on telephone communications that are indecent but not legally obscene[2] (*Sable v. FCC*, 1989).

When strict scrutiny is applied to a restriction on speech, the Court analyzes whether the regulation promotes a compelling state interest and whether it constitutes the least restrictive means to further that interest. The means by which the government interest is served must be narrowly tailored to achieve those ends, and the law must be reasonably restricted to the evil with which it is said to deal (*Sable v. FCC*, 1989).

When regulating indecent communication, the government typically argues that there is a compelling state interest because of the need to protect the well-being of the nation's youth (see e.g., *ACLU v. Reno*, 1996; *Ginsberg v. New York*, 1968). The protection of minors' physical and psychological well-being can satisfy the compelling state interest criteria of the strict scrutiny test. However, a mere governmental assertion that the nation's youth are in need of protection will not survive strict scrutiny. The government cannot "posit the existence of the disease sought to be cured," instead it must "demonstrate that the recited harms are real, not merely conjectural" (*Turner Broadcasting System v. FCC*, 1994, p. 531).

Even if there is a compelling state interest, legislation aimed at indecency may also be found unconstitutional because the means by which the government attempts to protect children cannot survive strict scrutiny.

One question asked about the means is whether the government's interest can be served by a law that is less intrusive on First Amendment freedoms. For example, in *Sable v. FCC* (1989), the Court held that a ban on indecent commercial telephone messages was not needed to prevent children from accessing the messages. Less intrusive means to protect children were available, such as requiring a credit card or access code before one could receive a message. The government could not prevail by asserting that these alternatives to a ban would be ineffective; instead, it would be the state's burden to prove that enterprising minors would be able to circumvent the rules.

A second question asked when applying strict scrutiny to the means of achieving a compelling state interest is whether the regulation would be successful in serving the asserted state interest. An example of how this principle is applied can be found in Justice Kennedy's dissenting opinion in *Denver Area Educational Telecommunications Consortium, Inc. v. FCC* (1996). The regulation at issue allowed cable system operators to prohibit the broadcasting of patently offensive programming on cable channels that they lease to other parties. Justice Kennedy's opinion noted that children could still see offensive programming in any locality in which the cable operator opted not to ban the offensive programming. Hence, this law was at most a "partial service of a compelling interest" (p. 943) and it could not survive strict scrutiny.

A third question asked about the means chosen is whether the costs to free expression imposed by the means are outweighed by any benefits achieved. In *Butler v. Michigan* (1957), a unanimous Supreme Court invalidated a statute that prohibited distribution to the general public of materials found to have a potentially harmful influence on minors. The Court reasoned that the law denied adults their free speech rights by allowing them to read only what was acceptable for children. Justice Frankfurter's opinion in *Butler* analogized the effect of this provision to "burn[ing] the house to roast the pig" (p. 383).

The Standards for Evaluating Broadcast Indecency

The government has a lower burden of justification when regulations apply to indecent expression in the broadcast medium. In *FCC v. Pacifica Foundation* (1978), the Supreme Court upheld the Federal Communications Commission's (FCC) power to impose sanctions when a radio station broadcast George Carlin's "Filthy Words" monologue[3] at 2 in the afternoon. The case arose when a father complained to the FCC because he heard the broadcast while driving with his young son. The monologue was not legally obscene, but it was found to be indecent.

The *Pacifica* opinion did not articulate a particular level of scrutiny for content-based regulations of broadcasting. Instead, the Court provided two justifications for giving the government greater power to punish indecent messages on the airwaves. First was the fact that the "broadcast media have established a uniquely *pervasive* presence in the lives of all Americans" (p. 748, italics added). The Court noted that indecent material on the airwaves can confront the citizen in the privacy of the home. An individual could turn on his or her radio and be subjected to indecent programming of which he or she had no prior notice. Justice Stevens' majority opinion rejected the argument that the harm of indecency could be remedied by turning off one's radio, analogizing this claim to "saying that the remedy for an assault is to run away after the first blow" (pp. 748-749).

Second, the Court noted that broadcasting is uniquely accessible to young children. The "government's interest in the 'well being of its youth' and in supporting 'parents' claim to authority in their own household'" (p. 749) justified a ban on indecent broadcasting, at least during times when children are likely to be awake.

The communicator faces a substantial detriment when the constitutionality of government restrictions is determined by the broadcasting standard rather than strict scrutiny. First, for highly protected communication channels, the less restrictive alternative of turning one's head is the remedy to offensive expression (*Cohen v. California*, 1971, p. 21). For pervasive modes of communication, if the receiver can be surprised by offensive words, the receiver's right not to be offended in the home trumps the free expression rights of the source.

Additionally, when strict scrutiny is applied, the government has a burden to prove that less restrictive alternatives to a ban on indecent expression would fail. This burden was not imposed in *Pacifica*. The government was not required to prove that radio station warnings would be unable to keep most children from hearing offensive programming. Alternatives such as parental programming of the radio buttons in the car, or a parental rule that only adults may tune in a station, were not considered.

Finally, the *FCC v. Pacifica Foundation* court did not ask whether the gains from banning indecent programming outweighed the cost. The majority opinion expressed concern that the listener could not be *completely* protected from offensive expression. The interest of the offended listeners was the only one considered. It was assumed that any harm caused by exposure to indecency was sufficient to outweigh the freedom of speech that is lost. The free expression right of the communicator and the right of willing adult listeners to hear the Carlin monologue were not even placed into the equation.

The *Denver Area* Test for Cable Regulation

The broadcast standard was not the only possible alternative to strict scrutiny that the Supreme Court might have applied to Internet regulations. In *Denver Area Educational Telecommunications Consortium, Inc. v. FCC* (1996), a Supreme Court plurality created a test for cable television regulations that could have very unpredictable results if applied to cyberspace cases.

Denver Area considered the constitutionality of Section 10a of the Cable Television Consumer Protection and Competition Act of 1992. That provision allowed the *operator* of a cable system to prohibit the broadcasting of programming that he or she reasonably believed to describe or depict sexual or excretory activities in a patently offensive manner on channels that he or she leased to a third party.

Justice Breyer's plurality opinion[4] (joined by Justices Stevens, O'Connor, and Souter) declined to apply strict scrutiny to this regulation. Instead, the plurality held that the Section 10a would be constitutional if it "properly addresses an extremely important problem, without imposing, in light of the relevant interests, an unnecessarily great restriction on speech" (p. 902).

Applying this alternative standard of review, Justice Breyer concluded that Section 10a did not violate the expression rights of those who leased cable channels. First, the provision had an "extremely important justification," namely, "protecting children from "exposure to patently offensive sex-related material" (p. 902). Second, the context of this provision was unique, involving the allocation of expression rights between system operators and those who leased channels from them, rather than a government ban on offensive programming. Third, the plurality held that the problem in this case was "remarkably similar to the problem addressed by the FCC in *Pacifica*" (p. 903). The restriction in *Pacifica* was constitutional because broadcasting is uniquely accessible to children, and cable broadcasting is "as accessible to children as over the air broadcasting if not more so" (p. 903). Finally, because Section 10a only permitted (rather than requiring) cable operators to limit offensive programming, the loss of expression would probably be less than that which would be imposed by a governmental ban.

The test articulated by the plurality in *Denver Area* would provide an uncertain method of analyzing restrictions of Internet expression or any future communication media. The plurality's standard focused on two questions. First, does the restriction focus on an "extremely important" problem? Second, does the restriction impose an unnecessarily great restriction on speech in light of the relevant interests? Justice Breyer's opinion cited no case law in support of these standards. The plurality gave no definition of these terms and they failed to compare or contrast them with the strict scrutiny. Although they noted that this case was similar to *Pacifica* because cable channels are also pervasive, the plurality did not explain how their new standard changed or maintained the level of scrutiny applied in *Pacifica*. Justice Kennedy argued that the plurality opinion "clutter[ed] our First Amendment case law by adding an untested rule with an uncertain relationship to the others we use to evaluate laws restricting speech" (*Denver Area*, 1996, p. 930).

The Choice of a Standard in *Reno* Would Have Significant Consequences

The choice of a standard of review would have a major influence on the Supreme Court's holding in *Reno v. ACLU* and also on subsequent challenges to regulation of the content of Internet communications. If the Court decided to use strict scrutiny, the government would have to meet a heavy burden of justification. Few regulations on the content of speech can satisfy that analysis (*U.S. v. Playboy Entertainment Group*, 2000). Conversely, if the Court concluded that the Internet was pervasive and applied the *Pacifica* standard, the Court would give much greater deference to the government's asserted justifications for regulation. Finally, if the Court decided that the Internet was similar to cable television and applied the *Denver Area* test, the outcome would be uncertain. A new strand of case law would evolve, as the terminology in *Denver Area* was operationalized and refined in *Reno* and in future challenges to government restrictions.

THE *RENO V. ACLU* OPINION APPLIES STRICT SCRUTINY

Content-Based Restrictions on Internet Expression Are Subject to Strict Scrutiny

By a 7-2 majority, the Supreme Court ruled that the challenged provisions of the CDA were unconstitutional. The key passage in Justice Stevens' majority opinion noted that a high level of constitutional protection should be provided for Internet communication. In his words, "our cases provide no basis for qualifying the level of First Amendment scrutiny that should be applied to this medium" (p. 897).

The *Reno* majority explicitly declined to apply the *Pacifica* reasoning to the Internet. The Court held that "the Internet is not as 'invasive' as radio or television" (p. 896). The majority cited the *Reno* district court's findings that "the risk of encountering indecent material by accident is

remote" (pp. 894-95) and that "[a]lmost all sexually explicit images are preceded by warnings as to the content" (p. 896). Another difference between
Pacifica and *Reno* was that whereas the FCC had regulated broadcast stations for decades, application of the CDA would not be determined by an
agency that was "familiar with the unique characteristics of the Internet"
(p. 894). The majority further noted that the *Pacifica* opinion "expressly
refused to decide whether the indecent broadcast would justify a criminal
prosecution," (p. 894), and criminal sanctions were the potential conse-
quence for CDA violators.

Instead of likening the Internet to the broadcast media, the Court
found it more analogous to for-profit telephone message services. When the
Supreme Court analyzed a prohibition on indecent telephone messages in
1989, the Court had declined to hold that the "dial-it" medium was analogous to broadcasting. This is because that medium "requires the listener to
take several affirmative steps to receive the communication," hence, "placing a telephone call . . . is not the same as turning on a radio and being taken
by surprise by an indecent message" (*Sable Communications of California,
Inc. v. FCC*, 1989, pp. 127–128). Using similar reasoning, the *Reno* majority noted that "[c]ommunications over the Internet do not 'invade' an individual's home or appear on one's computer screen unbidden. Users seldom
encounter content 'by accident'" (p. 896).

The *Reno* majority did not focus on the *Denver Area* test as a potential
standard for analyzing restrictions on Internet communications. No comparison was made between Internet communication and cable television.
Justice Stevens did note that the *Denver* case stood for the proposition that
the Court had an "overarching commitment to make sure that Congress
had designed its statute to accomplish its purposes without imposing an
unnecessarily great restriction on speech" (p. 900).

He did not elaborate on the meaning of this test, nor did he explain
how it compares to strict scrutiny.

The CDA Failed to Survive Strict Scrutiny

The *Reno* majority acknowledged that the government had an interest in
protecting children from harmful materials. However, the Court determined that the CDA was not narrowly tailored to achieve that objective
because it restricted too much constitutionally protected expression and
because less restrictive alternatives could be used to protect minors.

The Scope of the CDA's Prohibition is Unprecedented. The Court
determined that "the CDA effectively suppresses a large amount of speech
that adults have a constitutional right to receive and to address to one
another" (p. 899), noting that "the breadth of the CDA's coverage was

wholly unprecedented" (p. 901). The opinion noted that the expression that could be classified as indecent or patently offensive includes "large amounts of nonpornographic material with serious educational or other value" (p. 901). Examples include discussions about safe sex or prison rape, artistic images that include nude subjects, and any of the seven dirty words used in the George Carlin monologue.

The Court rejected the government's claim that the CDA would not interfere with adult-to-adult communication. Many Internet communications, such as a statements made in a chatroom, will inevitably reach minors as well as adults because there is no reliable method of verifying the age of those who access the communication. In many Internet contexts, adults would need to refrain from protected adult communication because the message would be likely to reach minors, too.

The majority also noted that the vague terms of the CDA, along with its criminal sanctions, created a chilling effect that would magnify the act's impact on protected expression. Justice Stevens noted that terms such as "indecent" and "patently offensive sexual activities and organs" were not defined. Thus, a communicator could not confidently assume that a serious discussion about homosexuality or birth control methods would be permitted under the CDA. The severe criminal sanctions imposed by the CDA could easily cause speakers to remain silent, rather than communicate even arguably illegal words, images, or ideas.

The CDA is not the Least Restrictive Alternative. The government also failed to satisfy the strict scrutiny analysis because the CDA was not the least restrictive alternative available to achieve the state interest of protecting minors.

The Court discussed several different alternatives. For example, receivers could limit sexually explicit material in their own home without burdening the rights of adults to access material that might be deemed indecent. Citing the *Reno* district court opinion, Justice Stevens noted that parents could install software that would be reasonably effective in preventing their children from gaining access to sexually explicit material or other information that they deem inappropriate for children. He noted that other alternatives to prohibition, such as tagging indecent material in a way that would facilitate parental control, or making an exception in the CDA for material with artistic or educational value, had been proposed during oral argument.

The majority refused to accept the government's argument that the Court should defer to a congressional assertion that nothing short of the CDA could limit minors' access from harmful materials. The fact that Congress passed the CDA without holding hearings or making any detailed findings made the government's claim that the act was a necessary remedy particularly unpersuasive to the Court.

Consequently, the CDA failed under a strict scrutiny analysis. The decision to apply strict scrutiny had an important effect on freedom of expression in cyberspace. If the Internet had been found analogous to radio and television, the *Pacifica* reasoning could have been used to uphold the CDA. The Court would have placed greater importance on the need to keep minors from encountering indecent communications and less on the rights of adults to communicate. The Court would have granted more weight to the government's assertion that less onerous alternatives to the CDA would fail. Because the Court determined that strict scrutiny was the appropriate standard, the extensive burden on the rights of adults to send and receive messages online received primacy, and the burden was on the government to prove that the CDA was necessary to protect children. The Reno opinion also set a precedent for strict scrutiny of future government regulation of cyberspace communication.

JUDICIAL REVIEW AFTER *RENO V. ACLU*

ACLU of Georgia v. Miller

A Georgia statute (*O.C.G.A.*, Section 16-9-93.1) made it a crime for a person to transmit data through a computer network if the data uses any individual name to falsely identify that person. Furthermore, the statute prohibited computer transmission of data that used a trade name, trademark, official seal, or similar item if it was falsely stated or implied that permission to use that item had been obtained. The state of Georgia argued that this law was necessary to prevent fraud.

In *ACLU of Georgia v. Miller* (1997), the U.S. District Court for the Northern District of Georgia granted a preliminary injunction against the enforcement of that statute. (The injunction was not appealed.) The court noted that the identity of the speaker is no different from any other component of a document's contents that the author may choose to include or exclude. Thus, the prohibition of Internet transmissions that falsely identify the speaker is a content-based restriction and subject to strict scrutiny.

The district court agreed that fraud prevention was a compelling state interest. However, the court noted that the statute was not narrowly tailored to achieve that objective. Instead, it included innocent speech within its scope. There are nonfraudulent reasons that a person might use false identification, such as to avoid ostracism, prevent discrimination, or protect privacy. In addition, a ban on the use of trade names or logos for noncommercial educational purposes, or in news or commentary, is not permitted by the First Amendment. Citing *ACLU v. Reno*, the court issued a preliminary injunction because "the public interest weighs in favor of having access to a free flow of constitutionally protected speech" (p. 6).

ACLU v. Johnson

In 1998, New Mexico passed a statute which criminalized the dissemination by computer of material that is harmful to minors. In *ACLU v. Johnson* (1999), the Tenth Circuit Court of Appeals affirmed a district court grant of a preliminary injunction against that statute. The appellate court noted that "the Court made clear in *Reno v. ACLU* that content-based regulation of Internet speech is subject to . . . strict scrutiny" (p. 5). The appellate court noted that in the absence of a viable means to verify age, any source of an Internet message that could be harmful to minors could be subject to liability under the law. Thus, the statute, "like the CDA, unconstitutionally burdens otherwise protected adult communication on the Internet" (p. 8).

Mainstream Loudoun v. Board of Trustees

The Loudoun County Library Board of Trustees passed a requirement that all library computers be equipped with software that would block all sites displaying material that was harmful to juveniles. The U.S. District Court for the Eastern District of Virginia enjoined the enforcement of this policy in *Mainstream Loudoun v. Board of Trustees of the Loudoun County Library* (1998). The library board argued that its policy was necessary to minimize access to pornography and avoid the creation of a sexually hostile environment. The court reasoned that "because the policy limits the receipt and communication of information through the Internet based on the content of that information, it is subject to a strict scrutiny analysis" (p. 9).

The library policy failed to pass a strict scrutiny analysis. The district court first noted that the defendant bears the burden to prove that the threat of disruption is actual, material, and substantial because, according to *Reno v. ACLU*, "the interest in encouraging freedom of expression in a democratic society outweighs any theoretical but unproven benefit of censorship" (p. 11). The defense could only point to three complaints in libraries outside Virginia and one elsewhere in that state. As a matter of law, the court held that this evidence was insufficient to show that the policy is reasonably necessary (p. 11).

The court also held that less restrictive means were available to further the defendant's interests. For example, the library could install privacy screens on its computers, require the library staff to regulate inappropriate use (as they have done in the past, for example, when prepubescent boys were giggling over gynecological pictures in a medical book), or install filtering software only on computers that would be available for minors (p. 12).

Ashcroft v. ACLU (ACLU v. Reno II)

In the aftermath of the first *ACLU v. Reno* decision, Congress passed the Child Online Protection Act (COPA). COPA banned communication for commercial purposes on the World Wide Web that is available to minors and includes any material that is harmful to minors according to contemporary community standards. In *ACLU v. Reno II*, the Federal District Court for Eastern Pennsylvania granted a preliminary injunction against enforcement of this statute. The district court emphasized that "as a content-based regulation of [non-obscene sexual] expression, COPA is presumptively invalid and is subject to strict scrutiny by this Court" (p. 493). The court held that COPA would be likely to fail a strict scrutiny analysis because the law imposes a burden on speech that is protected for adults and that the government would be unlikely to meet its burden to prove that COPA is the least restrictive means of preventing minors from accessing harmful material.

The Third Circuit Court of Appeals affirmed the district court's decision in June 2000. That decision emphasized the fact that "because of the peculiar geography-free nature of cyberspace, [COPA's] community standards test would essentially require every web communication to abide by the most restrictive community's standards" (p. 175). The appellate court concluded that the government had not met its burden to prove that standards for what is harmful to minors is reasonably constant across America. This case was appealed to the Supreme Court.

The Supreme court vacated the Third Circuit's community standards analysis; however, the Court did not deny the appropriateness of a strict scrutiny analysis. In *Ashcroft v. ACLU*, the Supreme Court considered the narrow question of whether COPA's "use of 'community standards' to identify 'material that is harmful to minors' violates the First Amendment" (p. 585). A majority agreed that COPA's use of community standards did not render the law facially invalid. However, the Court made it clear that it was not reviewing the District Court's conclusion that COPA will not survive strict scrutiny (p. 585–586).

Cyberspace Communications, Inc. v. Engler

Michigan passed Public Act 33, criminalizing the dissemination or display of sexually explicit material over the Internet if it was harmful to minors. The U.S. District Court for the Southern District of Michigan permanently enjoined the enforcement of that act in *Cyberspace Communications, Inc. v. Engler* (2001). Judge Tarnow's opinion noted that the Michigan law was a content-based limitation on speech, and therefore, the would be subjected to strict scrutiny. His opinion recognized that protection of minors was a compelling state interest. However, there were less restrictive means available for achieving that goal. For example, parents could use filters or child-friendly software. Additionally, the Court noted that "every computer is manufactured with an on/off switch, that parents may utilize, in the end, to control the information which comes into their homes via the Internet" (p. 3).

The Impact of *Reno v. ACLU*: A Summary

The Supreme Court's holding that content-based restrictions on Internet expression should be subjected to strict scrutiny has played an important role in preserving the free flow of information in cyberspace. In *Reno* and subsequent decisions, the burden of proof on the government has been high. The government has been required to prove that the state interest asserted is real, that the regulation serving that interest does not excessively burden protected communication, and that there are no less restrictive alternatives for achieving the government interest. As a result, content-based restrictions on Internet expression have failed to pass constitutional muster.

Although *Reno v. ACLU* has given Internet communication the higher level of protection afforded to the print media and public speakers, rather than relegating it to the lower standing of radio and television, it should be noted that Reno did not grant absolute protection to online expression.

Other rationales that are used to justify restrictions on expression can still be applicable, even if the expression is online. For example, rights may be limited in the context of government-funded speech. In *Urofsky v. Gilmore* (1999), the Fourth Circuit Court of Appeals upheld a Virginia law that prohibited state employees from sexually explicit communication on the Internet. This case was analyzed as a public employee speech issue. Public employees have a right to free speech on matters of public concern (*Pickering v. Board of Education*, 1967); however, the Fourth Circuit concluded that job-related speech is not a matter of public concern.

In *U.S. v. American Library Association*, the Supreme Court considered the constitutionality of the Children's Internet Protection Act (CIPA), a law that links library funding to the use of blocking software on Internet terminals used by both adults and minors. The Supreme Court did not apply strict scrutiny to this restriction. A four justice plurality held that CIPA does not violate the First Amendment because when the Government appropriates public funds to establish a program, it is entitled to broadly define that program's limits (p. 236). Justice Kennedy (p. 238) and Justice Breyer (p. 241) concurred in the judgment on other grounds. In their opinions, both justices argued that CIPA imposed a minimal burden on adults because the statute allowed libraries to unblock filtered material or disable the filter at the adult user's request.

However, the fact that Internet communication may be restricted in contexts where freedom of speech receives less protection (such as when the speech is government funded) should not obscure the importance of *Reno v. ACLU*. Reno included Internet communication with the channels that receive the highest level of protection, and courts have subsequently followed Reno by invalidating content-based restrictions on Internet expression.

CONCLUSION

During the past decade, the Internet became a major channel of communication. In the United States, the federal government and many state governments sought to control the content of expression on this fast-growing channel of communication.

The standard that courts used to review constitutional challenges to government restrictions on the content of Internet communication would have a significant impact on freedom of expression. If the courts applied strict scrutiny to the government's justification for regulation, content-based restrictions would likely be found unconstitutional. If Internet restrictions were subjected to the standard imposed in the broadcast media context (*FCC v. Pacifica Foundation*), the courts would be more likely to accept the government's justification for regulation. An increasingly great percentage of communication in the U.S. could be subjected to heightened government control.

Thus, the stakes were high when the Communications Decency Act was subjected to judicial review in *Reno v. ACLU*. In *Reno*, the Supreme Court determined that there was "no basis for qualifying the level of First Amendment scrutiny that should be applied to" the Internet (p. 897). The CDA was subjected to strict scrutiny and it failed because the act excessively burdened protected adult communication and because there were less restrictive means for shielding minors from indecent communication.

Reno set an important precedent for judicial review of content-based restrictions on Internet communication. In subsequent cases, courts have applied strict scrutiny to invalidate state and federal legislation aimed at expression in cyberspace. Although *Reno* did not establish absolute protection for Internet communication, it did provide the Internet with the higher level of protection afforded print communication and speech, rather than the lesser protection extended to the broadcast media.

NOTES

1. The CDA prohibited the knowing transmission, by means of a telecommunications device, of "obscene or indecent" communications to any recipient under 18 years of age (47 U.S. Code, Section 223a.) The act also banned the knowing use of an interactive computer service to send to a specific person under 18 years of age, or to display in a manner available to a person under 18 years of age, communications that, in context, depict or describe, in terms "patently offensive," as measured by contemporary community standards, sexual or excretory activities or organs (47 U.S. Code, Section 223d). Penalties included a fine and up to 2 years imprisonment (Reno v. ACLU, 1997).

2. Indecency and obscenity are not synonymous concepts in First Amendment law. The Supreme Court settled on the criteria for obscenity in *Miller v. California* (1973), and subsequent decisions have made it clear that material must depict patently offensive hard core sexual conduct (*Jenkins v. Georgia*, 1974) and lack serious literary, artistic, political, or scientific value. Obscenity is not protected by the First Amendment (*Roth v. U.S.*, 1957). *Indecency* is a broader term than obscenity. It refers to material that does not conform with accepted standards of morality (*FCC v. Pacifica Foundation*, 1978). Communication that does not describe "hard core" sexual conduct may nevertheless be indecent because it contains offensive words pertaining to sex or excretion (*FCC v. Pacifica Foundation*). Expression that could be prosecuted on indecency grounds includes the text of a Tony-winning Broadway play which portrayed homosexuality and AIDS in graphic language, news articles and chat room discussions regarding the practice of female genital mutilation, and travel magazine photographs of sculptures in India depicting copulating couples (*ACLU v. Reno*, 1996). Political expression containing indecent words, such as "Fuck the CDA," could also be sanctioned (*ACLU Brief*, 1997).

3. "Filthy Words" was a satirical monologue about words that could never be said on the airwaves. The original seven words on George Carlin's list were "shit, piss, fuck, cunt, cocksucker, motherfucker, and tits." Carlin noted that the words would "curve your spine, grow hair on your hands and maybe even bring us, God help us, peace without honor. . . ." (*FCC v. Pacifica Foundation*, 1978).

4. Three justices (Thomas, Rehnquist, and Scalia) agreed with the plurality that Section 10a did not violate the First Amendment. They based their holding on the fact that the expression rights of cable system operators generally took primacy over the rights of those who leased channels from the operators (*Denver Area*, 1996.

REFERENCES

ACLU Brief of Appellees. (1996, October). Submitted to the Supreme Court in the matter of *Reno v. ACLU, No. 96-511.*

ACLU v. Johnson, 194 F.3d 1149. (1999).

ACLU v. Reno, 929 F.Supp. 824 (1996), aff'd,. *Reno v. ACLU, 521 U.S. 844.* (1997).

ACLU v. Reno II, 31 F.Supp.2d 473 (1999), aff'd. 217 F.3d 162 (2000), remanded
    Ashcroft v. ACLU, 535 U.S. 564. (2002).
ACLU of Georgia v. Miller, 977 F. Supp. 1228. (1997).
Ashcroft v. ACLU, 535 U.S. 564. (2002).
Butler v. Michigan, 352 U.S. 380. (1957).
Cohen v. California, 403 U.S. 15. (1971).
Cyberspace Comm. Inc. v. Engler, 142 F. Supp.2d 827. (2001).
*Denver Area Educational Telecommunications Consortium, Inc. v. FCC. 518 U.S.
    727.* (1996).
FCC v. Pacifica Foundation, 438 U.S. 726. (1978).
Ginsberg v. New York, 390 U.S. 629. (1968).
Greenhouse, L. (1997, March 24). What level of protection for internet speech? *The
    New York Times*, p. D5.
Jenkins v. Georgia, 418 U.S. 153. (1974).
*Mainstream Loudoun v. Board of Trustees of the Loudoun County Library, 24
    F.Supp.2d 552.* (1998).
Markoff, J. (1994, Jan. 23). Building the electronic superhighway. *The New York
    Times*, p. 6.
Miller v. California, 413 U.S. 15. (1973).
Number of new internet users is growing (2001, June). *Pediatrics, 107,* 1380.
Numbers (2000, July 31). *Time*, pp. 156, 17.
O'Connor, R.J. (1995, May 12). Cyberspace hate speech, bomb data raising ques-
    tions. *Fresno Bee*, p. A6.
Pickering v. Board of Education, 391 U.S. 563. (1967).
Reno v. ACLU, 521 U.S. 844. (1997).
Roth v. U.S., 354 U.S. 476. (1957).
Sable Communications of California, Inc. v. FCC, 492 U.S. 115. (1989).
U.S. v. American Library Association, 539 U.S. 194, 156 L.Ed. 2d 221. (2003).
U.S. v. Playboy Entertainment Group, 529 U.S. 803. (2000).
Urofsky v. Gilmore, 216 F.3d 401. (2000), *cert. denied*, 531 U.S. 1070 148 L.Ed.2d
    662. (2001).
Volkoh, E. (1995). Cheap speech and what it will do. *Yale Law Journal, 104,* 1848.

5

Moving the Boxes Around

In Loco Parentis and The Child Online Protection Act (COPA)

Joseph Tuman
San Francisco State University

Joseph S. Tuman compares the Communications Decency Act (CDA) and the Child Online Protection Act (COPA). Both laws were designed to regulate the Internet in the name of the public interest in shielding children from material produced for "commercial purposes" that are "harmful to children." He argues that these two Federal laws passed in the United States addressing the regulation of obscenity and indecency on the Internet are very similar. He raises the question of whether given the finding that the CDA was unconstitutional, can COPA pass constitutional muster? The author calls for the thoughtful consideration of what parental and governmental responsibilities towards children should be in cyberspace.

As a student at the University of California (Berkeley), I would often finish the school year with perhaps $20 in my meager checking account, and hastily beat a path back to the San Joaquin valley, where I had spent much of my late childhood. There at my parents' home could be found a warm bed and a still full refrigerator and the opportunity to seek summer employment to pay for the next school year. Over the course of several years, I spent those summers in the employ of the U.S. government, as an inspector for the Department of Agriculture. Every morning I would drive to a different location in a territory that stretched between Stockton and Fresno, California, visiting different ranches and farms where California peaches were grown. My job was to inspect the fruit for size, quality, infestation, and potential rot. If I certified the fruit I inspected with a passing grade, it would be sold to local vendors or canneries. If I rejected a load of peaches, I was in effect saying they could not be sold for the same vendors or canneries. I was the judge and the jury.

Although the locations for these inspections differed, the set-up was always the same. I would sit with my tools and scales, beside a large table, all placed beneath a narrow corrugated tin roof, with a long dirt road leading from the peach orchards. These stations would be visited daily by growers in the area, who delivered their fruit for inspection on the back end of a long flat bed truck, usually filled with anywhere from 8 to 20 large wooden boxes—also known as bins—inside of which were the precious fruit.

To ensure that the sampling of fruit we inspected (usually three buckets worth from the bins) was truly a random sample, we inspectors carried a set of cards, changed by our supervisors on a daily basis, which provided random numbers of bins from which to draw. We counted the boxes, beginning with those closest to the truck cab, and moving backward. We marked the boxes we inspected, by drawing a colored chalk slash diagonally across their width. Because a different card was used for each delivery, and because the cards themselves were changed daily, the growers never really knew which box we would inspect, and thus there was no chance for them to stack the deck, as it were, by putting their best fruit only in those boxes they knew we would check.

This much seemed fair and reasonable. Very quickly, however, I observed that when I did reject a load of fruit for reasons including split-pits or inadequate size, the grower would usually say something unkind, and then jump into the truck and drive back into the orchards.

Invariably, 30 to 40 minutes would pass, and then the same grower would reappear, with supposedly new boxes on the back of the truck. Because this was technically a new load, I would go through the process again, examining my cards and randomly selecting boxes to sample for inspection. Often, the second inspection would end up the same as the first—with a rejection. The drama in the orchards would then play itself out a third, and sometimes a fourth and a fifth time, with the grower disappearing and returning with "new boxes." Sometimes, they passed by the end of it all.

Of course, the truth of the matter was that the grower would simply drive his truck back to a spot in the orchards, out of my eyesight, where his workers could rotate the boxes around, concealing my chalk marks, and outwardly creating the appearance of new boxes with new fruit. Because I never observed this practice in person, I was not allowed to challenge them. Instead, I continued to do my tests, as if each inspection of fruit was for the first time. But I knew what they were doing. They knew that I knew what they were doing. And I knew that they knew!

In my later years, I would observe that the growers with whom I worked in those long hot summers were not the only ones to try moving the boxes around. The U.S. Congress often acts in very similar fashion whenever a key piece of legislation is challenged in the court system and ultimately overturned by the Supreme Court.

For example, in 1998, Congress passed the Child Online Protection Act (COPA) into law, severely restricting any speech on the World Wide Web (henceforth, Web) which is "harmful to minors." Congress acted because only one year earlier, the United States Supreme Court, in *Reno v. American Civil Liberties Union, et al.,*[1] had declared an earlier Congressional attempt to regulate indecent speech on the Web, in a law called the Communications Decency Act (CDA), unconstitutional for violating the First Amendment.

At first glance, COPA does appear to be a different and more focused type of regulation for the Web than that offered in the CDA. COPA, as its name implies, is about protecting children. Government here realizes the classic ideal of *in-loco parentis*, acting in the place of the parents, to protect the child. COPA, as well, applies to obscenity and not just indecency, and is focused on those who produce "for commercial purposes" obscene material that is harmful to minors.

On closer observation, however, the differences between COPA and the CDA are not so clear. This chapter argues that the two laws are in fact very much alike. Perhaps more alike than they are different. And the question thus remains, in passing the COPA, did Congress simply drive the truck back into the orchard and move the boxes around?

BACKGROUND TO COPA: THE CDA

The origins for the legislation in COPA can be found in the CDA, which itself was tacked on as a piece of the Telecommuncations Act of 1996. In the years leading up to this act there had been increasing awareness of the potential for explosive growth in the Internet, with the result that more households began acquiring personal computers for individual word processing needs, and most especially—Internet access. By 1995, it was reported that 35% of all U.S. households had at least one personal computer (Negroponte, 1995). More to the point, in that same time, 70% of new sales of computers were for the home market, as families with children began to buy computers, creating the possibility of successive generations of computer-literate people—but also meaning that successively younger generations of children would have more access to the Internet. Without parental supervision, it was easy to assume these children might find themselves exposed to material that could be considered indecent or obscene.

Knowing a potential election year issue when it saw one, Congress jumped into this controversy and passed the aforementioned CDA.[2] The act provided in part that any person in interstate or foreign communication who "by means of a telecommunications device, knowingly . . . makes, creates, or solicits" and "initiates the transmission" of "any comment, request, suggestion, proposal, image, or other communication that, in context, depicts or describes, in terms patently offensive as measured by community standards, sexual or excretory activities, regardless of whether the user of such service placed the call or initiated the communication . . . knowing that the recipient is under 18 years of age . . . shall be criminally fined or imprisoned." In practice, the CDA would have imposed criminal penalties of up to $250,000 in fines, and as much as 2 years in prison for each transmission of obscene or indecent communication.

Diverse groups, including publishers, librarians, content and access providers, and civil liberties groups, quickly organized in legal opposition to the CDA, alleging a violation of the First Amendment. The Clinton administration, ordinarily more in sync with civil liberties issues, suddenly found itself forced to defend a law that appeared to violate free speech. Other groups, including the American Library Association, would later file separate actions against the CDA, and eventually all suits against this law were consolidated under one three-judge panel in the Third Circuit Court of Appeals (*ACLU v. Reno*, 1996). The three-judge court found the CDA unconstitutional—albeit each for different reasons. For Chief Judge Delores Sloviter, the CDA's challenged provisions failed strict scrutiny, both because they reached constitutionally protected speech, and because they were not narrowly drawn to achieve the desired result. For Judge Ronald Buckwalter, the constitutional problems grew out of the imprecision of the government's use of the terms *indecency* and *patently offensive*. And the difficulty of applying community standards for what appeared to be a Congressional attempt at promulgating national standards. For Judge Stewart Dalzell, the issue was approached differently, focusing on a failed justification for the CDA, grounded in a dated rationale for government regulation—from the *FCC v. Pacifica*[3] opinion—the "scarcity" rationale, which made sense for controlling and conserving the scarce resource of television and radio broadcast frequencies, but made little sense when applied to new mediums like cable television, or in this case, the Internet.

In 1997, the U.S. Supreme Court heard an appeal of the Third Circuit ruling, and in an opinion signed by all nine Justices, rejected every argument the government offered in support of the CDA. Only Chief Justice William Rehnquist and Justice Sandra Day O'Connor concurred and dissented in part, and both authored separate opinions to that effect. For the majority opinion, authored by Justice Stevens, the CDA was seen to be vague and overbroad in its blanket prohibitions of material that was both indecent and patently offensive. The majority opinion noted that "the many ambiguities concerning the scope of [the CDA's] coverage render it problematic for the purposes of First Amendment coverage." For instance, each of the two parts of the CDA uses a different linguistic form. The first uses the word *indecent*, whereas the second speaks of material that "in context, depicts or describes, in terms patently offensive as measured by contemporary community standards, sexual or excretory activities or organs." Given the absence of a definition of either term, this difference in language will "provoke uncertainty among speakers about how the two standards relate to each other and just what they mean" (p. 871). The majority did acknowledge that protecting children from exposure to indecent material was a laudable goal, but nevertheless concluded that in its rush to achieve this result, the CDA would also suppress too much speech among adults, as well as between parents and children.

Instead, the Court felt, the Internet should be recognized as a powerful "new marketplace of ideas," and a "vast democratic for[um]" that is "dramatic[ally] expand[ing] in the *absence* of government regulation" (p. 885). They thus upheld the Third Circuit opinion, and found the CDA unconstitutional.

At that point, Congress was forced to reconsider how to proceed with regulating this material on the Web. The result of their reconsideration was COPA.

CONGRESS RETOOLS WITH COPA

In COPA, Congress would handle things differently than it had with the CDA. Focusing on the Court's admission that protecting children from objectionable material online was a worthy goal, the new law provided that "Whoever knowingly and with knowledge of the character of the material, in interstate or foreign commerce by means of the World Wide Web, makes any communication for commercial purposes that is available to any minor and that includes any material that is harmful to minors shall be fined not more than $50,000, imprisoned not more than six months, or both" (47 USC section 231, (a), (1), 1998).

The emphasis in COPA was on protecting children, and prohibiting objectionable material only when offered for commercial purposes. Seeking to avoid the pitfalls found in the CDA, the new law also stipulated that Internet carriers and other service providers would not be targeted under this legislation, thus avoiding the possibility that any of these commercial providers would be affected by or bring action against COPA (47 USC 231, (b) 1998). Affirmative defenses were offered, which would hopefully narrow the reach of the new law, thereby avoiding any questions of overbreadth under the First Amendment. The new law provided that "It is an affirmative defense to prosecution under this section that the defendant, in good faith, has restricted access by minors to material that is harmful to minors—(A) by requiring use of a credit card, debit account, adult access code, or adult personal identification number (pin); (B) by accepting a digital certificate that verifies age; or (C) by any other reasonable measures that are feasible under available technology" (47 USC 231, (c), 1998).

To avoid any accusation of vagueness in the meaning of the new law, Congress further provided definitions for two key parts of COPA: "commercial purposes" and "material that is harmful to minors."

The new law provided that "A person shall be considered to make a communication for the commercial purpose only if such person is engaged in the business of making such communications" (47 USC 231 (e) (2) (A) 1998). Clarifying a part of this definition, the law then added:

> The term "engaged in the business" means that the person who makes a communication, or offers to make a communication, by means of the World Wide Web, that includes any material that is harmful to minors, devotes time, attention, or labor to such activities as a regular course of such person's trade or business, with the objective of earning a profit as a result of such activities (although it is not necessary that the person make a profit or that the making or offering to make such communications be the person's sole or principal business or source of income). A person may be considered to be engaged in the business of making, by means of the World Wide Web, communications for commercial purposes that include material that is harmful to minors, only if the person knowingly causes the material that is harmful to minors to be posted on the World Wide Web or knowingly solicits such material to be posted on the World Wide Web. (47 SC 231 (e) (2) (B) 1998)

Clarifying any ambiguity about what material was targeted, the new law then added:

The term "material that is harmful to minors" means any communication, picture, image, graphic image file, article, recording, writing, or
other matter of any kind that is obscene or that—(A) the average person, applying contemporary community standards, would find, taking
the material as a whole and with respect to minors, is designed to
appeal to, or is designed to pander to, prurient interest; (B) depicts,
describes, or represents in a manner patently offensive with respect to
minors, an actual or simulated sexual act or sexual contact, an actual or
simulated normal or perverted sexual act, or a lewd exhibition of the
genitals or post pubescent female breast; and (C) taken as a whole, lacks
serious literary, artistic, political or scientific value for minors. (47 USC
(e) (6) 1998)

Minors were defined as "any person under 17 years of age." (47 USC
(e) (7) 1988)

Almost immediately, COPA was opposed in federal court by multiple
groups, including the American Civil Liberties Union (ACLU),
Androgyny Books, American Booksellers Foundation For Free
Expression, Artnet Worldwide Corporation, Blackstripe, Addazi Inc.,
(d.b.a. Condomania), Internet Content Coalition, Electronic Frontier
Foundation, Electronic Privacy Information Center, Free Speech Media,
OBGYN.net, Philadelphia GayNews, PlanetOut Corporation, Powell's
Bookstore, Riotgrrl, Salon Internet Inc., and West Stock (now known as
ImageState North America). The plaintiff, Internet Content Coalition,
would eventually go out of existence and be dropped from the list of those
in opposition to the law.

In February 1999, the case, which was then known as *ACLU v. Reno*,[4]
would achieve an initial victory of sorts for the plaintiffs arguing in the
District Court for the Eastern District of Pennsylvania, as Judge Lowell A.
Reed granted a motion for preliminary injunctive relief, barring enforcement of COPA, and following his grant of a temporary restraining order.[5]
A motion for preliminary injunctive relief requires a showing by plaintiffs
that a credible threat of prosecution against them or a showing that they
will imminently suffer injury sufficient to establish their standing to bring
the lawsuit. To do this, the plaintiffs in opposition to COPA had to prove:
"(1) a likelihood of success on the merits; (2) irreparable harm; (3) that less
harm will result to the defendant if the preliminary injunction issues than
to the plaintiff if the preliminary injunction does not issue; and (4) that the
public interest, if any, weighs in favor of plaintiffs" (*Pappan Enterprises,
Inc., v. Hardee's Food Systems, Inc.,* 143 F. 3d 800, 803, 1998). Judge Reed's
opinion made clear that the plaintiffs had indeed established, after only 5
days of testimony and 1 day of arguments, that they would likely succeed
on the merits in a full trial. He was particularly troubled by
the affirmative defenses offered in COPA, particularly the requirement of

credit card use and adult verification screens that he felt might deter adult users from ever trying many Web sites. This would in turn place an economic burden or harm on plaintiffs, who might have no choice but to self-censor to avoid the costs of these defenses. Their censorship would definitely include material that would not be harmful to minors. Additionally, Reed noted that there was no real effective way "to restrict the access of minors to harmful material in chat rooms and discussion groups, which the plaintiffs assert draw traffic to their sites, without screening all users before accessing any content, even that which is not harmful to minors, or editing all content before it is posted to exclude material that is harmful to minors" (*ACLU v. Reno*, 1996, p. 492). Asserting that although plaintiffs had the burden of proving their motion for preliminary injunctive relief, it was the defendant government that had the burden of establishing that COPA was narrowly tailored and was the least restrictive means of meeting its objective—protecting children by regulating commercial pornographers. The court noted that as of that date, the government had not shown that COPA was narrowly tailored or the least restrictive means—because the law reached potentially protected speech under the First Amendment—and because the objective of protecting children from commercial pornographers might also be achieved by blocking or filtering software used by parents.

The government appealed to the Third Circuit Court of Appeals. There, a three-judge panel made up of Judge Theodore Alexander McKee, Judge Leonard I. Garth, and Judge Richard Lowell Nygaard, heard the government's appeal, but ultimately affirmed the district court's ruling, albeit for a different reason. In a unanimous decision, the circuit court opinion[6] noted strong concern that allowing COPA to go forward as written would establish a national standard for obscenity, something the Supreme Court had very explicitly rejected in *Miller v. California*.[7] This would be achieved, the court noted, because the law would privilege one "community standard" above all others. Said the court: "Because of the peculiar geography-free nature of cyberspace, a 'community standards' test would essentially require every Web communication to abide by the most restrictive community's standards" (p. 175).

Following this loss at the circuit court level, government lawyers were faced with only three options: let the decision stand and no longer seek enforcement of COPA; return to the district court level and motion for a full trial; on May 13, 2002, the Supreme Court issued a fractious 8–1 opinion in *Ashcroft vs. ACLU*,[8] vacating a decision of the 3rd Circuit, and remanding for further consideration. As is often the case with volatile court decision,s, different camps saw reason for victory in the high Court's ruling. For proponents and supporters of COPA, the 8–1 decision appeared to reflect general support by a vast majority of the Justices for government attempts to regulate obscenity and indecency online. For opponents and detractors, however, the decision was but one step in a lengthy path that seemed destined to lead back to the Supreme Court a second time, with possibly dire results for COPA.

Justice Clarence Thomas authored the majority opinion, joined by Chief Justice Rehnquist and Justice Scalia. Justices O'Connor and Breyer concurred in part with the majority reasoning, and with the judgment. Justices Kennedy, Ginsburg, and Souter concurred only with the judgment. O'Connor, Souter, and Kennedy (joined by Ginsburg and Souter) filed separate concurring opinions. Justice Stevens dissented outright.

Thomas' majority opinion focused on the narrow question of the accuracy of the 3rd Circuit's claim that COPA's use of "community standards" to "identify material that is harmful to minors" violated the First Amendment. Refining this, Thomas suggested the more precise issue was whether "community standards" could be imposed on Web publishers since they had no ability to control the "geographic scope of the recipients of their communications."[9] The ACLU argued that imposition of this kind of standard would force jurors to impose local standards on Web content, which would be impossible for a Web publisher to know in advance. The result of this would be that Web publishers would self-censor to avoid imposition of fines or penalties under COPA, even if their Web content included material that should or would be accessible to adults.

Thomas disagreed, suggesting that COPA was very narrow in its focus to only prohibit material harmful to minors, while also employing an established legal standard from *Miller vs. California*. Thomas also noted that in other cases, the Court held that requiring a communicator disseminating material to a national audience to observe community standards does not violate the First Amendment. Citing *Hamling vs. United States*,[10] and *Sable Communications Inc., vs. FCC*,[11] he asserted that both individuals and businesses that sent obscene material across geographical boundaries (using land mail) or individuals providing dial-a-porn (with telephone lines extending across different states and localities) were held responsible for knowing if their expression would violate the local community standards of any area in which it appeared. Applying this reasoning to Web publishers under COPA, Thomas concluded: "We do not believe the medium's 'unique characteristics' justify a different approach than that set forth in *Hamling* and *Sable*. . . . If a Web publisher chooses to send its material into a particular community, this Court's jurisprudence teaches that it is the publisher's responsibility to abide by that community's standards."[12]

Justice O'Connor's concurring opinion suggested a preference for doing what the Court had avoided in *Miller*: establishing a national standard for obscenity. Employing such a standard for online expression would help avoid situations in which Web publishers had to guess the community standards of the area where their work might appear.[13] Justice Breyer agreed with O'Connor, and in his separate opinion asserted that the meaning of "community" in COPA was intended as a standard that was "national and adult."[14]

By contrast, Justice Kennedy's separate concurring opinion (joined by Ginsburg and Souter) read more like a dissenting opinion. Kennedy made clear that his concurrence was based only on the very narrow question of the correctness of the 3rd Circuit ruling, arguing that there were a host of other questions for the appellate court to consider. Furthermore, he clearly said if the Circuit Court had considered these questions and addressed them, their action "might well justify enjoining enforcement of the Act (COPA)."[15] Kennedy's questions for the 3rd Circuit Court included (a) what is the breadth of COPA's coverage?[16] and (b) what are the community standards being invoked?[17] He wondered what *Miller's* language, repeated in COPA, referencing obscene material "taken as a whole" meant when discussing the world wide web?[18] Does it, for example, consider an allegedly obscene photo image on a web page in reference to all the other photos on the same page (e.g., if there are multiple thumbnail pictures)? Or one web page in relation to other web pages linked to a home page or Web site? Or does the sum total "whole" refer to everything on the world wide web?

Justice Stevens' dissent rejected Thomas' assumptions that *Hamling* or *Sable* could be used to justify forcing Web publishers to anticipate local community standards. Suggesting this could easily be done in the real world for mediums like land-based mail (as in *Hamling*) by examining the zip code of the place to which one was sending obscene material, or over the telephone (as in *Sable*) by addressing the area code of the place the call was being made to, Stevens distinguished online publishing because "a provider who posts material on the internet cannot prevent it from entering any geographic community."[19]

Stevens' dissent, coupled with Kennedy's tentative concurring opinion (joined by Ginsburg) makes this decision read more like a 5–4 than an 8–1. It also means that traditional swing votes provided by Justices O'Connor and Breyer, who also expressed some reservations with Justice Thomas' reasoning, are not a certainty for future appeals.

In March 2003, the 3rd Circuit reconsidered the case,[20] addressing all of the questions set forth by the majority, and most especially by Justice Kennedy. In the end, however, they once again declared COPA unconstitutional, justifying the lower court's earlier injunction of the Act. One year later, in March 2004, the Supreme Court once again heard arguments on a new appeal of the 3rd Circuit ruling. In June 2004, the Supreme Court handed down a different ruling affirming the decision of the Third Circuit, and suggesting that enforcement of COPA should be enjoined because the statute likely violates the First amendment.[21] This time, five members of the

Court (Kennedy, Stevens, Ginsburg, Souter, and Thomas) joined in the majority, while Scalia, Rehnquist, O'Connor, and Breyer dissented. The majority opinion, authored by Justice Kennedy, focused on the narrow issue of least restrictive means, suggesting that the injunction against enforcement of COPA would only be allowed it the government could show that there were o less restrictive means (in this case, blocking and filtering software) that would be more effective than the federal law. Writing for the majority, Justice Kennedy stated: "Filters are less restrictive than COPA. They impose selective restrictions on speech at the receiving end, not universal restrictions at the source. Under a filtering regime, adults without children may gain access to speech they have a right to see without having to identify themselves or provide their credit card information. Even adults with children may obtain access to the same speech on the same terms simply by turning off the filter on their home computers. . . . Filters also may well be more effective than COPA. First, a filter can prevent minors from seeing all pornography, not just pornography posted to the Web from America . . . forty percent of harmful-to-minors content comes from overseas . . . [F]ilters may also be more effective (than COPA) because they can be applied to all forms of internet communication, including e-mail, not just communications available via the World Wide Web."[22]

As of this time, the government is considering whether to contest the remand in the Circuit Court, but in all likelihood, enforcement of COPA may be finished unless new arguments about the ineffectiveness of filtering can be mustered to justify one more pass at the Supreme Court. Given that the last decision of the high Court was only a 5–4 split (with Thomas now being a swing voter), the temptation for government lawyers might be high. But after successive defeats with the CDA and now COPA at the district court, and now Supreme Court level, is it worth the effort?

MOVING THE BOXES AROUND

Any success with the Supreme Court in a new appeal would depend in no small part on the government's ability to fully distinguish COPA from the CDA. Despite the supposed new focus in this law, however, it is difficult to see how it is really very different from its predecessor.

To begin with, both COPA and the original CDA were written as criminal statutes—mandating not only fines *but also serious jail time* for noncompliance. The former might prove costly in a now technology-poor economy for Web site communicators—but most surely, the latter would invariably lead to self-censorship, as individuals weigh the risk of prison sentences, even for speech that be protected by the First Amendment. This much was true for the CDA, and it is no less true for COPA.

Second, both the CDA, which targeted "indecent" and "patently offensive" expression for minors, and COPA, which targets "material that is harmful to minors," invariably punish adults, because there is no real way to prevent access by minors without also burdening and deterring access by adults. Both laws in this respect offered affirmative defenses (which were nearly identical), along with the government's assurance—particularly for COPA—that used properly, would fully protect access for adults. But as was the case for the CDA—and so for COPA—the affirmative defenses do not offer an effective way of insuring that protected adult access will not also be limited, when the effort is made to deter access by minors.

As to this latter point, the district court findings in the COPA challenge noted that digital certificates guaranteeing an individual's age do not currently exist, which leaves the other affirmative defenses (credit cards, debit cards, adult access codes or adult personal identification numbers) as the only possible means of preventing a COPA prosecution. Note that these same defenses were considered in the CDA case and rejected as unfeasible by the Supreme Court.[23] These defenses, as any parent knows, are far from fool-proof. It is easy for a child to take a credit or debit card from a parent's purse or wallet. Unfortunately, many parents are also lax about leaving pin numbers or access codes, written on notepaper, conveniently beside a computer monitor for easy access. These are hardly barriers for an industrious child.

More to the point, perhaps, is the fact that this kind of affirmative defense would effectively preclude access for adults who did not possess credit cards or debit cards, or those who lack the resources to obtain such cards.

As to those adults who do possess credit and/or debit cards, it is likely that such a defense imposition on Web sites would lead to self-deterrence by adult users. Most people with credit or debit cards, who are inclined to use them online, only do so when purchasing a product or service. Most see the requirement for such cards in an economic context, and not as a requirement for proof of identification. It is likely, therefore, that adults would be deterred from entering sites seeking information, if they felt that getting into the site involved a commercial transaction. A credit or debit card creates an entirely different atmosphere and context for a Web site that might otherwise be only a nonprofit, public information site.

This point about context also has implications for adult access codes and pin numbers. These are currently required, voluntarily, for many pornography websites. It is likely that requiring these for nonprofit, public information sites would create the impression that these sites as well offered pornographic material. That context might well deter adult users who wanted to avoid association with pornography, but were interested in learning information about legal—albeit objectionable—matter.

Third, COPA, like the CDA before it, makes ineffective and inappropriate use of the term "contemporary community standards," as suggested by the aforementioned landmark decision on obscenity, *Miller v. California.* The language in COPA even goes so far as to quote *Miller's* test: "the average person, applying contemporary community standards, would find that the work, taking the material as a whole, appeals to the prurient interest" and only adds the words "and with respect to minors, is designed to appeal to, or designed to pander to" between "whole" and "prurient interest." Essentially, COPA only formally adds language about minors, creating the illusion that this law is about protecting minors, but using a standard from the real world that applies to obscenity generally.

As the Court in the CDA case found,[24] Web-based communicators are unable to determine what geographic location or community their messages may reach, let alone preventing such messages from reaching any such community. The fallacy for the CDA, as it is for COPA, is that in cyberspace there are no geographically based entities. The Internet completely obliterates geopolitical boundaries. At any given moment, a communicator may be interacting with other users from other parts of the country, or from other parts of the world. In cyberspace, therefore, our real-world sense of "community" does not apply; rather, because of the high volume of interactivity on the Internet, what we see instead are *virtual communities*, made up of users, subscribers, and interested parties, usually sharing a common interest in a given subject matter, whether it be dog grooming, nuclear proliferation, or the best places to fish in Minnesota. Unlike real-world communities, whose bonds are reinforced by the physical roots of existence, virtual communities may be only temporary, existing only in the moment of interaction. They are, nevertheless, communities— but fundamentally different from anything in the real world.

Laws like COPA and the CDA, however, impose a real-world community standard for determining obscenity in a place where there is no real-world community—only a virtual world. Both these laws would use the physical location of the offended user's computer hard drive and monitor as the location for a community whose standards might govern the question of obscenity. But this kind of dated reasoning ignores the already described dynamic of cyberspace. Why should the community within which the information appears on a screen necessarily be the community of record?

This leads to a fourth similarity between the two laws: Both were clearly overbroad in their regulation of expression on the Internet. The CDA restricted speech that would otherwise be protected for adults, a fact the Supreme Court and the lower courts noted in declaring the unconstitutional. COPA is no different. It too reaches expression that should be protected for adults and both restricts access **and** creates a chilling effect of self-censorship.

Finally, just as the CDA ultimately failed strict scrutiny analysis by not being narrowly tailored to further the government's interest in protecting children, COPA suffers from nearly identical defects. If COPA, like its predecessor, uses affirmative defenses that do not achieve a balance between protecting children and protecting the rights of adults to various forms of expression, then the restriction is not narrowly drawn. Worse, if COPA, like the CDA, makes use of affirmative defenses that can easily be defeated by even remotely industrious minors, it does not further the interest in protecting them.

IN LOCO PARENTIS AND PARENTAL RESPONSIBILITY

Perhaps the more profound and reaching impact of laws like COPA and the CDA can be found in the question they raise about the realities of child-drearing, the responsibilities of parents, and the role government plays when parents fail or are unable to meet those responsibilities. *In loco parentis*, an age-old concept, literally means "in the place of the parent." Congressional attempts at protecting children from objectionable material on the Internet were both election-year grandstanding and a sad commentary on the inability or incapacity of many parents to adequately supervise what their children do when online. This is hardly a new role for government. Across the country, various child protective service agencies have and will continue to assert responsibility in homes where domestic abuse or neglect occurs, acting in the place of the parent. When children are not in school, police and truant officers will do what parents sometimes do not want to do, or cannot do, and find these children, returning them to school. Where unsupervised children may be exposed to legal products such as tobacco or alcohol, government has acted in the place of the parent to mandate tougher penalties for merchants who might sell such products to minors. In cases of other kinds of technology, government has routinely asserted authority over broadcast media in television and radio, to protect children from harmful or offensive messages. In this case, government acted in the place of the parent, because over time, television became a convenient babysitter for families with working parents. With such a history, it is hardly surprising that Congress would seek to act where cyberspace and children became connected, leaving government once again to act in the place of a parent.

Unlike other forays into child protection, however, both CDA and later COPA sought to protect children in ways that unlawfully burden, and potentially restrict or even eliminate adult communication and expression.

The closest parallel justification for *in loco parentis* with COPA might be a comparison to rules limiting what broadcasters can allow on the air, during times when minors might be in an audience. But even this parallel becomes inadequate if such regulations for broadcast do not restrict or lead to self-censorship of lawful adult communication.

In this respect, Congressional attempts at acting in the place of the parent to protect children online have been unique, and perhaps beg the question whether government is really the proper authority to address what children may be exposed to with this medium. The Internet and computer-mediated communication are the next step in the evolution of the telephone, computer technology, and even broadcast technology. The potential for unsupervised exposure by children to this medium is much greater than it ever was for children who grew up with the television as a babysitter. As indicated earlier, most of the growth in computer purchases has come from families, purchasing computers so that children may use them for school and for entertainment. Unlike the television, which may have been used by children when adults were not home, a family's computer—or computers—will likely be in use throughout different times of the day, and very likely in the evenings after school hours, when parents are at home. In this way, parents will always have a greater potential impact for supervising what is appropriate for a child to interact with online, rather than abrogating this responsibility to government. Filtering and blocking software can assist in this process, used at the discretion of a parent—but no technology will ever replace the impact of supervision and involvement of a parent for a child. Rules like COPA, well-intentioned although they may be, are dangerous not only because they clearly violate the First Amendment, but also because they too easily let parents off the proverbial hook.

BACK TO THE ORCHARDS

Regulations like COPA do not pass careful Constitutional scrutiny. COPA itself is really no different than the law that preceded it—the CDA—and it clearly deserves the same fate. It is highly unlikely, however, that a Supreme Court opinion that declared COPA unconstitutional would prevent Congress from trying again. This is and continues to be a volatile election-year issue. And like the farmers who drove their peach trucks back to the orchards so that they might move the boxes around, hiding my chalk marks, and pretending that the next shipment they brought was a new harvest of fruit, Congress will likely go down the same path, recycling perhaps a third version of this regulatory scheme. Barring innovative thinking about the uniqueness of the Internet medium and the communities that inhabit it, not to mention a thoughtful discussion of what parental and governmental responsibilities towards children should be in cyberspace, there is no reason to expect that any other effort would make a passing grade either.

NOTES

1. 521 U.S. 844 (1997)
2. 47 U.S.C. section 223 et. seq.
3. 438 U.S. 726 (1978)
4. 31 F. Supp. 2d 473 (1999)
5. The TRO had been granted November 20, 1998.
6. 217 F. 3d 162 (3rd Cir. 2000)
7. 413 U.S. 15 (1973)
8. 535 U.S. 564 (2002)
9. 217 F. 3d., at 180.
10. 418 U.S. 87 (1974)
11. 492 U.S. 115 (1989)
12. 535 U.S. 564 at 583.
13. Id. at 587.
14. Id. at 590.
15. Id. at 593.
16. Id. at 592.
17. Id.
18. Id.
19. Id. at 606 to 607.
20. 322 F. 3d 240 (3rd Cir. 2003)
21. *Ashcroft vs. ACLU* 542 U.S.—(slip opinion, 2004)
22. Id. at 8–9 of slip opinion.
23. 521 U.S. at 861.
24. Id. At 853.

6

History and Decency

Overcoming the Threat of an Inside–Out Approach[1]

Eric M. Freedman
Hofstra Law School

In a comprehensive article in the Iowa Law Review, which has since proved to be prophetic, Eric M. Freedman argued for the repudiation of what he called the inside–outside approach to First Amendment analysis, an approach under which certain categories of expression are deemed to have such low value as to be "outside" the protection of the First Amendment. In "A Lot More Comes into Focus When You Remove the Lens Cap: Why Proliferating New Communications Technologies Make it Particularly Urgent for the Supreme Court to Abandon its Inside-Outside Approach to Freedom of Speech and Bring Obscenity, Fighting Words, and Group Libel Within the First Amendment," Professor Freedman called on the Supreme Court to reject this longstanding framework,persuasively contending that to do otherwise renders free speech interests, particularly those of new media modalities, vulnerable to unjustifiable attacks. What follows is an excerpt from the article, laying out Professor Freedman's viewpoint (Section 1 below), followed by his application of the argument to the issues raised by the Communications Decency Act of 1996 (Section 2 below), the Child Pornography Protection Act of 1996 (Section 3 below), the Child Online Protection Act of 1998 (Section 4 below), and a conclusion discussing the broader implications (Section 5 below).

SECTION 1: THE PROBLEM

Current free speech law resembles the Ptolemaic system of astronomy in its last days. Just as that theory grew increasingly incoherent in an attempt to incorporate new empirical observations that were inconsistent with its basic postulates, so is First Amendment doctrine disintegrating as cases reviewing restraints on speech strive to paper over the fact that analyses based on presuppositions as to the value of particular kinds of expression are inconsistent with the premises of the First Amendment itself.

Most readers of the opinions in *R.A.V. v. City of St. Paul*,[2] for example, will surely find it difficult to shake the feeling that all nine Justices are missing the forest for the trees, disputing hoary categories like "fighting words"[3] in a case whose true conflict bears no relationship to those categories.[4]

The explanation for the Justices' performance is that they are viewing the free speech universe through the distorting lens of an outmoded paradigm, one in which only certain speech is "within" the First Amendment. When the state seeks to regulate such speech, the key questions are:[5]

1. *Is the purpose of the regulation to restrict speech?*

In some cases, the answer may be no. For example, the regulation's purpose may be to suppress non-speech conduct (e.g., heroin sales, consumer fraud) with the restraint on speech being merely incidental.[6] Because, in many areas, simply asking the question comprehensively[7] goes a long way towards answering it, this issue rightly plays a central role in traditional First Amendment analysis.[8]

2. *If so, has the state demonstrated a compelling reason consistent with First Amendment values for restricting this speech?*

This inquiry is inevitably the controversial one. But asking it focuses discussion on the right subject, making explicit the policy choices that close cases will necessarily involve.[9]

3. *If so, has the state demonstrated that the regulation has been narrowly tailored towards achieving its permissible purpose?*

As the Supreme Court has long recognized, this standard plays an important practical role in keeping the government within whatever boundaries the legal system has determined are legitimate.[10]

In contrast, according to the Court, speech which falls into the categories of group libel, fighting words, and obscenity is "outside" the First Amendment.[11] Although the Justices disagree about precisely what it means for speech to be "outside" the First Amendment,[12] the underlying concept is clear: the speech categories "outside" the First Amendment are less socially valuable than the ones "inside" it, so governmental restraints on the former are free of the rigorous judicial scrutiny given to governmental restraints on the latter.

There are at least three major problems with this vision of the First Amendment.

First, its simplistic dualism is empirically false as a description of the legal landscape. All libel is plainly "within" the First Amendment.[13] Fighting words, although formally remaining outside it, are for all practical purposes within it.[14] That is, the Court, in addressing the problems posed by those categories of speech, has demonstrated a commendable focus on the three questions listed above. Only obscenity (and a widening sphere of erotically-oriented speech that is not technically obscene) remains truly "outside" the First Amendment,[15] in the sense that the Court has relieved itself of the obligation to address those questions.[16]

Second, the "inside-out" model of the First Amendment, and the obsolete doctrine it perpetuates, clouds clear thinking and reduces the likelihood of correct results on numerous free speech problems. The issue goes far beyond the logical desirability of improving doctrinal tidiness.[17] The current disarray in the law provides ammunition for a variety of attacks on free expression.

As long as certain categories of speech may be defined as "outside" the First Amendment because judges believe them to be unworthy of its noble protections, there is no logically consistent reason why any number of other forms of socially unpopular expression should not be similarly categorized.[18] This would allow their summary suppression without the need for serious consideration of the issues at stake.[19]

Third, the ability to cast certain forms of expression beyond the First Amendment pale poses a special danger to technologically novel communications media. Thus, for example, just as movies originally were placed "outside" the First Amendment because they were thought to be such a threateningly powerful medium of expression,[20] so it is now proposed that the unique characteristics of computers justify imposing special restraints on the communications they transmit.[21]

In response to these problems, this Article proposes that the Supreme Court repudiate the view that some forms of expression, whether defined by their content or by their mode of delivery, are "outside" the First Amendment. This proposal is not designed to provide a "theoretical basis for free speech that is at once true and elegant."[22] In particular, it assumes *arguendo* a continuation of the current proliferation of judicially-recognized sub-categories of speech "within" the First Amendment.[23] The merits of that development have been much debated elsewhere,[24] and are not addressed here.[25] For the categorization questions only arise with respect to speech that is already "inside" the First Amendment;[26] once it has achieved that status, judicial definition of the extent of legal protection requires an explicit discussion of First Amendment values.[27] Thus, just as freedom of expression was enhanced when libel and commercial speech were moved from "outside" the First Amendment to "inside" it, albeit each in its own category and subject to its own rules, so too will freedom of expression be enhanced when all speech is "inside" the First Amendment.

SECTION 2: THE COMMUNICATIONS DECENCY ACT

Specifically, and of special importance for the concerns of this volume, a rule that all forms of speech are "within" the First Amendment will ensure the nondiscriminatory coverage of all current or future methods by which expression may be conveyed. A glance at current developments in the light of history demonstrates the importance of this advantage.

Early in 1996, President Clinton signed the Communications Decency Act (CDA). This legislation subjected to fines and imprisonment for up to 2 years:

(a) The knowing transmission of "any comment, request, suggestion, proposal, image, or other communication which is obscene or indecent, knowing that the recipient of the communication is under 18 years of age, regardless of whether the maker of such communication placed the call or initiated the communication."

(b) The knowing use of "any interactive computer service to display in a manner available to a person under 18 years of age, any comment, request, suggestion, proposal, image, or other communication that, in context, depicts or describes, in terms patently offensive as measured by contemporary community standards, sexual or excretory activities or organs, regardless of whether the user of such service placed the call or initiated the communication."

By all ordinary First Amendment standards, these provisions were manifestly invalid. Briefly put:

1. Regulation on the basis of indecency (as opposed to the much narrower category of "obscenity") was pointedly limited by the Supreme Court in *F.C.C. v. Pacifica Foundation* (1978) to the broadcast media, a context in which it was claimed to be justified on the basis of spectrum scarcity and the special intrusiveness of those media (Kim, 1995). The Internet is not a physically limited medium; on the contrary, it is infinitely expandable as people set up additional nodes (Berman & Weitzner 1994). Nor is the medium intrusive; on the contrary, one has to search with considerable diligence to find what one is seeking (Rigdon, 1996).

2. Assuming regulation on the basis of indecency were permissible, the term was not defined in the provision quoted in paragraph *a* above, and the definition quoted in paragraph *b* did no more than reiterate that of the FCC in the broadcast context, which had been universally denounced on the grounds of vagueness, overbreadth and potential for selective enforcement (Goldsamt, 1995; Phelan, 1995).

3. In any event, in contrast to the broadcast media (and analogously to the case of dial-a-porn services, which the Supreme Court refused to allow Congress to outlaw (*Sable Communications v. F.C.C.*, 1989), there were less restrictive alternatives to a total ban available, in the form of a variety of access control and content-labeling systems (Lewis, 1995; Markoff, 1995).

4. Technical considerations made the statute so extremely unlikely to achieve its stated purpose—while so extremely likely to suppress speech that is protected by any standard—as to render it invalid under the First Amendment on the grounds of simple irrationality, like the alcohol-content labeling statute at issue in *Rubin v. Coors Brewing Company* (1995).

In light of the overwhelming force of this attack, how could anyone have given even a moment's credence to the possibility that the Supreme Court might uphold the statute? The answer is that historical experience—with, among others, printing presses (Ringel, 1970; Shackelton, 1975), secular dramatic troupes (Heinemann, 1993), rock music (Hill, 1991), comic books (and before that, dime crime novels) (Johnston, 1994; Klapper, 1960), sexually explicit telephone services (Woolfall, 1994), and video games (Zito, 1993)—shows that each new medium is seen at first as uniquely threatening, because uniquely influential, and therefore a uniquely appropriate target of censorship. Thus, "When Thomas Edison started making short films around the turn of the century, patrons ran from theatres in

horror when they saw a steam engine barreling directly toward the front
row seats" (Zito, 1993, p. A25). And, as mentioned in Section 1, in 1915 the
Supreme Court held that there was no First Amendment violation in the
creation of a government system for the censorship of movies, because
movies formed no part of the "press" (*Mutual Film Corp. v. Industrial
Commission of Ohio,* 1915). In other words, movies—like pornography—
were defined as "outside"the First Amendment.

To its credit, the Supreme Court in *Reno v. ACLU* (1997) resisted the
temptation to use this escape hatch in the case of the CDA and (in accordance with the views of commentators expressed in the first edition of this
volume and elsewhere) invalidated the statute on substantially the basis
outlined above. But the government continues to react with near-hysteria
to the possibility of the creation, dissemination, and viewing through the
use of computer technology of messages even vaguely related to sexuality
(Freedman, 1996)

SECTION 3: THE CHILD PORNOGRAPHY PROTECTION ACT

Even before *Reno* had been decided, Congress, in an effort at thought
control that flatly defied the First Amendment, smuggled into an omnibus
budget bill the Child Pornography Prevention Act of 1996. Introduced by
Senator Orrin G. Hatch of Utah, this legislation broadly criminalized the
dissemination of all visual images that "appear to be" ones of children
engaging in "sexually explicit" conduct, notwithstanding that the images
were generated purely electronically, without the use of any children (or
adult actors, for that matter) at all. According to the legislative findings
contained in § 121(1)(4) of the act, viewing such images "can desensitize
the viewer to the pathology of sexual abuse or exploitation of children, so
that it can become acceptable to and even preferred by the viewer."
Moreover, according to §121(1)(11)(B), such images create an unwhole-
some moral environment.

Thought control is not a legitimate First Amendment purpose even if—
perhaps especially if—the thoughts are ones that the majority considers
socially undesirable, as was true, for instance in the very recent past of
beliefs in the propriety of homosexual conduct and interracial marriage.
For example, when D.H. Lawrence's work *Lady Chatterly's Lover,* whose
subject is a woman who finds greater satisfaction with a gamekeeper than
with her husband, was made into a movie, the State of New York sought to
ban it. The government's rationale was that the "presentation of adultery as
a desirable, acceptable and proper pattern of behavior" was "contrary to
the moral standards, the religious precepts and the legal code of its citizen-

ry." Invalidating the state's effort as a violation of the First Amendment, Justice Potter Stewart wrote for the Court, "This argument misconceives what it is that the Constitution protects. Its guarantee is not confined to the expression of ideas that are conventional or shared by a majority. It protects advocacy of the opinion that adultery may sometimes be proper no less than advocacy of socialism or the single tax. And in the realm of ideas it protects expression which is eloquent no less than that which is unconvincing" (*Kingsley International Picture Corp.*, 1959).

Hence, defenders of the 1996 statute had to retreat to the argument that the banned material would incite people to commit misconduct, whether direct sexual assaults or the seduction of children. But modern First Amendment doctrine looks with extreme suspicion on the argument that some communication should be suppressed because it will have "a natural tendency" to induce its recipients to behave in an antisocial manner. Repeated experience—from prosecutions by the English Crown for seditious libel to American prosecutions of opponents of World War I, socialists in the early 1920s and Communists in the 1950s (Freedman 1996)—has shown that justification to be highly susceptible to the twin dangers of misprediction and official abuse. Thus, when *Brandenburg v. Ohio* (1969) held that the government could only suppress speech on this basis that proved that the communication is "directed to inciting or producing imminent lawless violence and is likely to incite or produce such action," the case built on a number of basic principles.

One of these is exemplified by *Butler v. Michigan* (1957), which struck down a law aimed at violent comic books because they were publications "manifestly tending to the corruption of the morals of youth." That law violated the First Amendment, Justice Frankfurter wrote, because, "The effect of this enactment is to reduce the adult population of Michigan to reading what is only fit for children." So too, even if some pedophile might be inflamed by images of juvenile sexuality, one has to base one's enactments on a reasonable viewer lest the law reduce the entire population of the country to viewing what is only fit for child molesters (Freedman, 1996).

In the words of Justice Brandeis, "Among free men the deterrents ordinarily to be applied to prevent crime are education and punishment for violations of the law, not abridgement of the rights of free speech and assembly" (*Whitney v. California,* (1927). If after viewing sexually explicit material someone commits a crime, the First Amendment mandates that the criminal be arrested, not the creator or distributor of the material.

Yes, came the reply, but in *New York v. Ferber* (1982) the Supreme Court decided that a broad range of "child pornography" was "outside" the First Amendment. This is misleading shorthand. The Court upheld a prohibition on such material on the basis of the following:

1. The state's interest was not in preventing the public from viewing the material, but rather in protecting children from being used in its production, and "[t]he prevention of sexual exploitation and abuse of children constitutes a government objective of surpassing importance."
2. A ban on the distribution of materials depicting sexual activity by juveniles furthers this interest because (a) "the materials produced are a permanent record of the children's participation and the harm to the child is exacerbated by their circulation," and (b) "the distribution network for child pornography must be closed if the production of material which requires the sexual exploitation of children is to be effectively controlled."

Of course, none of these justifications apply to purely imaginary children. Hence, the depiction of those is protected by the First Amendment. This is a statement that can be made with some confidence because in *Ferber* itself the Court noted that little or no communication was being suppressed inasmuch as creators could use over-age actors who looked younger, or simulate the scenes. In short, one key reason the Court upheld the statute at issue in the case was that creators would still be able produce works indistinguishable from ones employing actual children.

Ignoring this, committee report in support of the Child Pornography Protection Act simply declared that the legislation "is needed due to technological advances" in the creation of visual images, "particularly through the use of computers," that have "made possible the production of visual depictions that appear to be of minors engaging in sexually explicit conduct" (Senate Report, 1996). The authors of this rationalization were either ignorant of, or choose to ignore, history as well as the law. "Photography became a frequent censorship target in the late nineteenth century because it was supposedly more graphic and realistic than painting" (Meyer, 1994, pp. 1189-1190). Around the same time, magic lantern shows were often so shocking to audiences that, historian Peter Bacon recounts, "they fainted, cried, or talked back to the lantern-slide screen" (Roberts, 1995, p. H28). Are we now supposed to believe that images that could no longer be banned if shown in those media can be suppressed if generated by computer animation software, because the latter are too vivid?

The reality is that new media achieve their initial marketplace success precisely because they are for some purposes a more effective form of communication than pre-existing ones. This should be seen as an advance in human enlightenment, rather than as an excuse for otherwise impermissible state censorship.

Yet the Child Pornography Protection Act covered all images that "appear to be" ones of children engaging in "sexually explicit" conduct. It thus included innumerable works of art, like cartoons or cherubs cavorting at the edges of paintings, that "appear to be" images of such conduct because that is precisely what they are, although presumably the law was not aimed at them. Instead, the purpose of the statute seemed to be to proscribe any image that is so closely indistinguishable from one of a real juvenile engaging in sexual activity that a reasonable person could not tell that it was not. But that is hopelessly vague as a legal definition, and substantively unconstitutional as well. Mainstream movies such as *Romeo and Juliet*, *Traffic*, *The Blue Lagoon*, and *The Tin Drum*, all contain images of sexual activity by minors that seek to be accurate simulations, and not even the government was proposing to suppress such works (Freedman, 2002).

Confronted with this legislative botch, the U.S. Court of Appeals for the Ninth Circuit took the only sensible course and invalidated the statute (*Free Speech Coalition v. Reno*, (1999). The government promptly sought and gained review in the Supreme Court. In a ringing re-affirmation of the basic principles just outlined, the Court rejected the argument that the First Amendment applied differently to computer-generated images than to others, and affirmed (*Ashcroft v. Free Speech Coalition*, 2002).

SECTION 4: THE CHILD ONLINE PROTECTION ACT OF 1998

Meanwhile, in *Ashcroft v. ACLU* (2002), the government was appealing a decision of the U.S. Court of Appeals for the Third Circuit striking down the Child Online Protection Act (COPA), which had been law enacted by Congress in response to the invalidation of the CDA.

The case presented a tangle of legal intricacies that could be unraveled relatively easily by the application of some basic technology-neutral First Amendment principles. The statute prohibits the dissemination over the Internet of material that is obscene as to minors, a category recognized some years ago by the Supreme Court (*Ginsberg v. New York*, 1968). The problem arises because *Miller v. California* (1973) requires obscenity to be judged by "contemporary community standards," meaning local ones. Of course, applying this standard to the Internet would reduce the entire population of the country to viewing only that which would pass muster in the least tolerant locality. Because there was no technologically feasible solution to this problem, the Third Circuit held, the statute violated the First Amendment rights of both creators and recipients.

Although it reached the right result, the Third Circuit's legal reasoning was flawed. The problem at hand has nothing to do with the Internet. Rather, it arises from the long-observed fact that, as it was intended to be, the practical effect of *Miller*'s "community standards test" is to seriously limit the rights of national publishers in any medium. This is simply inimical to the First Amendment, one of whose purposes is to prevent an aroused local majority from imposing its views on a local minority (Freedman 1996). *Miller* was only possible because of the doctrinal fiction that obscenity is "outside" the First Amendment.

But as predicted in the first edition of this volume, when confronted with a choice between abandoning "obscenity" as a legal category and abandoning "local community standards," the Supreme Court chose the latter (*Ashcroft v. ACLU, 2002*). While the immediate effect appeared to be a defeat for free speech interests, the ultimate result was not. On remand, the Third Circuit, doing what it should have done in the first place, focused on the substantive coverage of the statute rather than the circumstance that the material was being distributed over the Internet and reaffirmed its earlier invalidation of the statute—this time on the entirely correct basis that "COPA endangers a wide range of communications, exhibits, and speakers [that is not] obscene as to minors" (*ACLU v. Ashcroft*, 2003).

SECTION 5: CONCLUSION

Notwithstanding the commendable results they have reached in recent cases, there remains a need for the courts to declare explicitly that they will enforce the First Amendment in the context of new methods of communication just as they do in the context of old ones. Until this happens, the ability to declare certain technologically defined categories of speech "outside" the First Amendment provides the courts an ever-available escape hatch from the need to provide coherent justifications for imposing otherwise impermissible regulations on just those communications formats in which the public has the liveliest interest.

Such discrimination against new technologies is not only unjustifiable, but unnecessary. For the marketplace will tend to do effectively—perhaps too effectively—that which would be a threat to civil liberties if done by the government. Today, for example, as all consumers know, standards for sexual explicitness differ among the commercial broadcast, cable, and movie industries, and, within the movie industry, between productions designed to be seen in movie theaters and in hotel rooms. So too, there was greater reluctance among the long distance telephone carriers than the local ones to carry "dial-a-porn" services, even though the latter were subject to more stringent legal regulations. In all of these cases, marketplace considerations, not legal ones, have determined the outcomes.

However distressing those outcomes may be to some aesthetic or political tastes, this process represents the First Amendment working as it usually does in fact. Just as the Constitution provides a quite lax outer framework within which day-to-day politics operate to produce policy results that, whatever one may think of their substance, have been determined after a generally unimpeded contest between political groups of varying power, so does it provide very broad limits within which the marketplace operates to disseminate that which the public—often making its desires known through aggressive political and media campaigns—wishes to obtain (Collins & Skover, 1993; Price, 1994). The key constitutional concern is that control rest with the people, not the government.

To be sure, there is implicit in this view the realization (which one may, according to taste, label realistic or cynical) that the political/economic marketplace, not the legal system, will determine the ultimate extent of speech regulation, a conclusion that may initially cause all of those sparring over First Amendment standards to wonder why they are bothering. The Supreme Court does not exist apart from the culture that it both shapes and reflects (Marshall & Ignagni, 1994), and Americans will in the long run have just as much freedom of speech as the majority desires.

But "in the long run we are all dead" (Keynes, 1923). As the now-vanished flag-burning uproar illustrates, First Amendment doctrine makes a difference in keeping the channels of discourse—and hence the possibilities of change—open during the interval that elapses between the initial urge toward suppression and the time, if ever, that the majority overcomes the Constitutional obstacles to the exercise of its will. As the rapid pace of modern communications works to shorten that interval, the importance of robust First Amendment standards increases.

NOTES

1. Section 1 of this chapter is an excerpt from a work originally published in 81 *Iowa Law Review* 4 (1996, pp. 883-968). Reprinted with permission. For this reason, we have maintained the original *Blue Book* citation format in that Section. We have also left intact the original cross-references to parts and footnotes of the original article, although only some of them appear in this volume.
2. 505 U.S. 377 (1992). For a full-length account of the case by counsel for the defendant, see Edward J. Cleary, *Beyond the Burning Cross: The First Amendment and the Landmark R.A.V. Case* (1994). See also *United States v. Juvenile Male J.H.H.*, 22 F.3d 821 (8th Cir. 1994) (affirming conviction of R.A.V. and others on federal civil rights charges arising out of same incident that led to state charges in *R.A.V.*).
3. See Kent Greenfield, Our Conflicting Judgments About Pornography, 43 Am. U. L. Rev. 1197, 1216-17 (1994); Steven H. Shiffrin, Racist Speech, Outsider Jurisprudence, and the Meaning of America, 80 Cornell L. Rev. 43, 46 (1994) (commenting that the "Court simply bungled the first amendment job"); Tona Trollinger, Reconceptualizing the Free Speech Clause: From a Refuse of Dualism to the Reason of Holism, 3 Geo. Mason Indep. L. Rev. 137, 172-73 (1994); Michael S. Degan, Note, "Adding the First Amendment to the Fire":

Cross Burning and Hate Crime Laws, 26 Creighton L. Rev. 1109, 1135 (1993) ("The fundamental flaw in *R.A.V.* is the Court's attempt to analyze the St. Paul ordinance under the fighting words doctrine."). The bankruptcy of the "fighting words" doctrine is discussed infra Part III.A.

4. *See* infra text accompanying notes 348-50. See generally Larry A. Alexander, Trouble on Track Two: Incidental Regulations of Speech and Free Speech Theory, 44 Hastings L.J. 921, 957-60 (1993).

5. The doctrinal framework is presented slightly more formally at infra note 25.

6. For more controversial examples than those in the text, see Arcara v. Cloud Books, Inc., 478 U.S. 697 (1986), *on remand* 503 N.E.2d 492 (N.Y. 1986); Konigsberg v. State Bar of California, 366 U.S. 36, 50-51 (1961). See generally Frederick Schauer, The Aim and the Target in Free Speech Methodology, 83 Nw. U. L. Rev. 562, 562-64 (1989). There is a full discussion of the speech-conduct distinction infra text accompanying notes 136-50.

7. In particular, the Court must assess the state's real purpose as well as its articulated one. See Edwards v. Aguillard, 482 U.S. 578, 586-87 (1987); Cornelius v. NAACP Legal Defense and Educ. Fund, 473 U.S. 788, 812-14 (1985).

8. E.g., Lillian R. BeVier, The First Amendment and Political Speech: An Inquiry Into the Substance and Limits of Principle, 30 Stan. L. Rev. 299, 300 (1978); Robert C. Post, The Constitutional Concept of Public Discourse: Outrageous Opinion, Democratic Deliberation, and Hustler Magazine v. Falwell, 103 Harv. L. Rev. 603, 683 (1990).

9. See Robert C. Post, Racist Speech, Democracy, and the First Amendment, 32 Wm. & Mary L. Rev. 267, 278-79 (1991); Steven Shiffrin, Defamatory Non-Media Speech and First Amendment Methodology, 25 U.C.L.A. L. Rev. 915, 955 (1978). In a forthcoming article whose proofs he has kindly shared with me, Eugene Volokh emphasizes the importance of the inquiry into constitutional values in answering this question. *See* Eugene Volokh, Freedom of Speech Beyond Strict Scrutiny, 144 U. Pa. L. Rev. (forthcoming 1996).

10. See, e.g., Sable Communications v. FCC, 492 U.S. 115, 126 (1989); Schad v. Mount Ephraim, 452 U.S. 61, 75-76 (1981); Martin v. Struthers, 319 U.S. 141, 145-49 (1943); Jamison v. Texas, 318 U.S. 413, 416 (1943); Schneider v. State, 308 U.S. 147, 164-65 (1939); Lovell v. Griffin, 303 U.S. 444, 451-52 (1938).

Thus, in Ladue v. Gilleo, 512 U.S. 43 (1994), the Court, in a case involving an individual who had posted an antiwar sign in the front window of her house, indulged in the entirely implausible assumption that the municipality's ban on residential signs was content-neutral (an assumption that saved the ban from summary invalidation under tests deriving from the second question), but went on to hold the ordinance unconstitutional because "more temperate measures could in large part satisfy Ladue's stated regulatory needs without harm to the First Amendment rights of its citizens." Id. at 2047. See generally Mark Cordes, Sign Regulation After *Ladue* : Examining the Evolving Limits of First Amendment Protection, 74 Neb. L. Rev. 36 (1995).

11. See R.A.V. v. City of St. Paul, 505 U.S. 377, 382-83 (1992); New York v. Ferber, 458 U.S. 747, 754, 763-65 (1982); see also infra note 115 and accompanying text (discussing incitement).

12. In *R.A.V.*, Justice Stevens (speaking on this point for himself alone) announced that he would conduct a holistic analysis of the speech in question and the regime of regulation being applied to it in order to determine the First Amendment issue. *R.A.V.*, 505 U.S. at 427-31. Justice White (whose views were joined by Justices Blackmun and O'Connor) wrote that the proper approach was to determine whether the speech fell within a category traditionally unprotected because of its absence of social value (e.g., obscenity, fighting words) and to permit or prohibit regulation accordingly. Id. at 398-402. The Court, in an opinion by Justice Scalia (joined by Chief Justice Rehnquist and Justices Kennedy, Souter, and Thomas) explained that the classification of the speech as protected or unprotected bore on, although it was not dispositive of, the issue of the degree of permissible government regulation. Id. at 386-88; see infra note 350.

13. See New York Times v. Sullivan, 376 U.S. 254, 268-69 (1964); infra note 331-45 and accompanying text; see also *R.A.V.*, 505 U.S. at 382-83.

14. This topic is discussed in greater detail infra Part III.A.

15. *See* infra Parts II.C.1-2. Although the issue of definition is one of some independent importance, see infra text accompanying notes 173, 191-96, 237-46, the argument presented here does not depend on how the legal system may choose to demarcate the material at issue. Hence, for present purposes, I use the terms "pornography" and "obscenity" interchangeably to mean any sexually explicit expression that the state seeks to suppress. *See* Ronald K.L. Collins & David M. Skover, The Pornographic State, 107 Harv. L. Rev. 1374, 1377 (1994) (adopting same approach); Steven G. Gey, The Apologetics of Suppression: The Regulation of Pornography as Act and Idea, 86 Mich. L. Rev. 1564, 1596 n.149 (1988) (same); Frederick Schauer, Response: Pornography and the First Amendment, 40 U. Pitt. L. Rev. 605, 607-08 (1978-79) (distinction between "obscene" and "pornographic" is "constitutionally uninteresting") [hereinafter Schauer, Response]. But cf. Edward De Grazia, Girls Lean Back Everywhere: The Law of Obscenity and the Assault on Genius 298 (1992) (stating that at the time of Roth v. United States, 354 U.S. 476 (1957), "everyone realized—even if no one could define either term—that there *was* a difference between them," and although reputable people could fight for an end to controls on obscenity, "'pornography' was very widely thought of as abominable stuff that no reputable lawyer or judge would care to be found defending"); Frederick F. Schauer, The Law of Obscenity 1 n.1 (1976) ("'Obscene' refers to that which is repugnant or disgusting. . . . Except as used in the law, it does not necessarily have any sexual connotations. 'Pornography,' on the other hand, . . . is limited to depictions of sexual lewdness. . . . Definitionally, obscenity may or may not be pornographic, and pornography may or may not be obscene.") [hereinafter Schauer, The Law of Obscenity]. See generally Nicholas Wolfson, Eroticism, Obscenity, Pornography and Free Speech, 60 Brook. L. Rev. 1037 (1994); William Safire, "Explicit" is not a Dirty Word, N.Y. Times Mag., May 26, 1991, at 8.

16. *See* Frederick Schauer, Codifying the First Amendment: New York v. Ferber, 1982 Sup. Ct. Rev. 285, 303 [hereinafter Schauer, Codifying].

17. See Harry Kalven, Jr., The Metaphysics of the Law of Obscenity, 1960 Sup.
     Ct. Rev. 1, 25-26 ("It is abundantly clear that the effort of the Court to deal
     with obscenity within its commitment to free speech has opened issues about
     free speech which transcend in importance the limited problem of obscenity.")
     [hereinafter Kalven, Metaphysics].

18. See Floyd Abrams, Hate Speech: The Present Implications of a Historical
     Dilemma, 37 Vill. L. Rev. 743, 752 (1992) ("Every major new doctrinal excep-
     tion to the general rule that speech may not be infringed leads in turn to new
     demands for further exceptions. What else would one expect?") (citation omit-
     ted); infra text accompanying notes 300-306, 351-355 (describing use of pre-
     sent doctrine to support proposals to curb violent entertainment, rap music,
     and "morally abhorrent speech").

19. See Elliot Mincberg, A Look at Recent Supreme Court Decisions: Judicial
     Prior Restraint and the First Amendment, 44 Hastings L.J. 871, 872 (1993):

     In other words, if before reaching the question of whether a restriction is
     valid under one of the demanding First Amendment tests, such as strict scruti-
     ny, the Court decides *a priori* that the First Amendment does not apply . . .
     then the conflict is resolved because the Court does not have to get into the
     First Amendment and strict scrutiny at all. . . . [W]e often say that application
     of the First Amendment "triggers" strict scrutiny. This method of analysis
     puts a trigger lock on the First Amendment.

20. See infra notes 364, 381 (discussing Mutual Film Corp. v. Industrial Comm'n
     of Ohio, 236 U.S. 230 (1915), *overruled by* Joseph Burstyn, Inc. v. Wilson, 343
     U.S. 495, 502 (1952)).

21. See infra text accompanying notes 371-81.

22. Charles Fried, The New First Amendment Jurisprudence: A Threat to
     Liberty, 59 U. Chi. L. Rev. 225, 231 (1992).

23. These legal subdivisions are multiplying at a rate that almost insures that any
     description will be obsolete by the time it sees print. See infra note 294.

     Thus, for example, the text accompanying supra notes 7-12 presents only a
     skeletal description of the questions that are asked in the analysis of restraints
     on speech "inside" the First Amendment. Actually, as helpfully summarized
     in John T. Haggerty, Note, Begging and Public Forum Doctrine in the First
     Amendment, 34 B.C. L. Rev. 1121, 1123-30 (1993), the Court first decides:

     (a) that a certain activity is "speech," see infra text accompanying notes 136-
         50; and

     (b) that it is "within" the First Amendment; and

     (c) that it should not be shunted off to one of a number of special tracks
         reserved for such matters as:

         (i) commercial speech, see Virginia State Bd. of Pharmacy v. Virginia
             Citizens Consumer Council, 425 U.S. 748, 775-81 (1976) (Stewart, J.,
             concurring) (comparing and contrasting special track categories to
             each other and to political speech); Laurence H. Tribe, American
             Constitutional Law 929-34 (2d ed. 1988) (describing how commercial
             speech moved from "outside" the First Amendment to within it but
             in a lower-value category); Steven M. Simpson, Note, The
             Commercial Speech Doctrine: An Analysis of the Consequences of

Basing First Amendment Protections on the "Public Interest," 39
N.Y.L. Sch. L. Rev. 575, 605-06 (1994) (criticizing the Court for analyzing such cases by deciding for itself the social utility of the speech,
instead of treating "free speech as a right, rather than a privilege").
But cf. Jerome L. Wilson, Commercial Speech Approaches Full
Protected Status, N.Y. L.J., Dec. 27, 1993, at 1 (reviewing recent
decisions); or

(ii)   speech in one of three distinct categories of public forum, *see* infra
note 196; Daniel A. Farber & John E. Nowak, The Misleading
Nature of Public Forum Analysis: Content and Contest in First
Amendment Adjudication, 70 Va. L. Rev. 1219, 1226-29 (1984) (criticizing the Court for diverting cases at this point, rather than proceeding to remainder of analysis).

The Court then places the speech onto one of two main tracks:

(1)   On what the commentators label Track One are content-based restrictions on speech, which are supportable only if "necessary" to the
achievement of a "compelling" state interest and if they are no broader
than necessary to serve that interest. *E.g.*, National Bank of Boston v.
Bellotti, 435 U.S. 765, 786 (1978);

(2)   On Track Two are content-neutral regulations, which will be upheld if
the state interest is "important" or "substantial" or "significant," and the
regulation is "narrowly tailored" to achieve this interest. See Ward v.
Rock Against Racism, 491 U.S. 781, 796-98 (1989).

Track Two owes its origins to United States v. O'Brien, 391 U.S. 367,
377 (1968) (discussed infra note 358), in which defense counsel took the
position that O'Brien's burning of his draft card during a protest against
the Vietnam War was pure speech, so that the case should be evaluated as
though O'Brien had "held aloft his Registration Certificate and said
words to the effect that 'I detest and execrate this piece of paper and
everything for which it stands,'" Brief for Respondent at 48-49, United
States v. O'Brien, 391 U.S. 367 (1968) (Nos. 232, 233), while counsel for
the government took the position that it was pure conduct, so that no
First Amendment issue was presented at all, Brief for Petitioner at 12-21,
United States v. O'Brien, 391 U.S. 367 (1968) (Nos. 232, 233).

24.   *Compare, e.g.*, Tribe, supra note 25, § 12-18 (generally disapproving of the
development) *and* Nina Kraut, Speech: A Freedom in Search of One Rule, 12
Cooley L. Rev. 177, 178 (1995) (same) *with* Schauer, Codifying, supra note 18,
at 314-17 (generally approving) *and* Steven Shiffrin, The First Amendment
and Economic Regulation: From a General Theory of the First Amendment,
78 Nw. U. L. Rev. 1212, 1251-53 (1983) (same). Larry Alexander, Cass
Sunstein, and Frederick Schauer have debated the issue of whether the judicial
system should recognize categories of "low value" speech in the interchange.
Legal Theory: Low Value Speech, 83 Nw. U. L. Rev. 547 (1989).

25.   See generally infra note 294.

26.   See Tribe, supra note 25, at 895; Schauer, Codifying, supra note 18, at 293
n.47.

27.   See infra text accompanying notes 294-95.

REFERENCES

ACLU v. Ashcroft, 322 F.3d240-253 (3d Cir. 2003).

Ashcroft v. ACLU, 535 U.S. 564. (2003).

Ashcroft v. Free Speech Coalition, 535 U.S. 234. (002).

Berman, J., & Weitzner, D. J. (1994). Abundance and user control: Renewing the Democratic heart of the First Amendment in the age of interactive media. *Yale Law Journal 104*, 1619, 1623-1624.

Brandenburg v. Ohio, 395 U.S. 444, 447. (1969).

Butler v. Michigan, 352 U.S. 380, 383-384. (1957).

Collins, R. K., & Skover, D. (1993). Commerce and communication, *Texas Law Review, 71*, 697.

F.C.C. v. Pacifica Foundation, 438 U.S. 726. (1978).

Free Speech Coalition v. Reno, 198 F.3d 1083 (9th Cir. (1999). *aff'd.* Ashcroft v. Free Speech Coalition, 535 U.S. 234. (2003).

Freedman, E.M. (2002). The fate of the Child Pornography Act of 1996: Digitized pornography meets the First Amendment. *Cardozo Law Review, 23*, 2011, 2016, n.36.

Ginsberg v. New York, 390 U.S. 629. (1968).

Goldsamt, S. (1995). "Crucified by the FCC"? Howard Stern, the FCC, and Selective Prosecution. *Columbia Journal of Law and Social Problems, 28*, 203, 250-252.

Heinemann, M. (1993). *Drama and opinion in the 1620s: Middleton and Massinger*. In J.R. Mulryne & Margaret-Shewring (Eds.), *Theatre and government under the early Stuarts*. New York: Cambridge University Press.

Hill, T. (1991). The enemy within: Censorship in rock music in the 1950s. *South Atlantic Quarterly, 90*, 675.

Human Rights Watch. (1996, May). Silencing the net: The threat to freedom of expression on-line. *Human Rights Watch, 8*, No. 2 (G). Available online at http://www.epic.org/free_speech/intl/hrw_report_5_96.html.

Johnston, G. (1994). It's all in the cards: Serial killers, trading cards, and the First Amendment. *New York Law School Law Review, 39*, 549, 552 553, 555 557.

Keynes, J.M. (1923). *A tract on monetary reform* (p. 80). London: MacMillan and Co. Ltd.

Kim, J.H. (1995). Cyber-porn obscenity: The viability of local community standards and the federal venue rules in the computer network age. *Loyola Law and Entertainment Law Journal, 15*, 415, 435 438.

Kingsley International Picture Corp. v. Board of Regents, 360 U.S. 684, 688-689. (1957).

Klapper, J.T. (1960). *The effects of mass communications* (pp. 143-159). Glencoe, IL: Free Press.

Lewis, P.H. (1995, July 3). Microsoft backs ratings system for the Internet. *The New York Times*.

Marshall, T.R., & Ignagni, J. (1994). Supreme Court and public support for rights claims. *Judicature, 78*, 146, 151.

Markoff, J. (1995, July 3). New Internet features will make voluntary ratings possible. *The New York Times*.

Meyer, C. (1994). Sex, sin, and women's liberation: Against porn-suppression. *Texas Law Review, 72,* 1097, 1189-1190.

Mutual Film Corp. v. Industrial Commission of Ohio, 236 U.S. 230 (1915), *overruled, Joseph Burstyn, Inc. v. Union,* 343 U.S. 495, 502. (1952).

New York v. Ferber, 458 U.S. 747, 763. (1982).

Phelan, T. (1995). Selective hearing: A challenge to the FCC's indecency policy. *New York Law School Journal on Human Rights, 12,* 347, 390-392.

Price, M.E. (1994). The market for loyalties: Electronic media and the global competition for allegiances. *Yale Law Journal, 104,* 667, 691-694.

Reno v. ACLU, 521 U.S. 844. (1997).

Rigdon, J.E. (1996, January 25). For some, the web is just a slow crawl to a splattered cat. *The Wall Street Journal.*

Ringel, W.E. (1970). *Obscenity law today* (pp. 148-149). Jamaica, NY: Gould Publications.

Roberts, S. (1995, January 19). Giving poverty and hardship a human face. *The New York Times.*

Rubin v. Coors Brewing Co., 115 S.Ct. 1585, 1592. (1995).

Sable Communications v. F.C.C., 109 S. Ct. 2829, 2836-2837. (1989).

Shackleton, R. (1975). *Censure and censorship: Impediments to free publication in the age of enlightenment* (p. 11). Humanities Research Center, University of Texas at Austin.

Senate Report. (1996). No. 104358, 104th Cong., 2d Sess., pt. I, p. 7.

Virginia v. American Booksellers Association, 484 U.S. 383, 389. (1988).

Whitney v. California, 274 U.S. 357, 377. (1927) (Brandeis, J., concurring)

Woolfall, B.D. (1996). Comment, implications of a bond requirement for 900-number dial-a-porn providers: Exploring the need for tighter restrictions on obscenity and indecency. *California Western Law Review, 30,* 297, 310-311.

Zito, T. (1993, Dec. 17). Senate demagoguery; Leave my company's video game alone. *The Washington Post.*

7

The Regulation of Indecency on the Internet

The CDA, COPA, and CIPA

Sharon Docter
California Lutheran University

Governmental and societal efforts to regulate "indecent" communica-tion are not new. Sharon Docter offers a critique of the rationale for regulating indecent speech across various media. She explores the his-torical nature of these efforts and then considers the challenges posed by the unique characteristics of the Internet through a comparison with the broadcasting and cable television models of regulation. Given that the United States Congress has made several attempts to address sexually explicit non-obscene content on the Internet, this chapter criti-cally examines these laws by comparing the Communications Decency Act, the Child Online Protection Act, and the Children's Internet Protection Act.

The rapid growth of the Internet in recent years presents policymakers and the courts with increasing challenges concerning the ways in which this technology should be regulated. It is estimated that approximately 56% of Americans are now regular users of the Internet; moreover, the diversity of Internet users is expanding rapidly (Rainie & Packel, 2001; UCLA Center for Communication Policy, 2001; U.S. Department of Commerce, 2000).

Because the Internet is a speech medium, policy themes have arisen concerning how proposed and existing regulation implicates the First Amendment.[1] One important policy theme concerns the regulation of indecent messages on the Internet. Internet Service Providers (ISPs) allow large numbers of persons, including minors, to access Web sites, E-mail and bulletin board (BB) messages that might contain indecent words or pictures. Rimm (1995) conducted a content analysis of pornography on the Internet and concluded that three of the five most popular Usenet newsgroups worldwide contained pornographic images, stories, or discussions. Another study estimated that the eight top adult Web sites had each been visited by at least 1 million users (Roodenberg, 2001). A House of Representatives Report issued in 1998 estimated that about 28,000 Web sites generate approximately $925 million a year in pornography (H.R. Rep. 105-775, 1998).

The proliferation of indecent messages has become a concern of both policymakers and information service providers. In late 1995, CompuServe suspended access to at least 200 Internet newsgroups worldwide in response to an order by German authorities who had deemed the newsgroups indecent and in violation of German law. The order affected all 4 million users in 147 countries, including the United States (Kaplan, 1995). In late 2001, the European Union's (EU) European Cybercrime Convention recommended adopting policies that would outlaw child pornography on the Internet as well as the propagation of racist and xenophobic ideas (Smyth, 2001).

In China and Singapore, government officials have at times required that objectionable Internet traffic be routed through government-owned servers so that government officials could monitor Internet content and preclude access to content deemed to be objectionable (Smith, 2001). Similarly, a Harvard Law School study found that government filtering systems prevent Saudi citizens from accessing sexually explicit content and also a wide array of nonsexually explicit content, such as content pertaining to religion, humor, music, movies, and homosexuality (Zittrain & Edelman, 2002). Although the content blocked in Saudi Arabia concerned sexually explicit material and personal freedom issues, in China, the government is more concerned about content pertaining to political expression. For example, in August 2002, a former Beijing policeman was sentenced to 11 years in prison for downloading and printing counter-revolutionary essays

(Qiang & Beach, 2002). Even in countries, such as the United States, with strong traditions of free expression, Congress has attempted to impose criminal penalties on the display of indecent messages through the Communications Decency Act (CDA) and the Child Online Protection Act (COPA).

The proliferation of indecency on the Internet and the subsequent concern of policymakers are not surprising, as speech pertaining to sex has accounted for the early use of many new technologies. Many initial sales of videocassette recorders, for example, were attributable to consumers' desires to view pornography in the privacy of their home. Similarly, sexually related speech accounted for the early adoption of pay-per-view TV, laser discs, and 976 calling (Harmon, 1993). Historically, as new media have developed, the courts have allowed the government to regulate indecent speech transmitted via these media. However, the courts have emphasized that policies that completely ban indecent speech from a particular medium are unconstitutional. As issues concerning the regulation of indecent speech communicated over other new technologies have arisen, the courts have generally attempted to fashion unusual remedies that accommodate the interests of both those who would like to receive indecent messages and those who would like to prevent indecent messages form the entering their home.

The Federal Communications Commission (FCC) defined "indecent speech" as "language that describes, in terms patently offensive as measured by contemporary community standards . . . sexual or excretory activities or organs" (In the Matter of Enforcement Prohibitions Against Broadcast Indecency in 18 U.S.C. 1464, 1990, p. 5300). Obscene speech, however, is patently offensive speech that lacks "serious, literary, artistic, political or scientific value" and that appeals to a prurient interest in sex, as measured by contemporary community standards (*Miller v. California*, 1973). Whereas indecent speech is protected by the First Amendment, obscene speech constitutes a category of speech that falls outside the scope of First Amendment protection. Because obscenity is not protected by the Constitution, obscenity may be prohibited uniformly across all media. Indecent speech, however, is not uniformly prohibited. Instead, whether or not indecency is regulated when communicated over a given medium depends on the unique characteristics of the communication technology. The regulations concerning indecent speech, for example, differ when the indecency is transmitted via the broadcast medium, cable television, the telephone, or a newspaper.

In this chapter, I examine and critique the rationale for regulating indecent speech and provide an historical overview of the regulation of indecency in broadcast and cable television. The chapter will then analyze Congressional attempts to regulate indecent speech on the Internet by comparing and contrasting the CDA, the COPA, and the CIPA.

JUSTIFICATIONS FOR THE REGULATION OF INDECENT SPEECH

Because indecent speech is a content-based regulation, the government may regulate indecent speech only to promote a "compelling interest" and only if the regulation is the least restrictive means of achieving the government's interest (*Sable Communications of California, Inc. v. FCC*, 1989; *Reno v. ACLU*, 1997).

Protecting Children From Harm

One compelling interest that the government has identified and that the courts have accepted as a rationale for regulating indecent speech is the interest in protecting the physical and psychological welfare of children (*Sable Communications of California, Inc. v. FCC*, 1989). This rationale was considered a compelling interest in the context of the Internet (*Reno v. ACLU*, 1997).

Embedded in this justification for the regulation of indecent speech is the assumption that indecent speech, whether broadcast via radio or television or communicated over telephone lines, causes harm to children. However, there is no empirical evidence that supports the proposition that indecent messages harm children. In an assessment of all the available social scientific literature concerning the effects of indecent speech on children, Donnerstein, Wilson, and Linz (1992) concluded "relevant empirical research provides no reasonable evidence to suggest harmful effects result from, exposure to such [indecent] content" (p. 111). The dissent in *Action for Children's Television v. FCC* (1995) recognized that this lack of evidence undermined the protection of minors from harm as a compelling interest:

> There is not one iota of evidence in the record to support the claim that exposure to indecency is harmful—indeed the nature of the alleged "harm" is never explained. There is significant evidence suggesting a causal connection between viewing violence on television and antisocial behavior; but . . . the FCC has pointed to no such evidence addressing the effects of *indecent* programming. (p. 671, Edwards dissenting)

The lack of empirical evidence concerning a relationship between indecent speech and harmful effects on children suggests that this justification for regulating indecency is not appropriate. The government can hardly claim a "compelling" interest in protecting children from indecent messages when no record of harm to children can be established.

However, the court in *Action for Children's Television v. FCC* (1995) held that a showing of harm is not necessary to justify the protection of minors from harm as a compelling interest. The court noted "a scientific demonstration of psychological harm is [not] required in order to establish the constitutionality of measures protecting minors from exposure to indecent speech" (pp. 661-662). The court instead rests its justification on normative considerations concerning children's moral and ethical development. However, even though a clear scientific demonstration of harm should not be required to justify a compelling interest, it appears that at least some demonstration of harm is necessary. Otherwise, the distinction between "a reasonable basis" for regulation, a "substantial interest," and a "compelling interest" become blurred. Moreover, the need for at least some demonstration of harm is particularly important when Congress seeks to suppress constitutionally protected expression. Without at least some demonstration of evidence, it would become increasingly easy for Congress to ban marginalized speech based on a claim that such speech undermines the moral and ethical standards of society. This principle is counter to the bedrock of the First Amendment.

The lack of evidence linking indecency and harm to children is of particular concern when one considers that the reason for denying individuals a right to express constitutionally protected speech has been based on a tenuous assumption. Unlike regulations of media that are designed to enhance speech by promoting diversity (such as the Fairness Doctrine), the curtailment of indecent speech in this context abridges speech by narrowing the diversity of messages and by directly burdening the free speech rights of those who seek to express and those who seek access to indecent speech.

Protecting Unsuspecting Adults

In *FCC v. Pacifica Foundation* (1978), the Court justified regulating indecent speech by identifying an interest in protecting unsuspecting adults from receiving shocking messages in "the privacy of the home, where the individual's right to be left alone plainly outweighs the First Amendment rights of an intruder" (p. 748). The court, in a plurality opinion, noted that the broadcast medium is uniquely pervasive and, therefore, "unconsenting viewers may tune into a station without any warning that offensive language is being or will be broadcast" (p. 732, n. 2). Viewers, then are considered a captive audience who lack the ability to control and monitor the messages they see and hear.

The justification that indecent speech may be regulated because it might shock unsuspecting adults also runs contrary to the principles of the First Amendment. In *Cohen v. California* (1971), the Court held that speech cannot be banned simply because it is offensive to some people.

In the Cohen case, a young man was criminally prosecuted for wearing a jacket that said "Fuck the Draft" in a courthouse. In reversing the conviction, the Court held that it is not the function of government to maintain what it regards as a suitable level of discourse within society. The free speech rights of individuals cannot be abridged simply because exercising those rights might create a danger that some will be offended: "The ability of government, consonant with the Constitution, to shut off discourse solely to protect others from hearing it is . . . dependent on a showing that substantial privacy interests are being invaded in an essentially intolerable manner. Any broader view of this authority would effectively empower a majority to silence dissidents simply as a matter of personal predilections" (p. 18).[2]

Moreover, the Court noted that if individuals were offended by Cohen's message, they could simply avert their eyes to avoid further exposure to the message because they were not a captive audience. Similarly, the viewers and listeners of indecent messages via broadcast media hardly can be considered a captive audience; to the extent that viewers are offended by indecent messages, they possess the ability to simply turn the channel.[3] Users of the Internet also cannot be considered a captive audience as they possess even greater control over which pages and images they wish to display or ignore than can viewers and listeners of radio and television (see *Reno v. ACLU*, 1997). To the extent that users come across offensive messages, they can electronically and instantaneously "avert their eyes" by proceeding to the next message.

In balancing the First Amendment rights of those who wish to disseminate and receive indecent messages versus those who are offended by indecent messages, the balance should tip in favor of the free dissemination of ideas, especially given the power of those offended by the messages to choose to ignore them. The justification, then, that indecent speech should be regulated because it offends unsuspecting adults is not a valid rationale for regulating indecent speech communicated via any media, but it is particularly inappropriate when applied to the Internet.

PROTECTING PARENTS' RIGHTS TO DIRECT THE REARING OF THEIR CHILDREN

A final justification for regulating indecent speech recognizes the interests of *parents* to raise their children in a manner as they see fit. In this regard, the government does not seek to regulate indecent speech because it assumes that indecent speech will harm children or offend adults; rather, the government regulates indecent speech only during times of the day when unsupervised children are likely to be in the audience. The goal is to protect the decision of some parents to prevent their children's exposure to indecent speech. The government, in this view, has a "compelling interest" in facilitating parents' choices about the kinds of programs they will allow their children to view (*Action for Children's Television v. FCC*, 1988).

The government interest in protecting parents' right to direct the rearing of their children was initially recognized in the context of the broadcast of indecent messages in the *FCC v. Pacifica* (1978) case. The D.C. Court of Appeals also relied specifically on the government's interest in facilitating parent's programming choices in its initial decision concerning the constitutionality of the FCC's 24-hour ban on indecent speech (*Action for Children's Television v. FCC*, 1988). The court repeatedly stressed that the government had an interest in "assist[ing] parents in controlling the material young children will hear" (p. 1223). Relying primarily on testimony from the FCC General Counsel, the court held that the government may regulate the broadcast of indecent speech *not* because the government has made an independent determination that a child's exposure to indecent material is morally wrong or harmful, but because the government has an interest in protesting parents' rights to control the material that their children may view. As the court noted, "the government does not propose to act *in loco parentis* to deny children access *contrary* to parents' wishes" (p. 1343). Instead, the court held that the government may regulate indecent speech broadcast over the airwaves only to the extent that the regulation will promote parental control of viewing choices and will balance the interests of those parents who object to their children viewing indecent programming versus those parents who allow it.

To the extent that the government continues to identify an interest in assisting parents in controlling their children's exposure to indecent messages, it finds a valid justification for regulating indecent speech, at least for those media that are accessible to unsupervised children. Importantly, this justification is independent of any harmful effects of indecent speech on minors as well as any offensive effects of indecent speech on unsuspecting adults.

THE BROADCASTING MODEL

Unlike the print medium, the broadcast medium historically has been regulated by the government. The classic justification for allowing the government to intrude into areas traditionally protected by the First Amendment and regulate the speech of its citizens is that there exists a scarcity of the electromagnetic spectrum (*Red Lion v. FCC*, 1969). Although theoretically anyone can have access to the print medium to disseminate views, the nature of the broadcast medium requires that only a limited number of voices can be communicated over the airwaves at one time. Thus, the government must act as a "traffic cop," granting licenses to a limited number of individuals and guaranteeing limited rights of access in certain instances. Additionally, the scarce nature of the broadcasting medium has been used as a justification for enacting regulations designed to ensure that a diversity of viewpoints are heard over the airwaves.

The scarcity rationale for regulation of the broadcast medium has come under increasing criticism (see Pool, 1983), and there have been signs from the Court that it will no longer accept scarcity as a valid justification for regulating broadcasting (*FCC v. League of Women Voters,* 1984). Scarcity of the electromagnetic spectrum, however, only justifies regulations that are designed to enhance speech by *increasing* the diversity of voices. The Fairness Doctrine and the limited rights of access for federal political candidates are examples of such speech-enhancing regulations. In contrast, regulations that *curtail* indecent speech cannot be justified through the scarcity argument, for regulations that abridge speech inevitably limit the range of viewpoints. As noted previously, the curtailment of indecent speech communicated over the broadcast medium has been permitted because radio and television are "uniquely pervasive" and "uniquely accessible to children" (*FCC v. Pacifica,* 1978, p. 748).

Relying on the rationale that broadcasting is uniquely accessible to children, the FCC, during the late 1980s, and pursuant to a directive from Congress, promulgated regulations that completely banned indecent speech from the broadcast medium. The D.C. Court of Appeals then issued a stay on enforcement of the ban; the court then voided the 24-hour ban as unconstitutional because the 24-hour ban impermissibly infringed on the First Amendment rights of those who wanted access to indecent messages (*Action for Children's Television v. FCC,* 1988, 1991). The court held that "the FCC may regulate such [indecent] material only with due respect for the high value our Constitution places on freedom and choice in what the people say and hear" (*Action for Children's Television v. FCC,* 1991, p. 1508). Implicit in the court's opinion is the assumption that the government cannot reduce public debate to a level that is only appropriate for children (see *Ginsberg v. New York,* 1968). However, given that "the power of the state to control the conduct of children reaches beyond the scope of its authority over adults" (*Action for Children's Television v. FCC,* 1995), the court permitted some regulation of indecent messages such as a requirement that indecent speech be broadcast during the late evening hours when children are not likely to be in the audience (*Action for Children's Television v. FCC,* 1991).

There are many reasons why the broadcast model cannot be applied to the Internet. Electronic communications are not as accessible to children as broadcasting. There can be no doubt that television is accessible to children.

Turning on a television or radio requires only that children turn on one switch. Children as young as 3 years old, for example, can generally understand how to turn on a television. One can argue that accessing the Internet requires a much more sophisticated understanding of the technology. Because the Internet is still primarily a text-based medium, children must be able to read to use the Internet effectively. Moreover, the Internet is less pervasive than broadcasting. As noted by the Court in *Reno v. ACLU* (1997), it is unlikely that adults will come across indecent material by accident. For these reasons, the Court has declined applying the highly regulatory broadcast model to the Internet (*Reno v. ACLU*, 1997).

THE CABLE TELEVISION MODEL

Unlike the broadcasting model, the courts have held that indecent material may not be restricted to the late evening hours on cable television (*Community Television of Utah, Inc. v. Roy City* , 1982; *Jones v. Wilkinson*, 1986). In reaching this holding, the courts noted that the fundamental differences between cable and broadcast television require that cable television be treated differently with regard to indecent material than the traditional broadcast model. One of the most important distinctions between cable and broadcast television is the viewer's choice over programming content. According to the courts, subscribers to cable television have a greater degree of choice than do viewers of broadcast television. First, viewers may choose to subscribe or not, and "a similar choice is not available with broadcast television" (*Community Television v. Roy City*, 1982, p. 1166).[4] Additionally, subscribers to cable television may select from varying tiers of service. There is the sense, then, that viewers of cable television are aware that programs on the higher tiers of service (such as Home Box Office) may contain more indecent material. By actively selecting tiers of service in which indecent material is likely to be present, the viewer implicitly consents to allowing the material into his or her home: "Cable signals travel over wires, not in the air. Such signals do not travel except on request. They are asked for. They are invited" (p. 1166). Finally, the subscriber to cable television may choose to terminate this service. A viewer of broadcast television, however, "cannot terminate his subscription to a publicly allocated broadcast channel" (p. 1166).

Given that the government cannot restrict the hours that indecent material may be cablecast, Congress used other means to accommodate the interests of parents who would like to ensure that their children not be exposed to indecent material. The Cable Communications Policy Act of 1984 provides that cable companies must make lock boxes available to subscribers at a reasonable price (47 U.S.C. section 624 (d)(2)(A), 1984). Lock boxes are devices that are installed on the cable box, which allow parents to lock out their access to cable television.[5]

In recent years, the Supreme Court affirmed the principle that cable television subscribers would receive greater First Amendment protection than broadcast viewers. In *United States v. Playboy Entertainment Group* (2000), the Supreme Court held as unconstitutional Section 505 of the Telecommunications Act of 1996 that attempted to regulate indecent programming on cable. Section 505 dealt with the problem of "signal bleed." Section 505 required that cable operators (and also satellite companies) completely scramble or block sexually explicit adult programming or show it only between the hours of 10 p.m. and 6 a.m. The practical effect of the legislation was to channel the indecency into the late evening hours because at the time, there was not technology available that would allow signals carrying sexually explicit programming to be fully blocked.

Section 504 of the Telecommunications Act required that cable operators fully block channels that a subscriber requests. The channel is blocked because the operator has the obligation to provide a lock box free of charge. Thus, signal bleed would only occur for that category of viewer who did not request the programming but also who did not request that the programming be blocked.

In balancing the burdens of those who seek access to sexually explicit programming versus those who seek to block access, the Court balanced the burdens in favor of those seeking access. Cable subscribers have a right to receive constitutionally protected expression at all times of the day. Thus, those who wish to block access should have the burden of affirmatively requesting the blocking technology (*United States v. Playboy Entertainment Group*, 2000).

Similarly, in *Denver Area Educ. Telecomm. Consortium v. FCC* (1996), the Court balanced the burdens in favor of those seeking access to sexually explicit speech, as in the *Playboy* case. In *Denver Area Educ. Telecomm. Consortium v. FCC* (1996), the Court considered challenges to sections of the Cable Consumer Protection Act of 1992. Section 10(b) of the Act required that sexually explicit material on leased access channels only be segregated to a single channel, blocked, and required that subscribers request access in writing. The Court found this scheme of segregating/blocking/written access was too burdensome on those who wished access. The burden instead should be placed on subscribers who wished to block access, as this process had worked for nonleased access channels.

The *Playboy* (2000) and *Denver* (1996) cases provide useful models that can be applied to the Internet. Legislation, for example, has required that public libraries install blocking technology on all computer terminals.

Users can request that the blocking technology be disabled (see discussion of the CIPA). This approach is counter to the *Playboy* and *Denver* cases and counter to First Amendment values because it places the burden on those seeking access to constitutionally protected expression to make an affirmative request for access. This inevitably will lead to a chilling effect on the right to receive information. The burden, then, should be placed on those who wish to block access to affirmatively make a blocking request.

POLICY RESPONSES

This section critiques three attempts to regulate indecent speech on the Internet: the CDA, the COPA, and the CIPA.

The Communications Decency Act

In 1996, Congress passed the CDA, which represented Congress' first attempt to restrict children's access to indecent messages on the Internet. The CDA prohibited the "knowing transmission of obscene or indecent messages to any recipient under 18 years of age" (CDA, section 223(a)). It also prohibited the "knowing sending or displaying of patently offensive messages in a manner that is available to a person under 18 years of age" (CDA, section 223 (d)). With the possible exception of one-to-one E-mail communication, it is impossible for Internet users to discern the age of those individuals who are likely recipients of messages (*Reno v. ACLU*, 1997). The CDA, then, constituted a virtual 24-hour ban on indecency in electronic communications.

The CDA did provide two affirmative defenses. If a person instituted a good faith effort to restrict minors' access to indecent or patently offensive messages by requiring a credit card verification, adult access code, or an adult personal identification number, then the person would be absolved of liability (CDA, section 223 (e)(5)). However, if a person violated the Act, they would be subject to criminal penalties, including up to 2 years in prison.

Shortly after its passage, the American Civil Liberties Union (ACLU) filed suit claiming that the CDA was unconstitutional on its face. The case reached the Supreme Court in 1997. The case is significant because it provides the first definitive holding that the Court is most likely to apply the print model to the regulation of the Internet.

Because the CDA is a content-based regulation, the Court concluded that it must be justified by a compelling government interest and must be the least restrictive means of achieving the government's interest (*Reno v.*

ACLU, 1997). The Court acknowledged that the government has an interest in protecting children from harmful materials. However, the CDA is
not the least restrictive means of achieving the government's interest.

In defending the CDA, the government argued that the CDA's affirmative defenses were the least restrictive means of achieving the government's interest. The Court, however, rejected this argument, finding that
the affirmative defenses did not save the statute. The Court found that age
verifications were ineffective. "There is no effective way to determine the
identity or age of a user who is accessing material through e-mail, mail
exploders, newsgroups or chat rooms" (*Reno v. ACLU*, 1997, p. 855).
Similarly, credit card authorizations also are ineffective. A credit card
authorization system or adult password system would impose tremendous
costs, particularly on noncommercial Web sites. The costs would be so
great that these sites might have to be shut down.

The government argued that the CDA was unconstitutional under
prior decisions, yet the Court distinguished each of the cases. The Court
found that the CDA was not analogous to laws prohibiting the selling of
indecent materials to minors under *Ginsberg v. New York* (1967). The
statute at issue in *Ginsberg* did not preclude parents from purchasing indecent material for their children, yet under the CDA, even if a parent consents to his or her child being exposed to indecent material, the parent
would be subject to criminal penalties. The statute at issue in the *Ginsberg*
case also offered a more precise definition of indecency and required that
the material be utterly without redeeming social importance (*Reno v.
ACLU*, 1997). Neither of these was present in the CDA. In fact, the Court
found the CDA to be unconstitutionally vague. Users and information
providers, fearing criminal prosecution because of minors' access to such
material, may avoid exercising their First Amendment rights by receiving
or initiating indecent communications. The risk of the chilling effect is even
greater when the initiators of the communication may face criminal prosecution, as is the case with the CDA.

The Court in *Reno v. ACLU* (1997) also distinguished the *FCC v.
Pacifica* (1978) case and explicitly rejected application of the broadcast
model to regulation of the Internet. Unlike the Internet, broadcasting is not
a scarce medium and historically has been regulated by an agency familiar
with its characteristics. The Internet has no such history. Moreover, the
Internet is not as accessible to children as broadcasting. "Unlike communications received by radio or television, the receipt of information over the
Internet requires a series of affirmative steps more deliberate and directed
than merely turning a dial. A child requires some sophistication and some
ability to read to retrieve material and thereby to use the Internet unattend-
ed" (*Reno v. ACLU*, 1997, p. 887). Moreover, the Court found that the
Internet was not as pervasive as the broadcast medium because the end user

has greater control over what material he or she accesses. Finally, the *Pacifica* case did not involve a complete ban of indecency but only channeled indecency into the late evening hours. The practical effect of the CDA is a complete ban on indecent speech.[6]

Thus, although the Court upheld the ban on obscene communications over the Internet, sections of the CDA that banned the communication of indecent or patently offensive speech were held unconstitutional. The Court recognized a compelling interest in protecting children from psychological harm. However, less speech restrictive means of protecting this interest, such as the use of blocking or filtering software, could protect the interests of parents who want to keep indecency from their children, while accommodating the interests of adults who seek access.

The Child Online Protection Act

In response to the Court's holding in *Reno v. ACLU* (1997), Congress passed the COPA in 1998. COPA assigns criminal and civil penalties to persons who "knowingly and with knowledge of the character of the material, in interstate or foreign commerce by means of the World Wide Web, makes any communication for commercial purposes that is available to any minor and that includes any material that is harmful to minors" (COPA, 47 U.S.C. 231 (a)(1) (1998)). In defining material that is harmful to minors, Congress closely paralleled the language of obscenity as defined in the *Miller v. California* (1973) case and the harmful to minors statutes at issue in the *Ginsberg v. New York* (1968) case:

> (A) the average person, applying contemporary community standards, would find, taking the material as a whole *and with respect to minors,* is designed to appeal to, *or is designed to pander to,* the prurient interest;

> (B) depicts, describes, or represents, in a manner patently offensive *with respect to minors,* an actual or simulated sexual act or sexual contact, an actual or simulated normal or perverted sexual act, or a lewd exhibition of the genitals *or post-pubescent female breast*; and

> (C) taken as whole, lacks serious, literary, artistic, political, or scientific value *for minors.* (COPA, 47 U.S.C. 231 (e)(6), 1999; italics added)

COPA contains many provisions that are different than the CDA. First, COPA applies only to the Web and not to the Internet. Thus, COPA attempted to address the concerns articulated in *Reno v. ACLU* (1997) that age-screening devices could not be applied to the Internet as a whole by narrowing the scope of COPA to the Web. COPA also attempts to define more precisely the term *patently offensive*. COPA requires that material harmful to minors appeal to a prurient interest and lack serious value for minors (*Ashcroft v. ACLU*, 2002). Whereas the CDA applied to all transactions on the Internet, COPA applies only to speech designed to make a profit. Thus, nonprofit entities that may not be able to afford the cost of age-screening would be exempt from the statute. The government also has argued that COPA is distinguishable from the CDA because the CDA constituted a flat ban on indecency and, therefore, even parents who consented to their children seeing indecent materials would be subject to criminal penalties. On the other hand, under COPA, parents may consent to have their children see material that might be deemed harmful. Finally, the CDA applied to persons under 18 years of age and thus may apply to individuals in their first year of college; COPA applied to individuals under seventeen years of age (*Ashcroft v. ACLU*, 2001, Brief for Petitioner; Roodenburg, 2001).

Shortly after its passage, the ACLU and several other groups filed suit alleging that COPA was unconstitutional on its face. Both the district court and the Third Circuit Court of Appeals stayed enforcement of COPA. The Third Circuit issued a rather narrow ruling, holding that the "contemporary community standards" definition of material harmful to minors under COPA could not be applied to the Internet. Therefore, Web sites would be forced to comply with the standards of the most speech-restrictive community (*Reno v. ACLU*, 3rd Cir. 2000). In 2002, the Supreme Court vacated the Third Circuit ruling, finding that the application of contemporary community standards did not make COPA facially invalid. In a significant departure from other precedent, a majority of justices found that applying a national standard for what constitutes material that is "harmful to minors" is constitutional as applied to the Internet. The Court found that community standards need not refer to a precise geographic locale, but rather could refer to the standards of the adult Internet community as a whole. The Court remanded the case to the lower court to consider whether COPA would survive strict scrutiny (the compelling interest test), is overbroad, or is unconstitutionally vague (*Ashcroft v. ACLU*, 2002).

In defending the constitutionality of COPA, the government relied heavily on *Ginsberg v. New York* (1968), which upheld the constitutionality of precluding vendors from making available to minors materials that are indecent. The government argued that adult verification screens are analogous to blinder racks at news stands and magazine racks and that COPA merely requires that harmful material be put behind an age-verification screen. Furthermore, they argued that, contrary to the holding of the Third Circuit, the "community standards" clause does not invalidate the statute (*Ashcroft v. ACLU*, 2001, Brief for the Petitioner).

Despite the government's arguments, COPA should not withstand strict scrutiny. Although there may be a compelling interest in protecting children from harm, credit card authorizations and adult access codes are not the least restrictive means of achieving the government's interest. As articulated by the respondents in *Ashcroft v. ACLU* (2001, Brief for the Respondents), most of the information on the Web is provided for free; the Web is an advertiser-based medium that is dependent on "hits" that are usually linked to advertising dollars. Credit card authorizations and/or adult access codes will most assuredly limit the flow of information, as users have consistently reported that they are inhibited from using credit cards on the Web because of fears of privacy and security. In fact, a synthesis of public opinion data revealed that between 57% and 96% (mean = 86%) of users report being very or somewhat concerned about credit card security (Fox, 2000; Green, France, Stepanek, & Borrus, 2000; Jones & Carlson, 2001; National Consumers League, 2000; UCLA Center for Communication Policy, 2000). Moreover, credit card authorizations and access codes will inevitably deter users from accessing indecent speech, particularly because the nature of the speech is so personal in nature. This, then, impermissibly burdens the rights of both speakers and listeners. Thus, like the CDA, the affirmative defenses contained in COPA cannot save an otherwise unconstitutional statute (see *Reno v. ACLU*, 1997). Like the CDA, COPA also assigns criminal penalties unless a Web site operator complies with the affirmative defenses, thereby creating a chilling effect on constitutionally protected expression.

Although the government argues that the scope of COPA is not as great as the scope of the CDA because COPA applies to the Web whereas the CDA applies to the Internet as a whole, COPA's scope is actually quite broad. Many Web sites contain interactive components, such as chatrooms and BBs. Interactive fora are important to attracting new users to Web sites (*Ashcroft v. ACLU*, 2001, Brief for the Respondent). COPA essentially requires that Web site operators put all content behind age verification screens, as Web site operators can never be sure whether or not individuals might post material that is harmful to minors and Web site operators would not want to risk criminal prosecution. This may have the effect, then, of reducing speech to a level that is appropriate for children, a principle that the Court has consistently held to be unconstitutional (*Ginsberg v. New York*, 1967).

COPA is overbroad for other reasons as well. COPA, for example, requires that the harmful material be "taken as a whole." Given that many Web sites contain interactive components, it is not clear what material should be evaluated. As Justice Kennedy noted, "it is unclear . . . what constitutes the denominator—that is, the material to be taken as whole—in the context of the World Wide Web" (*Ashcroft v. ACLU*, 2002, p. 68, Kennedy, J., concurring).

The Court's willingness to apply a national standard to the Web in determining what is harmful to minors also is problematic. Because the Web could reach any community in the United States, the standards of the most puritanical community could be used to determine what is "harmful to minors." As Justice Kennedy noted, the unique characteristics of the Web, unlike other forms of mass media, suggest that is it easier and cheaper to reach a worldwide audience than to reach a small, targeted audience:

> A Web publisher in a community where avant garde culture is the norm may have no desire to reach a national market; he may wish only to speak to his neighbors; nevertheless, if an eavesdropper in a more traditional, rural community chooses to listen in, there is nothing the publisher can do. As a practical matter, COPA makes the eavesdropper the arbiter of propriety on the Web. (*Ashcroft v. ACLU*, 2002, p. 59, Kennedy, J., concurring)

Justice Thomas' response to this argument is quite troubling, as he suggests merely that speakers should simply utilize a different medium. Eliminating access to a medium of expression directly contradicts the values of the First Amendment (*Ashcroft v. ACLU*, 2002, Kennedy, J., concurring).

Finally, COPA will not be successful at achieving its goal of protecting children from harmful materials. The Web represents a vast array of networks, with communications initiating both within the United States and internationally. A system that imposes criminal penalties for making available material that is harmful to minors does not preclude those outside the United States from making indecent communication available to minors, especially given that 40% of all Internet content originates outside the United States. Moreover, minors may still gain access to potentially harmful materials through non-Web-based protocols (*Ashcroft v. ACLU*, 2001, Brief for the Respondent).

COPA, then, is both overinclusive and underinclusive in achieving its goal of preventing minors from accessing harmful materials. Voluntary blocking software, although not perfect, is a much less speech-restrictive alternative and accommodates the interests of parents who want to block access without infringing on the rights of adults who might seek access.

The Children's Internet Protection Act

Congress' latest attempt to regulate indecency, the CIPA, was passed as a last-minute attachment to an appropriations bill in late 2000. Rather than imposing criminal penalties as the CDA and COPA did, CIPA requires that libraries and schools receiving federally funded technology install filtering software as a condition of funding.

Specifically, CIPA requires that those schools and libraries that receive Universal Service discounts (the "E-rate") for Internet access, Internet service, or internal connections install a "technology protection measure" or filtering software to prevent children from accessing indecent content. The technology protection measure must block or filter "visual depictions" that are obscene, constitute child pornography or are harmful to minors. CIPA contains provisions that allow librarians or school officials to disable the blocking software "to enable access for bona fide research or other lawful purpose" (CIPA, 3601 (3); 1712 (3)).

Because the rights of children are not the same as the rights of adults, CIPA has different constitutional implications for public libraries than for public schools.

CIPA's Application to Libraries. Shortly after its passage, the American Library Association (ALA) and the ACLU filed a constitutional challenge to the provisions of CIPA that require the installation of filtering software in public libraries as a condition of funding. In May 2002, the district court held that CIPA was unconstitutional (*ALA v. United States*, 2002). In 2003, the Supreme Court overruled the district court, holding that CIPA did not violate the First Amendment.

Like the CDA and COPA, the district court was correct in holding CIPA unconstitutional. CIPA should have been held unconstitutional as applied to libraries because it required libraries to infringe on the First Amendment rights of their patrons who have a right to receive constitutionally protected expression.

The *Reno v. ACLU* (1997) case clearly established that Internet users have the right to receive information and ideas over the Internet, even if that information is indecent. In determining what First Amendment rights are afforded library patrons, it is important to examine the nature of the forum. The First Amendment rights may differ depending on whether or not libraries are traditional public forums, limited public forums, or nonpublic forums. A "traditional public forum" is publicly owned property that has been traditionally used for expressive purposes. Streets, sidewalks, and parks are examples of traditional public forums (*Hague v. CIO*, 1938; *Police Department v. Mosley*, 1972). Traditional public forums are afforded the greatest degree of First Amendment protection and the government is in general precluded from imposing content regulations.

A "limited public forum" is public property "which the state has opened for use by the public as a place for expressive activity" (*Perry Ed. Assn. v. Perry Local Educators' Assn*, 1983). The state is neither required to open up nor indefinitely make available certain public property for expressive activity. However, once the government has invited expressive activity into a particular forum, it cannot make content discriminations concerning the type of expressive activity that it will allow. Libraries are most certainly public places that the state has opened for expressive purposes. They are places where individuals exercise their right to receive information. Some case law suggests that libraries are limited public forums (see *Brown v. Louisiana*, 1966, plurality opinion). In the *Brown* case, the Court held that civil rights demonstrators had the right to hold a silent demonstration at a segregated library because the demonstration did not interfere with other library patrons. Similarly, in *Mainstream Loudoun v. Board of Trustees of the Loudoun County Library* (1998), the court also suggested that public libraries are limited public forums.

In this sense, then, public libraries are very different than school libraries. In *Board of Education v. Pico* (1982), the Supreme Court considered whether a local school board may remove books from the school library because board members disagree with the content contained within the books. In the case, the Court held that a school board may not remove books from a library on the basis of content or viewpoint. However, because the public school has a special role in inculcating values, the board may remove books for reasons of educational suitability, such as, for example, if a book is pervasively vulgar (*Board of Education v. Pico*, 1983; *Mainstream Loudoun v. Loudoun County Library*, 1998). In reaching this holding, the plurality was clear that the holding was narrow and applied only to libraries within the public school context. Even the dissent acknowledged that there are fundamental differences between a school library and a public library. Justice Rehnquist, in his dissenting opinion, noted that "[u]nlike public libraries, elementary and secondary school libraries are not designed for freewheeling inquiry" (*Board of Education v. Pico*, 1983, p. 915). Moreover, in dissenting from the plurality, Justice Rehnquist argued that local school boards should be entitled to make removal decisions because the books would be available at public libraries. Thus, the *Pico* case suggests that public libraries may not make content-based decisions about what kinds of content to remove.

Both the limited public forum doctrine and the *Pico* case suggest that content-based decisions about filtering content from public libraries must be justified by a compelling government interest and filtering must be the least restrictive means of achieving the government's interest. In *ALA v. United States* (2002), the district court applied strict scrutiny based on the public forum doctrine. As is the case with the CDA and COPA, the government may argue that it has a compelling interest in protecting the physical and psychological well being of minors (*Reno v. ACLU*, 1997). However, requiring that libraries install filters at all computer terminals as a condition of funding is not the least restrictive means of achieving the government's interest. The terms of CIPA clearly require that filters be installed at "any" computer within the library. Thus, instead of requiring that particular terminals within the library have filters, the filtering requirement applies to all terminals, whether or not they are being used by children.

Moreover, it is well established that filtering software is both overinclusive, filtering content that may not be sexually explicit at all, and underinclusive in that inappropriate content still may come through. For example, a study of one of the most popular filtering software programs, Cyberpatrol, revealed that the program had blocked the Web sites for Planned Parenthood, Enviro-link (an environmental Web site), the AIDS Authority, the MIT Project on Mathematics and Computation, the University of Arizona Web site, and the Web site for the U.S. Army Corps of Engineers Research Laboratories (Horowitz, 2000). Popular filtering programs also have blocked the Web sites of Amnesty International, House Majority Leader Dick Armey, and an electronic copy of *Jane Eyre* (Hopper, 2000). Filtering programs also are underinclusive. A recent study by Consumer Reports reported that one in five adult-oriented sites were not blocked (Duffy, 2001). Even the makers of popular filtering software, such as Net Nanny and Cybersitter, admit that it is impossible to create software that will block all pornography while at the same time not block protected speech (Brickley, 2001). In *ALA v. United States* (2002), the district court conducted an extensive analysis of filtering software and found that blocking technology was both overinclusive and underinclusive because of "limitations on the technology that software filtering companies use to gather and review Web pages, limitations on resources for human review of Web pages, and the necessary error that results from human review processes" (*ALA v. United States*, 2002, p. 18).[7]

The government has argued that the provisions within CIPA allowing librarians to disable the filtering software on the request of the library patron cures the statute of its constitutional flaws because adults, then, could request access to constitutionally protected expression. The disabling provision of CIPA states that a library official "may disable the technology protection measure concerned to enable access for bona fide research or other lawful purposes." This places the burden on those who seek access to affirmatively request permission to receive constitutionally protected expression. This will have a severe chilling effect on library patrons, who may be hesitant to request access because of the social stigma attached to such a request, particularly given the nature of the speech at issue. In balancing the burdens between those who wish to restrict access versus those who seek access, the courts should tip the balance in protecting the right to receive constitutionally protected expression (see *Denver Area Educ. Telecommunications Consortium, Inc. v. FCC*, 1996, holding that it was unconstitutional to require that cable subscribers affirmatively request in writing access to patently offensive leased access cable channels; *United States v. Playboy Entertainment Group*, 2000).

In addition to chilling the right to receive information, the disabling provision suffers from another fatal flaw. It gives too much discretion to library officials to determine under what circumstances disabling is appropriate. The statute, as previously noted, provides that librarians "may" disable the filters. However, the statute does not provide any guidance or standards to librarians concerning when they may disable the filters, other than for a "lawful purpose" or for "bonafide research." For example, there is no definition concerning what constitutes "bonafide research." The librarian in this instance, then, represents a government actor who has the power of the gatekeeper and may use his or her individual discretion in deciding when to disable the software (*American Library Association v. U.S.*, 2001, Defendant's Brief in Opposition to Motion to Dismiss).

The *Mainstream Loudoun v. Loudoun County Library* (1998) case is most applicable to CIPA. In *Mainstream Loudoun*, the library Board of Trustees required that filtering software be installed on all terminals in the public library in order to protect employees from sexual harassment. The court held that the policy unconstitutionally interfered with the right of library patrons to receive constitutionally protected materials. The court found that the policy reduced speech to a level that is fit for children. The court found that requiring filtering software gave too much discretion to companies who create the software; the decision concerning what material to filter is made based on secret criteria which are not disclosed to those seeking access and which may not bear any relationship to the legal definitions of speech outside the scope of the First Amendment, such as obscenity or child pornography.

Like CIPA, the policy at issue in *Mainstream Loudoun* also contained a disabling policy. The filtering software could be unblocked on a written request by library patrons seeking access to a particular site. The court found that such a policy impermissibly chilled speech of those seeking access. The court noted that there may be a "severe chilling effect of forcing citizens to publicly petition the Government for access to speech it clearly disfavored" (*Mainstream Loudoun*, 2001, p. 41, citing *Lamont v. Postmaster General of the United States*, 1965). Moreover, the *Mainstream Loudoun* court found that the unblocking policy gave unfettered discretion to library officials to determine when to grant unblocking requests, and this only increased the chilling effect. "[The unblocking policy] grants library staff standardless discretion to refuse access to protected speech . . . ." (p. 41).

Despite these arguments, the Supreme Court upheld CIPA in 2003. In a plurality opinion, the Supreme Court did not apply strict scrutiny because they did not find Internet access within public libraries to be public forums.

"A public library does not acquire Internet terminals in order to create a public forum for Web publishers to express themselves, any more than it collects books in order to provide a public forum for authors to speak" (*United States v. American Library Association*, 2003, p. 233). Moreover, the plurality found that strict scrutiny was not required because libraries have broad discretion to make content-based determinations about their collections even when those determinations block certain types of Internet content. Finally, the Court did not find that requirement that libraries install filtering software as a condition of funding to be over-inclusive because the disabling provision allows patrons to request that the filtering software be disabled if the filtering software erroneously blocked content or if the patron needs access to blocked content for bonafide research purposes.

Thus, despite the strong arguments articulated by the district court, the Supreme Court has upheld CIPA's application to libraries.

CIPA as Applied to Schools. The sections of CIPA requiring that filtering software be installed on computers in public schools should withstand constitutional scrutiny. In fact, there were no constitutional challengers to this section.

Unlike adults, children do not have a right to receive nonobscene sexually explicit forms of expression (*Ginsberg v. New York*, 1968). While children "do not shed their constitutional rights to freedom of speech or expression at the schoolhouse gate" (*Tinker v. Des Moines School District*, 1969), the Court has never held that the constitutional rights of children are the same as those of adults.

For example, in *Bethel School District v. Fraser* (1986), the Court held that a student could be disciplined for giving a speech that contained sexual metaphors. The Court held that the school has an interest in maintaining school discipline and in teaching students socially appropriate behavior. Thus, the interest in teaching students the boundaries of socially appropriate behavior outweighed the student's right to free expression in this instance. Similarly, in *Hazelwood School District v. Kuhlmeier* (1988), the Court held that school officials may censor content contained in school newspapers if the decision to delete content is reasonably related to legitimate pedagogical concerns. The *Hazelwood* Court distinguished the *Tinker* case. In *Tinker*, the Court held that students may not be prohibited from wearing black armbands as a means of protesting the Vietnam War. In *Tinker*, those students wearing black armbands were not necessarily engaged in a school-sponsored activity. In *Hazelwood*, on the other hand, the student newspaper was considered a school-sponsored activity and as such, school officials did not have to satisfy the compelling interest test but only show that the decision was reasonably related to legitimate pedagogical concerns.

Whether or not Internet use is a school-sponsored activity is an important factual question. Utilizing a school's computers probably will be considered school-sponsored, as students presumably will use the Internet during school hours for pedagogical purposes, such as research. As such, the lower standard of *Hazelwood* would apply, and school official could argue that there is a legitimate pedagogical concern in blocking access to sexually explicit speech, as schools have an obligation to inculcate socially appropriate values.

. The *Board of Education v. Pico* (1982) case is perhaps most relevant to the constitutionality of CIPA. As previously noted, the *Pico* case concerned a local school board's decision to remove books from a school library for content-based reasons. In *Pico*, the plurality of the Court held that school officials may not remove library books from shelves for narrowly partisan or political reasons, but may remove books for reasons of "educational suitability" such as "pervasive vulgarity." Decisions to block content through filtering software is analogous to decisions to remove books from library shelves because removal decisions do not require financial expenditures (*Mainstream Loudoun v. Board of Trustees of Loudoun County Library*, 1998). As applied to CIPA, school officials could successfully argue that filtering software is intended to block content that is not educationally suitable for children and that is vulgar or educationally unsuitable. Unlike filtering in public libraries, the courts need not consider the constitutional rights of adults to receive access to materials. Given that children do not have a constitutional right to receive images or words that may be considered vulgar, those sections of CIPA that require filtering software to be installed on computer terminals in public schools do not violate the First Amendment.

Although installing blocking software in schools raises no constitutional problems, policymakers should question whether this is wise policy, particularly in the context of secondary schools. Given the overinclusiveness of blocking software, students may be denied access to material that might be educationally beneficial. Perhaps a better alternative is the close monitoring of students' Internet use along with inculcating values in students so that they might develop the skills to make informed choices about their Internet use based on what content is socially appropriate.

CONCLUSIONS

Since 1996, Congress has made three attempts to regulate sexually explicit nonobscene content on the Internet through the CDA, COPA, and CIPA. With the exception of CIPA, all of these attempts unconstitutionally violate the First Amendment rights of adults seeking access to such content on the Internet.

It is not surprising that Congress appears willing to pass unconstitutional legislation, as taking a strong, public First Amendment stance is a politically risky position, particularly during an election year. Representatives opposing the CDA, COPA, or CIPA might appear as if they were supporting easy access to sexually explicit speech on the Internet, a highly unpopular position. The result, then, is that First Amendment concerns are absent from the debate surrounding the CDA, COPA, and CIPA. Instead, Congress appears willing to pass unconstitutional legislation and then leave it to the Courts to invalidate the statutes, as this is a politically safe position.

Rather than assigning criminal penalties for the dissemination of sexually explicit speech on the Internet (as the CDA and COPA do), or requiring the imposition of filters in public libraries (as CIPA does), a better alternative would be a system of voluntary blocking. This would place the burden on those seeking to block access to constitutionally protected speech. In balancing the burdens in the context of cable television, the Court in *United States v. Playboy Entertainment Group* (2000) and to some extent in *Denver Area Educ. Telecomm. Consortium v. FCC* (1996) adopted this approach; the "default" in these cases was to allow access; those who wished to block access had to make an affirmative request to do so. This same approach could be helpful in the context of the Internet whereby users should have broad access to all kinds of content, while those who seek to block access should take affirmative steps to do so. Any other approaches—particularly those that seek broad bans on particular kinds of speech—will hamper the free flow of information.

NOTES

1. Some of these policy themes include the degree of content regulation that is permissible, copyright issues, liability for defamation, guarantees of access, and privacy and security.
2. Interestingly, when considering indecency regulations in the broadcasting context, the court declined to address whether the "protection of the home against intrusion by offensive broadcasts" constituted a compelling interest justifying the regulation of indecency (*Action for Children's Television v. FCC*, 1995, pp. 660-661) *because other justifications were sufficiently compelling.*
3. *FCC v. Pacifica* (1978) can be distinguished from *Cohen v. California* (1971). In *Pacifica*, the Court distinguished *Cohen* by noting that there was no evidence any person was in fact offended by *Cohen*'s jacket. In *Pacifica*, however, there was evidence that at least one person was offended by the indecent radio broadcast. Moreover, the offensive speech communicated in *Cohen* and *Pacifica* did occur in different contexts. *Cohen* concerned indecent speech communicated in a public place. *Pacifica* concerned indecent speech communicated over the pub-

lic airwaves and brought into people's homes and car radios. One important justification for regulating indecent speech in Pacifica, then, concerned protecting unconsenting adults form being shocked in the privacy of their homes.

4. See also *Action for Children's Television v. FCC* (1995), in which the court noted that "unlike cable subscribers who are offered such options as 'pay-per-view channels' broadcast audiences have no choice but to 'subscribe' to the entire output of traditional broadcasters" (p. 660).

5. In 1992, Congress amended the Communications Act to provide that indecent programming on leased access channels must be carried on a single channel and will be blocked unless the customer requests access in writing. The number of leased access channels vary depending on the total number of cable channels available. However, leased access channels represent a relatively small percentage of the total number of channels. Moreover, the Senate has passed a bill requiring that cable operators scramble programming that is unsuitable for children. Passage of such legislation by the Hours appears likely.

6. The court also distinguished the *Renton v. Playtime Theatres, Inc.* (1986) case, which held that local governments may zone adult theaters into nonresidential neighborhoods. This represents a regulation of the time, place and manner of speech. The CDA, on the other hand, does not zone speech, but represents a flat ban on indecent speech that applies to the entire universe of cyberspace (*Reno v. ACLU*, 1997).

7. The district court also found that less speech restrictive alternatives were available such as posting clear Internet use policies, enforcing penalties on persons who violate use policies, requiring parental consent or presence when children seek access to unfiltered computer terminals, establishing a system of optional filtering, or requiring that unfiltered computer terminals be placed out of sightlines to prevent children and unconsenting patrons from exposure (*ALA v. United States*, 2002).

REFERENCES

Action for Children's Television et al. v. FCC, 852 F.2d 1332 (D.C. Cir.) (1988).
Action for Children's Television et al. v. FCC, 932 F.2d 1504 (D.C. Cir.) (1991).
Action for Children's Television et al. v. FCC, 58 F.3d 654 (D.C. Cir.) (1995).
American Library Association v. United States, Response in Opposition of Plaintiffs The American Library Association et al., to Defendant's Motion to Dismiss Plaintiffs' Complaint, Civil Action No. 0 1CV13 03; 01CV1322 (E.D. Penn. 2001).
American Library Association v. United States, 2002 U.S. Dist. LEXIS 9537 (E.D. Pa. 2002).
Ashcroft v. ACLU, Brief for the Petitioner, 2000 U.S. Briefs 1293 (2001).
Ashcroft v. ACLU, Brief for the Respondents, 2000 U.S. Briefs 1293 (2001).
Ashcroft v. ACLU, 122 S. Ct. 1700 (2002).
Bethel School District v. Fraser, 478 U.S. 675 (1986)
Board of Education v. Pico, 457 U.S. 853 (1982).

Brickley, P. (2001, October). Internet decency standards pose ethical and financial problems for many companies, schools and libraries. *Corporate Legal Times*, p. 80.

Brown v. Louisiana, 385 U.S. 863. (1966).

Child Online Protection Act, 47 U.S.C. 231 *et. seq.* (1998), *enforcement stayed* (2002).

Children's Internet Protection Act, 47 U.S.C. 254(h) *et .seq.*; 20 U.S.C. 9134 *et. seq.* (2000), *enforcement stayed* (2002).

Communications Decency Act of 1996, 47 U.S.C. 223 *et. seq.* (1996), *repealed* (1997).

Cohen v. California, 403 U.S. 15 (1971).

Community Television of Utah, Inc. v. Roy City, 555 F. Supp. 1164 (D. Utah) (1982).

Denver Area Educ. Telecomm. Consortium v. FCC, 518 U.S. 727 (1996)

Donnerstein, E., Wilson, B., & Linz, D. (1992). On the regulation of broadcast indecency to protect children. *Journal of Broadcast & Electronic Media, 3*(6), 111-117.

Duffy, S.P. (2001, March 21). Libraries, ACLU challenge new law. *The Legal Intelligencer, 1*.

FCC v. League of Women Voters, 468 U.S. 364. (1984).

FCC v. Pacifica Foundation, 438 U.S. 726. (1978).

Fox, S. (2000). *Trust and privacy online: Why Americans want to rewrite the rules.* Pew Internet & American Life Project report. Retrieved November 2, 2000, from http://pewintemet.org/reports/toc.asp?Report=19

Ginsberg v. New York, 390 U.S. 629. (1968).

Green, H., France, M., Stephanek, M., & Borrus, A. (2000, March 20). *It's time for rules in wonderland. Business Week/Harns poll: A growing threat.* Retrieved January 19, 2002, from http://www.businessweek.com/2000/00_12/b36 73010.htm

Hague v. CIO, 307 U.S. 496. (1939).

Harmon, A. (1993, December 29). The "seedy" side of CD-ROMs. *Los Angeles Times*, p. A26.

Hazelwood School District v. Kuhlmeier, 484 U.S. 260. (1988).

Hopper, D.I. (2000, December 20). ACLU to fight filtering plan. *The Legal Intelligencer*, p. 4.

Horowitz, A. (2000). The constitutionality of the Children's Internet Protection Act. St. *Thomas Law Review, 13*, 425-444.

In the Matter of Enforcement of Prohibitions Against Broadcast Indecency in 18 U.S.C. 1464, 5 F.C.C.2d 5297. (1990).

Jones, J.M., & Carlson, D.K. (2001, June 28). *Majority of e-mail users express concern about Internet privacy.* Gallup News Service.Retrieved January 24, 2002, from http://www.gallup.com/poll/releases/PrO 10628. asp

Jones v. Wilkinson, 300 F.2d 989. (10th Cir.) (1986).

Kaplan, K. (1995, December 29). Germany forces online service to censor Internet. *The Los Angeles Times*, p. Al.

Mainstream Loudoun v. Board of Trustees of the Loudoun County Library, 24 F. Supp. 2d 552. (E.D. Va 1998).

Miller v. California, 413 U.S. 15. (1973).

National Consumers League. (2000, October). *Online Americans more concerned about privacy than health care, crime, and taxes, new survey reveals.* Retrieved January 26, 2002, from http://nclnet.org/pressessentials.htm

Perry Ed. Assn. v. Perry Local Educators' Assn, 460 U.S. 37. (1983).

Police Department v. Mosley, 408 U.S. 92. (1972).

Pool, I. (1983). *Technologies of freedom.* Cambridge, MA: Harvard University Press.

Qiang, X., & Beach, S. (2002, August 25). The great firewall of China. *The Los Angeles Times,* p. M3.

Rainie, L., & Packel, D. (2001, February 18). *More online, doing more.* Pew Internet & American Life Project report. Retrieved January 19, 2002, from http://www.pewintemet.org/reports/toc.asp?Report=30

Red Lion v. FCC, 395 U.S. 367. (1969).

Reno v. ACLU, 521 U.S. 844. (1997).

Reno v. ACLU, 217 F.3d 162. (3rd Cir.) (2000).

Renton v. Playtime Theatres, Inc., 475 U.S. 41. (1986).

Rimm, M. (1995). Marketing pornography on the information superhighway: A survey of 917,410 images, descriptions, short stories and animations downloaded 8.5 million times by consumers in over 2000 cities in forty countries, provinces and territories. *Georgetown Law Journal, 83,* 1849-1934.

Roodenberg, J.M. (2001). Son of the CDA: The constitutionality of the Child Online Protection Act of 1998. *Communication Law and Policy, 6,* 227-257.

Sable Communications of California, Inc. v. Federal Communications Commission (FCC), 492 U.S. 115. (1989).

Smith, B.L. (2001). The third industrial revolution: Policymaking for the Internet. *Columbia Science and Technology Law Review, 3,* 1-44.

Smyth, J. (2001, September 21). Proposed monitoring of e-communications criticized. *The Irish Times.*

Tinker v. Des Moines School District, 393 U.S. 503. (1969).

UCLA Center for Communication Policy. (2001). *The UCLA Internet report 2001: Surveying the digital future: Year two.* Retrieved January 21, 2002, from http://www.ccp.ucla.edu

United States v. American Library Association, Inc., 539 U.S. 194 (2000).

United States v. Playboy Entertainment Group, 529 U.S. 803 (2000).

U.S. Department of Commerce. (2000, October). *Falling through the net: Toward digital inclusion. A report on Americans' access to technology.* National Telecommunications and Information Administration. Retrieved October 15, 2001, from http://digitaldivide.gov/reports.htm

Zittrain, J., & Edelman, B. (2002). *Documentation of Internet Filtering in Saudi Arabia.* Berkman Center for Internet & Society, Harvard Law School. Retrieved July 18, 2002 from http://cyber.law.harvard.edu/filtering/saud-arabia/

8

Filtering the First Amendment

The Trouble with Internet Content Filters in Public Libraries and Schools

Christopher D. Hunter
Trion Communications

Technological solutions have been sought to solve the problem of access to objectionable websites, particularly to minors. Legislative efforts have linked federal funding to libraries and schools to those institutions offering limited web access. Yet the limitations of filtering software products such as CyberPatrol, smutty, illegal or otherwise objectionable mean that no product in the roughly $250 million filtering software market can screen out objectionable websites without also blocking constitutionally protected sites. In this chapter Christopher Hunter explores the many reports detailing the often flawed performance of filters and examines, why as a technical matter, filters raise serious First Amendment issues when installed in public libraries and schools. This chapter sheds light on the June 2003 decision of the U.S. Supreme Court that upheld a federal law making filters a condition for public libraries to continue to receive federal subsidies and grants.

Since the Internet came to the fore of public attention around 1994, Americans have been obsessed with the scourge of easily accessed online pornography, violence, and hate speech. Newspaper and magazine articles have fed this fear with titillating stories about pornographic Web sites, hate groups, and online sexual predators. Indeed, according to research conducted by the Annenberg Public Policy Center, fully one fourth of news articles about the Internet from October 1997 to October 1998 were alarmist in nature and two thirds of these articles raised disturbing issues about the nature and content of the Web (Turow, 1999). Such coverage has led to high levels of concern among parents who fear for their children's online safety. For example, a February 2000 survey by the Annenberg Public Policy Center found that 72% of parents were concerned that their children might view sexually explicit images on the Internet, and only 51% felt that the Net was a safe place for children to spend time (Turow & Nir, 2000).

Widespread public concern and a perceived abundance of harmful material has led Congress to pass two laws, the Communications Decency Act (CDA) in 1996, and the Child Online Protection Act (COPA) in 1998, both aimed at criminalizing Internet content deemed obscene or harmful to minors. In conjunction with these legislative efforts, the software industry has developed its own technological solution, namely content-filtering software like Bess, CYBERsitter, Cyber Patrol, I-Gear, Net Nanny, SurfControl, WebSENSE, and so on. These programs claim to block between 90% and 95% of dangerous Net content (CYBERsitter, 2002; SurfControl, 2001), while allowing unfettered access to the net's vast quantities of valuable material.

Since their passage, courts have rejected both the CDA and COPA as unconstitutional restraints of First Amendment protected speech.[1] In overturning these legislative solutions, the courts pointed to the supposedly "equally effective" but "less restrictive alternative" of Internet-filtering software as the best way to keep the Internet a safe place for children. As a result, filter technologies have been championed as *the* solution for keeping inappropriate content at the edge of cyberspace, and away from children. These self-regulatory, market-driven technologies are seen as First Amendment friendly, and far preferable to direct government regulation of Internet content. In the wake of the CDA's defeat, no less than the Clinton administration endorsed this idea, noting that "Advanced blocking and filtering technology is doing a far more effective job of shielding children from inappropriate material than could any law" (White House, 1997).

Support for filters only intensified in the wake of the April 1999, Columbine High School shooting tragedy. In the days following the incident, the news media uncovered the fact that the shooters frequently used the Internet to access Neo-Nazi and bomb-making Web sites. In the rush to blame something for the inexplicable killing spree, both the public and politicians cast a collective pointed finger at the Internet. A CNN/*USA Today* poll conducted shortly after the killings found that 64% of respondents said the Internet contributed to the tragedy (cited in McCullagh, 1999). Responding to this perceived problem, Congress and the White House drafted a flurry of new laws and proposals to curb access to dangerous Internet content. Senator John McCain introduced an early version of the Children's Internet Protection Act (CIPA), requiring all schools and libraries receiving federal funds for Internet access to install filtering software. Another proposed law sought to require any Internet service provider (ISP) with more than 50,000 subscribers to distribute content blocking software to its customers (Bloomberg, 1999). The Federal Communications Commission (FCC) similarly endorsed filters. Speaking about Littleton at a May 1999 conference, FCC Chairman William Kennard (1999) noted "We need filtering software for families to use on their PCs. Just as you wouldn't send a child off alone in a big city, you wouldn't—and shouldn't—let them explore the vast landscape of the Internet without a chaperone." In a similar speech announcing a joint industry-White House "Parents Protection Site", Vice President Gore noted that filters were the best tool parents could use to protect children from the "free-fire zones and red light districts in cyberspace."

The Internet content industry has also thrown its support behind filter use. In September 1999, the Bertelsmann Foundation (1999) released a major self-regulation proposal seeking to "protect children online as well as guarantee free speech" (p. 8). To achieve this end, the proposal called for the development of a voluntary international content rating and filtering system.

Filters once again received strong support during the 2000 presidential election campaign. Candidates Elizabeth Dole, John McCain, George W. Bush, and Al Gore all supported some form of filter use. As Bush noted during one of the presidential debates, "There ought to be filters in public libraries, and filters in public schools, so that if kids get on the Internet, there's not going to be pornography or violence coming in" (cited in McCullagh, 2000).

Perhaps due to such high-profile endorsements, the vast majority of Americans support the use of filters. According to an October 2000 survey conducted by the Digital Media Forum, 92% of respondents said pornography should be blocked on school computers, whereas 79% said filters should be used to block access to hate speech (Weiner, 2000).

In December 2000, Internet content filters received official U.S. government endorsement with the passage of the CIPA (discussed in detail later). In a press release issued after the bill's passage, Sen. McCain (2000) commented that filters would "ensure that pervasive obscene and violent material is screened out and that our children are protected" (McCain, 2000).

Although the White House, Internet industry, Congress, and the general public may accept that content filters are the way to go, a number of scholars and civil libertarians have asked whether these technologies are indeed the best solution for protecting children from inappropriate Internet content. They point out that content-filtering software tends to block a great deal more speech than even government regulation would deem off limits. In many instances, filters seem to have a conservative political bias in blocking access to controversial, but certainly not pornographic material about gay and lesbian issues, sex education, and so on. Furthermore, such blocking decisions can be based on nearly any criteria, and are not open to public or institutional review because filter makers consider their lists of blocked sites proprietary trade secrets. Finally, many filters do not even work as advertised, failing to block many objectionable Web sites and thus giving parents a false sense of security. In short, Internet software filters championed as effective and First Amendment friendly, would seem to be anything but (ACLU, 1997).

In this chapter I will explore the many reports detailing questionable filter performance, why as a technical matter filters are systematically flawed and will likely always be so, and why these flaws raise serious First Amendment issues when filters are installed in public libraries and schools.

THE TROUBLE WITH FILTERS

Flaws in filtering software have been identified in numerous investigations into filter effectiveness conducted by journalists, academics, civil liberties groups, policy organizations, and even government-appointed commissions. This section reviews just a few of the more outrageous examples of faulty filters.

One of the first groups to identify politically motivated blocking decisions by filter makers was the gay and lesbian community. In June 1995, Christopher Kryzan (1995) sent out an e-mail advisory documenting 10 gay-related Web sites blocked by SurfWatch as pornographic. In November 1995, The Gay & Lesbian Alliance Against Defamation (GLAAD) released a similar report criticizing Cyber Patrol for blocking gay-related Web sites as pornography. The GLAAD (1995) press release noted that CyberPatrol blocked access to the following:

- The San Jose gay and lesbian paper OutNOW!
- Gay and lesbian community center sites in San Jose and New York.
- Guides from gay student groups at Berkeley and Stanford.
- A performing arts center in San Francisco.

- A guide to broadcast programs with gay themes or characters.
- Lesbian and gay employee groups.
- The site for the 1998 Gay Games.

CYBERsitter has also come under intense criticism for blocking access to gay- and lesbian-related resources, including the Web sites of GLAAD and the National Organization for Women. In response, CYBERsitter's president, Brian Milburn (cited in Weinberg, 1997), commented, "I wouldn't even care to debate the issues if gay and lesbian issues are suitable for teenagers. . . . We filter anything that has to do with sex. Sexual orientation [is about sex] by virtue of the fact that it has sex in the name."

GLAAD's *Access Denied* report nicely summarizes filters' politically motivated decision to block many gay and lesbian resources as if they were inappropriate pornography sites:

> The majority of software currently on the market, as well as new products in development, place informational Web sites serving the gay, lesbian, bisexual and transgender community in the same categories as sexually explicit sites. The software developers are either unable or unwilling to consider that information about sexual orientation and identity (e.g., a gay square dancing site) has nothing to do with sexual behavior, and everything to do with culture and identity. (GLAAD, 1997, p. v)

In February 1996, the online news source *Netsurfer Digest* reported that SurfWatch had blocked access to the official White House Web site. The apparent reason for the block was the presence of the key word "couples" on a page devoted to the presidential and vice presidential couples (Netsurfer Digest, 1996).

Hoping to provide more systematic evidence of filter flaws and thus persuade schools, libraries, and parents that filters might not be the best solution for protecting children from harmful Internet material, a group of programmers and civil libertarians formed the Censorware Project in 1997. One of the Censorware Project's (1997) first reports, *Blacklisted by Cyber Patrol: From Ada to Yoyo*, documented extensive, and quite bizarre overblocking by Cyber Patrol. Among the sites incorrectly blocked under Cyber Patrol's "FullNude" and "SexActs" categories were the following:

- The Creature's Comfort Pet Care Service Web page devoted to pets.
- The MIT Project on Mathematics and Computations.
- The National Academy of Clinical Biochemistry.
- The We the People of Ada Web site devoted to local politics in Ada, Michigan.

The report also identified a problem known as *virtual hosting*, where a filter's blocking of one site on an ISP results in *all* sites on the same ISP being blocked. The Censorware Project found that Cyber Patrol overblocked more than 50 ISPs hosting multiple Web sites on the same Internet protocol (IP) address.

In July 1999, the Censorware Project released *Passing Porn, Banning the Bible*, an analysis of the Bess filtering software in actual use in 10 public school systems around the country. The Censorware Project tested Bess against lists of pornographic sites as well as innocuous material to gauge both under and overblocking. The report found that Bess failed to block hundreds of easy to find pornographic Web sites, including the following:

069palace.com	koreax.com	straightnhard.com
amatuerxxx.com	legal-sex.com	stripshowlive.com
asianslut.com	livedancer.com	teen-photos.com
crazysmut.com	maleporn.com	teenpicts.com
digitaldesires.net	malestrippers.com	teenhotel.com
dynamicsex.com	nudedudes.com	teensnatch.net
eliteporn.com	orgasm.com	themaleroom.com
erotic-queens.com	orientalpussy.com	thenudiebar.com
freeadultsexpics.com	partyingsluts.com	this-is-your-wife.com
freexxxpictures.com	realgaystuds.com	webxtasy.com
freshgirl.com	redlightzone.com	weekly-weinee.com
galacticsex.com	sexpasswords.com	wickedonline.com
givemeporn.com	sexxxysnacks.com	wwwmen.com
guys4u.com	soft2hard.com	xxxfetish.com
hotasianfoxes.com	straight-hunks.com	

In addition to its poor performance in blocking access to pornography, Bess was found to overblock numerous educationally valuable Web sites, such as the following:

- *Mother Jones* magazine.
- *Redbook* magazine.
- Feminists Against Censorship.
- A site containing the *Jefferson Bible*.
- The Friends of Lulu site, promoting the idea that girls should read comic books too.

During the summer of 2000, the congressionally appointed COPA Commission heard testimony from filter makers, free speech advocates, and numerous other parties interested in protecting children online. At the July 20th hearing, Richard Schwartz (2000), CEO of ClickSafe, submitted a statement noting that, "ClickSafe's uses state-of-the-art, content-based filtering software that combines cutting-edge graphic, word and phrase-recognition technology to achieve extraordinarily high rates of accuracy in filtering pornographic content" (p. 1). Schwartz also commented that "ClickSafe can precisely distinguish between appropriate and inappropriate sites (i.e., it has both remarkably low underblocking and overblocking rates)" (p. 1). To verify these claims, the Internet free speech advocacy group, Peacefire (2000b), tested ClickSafe against the COPA Commission's own Web site, as well as the sites of organizations who testified before the Commission. Peacefire found that ClickSafe incorrectly blocked access to numerous pages on the COPA Commission's own site, including a Frequently Asked Questions page, and the biographies of Commission members Donna Rice-Hughes and Stephen Balkam. ClickSafe was also found to block access to the following:

- The Center for Democracy and Technology.
- Bible Study Tools from Crosswalk.com.
- The American Civil Liberties Union.
- The Electronic Frontier Foundation.
- The American Family Association, a conservative group that supports the use of filters in public schools and libraries.

Likely due to such reports of filter overblocking, the COPA Commission's final report to Congress failed to endorse the mandatory use of filters in public libraries and schools. The report concluded:

> This technology raises First Amendment concerns because of its potential to be over-inclusive in blocking content. Concerns are increased because the extent of blocking is often unclear and not disclosed, and may not be based on parental choices. . . . There are significant concerns about First Amendment values when server-side filters are used in libraries and schools. (pp. 19-20)

On election day 2000, Peacefire released *Blind Ballots*, a study detailing congressional candidate Web sites blocked by Cyber Patrol and Bess. Peacefire tested a list of roughly 1,000 active congressional candidate Web sites provided by the election resource site, NetElection.org. The report found that Cyber Patrol blocked nine candidate sites under its sexual content categories. Among the sites blocked was that of Jeffrey Pollock, a

Republican candidate in Oregon's third district, whose position page on Internet issues stated, "We should demand that all public schools and libraries install and configure Internet filters." Bess was also found to block numerous candidate Web sites, including that of Ed Markey, the powerful Congressman from Massachusetts's seventh district. Bess also blocked access to 19 third-party candidate sites. Many of these sites were blocked because they were hosted on free home page services like members.aol.com and zoom.com. Such free hosting sites provide third-party candidates with a low-cost way of reaching a potentially mass audience. However, because these sites have been found to contain some pornographic content, Bess blocks *all* free hosting services under its "Typical School Filtering" setting (Peacefire, 2000a). Given that the First Amendment provides the highest level of protection to core political speech like congressional candidate Web sites, it is quite troubling to realize that the blocked sites just mentioned would not have been available to students and citizens seeking political information at public libraries and schools with filtered Internet access.

A final area where filters have been shown to dramatically overblock valuable Internet content occurs when filters are confronted with privacy, translation, and archive Web sites that handle Web site addressing in non-standard ways. In a series of reports, programmer Seth Finkelstein documented how filtering software must block access to these sites in order to function. For example, Bess contains an undocumented "loophole" category that blocks access to privacy enhancing services such as "The Anonymizer" (Finkelstein, 2001). When a Web surfer uses this service, all Web page requests are sent through an Anonymizer proxy server that strips the request of any identifying information. In other words, even if a user requested the site www.xyz.com, the user's ISP would only see that a request had been made to anonymizer.com. So in the case of www.xyz.com, the Anonymizer service would return the request to the end user in the form of an address such as anon.free.anonymizer.com// www.xyz. com/. Because most filters block sites by their address, surfing through the anonymizer, which changes the address, defeats the filter. As a result, in order to remain effective filters must block *all* services that act in this way. This is quite troublesome because the blocking of anonymizers may prevent some library patrons or public school students from searching for highly sensitive information. As Nunberg (2001) commented, "An adolescent who wants to obtain information from a sex advice site or suicide prevention site might have qualms about accessing the site if she knows that the library might be logging her Web use" (p. 54). Such blocking due to technical addressing reasons also prevents access to useful language translation sites such as Bablefish.org (Finkelstein, 2000), and archive sites like the Waybackmachine.org, which allows users to view old versions of sites that have disappeared from the Web (Finkelstein, 2002).

WHY FILTERS FAIL

The many examples outlined here, and countless other reports and studies of filter performance conducted since 1995 have all found overblocking, underblocking, or both. But why is it that filters so consistently fail to work as advertised?

Currently available filtering products use a wide range of techniques (blacklists, whitelists, key word filtering, label-based filtering, customer reports, etc.) to find, classify, and block harmful Internet content. The most commonly used of these methods is the development of extensive black lists that contain hundreds of thousands of blocked Web sites, Web pages, Usenet newsgroups, and mailing lists. Blocked site lists are compiled using two primary methods. The first method is human review, in which companies hire professional surfers to explore the Internet looking for objectionable content. Filter makers generally employ between 20 and 40 full- and part-time Web site reviewers. When material that meets a filter maker's blocking criteria is found, the Web site, newsgroup, or the like, is added to the program's master blocked site list. Most filter makers claim that all of their blocking decisions are based on careful human review, but this claim is somewhat suspect due to the tremendous size and rapid growth of the Web.

Put simply, the Web is a vast space. There are currently more than 37 million Web sites (Netcraft, 2002), and more than 2.1 billion unique, publicly available Web pages (Cyveillance, 2000). Every day, 7 million new Web pages are created (Cyveillance, 2000), and more than 50 million existing pages change their content (Censorware Project, 2000). In addition to the publicly available web, there exists what is known as the "invisible" or "deep" web, comprised of pages residing in Web-accessible databases and other difficult-to-index locations. One estimate places the size of the "deep" Web at nearly 550 billion individual documents (BrightPlanet, 2000).

Combining the sheer size of the Web with its ever-changing nature, it is clearly impossible for any filter company, even with a staff of hundreds or even thousands, to review a majority of the Web's content for pornographic material. As Finkelstein and Tien (2001) outlined the problem:

> How fast can a person evaluate a Web page? A reasonable overall estimate is one page per minute. One page per minute is 60 pages per hour. That's 480 pages per eight-hour workday. Let's call it 500 pages per workday for ease of calculation. At 200 workdays per year, we have 100,000 pages per work-year. So one person doing only censorware evaluation could only do 0.1 million pages in a year. (p. 71)

Even if filter developers could review such a large percentage of Web content, they would still have to continually re-review the millions of Web pages that have updated their content (e.g., candyland.com was originally a pornography Web site until Hasbro bought the domain and converted it to a Candyland board game product site).

Because it is simply impossible for human reviewers to keep up with the ever-expanding web, filter makers must resort to the use of context-insensitive Web "spiders" that crawl from Web site to Web site and flag content due to the presence of key words like sex, breast, and so on. Filter makers like to claim that these routines use "revolutionary new artificial intelligence technology" to only identify sites that are truly pornographic. However, such claims are highly dubious. The use of computers to accurately understand and classify human language is a notoriously difficult problem. As Wallace (2001) commented, "the understanding of colloquial or everyday human content by a computer—often referred to as 'natural language processing'—is one of the most difficult problems that 'strong artificial intelligence' has yet to solve."

Filter makers further claim that their Web spiders do not automatically add sites to their master blocked site lists, but instead refer flagged Web content to human reviewers for final inspection. However, given the many obviously incorrectly blocked Web sites described previously, it is likely that some Web sites and Web pages are being added to blocked site lists without human review.

Another measure that many filter programs employ is key word filtering, also known as *string recognition*. If a site does not appear on the blocked site list, many filter programs will still "read" the page before it is displayed by a Web browser. If the filter encounters key words that have been deemed improper, it will either block out those words or completely deny access to the page. Unfortunately, key word filters are not advanced enough to understand the context of human language. In one humorous example of this problem, CYBERsitter's blocking of the word *homosexual* would render "President Clinton opposes homosexual marriage" to say "President Clinton opposes marriage" (Weinberg, 1997). Several filtering programs also use key word filtering to block users from searching the Web using phrases like "sex education."

Another problem associated with categorizing the vast volume of Web sites is *granularity*. Granularity refers to the level of a Web site at which a blocking decision is imposed. Take for example the following fictional domains:

1. http://www.xyz.com/
2. http://www.xyz.com/directory1/
3. http://www.xyz.com/directory1/page1.html

If a block were imposed on the first address, also known as the root level, the entire site xyz.com would be blocked. All subsequent directories and pages falling under the xyz.com domain would be off limits. If the second address were blocked, only that particular directory, "/directory1/," and all pages within that directory would be blocked. Finally, if the third address were blocked, only "page1.html" in "/directory1/" would be blocked, but the rest of xyz.com would be available.

The level at which a block is imposed is extremely important, because many Web sites have hundreds of subdirectories containing millions of individual Web pages. Therefore, blocking at the root level of the site playboy.com for example, would mean that all other content on the site would be blocked even if certain subdirectories and individual pages contained nonpornographic interviews, articles, editorials, and so on. Granularity of blocking is a particular problem on large Web sites like Geocities.com and Tripod.com, which allow millions of people to develop their own home pages for free within separate directories. These sites have been found to contain pornographic pages, and as a result many filter companies have blocked these sites at the root level. Therefore, this means that millions of nonpornographic, nonobjectionable pages are also blocked in the process, a form of collateral damage to free speech. Filter companies often block at the root level because it is too time consuming to surf through the millions of pages on such sites, looking for specific examples of off-limits content. This reality once again casts doubt on filter maker claims that all Web sites or Web pages they block have been reviewed by a human. It may be true that a reviewer examined the root level of a site, and perhaps a few subdirectories, but in many cases it would be simply impossible to review all directories and individual pages on a large-scale Web site.

Another problem related to granularity is presented by a technique known as *virtual hosting*. Behind every Web site is what is known as an IP address. So for example, the Web site of the civil liberties organization the Electronic Frontier Foundation is http://www.eff.org/, which is associated with the IP address 204.253.162.16. Filter companies often times block Web sites by IP address. However, using a technique known as virtual hosting, several separate Web sites, each with a different domain name, can share the same IP address. Therefore, if a filter company blocks a pornography Web site by IP address, but other nonpornographic sites share the same IP, then the other sites will be blocked as well. This problem is only likely to get worse, as there is actually a shortage of available IP addresses. As a result, the American Registry for Internet Numbers, the group that allocates IP numbers, encourages the widespread use of virtual hosting in order to conserve IP addresses.[2]

Compounding all of these problems is the fact that most filter makers consider their lists of blocked sites proprietary trade secrets, and therefore do not make them available for public scrutiny. Instead, filter makers encrypt their blocked site lists so that no one can review which sites they have decided to block and why.

The many structural problems with filtering software outlined here result in two outcomes. The first is underblocking, where filters fail to block access to pornographic or other types of objectionable material. The primary reason that such content slips past filters is the incredible size and rapid growth of the web. Filter companies simply cannot keep up with the volume of new pornographic Web sites coming online every day. Due to this problem, filter companies must resort to techniques such as context-insensitive Web spidering and key word filtering. This results in the second outcome, the systematic overblocking of benign, valuable speech.

CYBERSPACE FILTERING MEETS THE REAL WORLD

The many problems associated with filters make them a less than perfect parental empowerment tool. Nevertheless, parents implementing their values through the use of filters on home computers raises few if any constitutional concerns. However, when filters are introduced into public, government-sponsored institutions whose goal is the dissemination and receipt of valuable educational, political, and cultural speech, serious First Amendment issues are raised. Perhaps the most interesting and instructive example of where filters meet real-world information use is occurring in our nation's public libraries and schools. These cornerstones of our democracy are currently engaged in an intense public and legal debate about the appropriateness of installing filters to protect minors (and adults) from potentially harmful material. More than a decision about what filter program to use, the debate over filters in libraries and schools raises fundamental questions about the core nature of these institutions. As such, decisions made about filtering Internet access will have profound implications for education and the future of information access in our increasingly networked society.

THE LIBRARY FILTER DEBATE ROUND 1: LOUDOUN

The historical mission of public libraries has been the widespread dissemination of information in order to promote an educated and informed citizenry. The founders of the nation's first public library—the Boston Public Library, opened in 1854—wished "to promote equality of educational opportunity, to advance scientific investigation, to save youth from the evils of an ill-spent leisure, and to promote the vocational advancement of the workers" (Shera, 1949, p. 247). This progressive spirit of open access to information and educational empowerment remains the core principle of today's public library system. As the American Library Association's (ALA, 2002), Library Bill of Rights notes, "Books and other library resources should be provided for the interest, information, and enlightenment of all people of the community the library serves."

Given this background, it is unsurprising that public libraries have eagerly led the charge to "wire" citizens to perhaps the greatest repository of information ever created, the Internet. Today, approximately 95% of all public libraries provide public access to the Internet (Bertot & McClure, 2000). Although Internet access undoubtedly opens up a tremendous new world of information to library patrons, it also facilitates easy access to pornography, hate speech, and other forms of content that many people may find objectionable. As such, libraries have been confronted with community concerns about inappropriate Internet content, and calls to install filtering software.

Although it may appear that Internet access presents libraries with a difficult new choice between expanded access to information and protecting children and community values, it turns out that libraries have always wrestled with this issue. As Davis (2001) commented, "Public librarians from the earliest years have considered the welfare of their patrons in the selection process" (p. 3). For example, long before computers or the Internet, libraries in the 1920s struggled with purchasing decisions regarding "pornographic" fiction like *Lady Chatterley's Lover*, *Ulysses*, *Madame Bovary*, and *The Arabian Nights* (Cornog & Perper, 1991). In more recent times, libraries have debated the purchase of adult magazines like *Playboy*, and in the case of the Library of Congress, the translation of *Playboy* into braille (Cornog, 1991). Today, the addition of Internet access to most libraries presents yet another tough call; allow unfettered access to information on the Net, or use filters to block access to sexually explicit material, but due to overblocking, also block access to valuable material.

Those who support filtered Internet access in libraries note that libraries have always acted as filters. Through purchasing decisions, librarians evaluate, analyze, and authenticate information and materials. These "information quality" decisions are at the very core of the library profession (Bastian, 1997). As such, the Internet simply represents a new source of information that should be subject to traditional selection criteria. As Cronin (2001) commented, "Very few public libraries acquire pornography for their print collections. . . . Logically, therefore, one would expect professional librarians to make similar filtering choices in respect of digital pornography" (2001, p. 6).

Advocates of library filtering also argue that libraries have traditionally made selection decisions that reflect prevailing community norms. Davis (2001) for example, noted that "conscientious librarians make every effort to understand their communities . . . in order to select materials that will be optimally useful" (2001, p. 9). Given this role, filter advocates argue that libraries should block material that the communities they serve find harmful or offensive.

So, if the traditional role of libraries has been as a community-sensitive information filter for tangible books, magazines, and so on, why shouldn't they filter Internet access as well?

The simple answer, as abundantly illustrated here, is that blocking programs take information-selection decisions out of the hands of librarians, and place them into the unknown blocking criteria of a particular program. As discussed earlier, filter makers often refuse to reveal their blocked site lists and the criteria by which such sites are deemed off limits. As Lessig (1998) commented, "The lists are our day's banned books, yet unlike the past, we never see the actual list of books banned" (p. 33).

At a more fundamental level, many libraries argue that their purpose is to promote free speech, a goal they achieve by providing free books to individuals regardless of age or income. However, by using software filters over which they have little control, libraries will inevitably block access to a wide range of constitutionally protected speech. This runs afoul of both library tradition and the First Amendment. Realizing this potential danger, in 1997 the ALA came out strongly against filtered Internet access, noting in its *Statement on Library Use of Filtering Software* that:

> Libraries are places of inclusion rather than exclusion. Current blocking/filtering software prevents not only access to what some may consider "objectionable" material, but also blocks information protected by the First Amendment. The result is that legal and useful material will inevitably be blocked.

Despite the ALA's strong opposition to the use of filters, many public libraries started adopting the software beginning in 1997 and 1998. Among the first communities to implement filtered net access was Loudoun County, Virginia, where, in October 1997, the library's board of trustees decided to install blocking software on *all* public Internet terminals. They did so in fear of legal prosecution for making obscene material available to minors, as well as sexual harassment suits by employees forced to view objectionable material on library computer screens (Macavinta, 1998). In its final form, the library's "Policy on Internet Sexual Harassment" (Loudoun County Public Library, 1997) required that "site-blocking software . . . be installed on all [library] computers," in order to "block child pornography and obscene material (hardcore pornography)," and "block material deemed Harmful to Juveniles under applicable Virginia statutes and legal precedents (soft core pornography)."

In order to implement the policy, the library choose to purchase Log-On Data's X-Stop filtering program. According to X-Stop marketing material, the program only blocked sites deemed legally obscene under the Supreme Court's *Miller* (1973) test.[3] Doubting the accuracy of such claims, a local community group, Mainstream Loudoun, asked lawyer Jonathan Wallace to test the program. Similar to the results discussed earlier, Wallace found that X-Stop blocked far more than legally obscene Internet material. In his *The X-Stop Files* Wallace (1997), found that the program blocked the following nonobscene sites:

- The University of Chicago's Fileroom project, which tracks acts of censorship around the world.
- The *National Journal of Sexual Orientation Law.*
- The Banned Books page at Carnegie Mellon.
- The American Association of University Women, which describes itself as a national organization that "promotes education and equity for all women and girls."
- The Religious Society of Friends, better known as the Quakers.

Angered by such overblocking, Mainstream Loudoun filed suit claiming the policy was an unconstitutional restriction of patrons First Amendment right to receive information. Two free speech groups, People for the American Way and the ACLU joined the suit, *Mainstream Loudoun v. Loudoun County Library Board of Trustees*, which was settled in federal district court in November 1998.

In the court's decision, Judge Leonie M. Brinkema struck down the library's filtering policy, finding that it failed a number of First Amendment tests designed to protect free speech.

First, the court concluded that the policy did indeed implicate the First Amendment as a content-based restriction on speech. The Loudoun County library board had argued that installing filters was simply a selection decision, and that the "First Amendment does not in any way limit the decisions of a public library on whether to provide access to information on the Internet" (Loudoun County Library Board of Trustees, 1998, p. 2). The board further argued that "restricting Internet access to selected materials is merely a decision not to acquire such materials rather than a decision to remove them from a library's collection" (p. 793). To assess these claims, Judge Brinkema relied heavily on the Supreme Court's decision in *Board of Education v. Pico* (1982).

The Pico case was brought about when a New York school board removed a number of books from a school library for being "anti-American, anti-Christian, anti-Semitic, and just plain filthy" (p. 857). Students sued the school board for violating their First Amendment right to receive information. In a highly splintered plurality opinion, the Court affirmed this right, noting that "the Constitution protects the right to receive information and ideas" (p. 867). As such, the school board could not remove books merely because "they dislike the ideas contained in the books," and thus "seek by their removal to prescribe what shall be orthodox in politics, nationalism, religion, or other matters of opinion" (p. 872).

Judge Brinkema analogized the Loudoun County filtering policy to the unconstitutional book removal decisions made in the Pico case. She concluded that purchasing access to the Internet was like buying access to a "collection of encyclopedias" (Loudoun I, p. 794), and that filter use was akin to the selective removal of disfavored content. The library's decision to filter was therefore "more appropriately characterized as a removal decision" (Loudoun I, p. 794), and that "Having chosen to provide access, . . . the Library Board may not thereafter selectively restrict certain categories of Internet speech because it disfavors their content" (Loudoun I, p. 795-796).

Given that the filter policy was found to be a content-based restriction on speech implemented in the "limited public forum" of a public library, it was subject to an extremely demanding First Amendment test known as "strict scrutiny." The strict scrutiny test asks whether a government speech restriction is "necessary to serve a compelling state interest and . . . is narrowly drawn to achieve that end" (*Perry Education Ass'n v. Perry Local Educators' Ass'n*, 1983, p. 45).

Judge Brinkema found that although protecting children from pornography was indeed a compelling sate interest, the use of X-Stop was not the least restrictive means of achieving that end. Instead, the court listed acceptable use policies, privacy screens, librarian monitoring, time limits, and installing filters on selected child access computers (as opposed to all computers), as less restrictive alternatives.

Not only did the Loudoun County policy fail strict scrutiny, it was also deemed a prior restraint, as it blocked access to constitutionally protected speech without giving any blocking criteria, nor a well-defined procedural mechanism for reviewing blocking decisions. Noting the standardless and secretive blocking decisions made by X-Stop, Judge Brinkema concluded:

> The degree to which the policy is completely lacking in standards is demonstrated by the defendant's willingness to entrust all preliminary

blocking decisions—and, by default, the overwhelming majority of final decisions—to a private vendor, Log-On Data Corp. Although the defendant argues that X-Stop is the best available filter, a defendant cannot avoid its constitutional obligation by contracting out its decision making to a private entity. Such abdication of its obligation is made even worse by the undisputed facts here. Specifically, defendant concedes that it does not know the criteria by which Log-On Data makes its blocking decisions. It is also undisputed that Log-On Data does not base its blocking decisions on any legal definition of obscenity or even on the parameters of defendant's policy. (Loudoun II, p. 569)

Making matters worse, if a patron wanted to have a site unblocked, he or she would have to submit a written request to a librarian. The unblocking policy contained no guidelines about how to evaluate such sites, no time period for review, no notification requirement, and no provision for judicial review of blocking decisions.

For all of these reasons, Judge Brinkema found that the Loudoun County library filter policy "offends the guarantee of free speech in the First Amendment and is, therefore, unconstitutional" (Loudoun II, p. 570).

Although opponents of library filtering initially claimed the *Loudoun* decision as a major victory, a closer look reveals that it only settled a relatively narrow issue. The Loudoun County policy required that *all* library computers utilize filters, regardless of whether they were used by adults or children. The court overturned this policy as overbroad, but in its own ruling noted that filters may be appropriate if installed on computers designated only for children.

So, despite a seemingly strong ruling against library filtering, the practice has actually expanded dramatically since the *Loudoun* decision. According to a January 2002 survey conducted by *Library Journal*, some 43% of public libraries reported filtering Internet use, up from 31% in 2001 and 25% in 2000 (Oder, 2002).

THE LIBRARY FILTER DEBATE ROUND 2: CIPA

Although many public libraries currently employ some form of filtering software, filtered access may soon become universal due to Congressional passage of the CIPA, a new law requiring that public libraries and schools receiving federal Internet access subsidies install some form of blocking software on all Internet terminals.

Legislation similar to CIPA had been introduced by McCain in 1998 and 1999. Both of these bills failed to achieve passage through the normal legislative process, so in 2000, McCain, along with Senator Rick Santorum (R. PA) and Representative Ernest Istook (R. OK) attached CIPA as an amendment to the multibillion dollar Labor, Health, Human Services, and Education appropriation bill (J. Schwartz, 2000). Despite the *Loudoun* decision, the COPA Commission's failure to endorse filters, a Congressional Research Service report concluding the legislation might be unconstitutional (Smith, 2000), and White House opposition to the amendment, Congress passed CIPA on December 15, 2000. The appropriations bill, along with the CIPA amendment was signed into law by President Clinton on December 21, 2000.

CIPA requires that any public library or school receiving federal "e-rate" or Library Services and Technology Act (LSTA) grants, install a "technology protection measure" on *all* Internet access terminals, in order to block access to "visual depictions" that are obscene, child pornography, or harmful to minors. CIPA also contains a filter—disabling provision that specifies that an administrator "may disable the technology measure concerned, during use by an adult, to enable access for bona fide research or other lawful purpose."

Soon after CIPA's passage, the ALA and the ACLU announced that they would challenge the act's constitutionality on several grounds. First, CIPA's filtering requirements would distort the traditional role of public libraries as "resources for the communication and receipt of information and the free exchange of ideas" (ALA, 2001, p. 1). Second, CIPA would hurt low-income library patrons because some 70% of libraries serving communities with poverty levels in excess of 40% receive "e-rate" funding (ALA, 2001, p. 22). Finally, federally mandated library filters "inevitably will lead to the suppression of vast amounts of protected speech that would otherwise be available to public library patrons" (ALA, 2001, p. 3).

CIPA supporters responded to the ALA-ACLU lawsuit by noting that the act allows local libraries to decide which filter best fits their communities. As McCain (2001) noted in his response to the lawsuit, "This law gives communities the freedom to decide what technology they choose to use and what to filter out. It does not dictate any specific actions be taken by communities or apply a federal standard, it simply requires them to have some technology in place to protect children if they are using federal funds for Internet access." Supporters similarly pointed to CIPA's disabling provision as a saving grace for occasional filter overblocking of constitutionally protected material.

In March 2002, the constitutionality of CIPA was argued before a special three-judge panel in U.S. district court in Philadelphia, the same court that heard the initial challenges to the CDA and COPA.

At first glance, the issues presented by CIPA in the case of the *American Library Association v. United States* (2002) appear to be nearly identical to those raised by the *Loudoun* decision, and indeed they are similar. However, one significant difference does exist, and that is Congress's "power of the purse." The Department of Justice (DOJ), defending CIPA, argued that Congress has wide discretion in crafting funding schemes, and that if libraries do not like CIPA's filtering requirements, they "may simply decline to accept the subsidy" (DOJ, 2001, p. 16). Indeed, in a number of cases, the Supreme Court has indicated that Congress may condition funding on limiting the exercise of certain constitutional rights. For example, in *Rust v. Sullivan* (1991), the Court ruled that Congress could permissibly condition Title X family planning funds by requiring that doctors not discuss abortion or other family planning options with patients. By the same token however, the Court has also ruled that when Congress distributes funds to state and local governments, it can not "induce [those entities] to engage in activities that would themselves be unconstitutional" (*South Dakota v. Dole*, 1987, p. 210).

These seemingly contradictory opinions have been somewhat clarified by the Court's recent ruling in *Legal Services Corp. v. Velazquez* (2001). At issue in *Velazquez* was a federal law prohibiting lawyers who accepted funds from the Legal Services Corporation from bringing challenges to existing welfare laws. The Court struck down the condition as a violation of the First Amendment. In doing so, the Court drew a distinction between situations in which the government is the speaker, and situations where the government "does not itself speak or subsidize transmittal of a message it favors but instead *expends funds to encourage a diversity of views from private speakers*" (*Velazquez*, 2001, p. 1049, italics added). The Court argued that the counseling activities of doctors in the *Rust* decision were government speech and could therefore be limited. However, as in *Velazquez*, where the government regulation is "designed to facilitate private speech, not to promote a government message," the First Amendment applies with full force (*Velazquez*, p. 1049). The *Velazquez* decision also set forth another test to determine if a funding program inappropriately restricts private speech, whether "the government seeks to use an existing medium of expression and to control it . . . in ways which distort its usual functioning" (*Velazquez*, p. 1049).

Given the *Velazquez* decision, it would seem clear that CIPA imposes unconstitutional conditions on "e-rate" and LSTA library funding. First, the goal of these funding programs is to facilitate private speech, or perhaps more accurately, the receipt of private speech, by wiring America's libraries to the Internet. In this role, the government is clearly not the speaker, but a facilitator of private speech, and therefore the First Amendment should apply with full force. Second, CIPA's filtering requirements distort the normal functioning of both the Internet and public libraries. As the ALA and ACLU noted in their joint post trial brief:

> The blocking software mandated by CIPA fundamentally distorts the normal functioning of the marketplace of ideas that is the Internet . . . CIPA would also distort the normal functioning of public libraries, whose traditional mission is to provide a broad range of information to meet patrons' individual interests and needs, not to tell patrons what to read or think. (ALA & ACLU, 2002, p. 43)

Because CIPA's funding conditions are likely unconstitutional, additional First Amendment flaws, similar to those raised in *Loudoun*, can be explored. First, at trial, the ALA and ACLU both argued that CIPA, as written, is facially overbroad because any implementation of filtering software will inevitably lead to the blocking of vast amounts of constitutionally protected speech. To prove this point, several experts on filtering software were called to discuss their research into filter effectiveness. I was called as an expert by the ALA, and testified that "My conclusion after reviewing 40 studies is that filters are systematically flawed" (cited in Morgan, 2002a). The ACLU called Ben Edelman (2001), who conducted a study of four popular filters. The studies found that between 4,300 and 6,300 useful Web pages were incorrectly blocked. Attempting to counter this testimony, the DOJ called its own witnesses to testify to filter effectiveness. However, even their studies found significant overblocking. For example, DOJ witness Cory Finnell (2001) analyzed the log files of three libraries using filter software and found overblocking rates ranging from 5% to 15%. In real-world library use terms, this would mean that thousands of library patrons would be denied access to protected speech every year (ALA & ACLU, 2002, p. 14).

Perhaps realizing the weakness of their arguments about filter effectiveness, the DOJ also argued that a library's decision to filter was akin to traditional collection development policies that do not raise First Amendment issues. During closing arguments, DOJ lawyer Rupa Battacharyya stated that "There is no constitutional right to immediate, anonymous access to speech, for free, in a public library" (cited in Morgan, 2002b), and that filter use was merely a selection decision about what material libraries would make available to their patrons. In response, the ALA and ACLU argued, as in *Loudoun*, that filters are not at all like traditional collection development policies, because librarians have little or no role in selecting the sites that are blocked by filtering software. Given the precedent set in *Loudoun* that filter use is more akin to a removal decision, it is highly likely that CIPA's filter requirements will be found to be a content-based regulation of speech and thus subject to strict scrutiny.

In applying strict scrutiny, CIPA is once again found wanting. Although the government clearly has a compelling interest in protecting library patrons from illegal obscenity, child pornography, and harmful to minors content, no evidence was presented to support the contention that clumsy filtering software is the least restrictive means of achieving this end. Instead, as the ALA and ACLU point out, libraries can use numerous alternative methods to achieve the government's interest without significantly burdening patrons' free speech rights. Less restrictive alternatives to mandatory filter use on all library terminals include the *optional* use of filters, filters on child-only computers, acceptable use policies, privacy screens, Internet education classes, and so on (ALA & ACLU, 2002, pp. 23-24).

A final argument lodged against CIPA was that its filtering and disabling provisions constitute a classic prior restraint on speech. CIPA's filtering mandate gives standardless discretion about blocking decisions to secretive filter makers who refuse to release their lists of blocked Web sites. Making matters worse, it was uncontested at trial that filter makers blocking categories in no way correspond to the exacting legal definitions for determining obscenity, child pornography, and harmful to minors content (ALA & ACLU, 2002, p. 30). The DOJ, in response, argued that CIPA's disabling provision could overcome filter overblocking and permit adults access to protected speech. However, according to the ALA and ACLU, the disabling provision only makes CIPA's problems worse. The provision merely states that a librarian "may" disable a filter in response to an unblocking request. No standards are given for how this decision is to be made nor is there any definition of what a "bonafide research" purpose might be (ALA & ACLU, 2002, p. 30-33). Finally, the disabling provision requires an affirmative request from a library patron, thus creating "a dangerous chilling effect on the exercise of patrons' right to receive information anonymously by attaching a threat of stigma to the receipt of fully protected materials" (ALA, 2001, p. 5).

Given CIPA's many First Amendment flaws pointed out at trial, its similarity to the filtering policy overturned in the *Loudoun* decision, the law is likely to be found unconstitutional. Due to a provision written into CIPA however, the special three-judge panel's ruling will automatically be appealed to the Supreme Court.

THE SCHOOL FILTER DEBATE

Like libraries, public schools are confronted with multiple goals that are often in direct conflict. The primary goal of education, and the reason it is compulsory, is the creation of informed citizens, capable of the autonomous thought and action necessary for a vibrant democracy. To achieve this goal, schools must provide students with wide access to ideas, even those that may be offensive and contrary to prevailing norms. Through such open access and inquiry, education allows students to develop their own beliefs, and to critically weigh those of others.

Competing with the notion of open inquiry is the responsibility schools have to local communities and local values. This responsibility is set forth by the thousands of local school boards, who representing the views of their community, choose which topics to teach and what books to buy. Given this system, liberal school districts may teach sex education and evolution, whereas more conservative districts have the latitude to exclude such subjects as contrary to community norms. In this way, education is also about indoctrination into the norms and values of the surrounding community (Kubota, 1997, p. 704-705). Indoctrination clearly seems antithetical to open inquiry, where nothing is sacred and all norms are open to investigation. As one federal court noted in *James v. Board of Education* (1972) :

> Society must indoctrinate children so they may be capable of autonomy. They must also be socialized to the norms of society while remaining free to modify or even abandon those norms. Paradoxically, education must promote autonomy while simultaneously denying it by shaping and constraining present and future choices.

Given these somewhat contradictory goals, what are schools to do about the Internet? The Internet clearly facilitates near limitless access to information of all stripes and colors, however, this very access also has the potential to expose students to content which is contrary to community norms. Not surprisingly, many schools have turned to filters as a way of balancing access with indoctrination. As of 2000, 98% of public schools had access to the Internet, of which 74% used filtering software (National Center for Education Statistics, 2001). This percentage will only increase due to the passage of CIPA, which requires that public schools receiving "e-rate" funds install filters on all school computers.

As described earlier, filtering programs block significant amounts of constitutionally protected speech in the process of blocking the potentially harmful material that school systems rightly purchase filters to deal with. In the context of libraries, such overblocking has been found to be an impermissible restraint on patrons First Amendment right to receive information. But does the same logic hold within the walls of the schoolhouse? After all, as the Supreme Court famously stated in *Tinker v. Des Moines Independent Community School District* (1969, p. 506), "it can hardly be argued that either students or teachers shed their constitutional rights to freedom of speech or expression at the schoolhouse gate." On the other hand, however, the Court has also noted that school boards have wide discretion in selecting curricular materials and "to prescribe and control conduct in the schools" (Tinker, referring to *Epperson v. Arkansas*, 1968, p. 104). Is it therefore a violation of students free speech rights to block whitehouse.com (a pornography site), while also denying access to whitehouse.gov? What latitude do school administrators have in determining what Internet content is not acceptable to community norms and thus subject to blocking?

As in the *Loudoun* case and the current challenge to CIPA, *Pico* would seem to offer the closest analogy to a school's use of filtering software. Although the *Pico* Court found that a school board could not simply remove disfavored books from the school library, it also noted that schools could "claim absolute discretion in matters of curriculum by reliance on their duty to inculcate community values" (p. 868). *Pico* would therefore seem to imply that school administrators can filter Internet access if it is part of a predefined classroom curriculum. In essence, filters would mirror a school board's power to decide what text books are appropriate. However, if schools grant students unsupervised time to simply "surf the net" for research purposes, then filtering would not be permissible. As Kubota (1997, p. 713) noted, "The freedom of choice enjoyed by students while browsing the Internet is analogous to students searching the library and voluntarily choosing books of interest. Schools cannot claim to have any real curricular control over such an open-ended, free wheeling, and unsupervised activity."

Another potentially serious problem with school filtering is that school boards cannot truly claim to be making selection decisions when they install filters whose blocking decisions are made by a private company, unwilling to share its list of blocked sites. This opens school filtering up to a challenge on overbreadth grounds because schools "are likely to simply accept, without review, the filtering standards and product of the filtering software provided . . . this lack of involvement in the filtering process will preclude a school from making a convincing argument that its filtering blocks only constitutionally unprotected material" (Kubota, 1997, p. 727).

To date, there have been no First Amendment challenges to the use of filters in public schools. However, given that CIPA is likely to force most public schools into installing such software, a *Pico*-like challenge to filter overblocking in schools is likely.

CONCLUSION

The issue of inappropriate material on the Internet is not about to go away any time soon. Although the percentage of pornography on the Internet is likely only about 1% or 2% (Lawrence & Giles, 1999, p. 107), that still translates into more than 100,000 adult sites (Nunberg, 2001, p. 9), most of which are easily accessible to children. Research shows that minors are accessing these sites with some regularity. According to a December 2001 survey by the Kaiser Family Foundation, among all 15 to 17-year-olds who have ever gone online, 70% had accidentally stumbled across pornography online and 23% very or somewhat often.

Such statistics point to a real problem that must be addressed. As such, parents and legislators are likely to continue to tout filters as the best way to protect children from the dangers of the Net. However, as this chapter has abundantly illustrated, filters are a highly problematic "solution" to inappropriate Net content. All too often, they fail to block the pornography they are designed to screen out, and far more troubling, they block access to a wide range of valuable and constitutionally protected material. In the context of libraries and schools, filter overblocking implicates the important First Amendment rights of library patrons and students to receive information. Indeed, indiscriminate and secretive filter overblocking would seem to contradict the very purposes of these institutions, to provide wide access to information and to educate citizens for active engagement in the "marketplace of ideas" that is our democracy.

Due to these problems, policies like CIPA, which require filters on *all* public library Internet terminals, are likely to be found unconstitutional. This does not mean however, that filters have no place in public libraries. Used voluntarily on child-only computers, and in conjunction with other less restrictive means like acceptable use policies and privacy screens, filters may constitute a useful, and constitutionally acceptable method for limiting minors access to inappropriate Internet content without unduly burdening the rights of adult library users.[4]

In the context of public schools, filters may be given wider latitude, but again, they should not be thought of as *the* solution for protecting students from harmful material. Perhaps a better method would be to educate students about appropriate Internet use, how to evaluate Internet content for credibility, and what to do when they encounter adult content. As Willard (2001) commented:

> As educators, our primary focus must be to help young people learn to use the Internet in a safe, responsible, and effective manner. In other words, we need to help young people develop effective filtering and blocking systems that will reside in the hardware that sits on their shoulders.

In summary, filters are a seductively simple solution that promise to solve a long-standing problem by simply installing a piece of software. Unfortunately, complex social problems—like defining what is appropriate and for whom—cannot be reduced to lines of software code. Rather, social

problems call for social solutions, like community and parental involvement in decisions about how to best harness the tremendous potential of
the Internet. Software filters may be one part of the answer, but by themselves, they are a poor substitute for the sensitive human judgment and
expertise of parents, librarians, and educators.

NOTES

1. The CDA was struck down by the Supreme Court in the case of *Reno v.
   ACLU,* and COPA has been struck down by two federal circuit courts, and was
   appealed to the Supreme Court in November 2001.
2. See http://www.arin.net/.
3. In *Miller v. California* (1973), the Supreme Court fashioned a three-pronged
   test for determining obscenity: (a) whether "the average person, applying contemporary community standards" would find that the work, when taken as a
   whole, appeals to the prurient interest; (b) whether the work depicts or
   describes, in a patently offensive way, sexual conduct specifically defined by the
   applicable state law; and (c) whether the work, taken as a whole, lacks serious
   literary, artistic, political, or scientific value.
4. The use of filters on child-only library computers is not without controversy,
   however. As the Court found in *Pico,* even minors have a right to receive constitutionally protected speech. Therefore, a filter blocking a teen's access to a
   nonobscene sex education site for example, could be found to violate the First
   Amendment. For this reason, the *Loudoun* court noted that although filters on
   child-only computers may be a less restrictive alternative than filters on all
   library terminals, even this policy would not "necessarily be constitutional if
   implemented" (Loudoun II, p. 567).

REFERENCES

American Civil Liberties Union. (1997). *Fahrenheit 451.2: Is cyberspace burning?*
ACLU White Paper. Available: http://www.aclu.org/issues/cyber/
burning.html.

American Library Association. (1997). Statement on library use of filtering software. Available: http://www.ala.org/alaorg/oif/filt_stm.html.

American Library Association. (2001). Complaint for declaratory and injunctive
relief. Submitted in the case of the *American Library Association v. United
States of America,* Civil Action No. 01-CV-1303.

American Library Association. (2002). *Library bill of rights.* Available:
http://www.ala.org/work/freedom/lbr.html.

American Library Association and the American Civil Liberties Union. (2002).
Joint post-trial brief. Submitted in the case of the *American Library Association
v. United States of America,* Civil Action No. 01-CV-1303.

Bastian, J. (1997, October). Filtering the internet in American public libraries: Sliding down the slippery slope. *First Monday, 2*(10). Available: http://www.firstmonday.org/issues/issue2_10/bastian/index.html.

Bertelsmann Foundation. (1999, September). *Self-regulation of internet content.* Available: http://www.stiftung.bertelsmann.de/internetcontent/english/download/Memorandum.pdf .

Bertot, J., & McClure, C. (2000, September 7). *Public libraries and the internet 2000: Summary findings and data tables.* Report to National Commission on Libraries and Information Science. Available: http://www.nclis.gov/statsurv/2000plo.pdf.

Bloomberg News. (1999, May 13). Senate unanimously passes filtering bill. *Bloomberg News.* Available: http://www.news.com/News/Item/0,4,36540,00.html.

Board of Education V. Pico, 457 U.S. 853. (1982).

BrightPlanet. (2000, July). *The deep Web: Surfacing hidden value.* Available: http://www.brightplanet.com/deepcontent/tutorials/DeepWeb/index.asp.

Censorware Project. (1997, December). *Blacklisted by Cyber Patrol: From Ada to Yoyo.* Available: http://censorware.net/reports/cyberpatrol/ada-yoyo.html.

Censorware Project. (1999, July). *Passing porn, banning the bible: N2H2's Bess in public schools.* Available: http://www.censorware.net/reports/bess/.

Censorware Project. (2000, September 7). *Size of the web: A dynamic essay for a dynamic medium.*

COPA Commission. (2000, 20 October). *Final report of the COPA commission.* Available: http://www.copacommission.org/report/.

Cornog, M. (1991). A case study of censorship? The Library of Congress and the brailling of *Playboy.* In M. Cornog (Ed.), *Libraries, erotica, pornography.* Phoenix, AZ: Oryx Press.

Cornog, M., & Perper, T. (1991). For sex, see librarian. In M. Cornog (Ed.), *Libraries, erotica, pornography.* Phoenix, AZ: Oryx Press.

Cronin, B. (2001). Expert report of Blaise Cronin. Submitted by the U.S. Department of Justice in the case of the *American Library Association v. United States of America,* Civil Action No. 01-CV-1303.

CYBERsitter. (2002) Product literature. Available: http://www.cybersitter.com/gte/.

Cyveillance. (2000, July 10). *Internet exceeds 2 billion pages.* Available: http://www.cyveillance.com/web/newsroom/releases/2000/2000-07-10.htm.

Davis, D. G. (2001). Expert report of Donald G. Davis, Jr. Submitted by the U.S. Department of Justice in the case of the *American Library Association v. United States of America,* Civil Action No. 01-CV-1303.

Department of Justice. (2001). Defendant's memorandum of law in support of their motion to dismiss plaintiffs' complaints. Submitted by the U.S. Department of Justice in the case of the *American Library Association v. United States of America,* Civil Action No. 01-CV-1303.

Edelman, B. (2001). Expert report of Ben Edelman. Submitted by the ACLU in the case of *ACLU v. United States of America,* Civil Action No. 01-CV-1322. Available: http://cyber.law.harvard.edu/people/edelman/pubs/aclu-101501.pdf.

Epperson v. Arkansas, 393 U.S. 97, 104. (1968).

Finkelstein, S. (2000, November 16). *SmartFilter's greatest evils*. Available: http://www.sethf.com/anticensorware/smartfilter/greatestevils.php.

Finkelstein, S. (2001, August 14). *Bess's secret loophole (censorware v. privacy & anonymity)*. Available: http://www.sethf.com/anticensorware/smartfilter/greatestevils.php.anonymity). Available: http://www.sethf.com/anticensorware/bess/loophole.php.

Finkelstein, S. (2002, March 13). *The Pre-slipped slope—Censorware v. the Wayback Machine Web archive*. Available: http://www.sethf.com/anticensorware/general/slip.php.

Finkelstein, S., & Tien, A. (2001). *Blacklisting bytes*. In D. Sobel (Ed.), *Filters & freedom 2.0* (pp. 63-78). Washington, DC: Electronic Privacy Information Center.

Finnell, C. (2001). Expert report of Cory Finnell. Submitted by the Department of Justice in the case of the *American Library Association v. United States of America*, Civil Action No. 01-CV-1303.

Gay & Lesbian Alliance Against Defamation. (1995, November 14). *GLAAD criticizes blocking of gay and lesbian resources on the internet*. GLAAD Press Release. Available: http://www.glaad.org/org/press/index.html?record=2374.

Gay & Lesbian Alliance Against Defamation. (1997, December 2). *Access denied: The impact of internet filtering software on the lesbian and gay community*. Available: http://www.glaad.org/binary-data/GLAAD_PDF/pdf_file/12.pdf.

Gore, A. (1999, May 5). *Remarks on the Internet*. White House Office of the Press Secretary. Available: http://web1.archive.org/web/19991126111413/http://www.whitehouse.gov/WH/New/html/19990505-4219.html.

James v. Board of Education, 461 F. 2d 566, 573. (2d Cir. 1972).

Kaiser Family Foundation. (2001, December). *GenerationRx.com: How young people use the internet for health information*. Kaiser Family Foundation Survey. Available: http://www.kff.org/content/2001/20011211a/GenerationRx.pdf.

Kennard, W. (1999, May 4). Remarks of William Kennard at the Annenberg Public Policy Center conference on Internet and the family. Available: http://www.fcc.gov/Speeches/Kennard/spwek916.html.

Kryzan, C. (1995, 14 June). *SurfWatch censorship against lesbigay Web pages*. Available: http://cpsr.org/cpsr/lists/rre/SurfWatch_Censorship_Against_L.

Kubota, G. (1997). Public school usage of internet filtering software: Book banning reincarnated? *Loyola of Los Angeles Entertainment Law Journal, 17*, 687-731.

Lawrence, S., & Giles, C. L. (1999). Accessibility of information on the web. *Nature, 400*, 107-109.

Legal Services Corp. v. Velazquez, 121 S. Ct. 1043. (2001).

Lessig, L. (1998, May). *What things regulate speech: CDA 2.0 v. filtering*. Unpublished draft. Available: http://cyberlaw.stanford.edu/lessig/content/articles/works/what_things.pdf.

Loudoun County Library Board of Trustees. (1998, September 4). Defendants brief. Submitted in the case of *Mainstream Loudoun v. Loudoun County Library Board of Trustees*, Civil Action No. 97-2049-A.

Loudoun County Public Library. (1997, October 20). *Policy on internet sexual harassment.* Available: http://www.pfaw.org/courts/loudoun_harrass.html.

Macavinta, C. (1998, February 6). ACLU takes filtering to court. *News.com.* Available: http://news.com.com/2100-1023-207910.html.

Mainstream Loudoun v. Loudoun County Library Board of Trustees, 24 F. Supp. 2d 552, (E.D. Va. 1998) (Loudoun II).

Mainstream Loudoun v. Loudoun County Library Board of Trustees, 2 F. Supp. 2d 783, (E.D. Va. 1998) (Loudoun I).

McCain, J. (2000, December 15). *Congress passes internet filtering for schools, libraries.* Press Release. Available: http://www.senate.gov/~mccain/intfinal .htm.

McCain, J. (2001, March 20). *McCain: We must protect children on internet competition.* Press Release. Available: http://mccain.senate.gov/intfilt01.htm.

McCullagh, D. (1999, April 23). Looking for something to blame. *Wired News.* Available: http://www.wired.com/news/print/0,1294,19291,00.html.

McCullagh, D. (2000a, October 18). Gore, Bush favor filth filters. *Wired News.* Available: http://www.wired.com/news/print/0,1294,39529,00.html.

Miller v. California, 413 U.S. 15. (1973).

Morgan, D. (2002a, March 26). Experts say porn filters don't work. *Reuters.* Available: http://www.techtv.com/news/politicsandlaw/story/0,24195, 3378010,00.html.

Morgan, D. (2002b, April 4). Judges end U.S. library porn trial on skeptical note. *Reuters.* Available: http://www.forbes.com/newswire/2002/04/04/rtr55 9809.html.

National Center for Education Statistics. (2001, May). *Internet access in U.S. public schools and classrooms: 1994-2000.* National Center for Education Statistics. Available: http://nces.ed.gov/pubs2001/InternetAccess/.

Netcraft. (2002, April). *Netcraft Web server survey.* Available: http://www.net-craft.com/survey/.

Netsurfer Digest. (1996, February 19). White House accidentally blocked by SurfWatch. *Netsurfer Digest,* 2(5). Available: http://web1.archive. org/web/19970118151146/http://www.netsurf.com/nsd/v02/nsd.96.02.19 .html.

Nunberg, G. (2001). CIPA trial: Expert report of Geoffrey Nunberg. Submitted by the American Library Association in the case of the *American Library Association v. United States of America,* Civil Action No. 01-CV-1303.

Oder, N. (2002, January 15). The new wariness. *Library Journal.* Available: http://libraryjournal.reviewsnews.com/index.asp?layout=article&articleid= CA188739&publication=libraryjournal.

Peacefire. (2000a, November 7). *Blind ballots: Web sites of U.S. political candidates censored by censorware.* Available: http://www.peacefire.org/blind-ballots/.

Peacefire. (2000b, July). *Sites blocked by ClickSafe.* Available: http:// peacefire.org/censorware/ClickSafe/screenshots-copacommission.html.

Perry Education Association v. Perry Local Educators' Association et. al., 460 U.S. 37. (1983).

Reno v. ACLU, 521 U.S. 844, 870 (1997).

Schwartz, J. (2000, October 20). Support is growing in congress for internet filters in schools. *The New York Times*, p. A28.

Schwartz, R. (2000, July). *COPA commission testimony*. Available: http://www.copacommission.org/meetings/hearing2/schwartz.test.pdf .

Shera, J. H. (1949). *Foundations of the public library: The origins of the public library movement in New England, 1629-1855*. Chicago, IL: University of Chicago Press.

Smith, M. (2000, September). *Internet—protecting children from unsuitable material and sexual predators: Overview and pending legislation*. Congressional Research Service Report, RS20036.

South Dakota v. Dole, 483 U.S. 203. (1987).

SurfControl. (2001). Product literature. Available: http://web1.archive.org /web/20001212234100/http://www.surfcontrol.com/news/press_releases/ content/06_14_2000.html.

Tinker v. Des Moines Independent Community School District, 393 U.S. 503. (1969).

Turow, J. (1999). *The internet and family: The view from parents; The view from the press* (Annenberg Public Policy Center of the University of Pennsylvania, Rep. No. 27). Philadelphia, PA: Annenberg Public Policy Center.

Turow, J., & Nir, L. (2000). *The internet and the family 2000: The view from parents, the view from kids* (Annenberg Public Policy Center of the University of Pennsylvania, Rep. No. 33). Philadelphia, PA: Annenberg Public Policy Center.

Wallace, J. (1997). The X-Stop Files. *The Ethical Spectacle*. Available: http://www.spectacle.org/cs/xstop.html.

Wallace, J. (2001, September 1). N2H2's weak AI. *The Ethical Spectacle*. Available: http://www.spectacle.org/cs/bess2.html.

Weinberg, J. (1997). Rating the net. *Hastings Communication & Entertainment Law Journal, 19*, 453. Available: http://www.law.wayne.edu/weinberg/rating. htm.

Weiner, R. S. (2000, October 18). Survey finds support for school filters. *The New York Times*. Available: http://www.nytimes.com/2000/10/18/technology/ 18EDUCATION.html.

White House. (1997, July 16). Summary of the internet family empowerment white paper. White House meeting on Internet Parental Empowerment Tools. Available: http://www.cdt.org/speech/970716summary.html.

Willard, N. (2001). Supporting the safe and responsible use of the internet : A children's internet protection act planning guide. *Responsible Netizen*. Available: http://netizen.uoregon.edu/documents/cipa.html; http://responsiblenetizen. org/onlinedocs/documents/philandapproach.html

9

Copyright in a Digital World

Intellectual Property Rights
in Cyberspace

Donald Fishman
Boston College

Copyright, perhaps more than any other area of law has been challenged by the dual technological innovations of digitalization and the Internet. Experts argue that this is a critical time in the development of copyright law. In this chapter, Donald Fishman considers the continued relevance of the rationale for a copyright system in a digital world and examines unique challenges to regulating intellectual property rights in cyberspace now and in the future. The author examines underlying issues of copyright including defining the nature of a "copy" and "fixation" when in certain digital situations it is a necessary or inevitable component of accessing electronic information.

Copyright has increasingly become a focal point of attention as the United States moves forward into an information-oriented economy. As we proceed in the first decade of the new millennium, a large and growing number of professions and occupations play important roles as information producers. They may either create the original information, or they may acquire the initial information, add to it, and then re-distribute a new version of the data. This value-added process is an especially important characteristic of an information-oriented economy.

Moreover, as we move from analog to digital technology, the role of an information producer becomes increasingly easier to enact. The convergence of data, voice, and video into one digitally designed medium allows individuals and organizations to store, edit, format, and combine data in ways unimagined a generation ago. As more information becomes digital, the information becomes easier to copy, reformat, and redistribute. As Katsh (1995) observed, value in this new digital environment will lie not only in "owning and possessing the information," but also in the "opportunities presented to use and exploit the information" (p. 224). Katsh contended that secondary users of this information play a vital role by enhancing the original information so that there is an "evolutionary" quality in the transfer of the information from the first producer to the now second user-producer. Ginsburg (1995) insisted that there is a "collaborative" process to the authorship of this new data that did not exist in an analog world. But, this newly found capacity to create, reconfigure, and redistribute information, while adding value to the original work, raises issues that go to the heart of the traditional meaning of copyright law.

The concept of a vast network of linked computers with unlimited access to information and the capacity to redistribute that information directly challenges what in copyright law traditionally has been the one-dimensional relationship between the author-as-producer and the reader-as-user. Ginsburg (1995) identified three major components of this newly emerging system: "pervasive audience access" to information, the ability to copy easily, and on a large-scale, and the ability to distribute and redistribute information. From this perspective, the Internet may be thought of as one large and efficient copying machine with the capacity to make verbatim copies of data, audio, and video works on a massive and unprecedented scale.

Copyright, as we know it, is at a crossroads in its development. As Goldstein (1994) noted, "The digital revolution promises both new strains and new opportunities for copyright law" (p. 197). Samuelson (1990) depicted the digital revolution in terms of six characteristics: the ease of copying, the ease of transmitting works, the ease with which information can be "modified and manipulated" and thus customized and resold to targeted customers, the interchangabilty of works in digital forms as opposed to the medium-specific constraints that limit analog works, the compactness of digitized information, and the capacity for creating "new methods of searching digital space and linking works together" (pp. 324, 330). Overall, these six features characterize a high-volume information system composed of multiple networks that will make information transfers convenient, inexpensive, and widely accessible.

The digital revolution challenges two underlying assumptions of the copyright system. First, the older view held that an information producer was granted a copyright that provided the right to exclude others from unauthorized copying. The ambiguous terms in this formulation are "exclude" and "unauthorized copying." In our new environment, copying already has become a frequent, necessary, and even inevitable component of using electronic information. Saving or using a file requires making a copy of what is in memory. Downloading a file also requires making a copy. Reading a file involves not only making a copy but displaying previously copyrighted information on a screen. Katsh (1995) observed, "As we interact with the new media, our work experience inevitably changes since copying is an act that inevitably takes place on a new scale as one works with information in electronic form" (p. 216).

A second assumption rendered problematic by the digital revolution is the centrality of the "fixation standard" in copyright law. The fixation standard is a relatively new test. Reacting to the tedious process that the 1909 Copyright Act required in order to determine the eligibility of works for copyright protection, Congress, in the 1976 Copyright Act, set forth a resourceful, even forward-looking, approach to define the eligibility of new works for copyright.

To receive copyright protection, a work must be an "original work of authorship fixed in a tangible medium of expression, now known or later developed, from which they can be perceived, reproduced, or otherwise communicated, either directly or with the aid of a machine or device" (17 U.S.C. § 102). The act further defines fixation as a condition that is "sufficiently permanent or stable to permit it to be perceived, reproduced, or otherwise communicated for a period of more than transitory duration" (17 U.S.C. § 101). Yet, in an electronic format, a work can be fixed for a "transitory" moment, edited, reformatted, and then reconfigured in a way that the second work no longer resembles the original. The question then arises: Is the information that is temporarily used "fixed" or "unfixed"? And, if we conclude that the information is not fixed, or that fixation is a complex and nuanced procedure, then are we forced to reassess the meaning of the concept of "fixation" that during the past three decades has become one of the threshold elements of modern copyright law?

Less than a generation ago, terms like the "World Wide Web," "Information Superhighway," "Digital Age," "Electronic Marketplace," and the "Internet" were either nonexistent or confined to use by a small subculture. In 1984, William Gibson, in his book the *Neuromancer*, coined the term *cyberspace* to explain the paradigmatic shift from a print and broadcast-based society to the electronic era.

A year earlier, Ithiel de Sola Pool (1983) wrote his now classic book *Technologies of Freedom*, which explained the digital revolution in broad but useful generalizations. Pool argued that electronic modes of communication would displace print and broadcast technologies and that the computers would "become the printing presses of the twenty-first century" (p. 189). Pool's first chapter was entitled "A Shadow Darkens" because he envisioned confusion arising about the new technologies, and he predicted the emergence of newly discovered difficulties with the "norms that govern communication" (p. 10). As to the persistence of copyright, Pool was equally pessimistic:

> Established notions about copyright become obsolete, rooted as they are in the technology of print. The recognition of a copyright and the practice of paying royalties emerged with the printing press. With the arrival of electronic reproduction, these practices become unworkable. Electronic publishing is analogous, not so much to the print shop of the eighteenth century as to word-of-mouth communication, to which copyright was never applied. (p. 214)

Pool insisted that "[T]otally new concepts will have to be invented to compensate creative works in this new environment. The print-based notion of copyright simply will not work" (p. 215). Rose (1995) reaffirmed Pool's basic question when he inquired: "What can 'copyright' possibly mean when millions of people can download the information they find on the Internet?" (p. 112). There also is a growing literature that questions the role and efficacy of the Copyright Office in the context of the Information Superhighway (Samuelson, 1994; Schwartz, 1994; Weisgrau, 1994).

The rapid growth of the Internet has intensified the pressure to clarify the scope of copyright law. In 1994, an estimated 2.3 million Americans purchased personal computers for their home, and the number of computers in use by 1996 was estimated at 33.9 million (Stuckey, 1996). By 1999, approximately 90 million Americans were computer users (Kaye & Medoff, 2001). Most of these users had computers equipped with high-speed modems, making electronic communication one of the more popular uses. Information also is available through a plethora of networks and online services. The emergence of hypertext markup language (HTML), when coupled with the creation of hypertext transfer protocol (HTTP), a standard protocol that links thousands of servers to host computers, has prompted the explosive growth of the Internet. Equally important is that by 2003 there were approximately 545 million Internet users worldwide with an inestimable number of servers (Kaye & Medoff, 2001). An expanding system of interlinked and distributed servers has led to the creation of numerous new computer applications, more overall users, and more control and manipulation of data by information users. It is a scenario that frightens owners and creators of copyright materials. They fear that the electronic marketplace will displace the traditional owner-user relationship and undermine the meaning of copyright because of the largely unforeseen contexts in which the original information may be applied.

The purposes of this chapter are threefold. First, I discuss the rationale for why a copyright system is needed in a digital world to sustain creative works. Second, I identify several problems that occur in regulating intellectual property in cyberspace. Third, I examine five issues that are likely to be prominent in copyright litigation during the next decade.

A RATIONALE FOR A COPYRIGHT SYSTEM

Article I, Section 8, Clause 8 of the Constitution empowers Congress "to promote the Progress of Science and the useful Arts, by securing for Limited Times to Authors and Inventors the exclusive Right to their respective Writings and Discoveries." This clause is one of the few instances where the term *right* is explicitly used in the Constitution. The premise underlying the copyright clause is that an economic incentive should be provided to encourage authors and inventors to produce, and that society as a whole will benefit because the writings and inventions will create new ideas and new products. The emphasis is placed on providing incentives to individuals that will lead to producing a public benefit. In *Mazer v. Stein* (1954), the Court wrote that "[E]ncouragement of individual effort by personal gain is the best way to advance public welfare through the talents of authors . . ." (p. 201).

The notion that the copyright system should provide incentives to innovators sanctioned the legitimacy of proprietary rights for data, and this assumption allows information to be both privately owned and selectively distributed. The rationale for excluding others from copying, distributing, or displaying information is based on the need to foster attractive incentives for individuals to produce creative works and to allow them to reap the benefits of their labors. But these proprietary rights do not exist in perpetuity, and they are limited by the Constitution.

In fact, the actual language of the Constitution provides a framework for the copyright statutes that subsequently were enacted. One key phrase in the Constitution that guided statutory construction was "limited times." An individual was granted a monopoly, whether it be a copyright or a patent, for a limited amount of time. The first copyright statute used two terms of 14 years. The more widely known 1909 Copyright Act used two terms of 28 years. The 1976 Copyright Act extended the duration to the life of an author plus 50 years. The concept of a monopoly usually carries with it a pejorative status in U.S. law. In copyright law, however, the author or creator is given a monopoly for a limited period in order to encourage him or her to produce. According to the Constitution, authors and creators are thus guaranteed a period when they have an "exclusive right" to control the product in order to reap a profit. The Constitution probably would not permit a "perpetual right" to copyrighted materials. But it does allow Congress the latitude to develop a time frame in order to optimize the benefits of copyright protection. The word "writings" in the Constitution has been interpreted by Congress and the courts in an expansive way to include sculpture, videotapes, graphics, maps, paintings, and even computer software programs.

A copyright thus provides a monopoly to authors, artists, and creators for their respective writings and works. The author has the exclusive right to control the work and can deny authorization to use, reproduce, perform, or display the work for the statutory life of the copyright. This is the trade-off that Congress makes in order to promote intellectual, artistic, and creative work. The monopoly privileges have predetermined goals:

> The monopoly privileges that Congress may authorize are neither unlimited nor primarily designed to provide a special private benefit. Rather, the limited grant is a means by which an important public purpose may be achieved. It is intended to motivate the creative activity of authors and inventors by the provision of a special reward, and to allow the public access to the products of their genius after the limited period of exclusive control has expired. (*Sony Corporation v. University City Studio*, 1984, p. 774)

The 1976 Copyright Act provided a solution to disentangle copyright law from a difficult and recurrent problem. Prior to the 1976 Act, copyright relied on a categorical approach to subject matter. The Copyright Act of 1790 limited copyright to "books, maps, and charts." Later copyright acts added photography, movies, phonograph records, and cable television to the list of protected works. The categorical approach meant that the courts were compelled to examine each new communication format or technology to determine whether it could be interpreted as a "writing" within the constitutional scope of the copyright clause. Understandably, there was much judicial diffidence in approaching this difficult task. The courts believed it was the express responsibility of Congress to legislate whether a new technology should be covered under copyright protection.

In 1976, the categorical approach to copyright's subject matter was revamped. In the 1976 Act, Congress defined a copyright as an "original work of authorship fixed in a tangible medium of expression." The "fixation standard" was designed to cover existing, and yet to be discovered, technologies (Brandriss, 1996, pp. 237-238).

In theory, the fixation standard was a choice based on sound policy decisions. Congress could have selected various other points along a continuum as the place to begin the copyright protection for a work. For instance, Congress could have offered copyright protection at the point of creation; at the point of publication; at the point of registration; at the point of placing notice on a work; or at the point of depositing a work at the Library of Congress. The point of creation was problematic because it presented evidentiary problems and left no record for the innovator whose creation was still in his or her head. The points of registration, notice, and deposit were formalities that our European counterparts already had rejected. Because the United States was attempting to move closer in philosophy and administrative procedures to the countries that were signatories of the Berne Agreement, Congress decided not to make copyright dependent on fulfilling any one of these mechanical steps. Thus, the fixation standard, which goes into effect when a work is "fixed in a tangible medium of expression," became the new definition of copyright.

There were, however, two unforeseen problems with this definition. First, the fixation standard, which initially seemed far superior to the older categorical approach, encountered difficulties in the electronic age. Imagine a web browser that picks up an image and places it on a computer screen. When the image is placed on the screen, is it actually fixed? Can an individual use information that appears on the screen on the grounds that it is not fixed and therefore not copyrightable information? There were no clear-cut answers available to resolve this issue. But there is sufficient reason to believe that fixation will be a problem in a digital environment.

Second, the problem of judicial diffidence persisted. In the widely celebrated 1984 *Sony v. Universal Studios* case, Justice Stevens' majority opinion upheld home videotaping, but it also contained a strong protest that this was not the type of decision that the courts should be making. This complaint was more than a feigned sigh of anguish on the part of the Court in making a difficult decision. The Court felt ill-equipped to make such a decision where Congress had been silent on its intentions. Moreover, because Congress has the ability to conduct hearings, investigate industry policies, and legislate new initiatives, the Court understandably wanted to defer the decision making to an institutional setting that had more expertise. But the Court was forced to act as Congress defaulted on making a decision. In *Sony*, the Court ruled that commercial copying was presumptively unfair, but that copying in the privacy of one's home was permissible. For the digital age, this holding opened the door for massive copying so long as it occurred in one's domicile. In *Campbell v. Acuff Rose* (1994), the Court sought to narrow this holding, retreating from the expansive nature of allowing home reproduction. Home reproduction that looked benign in the eyes of the *Sony* Court was highly troublesome for the *Acuff Rose* Court. Among the changes that had occurred in the decade between the two decisions were the increasing reliance on a home office, the widespread use of personal computers, and the growth of the Internet, which gave a vastly different coloration to "working at home."

The 1976 Copyright Act sets forth the exclusive rights of copyright owners, but the meaning of these rights becomes increasingly more difficult to ascertain as the digital age unfolds. Section 106 of the Act enumerates the *five* exclusive rights of owners:

1. The right to make copies.
2. The right to prepare derivative works.
3. The right to publicly display.
4. The right to publicly perform.
5. The right to publicly distribute.

These five rights constitute the widely heralded "bundle of rights," and under copyright law, no one may exercise these rights without expressed authorization from the owner. The word "public," which seemed more straightforward in a predigital age, now assumes an ambiguous meaning when one talks about downloading materials in the privacy of one's home. In addition, the term *electronic transmission* is not addressed anywhere in the 1976 Act, and whether electronic transmission is an extension of "distribution" or itself a new medium with special "rights" is unclear and subject to widespread debate (Gailey, 1996; Kravis, 1993). Under traditional copyright law, rights not established by contract or developed under a work-for-hire situation are reserved for owners. This tradition, although occasionally modified by judge-made exceptions, serves as a formidable obstacle for users successfully to assert "new" or "unclaimed" rights in digitized information.

The chief exception to the "exclusive rights of owners" in Section 106 of the 1976 Copyright Act is the "fair use doctrine" in Section 107, which grants privileges to users of copyrighted works. The fair use doctrine is a device employed to minimize the conflict between owners and users of copyrighted materials (Crews, 1996). It is an affirmative defense to legitimize copying by a user. The 1976 Act gave statutory recognition to what had been a longstanding judicial doctrine. The doctrine has four criteria, and the courts attempt to apply all four when considering a given case:

1. **Purpose of the Use.** Courts are willing to grant a wider latitude for some purposes rather than others. Section 107 mentions six purposes that receive special attention: criticism, comment, news reporting, classroom teaching, scholarship, and research. In addition, courts have been willing to grant special breathing room to nonprofit activities. In *Sony*, the Court stated a "for-profit" enterprise should be treated as "presumptively unfair" (p. 774). The Court has been willing to read into the objectives of the "purpose category" activities that recast, transform, or constitute a creative use of the original work toward a desirable social objective. In *Sony*, the dissent argued vigorously that a distinction should be drawn between a productive and nonproductive use. A productive use involved something that was creative and that required the user to add an element to what previously had existed. A nonproductive use merely took the item and used it passively for entertainment. The dissent viewed videotaping off the air as a nonproductive use and contended it should never be treated as fair use (*Sony*, 1984, p. 774). This distinction between productive and nonproductive uses has appeared elsewhere in recent court decisions, making it a key ingredient in interpreting the "purpose of the work" provision of the fair use doctrine (Stuckey, 1996). Moreover, the productive/nonproductive dichotomy increasingly will become an important boundary-drawing test as commentators and courts focus on the value-added dimension of the second user-producer.

2. **Nature of the Work.** Some works are treated differently than others in the eye of the courts. News is treated with more leeway for the copier than a work of entertainment. A factual and nonfiction work receives less weight than a creative work. Items such as music sheets and workbooks are regarded as consumable items, and there is a presumption against using materials from them, whereas nonconsumable work may be treated with greater leeway. It is likely that items such as E-mail, bulletin board (BB) postings, electronic journals, and online, fact-based data bases will warrant different treatment, despite being common elements of the digital revolution.

3. **Amount Taken.** The courts examine the amount of material taken and weigh it against the work as a whole. Different ratios have been applied to different types of work. It is possible, for example, for a classroom teacher to take a chapter in a prose book if only one copy is handed out to each student, and the copying is regarded as spontaneous. At the same time, even

taking a limited number of words of poetry or music may trigger the claim of an unfair appropriation of another's work.
4. **Market Effect.** When the economic injury to the copyright holder can be demonstrated, making even a single copy or taking a limited appropriation, no matter how small the money involved in the case, may result in an infringement action. If the unauthorized use damages the market for the original work, then the courts have been reluctant to extend protection against infringement to the copyright users. Among the four criteria, the market variable has usually been given the greatest weight by the courts.

The fair use doctrine has been used in the past to make accommodations when new technologies have arisen. At present, it has become an important benchmark for determining attitudes toward regulation of information in an electronic age. A debate between copyright optimists and pessimists has raged in books, journals, convention papers, and industry-user conferences, but the discussion has produced mixed results. As Goldstein (1994) explained, copyright optimists believe that the fair use doctrine once again will be employed to accommodate the need of owners and users, granting reasonable compensation and use to each side.

Copyright pessimists, however, demur. They argue the digital revolution is not just a new mechanism to acquire information, but a completely new set of procedures that have far-reaching implications for most types of copyrighted materials. They acknowledge that the flexibility of the fair use doctrine has allowed it to serve as a useful device to resolve past difficulties. Yet, they argue that the scale of the digital revolution goes well beyond the dislocations made by any one single innovation in two key respects. First, the technological innovations now allow for value-added interactions, with additional links that permit users to pursue a subject at a depth and scope that the users, not the initiating author, establish. The user therefore "becomes a director, or creator, a driver or navigator, perhaps even an author, and much less of a subject or recipient of an author's message" (Katsh, 1995, p. 202). Second, cyberspace is not medium-specific as were the analog formats. Instead, digitized information covers several media and allows the user to interact simultaneously with multiple formats. According to copyright pessimists, digitized information represents a major departure from the medium-specific rules that traditionally have governed copyright.

There are, of course, many blue-sky predictions of what changes will likely occur because of the digital revolution, and why the label "information age" represents an astute characterization of an economy that is now the legitimate successor to the "agrarian" and "manufacturing" eras (Straubhaar & LaRose, 2002, pp. 15-17). Yet, despite the controversy about the nature and scope of the digital revolution, there is a growing consensus that Pool's (1983) earlier assessment is correct: The development of digital technology represents a paradigmatic shift on a scale that is difficult to imagine.

But the rationale behind the copyright system will continue to be important even in an information-oriented economy. Copyright exists to provide incentives to authors and creators so that they will undertake the labor to create new works. Without a system of incentives and a means to reap the benefits of their own labor, authors and creators will have less desire to provide society with intellectual property. Litman (1994) and Samuelson (1996) are correct in warning that the bargain society strikes with authors and innovators in cyberspace should not unduly "privilege" owners of copyrighted materials. They contend that care must be taken to protect the rights of the public against the many stakeholders and their accompanying attorneys who represent vested intellectual property interests at odds with providing reasonable access to information users.

Recently, the Supreme Court ruled in a case that sought to protect the public domain for information users. At issue was the meaning of the phrase "limited times" in the Copyright Clause of the Constitution, and the level incentives desirable to encourage the production of creative works.

Eldred v. Ashcroft (2003) challenged the constitutionality of the Sonny Bono Copyright Term Extension Act (CTEA). In 1998, that act extended the term of copyright protection for authors and creators from 50 to 70 years after the death of the creator, and it extended copyright protection to works owned by corporations to 95 years. The CTEA was widely perceived as having been passed to please the interests of corporate information owners, especially the Walt Disney Corporation whose chief character and corporate spokesperson, Mickey Mouse, would have entered the public domain in 2003. Eric Eldred, who initiated the lawsuit, published an online archive of classic literature that included books and poems. The other plaintiffs who joined with Eldred included an online vendor of sheet music, and a company that preserves and restores old films. Eldred et al. contended that old works "should flow continuously into the public domain" and that Congress capitulated to the interests of corporate information owners in passing the CTEA. Eldred maintained that a troubling trend was unfolding: "If the big publishers and media giants have their way, then basically they'll turn our culture into a pay-per-view event" (Carnevale, 2002, p. A35). Eldred insisted that a decision against him would slow down the process of digital archiving of old books, magazine, movies, and sound recordings, and it would hurt the distribution of free electronic versions of creative works that otherwise would have fallen into the public domain.

The *Eldred* lawsuit reflects an evolving controversy over whether the expansion of copyright has created a harmful set of entitlements for information owners that distorts the rationale underlying copyright. Fisher (1992) argued that the expansion of copyright in terms of duration and the types of works that it applies to "has grown steadily and dramatically from the eighteenth century to the present" and that "in the absence of any organized resistance" the lobbying process has heavily favored the expansion of the rights of information owners at the expense of unorganized consumers and information users. The public at large has been defended by a diffuse group of public interest activists, educators, and miscellaneous civic welfare organizations who lack political power. According to Fisher (1992), information owners "have had a strong financial interest in statutory reform that would protect them against nonpermissive use of their 'property,'" and they have been highly successful in lobbying Congress to enact legislation that favors their financial and legal well-being. This line of argument raises serious questions about whether entrenched interests, especially the large corporations, have maximized their own welfare at the expense of the public at large.

Moreover, Eldred was a novel case in that the Supreme Court has never previously accepted a lawsuit that challenged Congress' ability to extend the duration of copyright. In fact, the historical precedents indicate that Congress alone has the sole power to establish the scope and duration of copyright legislation. The Constitution authorizes this role, and since 1790, Congress has enacted five different copyright statutes without a challenge to its power. But the argument made by Eldred and his supporters is that Congress has overreached its constitutional authority by stretching the duration of copyright beyond desirable "constitutional" limits (Lessig, 2001, pp. 196-198). At its core, *Eldred* raised important economic questions about the level of incentives necessary to encourage the production of new works. Were the added 20 years that the CTEA provides necessary to stimulate the production of new works? And was the retroactive protection given to the older works consistent with the requirements of the Constitution to provide a right for "limited times" in order to stimulate *new* works?

In *Eldred*, the Court ruled 7–2 in favor of upholding the CTEA and granting owners of copyrighted works the extra 20 years. The Court held that the CTEA was a rational exercise of legislative power that violated neither the Copyright Clause nor the First Amendment. Writing for the majority, Justice Ginsburg maintained that the act was consistent with highly beneficial objectives of public policy. Among these goals were to (a) harmonize U.S. and European Law so that American authors receive the same protection as their European counterparts; (b) take advantage of demographic, economic, and technological changes affecting the value and commercial lifetime of a given work; and (c) "encourage copyright holders to invest in the restoration and public distribution of their works."

Ginsburg found that the CTEA was consistent with the "limited times" phrase of the Copyright Clause, and she declared that it was not the role of the Court "to second-guess congressional determinations and policy judgments of this order, however debatable or arguably unwise they may be." Ginsburg firmly concluded that Congress had engaged in a permissible exercise of its authority.

In his dissent in *Eldred*, Justice Breyer maintained the economic effect of the CTEA was to make the copyright term "virtually perpetual." The act's primary effect was to extend an economic benefit not to authors, but to "their heirs, estates, or corporate successors." Breyer also argued that CTEA would not harmonize U.S. law with European protections nor would the supposed conformity to European standards encourage new works. Instead, Breyer regarded the CTEA as providing private benefit to a small group of owners rather than promoting artistic creativity for the public good. "It is easy to understand," declared Breyer, "how the statute might benefit the private financial interests of corporations or heirs who own existing copyrights. But I cannot find any constitutionally legitimate, copyright-related way in which the statute will benefit the public."

Despite the controversy in *Eldred* (2003), there is still a widespread belief among commentators within the intellectual property community that attention should be devoted to protecting the rights of creators because "without authors, there are no works to use," and authors remain the primary vehicle for creating intellectual and artistic innovations and thus serving the public interest at large (Ginsburg, 1995 p. 1468). "The *sine qua non* of copyright," wrote the *Feist* (1991) Court, "is originality" (p. 345), and that authorship and originality are the chief reasons for giving special legal deference to authors and creators. However, copyright policy traditionally has been designed to maintain an equitable balance between encouraging authorship and providing reasonable access for users of copyrighted materials. This has been popularly known as the classic copyright bargain: A limited form of protection and monopoly power for authors in exchange for the creation of new works. Despite the novel problems posed by cyberspace, the long-standing rationale of balancing incentives for authors with reasonable access for users is likely to continue as Congress' primary objective.

PROBLEMS WITH DIGITAL PROPERTY

David Nimmer (1996) referred to the "familiar specter of technology leapfrogging legislative intent" when he considered the special problems posed by cyberspace. Despite the widely acclaimed flexibility of the Fair

Use Doctrine, new technologies have emerged that pose problems unanticipated by Congress or by the existing stakeholders in the copyright arena. Beginning in the 1960s, the new technologies have altered the traditional relationship between owners and users of copyrighted materials.

The first major battle with the new technologies was fought over the photocopier. Hand-copying was labor intensive, time-consuming, and ultimately created a copy that was inferior to the original printed work (Samuels, 2000). On the other hand, the photocopier made copying easy, inexpensive, and accessible to a large proportion of the population who otherwise would have purchased a book, a journal, back issues, or reprints from the copyright owner. As photocopying became more widespread, publishers vigorously protested what they perceived to be an infringement on their exclusive right to make copies. They also bitterly assailed the magnitude of the copying, claiming unquantifiable sums of lost potential revenue. But the courts, not wanting to stifle technological innovations, reluctantly affirmed the right of an individual to photocopy under the fair use doctrine, subject only to minor restrictions. In *William and Wilkins* (1973), the Court of Appeals held that photocopying by individuals constituted a fair use, and the Supreme Court allowed that decision to stand because of the 4–4 split among the justices on how to assess the photocopying process (Justice Blackmun did not participate in the voting because of his prior association with medical publishers while serving as counsel at the Mayo Clinic in Rochester, Minnesota).

Twenty years later, the market and submarket for photocopying had crystallized. The courts, therefore, began to identify particular segments of the photocopying industry that infringed on the legitimate rights belonging to authors and publishers. In *Basic Books v. Kinko's* (1991), *American Geophysical Union v. Texaco* (1994), and *Princeton University Press v. Michigan Documents Service* (1996), different courts set forth substantially narrower and more restrictive interpretations of fair use. These decisions, in turn, stimulated the creation and widespread use of a clearinghouse system for permissions for printed materials. Ironically, the clearinghouse for print permissions has been aided by other new technologies—the computer and fax machines—that allow permissions typically to be obtained within a 3-week period.

The second major battle with the new technologies was fought over the videocassette recorder (VCR). Videotape has existed for a long time, but the introduction of the VCR in 1976 made copying complete television programs easy and inexpensive (Lardner, 1987). In a controversial 5–4 decision, the Supreme Court interpreted videotaping in the home as a noncommercial use permitted by the Fair Use Doctrine. The Court contended that because the VCR had substantial non-infringing purposes, *Sony*, the manufacturer of the technology, could not be held liable for contributory infringement. But the courts have been vigilant in regulating videotaping when done in a commercial context or outside the privacy of an individual's house. In *Pacific & Southern v. Duncan* (1984), the court held that a videographer who taped newscasts and then contacted individuals mentioned in the news stories and offered to sell them a video copy of their appearance on a particular news broadcast infringed on the rights of owners of the television station. The court assailed not only the commercial nature of that entrepreneurial venture but stated that the "public" distribution of the videotapes from a company called "TV News Clips" militated against a finding of fair use for the defendant. Overall, the early videotape decisions strongly reinforced a private–public distinction in using copyright materials.

A third major battle over the new technologies has recently been fought over the downloading of digital music from the Internet. This is a highly vexing, ongoing situation that directly involves digital technologies and the Internet. During the early 1980s, digital music in the form of compact discs (CDs) began to replace the older analog version of recording music on vinyl albums. Digital music produced a higher quality sound recording, and it was more durable than vinyl albums. In 1987, an audio file format was developed to allow music to be digitally compressed into a fraction of its usual disk space. These compressed audio files could then be transmitted over the Internet and stored on the hard drive of another person's computer. This technology was called an MP3 file transfer protocol. During the early 1990s, the technology remained relatively isolated, appealing primarily to high school and college students who wanted to obtain free copies of the songs of their favorite musicians.

Subsequently, MP3 BBs, chatrooms, and Web sites emerged to provide users with the computer know-how regarding downloading freely available software, the mechanics of peer-to-peer music software sharing, and information about what sites to access in order to obtain music. Because MP3 files were unsecured, a person who acquired the music could then make an unlimited number of copies. The files retained a CD-quality sound no matter how many copies were made (Litman, 2001).

In 1999, Napster took the technology of Internet music one step further. Traditional search engines such as Yahoo! or Lycos contained many dead sites and outdated links, and the existing search process for finding Internet music was tedious. Napster's creator, Sean Fanning, a 19-year old freshman at Northeastern University, wrote a software program that made Internet music convenient and technically easy to use. Napster required a user to log-in and establish a user name. Once registered, a user could connect to a database of music owned by other Napster registrants. Napster's program soon became the most popular version of peer-to-peer software sharing. Napster also profited from a network effect: The more users that

Napster acquired, the more effective the system became for sharing music. In addition, Napster had an innovative hotlist function that allowed an individual to browse and access the MP3 files on another user's computer. Within a short time, Napster had 10 million subscribers, and by January 2001, it had 62 million subscribers (Levy, 2001).

The Record Industry Association of America (RIAA) sued Napster for contributory and vicarious copyright infringement. As much as 87% of the music being copied by Napster users was copyrighted with more than 70% of the music having been copyrighted by RIAA members (*A&M Record v. Napster*, 2001, p. 1013). Napster responded with a fair use defense that emphasized two major arguments. First, the company claimed that it lacked copyright liability because individual users were making personal, noncommercial copies of the music. Second, Napster contended it lacked any liability because it neither stored nor cached music on it servers. Napster instead insisted that it merely provided a central directory that allowed subscribers to make connections; it offered technical support for indexing and searching musical files; and it created chatrooms for users to meet and discuss music. The gist of Napster's position was that, if this case were considered in the offline world, the company would have been allowed to engage in activities that facilitated private acts of copying in keeping with the holding of the *Sony* Court regarding the multiple uses of VCRs.

In *A & M Records v. Napster* (2001), the Ninth Circuit Court of Appeal upheld a decision against Napster. While discussing the traditional four factors of the fair use test, the court's decision was noteworthy in two important respects. First, the court redefined a *commercial purpose* so that it now extended to home, or private, copying. The new definition defined a *use* as commercial if it involved "repeated and exploitative copying of copyrighted works, even if the copies are not for sale" (p. 1015). The court openly speculated about the harmful effects of free riders—Napster users who were getting something for free that they would ordinarily have to buy. Second, the court argued that the copyright holders should have the first opportunity to develop their own system for Internet music. Although the court noted that it was hard for the RIAA to quantify how much harm that Napster was doing to its actual record sales, the court worried about the evolving Internet market and its vast potential. As the court declared, "[A] lack of harm to an established market cannot deprive the copyright holder of the right to develop alternative markets for the works" (p. 1017). Moreover, the court refused to consider Napster's plea to establish a compulsory license system for Internet music that had been utilized in other troublesome areas of copyright litigation, such as coursepacks and jukeboxes. In *Napster*, the court argued that the right of an existing copyright holder to exploit the online market trumped a user's right to exploit that information. This decision was similar to the holding in *LA Times v. Free*

Republic (2000), where a district court held that the *Los Angeles Times* had the first right to develop an online market for viewing its own articles.

Understandably, the copyright decisions in a limited number of cases concerning the new technologies do not allow us to infer a "typical" pattern. Nonetheless, it is clear that the courts have developed a multi-tiered economic strategy in the treatment of the new technologies. It is evident that the courts have adopted one strategy for the formative period of a new technology and another strategy for the technology when the market begins to mature, and it is easier to identify which parties are benefiting or being harmed by the applications of the technology. A third strategy is designed for the unfolding online world to allow the existing copyright holders the first right to exploit and develop an Internet market for their works and to protect this market against exploitation by noncopyright owners. There is a very strong market orientation in these legal strategies. Gordon (1982) believes that "Markets are a system for consensual exchange of owned good" and that a market system in copyright law will develop and mature over time as the ability to handle problems such as transactions costs diminish (pp. 1605-1622). To the extent that the history of regulating the photocopier, VCR, and digital music provides any guidance, the Internet in 20 years will look vastly different than its current configuration. Yet there are several similarities in the uses of the new technologies that are worth noting. Cyberspace continues the technological trend of making copying easier and less expensive for users. In addition, it allows items to be copied, adapted, and distributed to other users in vastly changed formats (Samuelson, 1990). It is still too early to identify either the scope of this emerging system, the nature of the eventual relationship between owners and users of copyrighted materials, or even the types of online-service providers that will emerge as intermediaries between creators and end-users of materials. Like the photocopier and VCR, it will take time for the market structure and the entrepreneurial context to mature in cyberspace. For instance, Fisher (2001) suggested several provocative alternatives to the current scheme of retail outlets as the primary distributors of music as Internet music matures. Among his suggestions are a subscription contract with a digital service provider who licenses sought-after music, membership in an Internet club directly sponsored by a recording artist, and a restricted membership on a mailing list with ancillary benefits such as reserved seats in a concert hall. Gordon (1982) is correct in her assessment that what economists call a "market failure" may only be a temporary condition, and that a market structure for a given technological use may unfold only after the passage of an undefined period of time.

With new technologies, both Congress and the courts have followed what William James (1912) termed Kierkegaard's paradox: "[W]e live forwards but we understand backwards" (p. 238). The existing literature on

regulation of cyberspace devotes a disproportionate amount of space to discussing the photocopier, the VCR, and the cable industry because these are
concrete instances where the courts were forced to grapple with market
failure, new technologies, and where new rules eventually emerged. They
have become the templates to understanding the Information
Superhighway. Similarly, the Napster case will be scrutinized for the long-
term effects of the court's approach. The court stopped Napster, but the
MP3 revolution continues to flourish. In 2003, for instance, Kazaa had
more online users than Napster ever had, and the sale of recorded music in
retail stores had fallen an additional 16% since the *Napster* decision
(Anderman, 2003, p. N1).

It might have been more strategic for the RIAA to buy Napster and
then use it to showcase its own Internet music system rather than to go to
court to shut down the upstart company. The issues in *Napster* and the
emergence of a market structure for Internet music will bear careful watching in the coming decade, especially if compressed files for video, the next
generation of MP4 files, and multimedia technologies emerge to pose serious threats to existing media market structures.

FUTURE ISSUES IN COPYRIGHT LITIGATION

Despite the attempts to draw on the history of new technologies for guidance, several of the issues raised by cyberspace are truly novel. First, the
ease of technological copying substantially outstrips any notion of copying
currently in the 1976 Copyright Act or reflected in the development of
nondigital technologies. Second, as the *Napster* case demonstrates, users are
not only extremely numerous, but they are working from widely diverse
locations, often in their homes, and this makes the enforcement of any particular right more problematic (Ginsburg, 1995, p. 1489). Third, the concept of a user must be reformulated to reach a conception that there are
multiple types of users, several of whom will add value to the information.
The "simple end-users" who do not transform the original data may
become only a minor segment of a complex market structure.

But in what sense, if any, will end-users exist, or will we all be user-
producers and thus inadvertently infringe on the derivative rights of copyright owners under Section 106? At this stage in the development of the
Information Superhighway, the answer to this question is unclear.

The following is a list of five major issues dealing with copyright and
cyberspace. This is not an exhaustive list because new developments consistently force a reconfiguration of the central questions underlying the creation, development, and protection of intellectual property. Yet, this discussion attempts to address several troublesome copyright issues that may

require a new legislative or judicial approach. As O'Rourke (1994) astutely observed, "the law is a moving target," but some pivotal issues, nevertheless, may be identified (p. 511).

1. *The right to browse should be re-considered in light of the widespread confusion concerning the treatment of random access memory (RAM).* Certain parts of the Internet, such as web pages and BBs, invite people to browse. If the browsing is defined as glancing, browsing might be the functional equivalent to reading. Yet, in order to browse, computer users are required to download information into the RAM of their own computer. This process, and whether it constitutes making an illegal copy, is open to dispute. The key questions are: Does downloading information into RAM constitute fixation? and At what point should downloading trigger copyright infringement?

In *Advanced Computer Services of Michigan v. MAI* (1994), the district court of Virginia ruled that transferring a program or information onto the RAM of a computer constitutes making a copy, and it thus represents a copyright infringement. Plaintiffs had argued that "the nature of RAM is so ephemeral, so transitory, as to preclude a finding that a 'copy' of the program is made when it is transferred from a permanent memory source to the computer's RAM" (p. 362). Moreover, the plaintiffs contended that the threshold for fixation had not been actually reached because once the computer is turned off, the information in RAM disappears.

In rejecting the plaintiffs' arguments, the court concluded that the Copyright Act "does not require absolute permanence for the creation of a copy" (p. 363). Rather, the court stated that the test for copying should be whether the information is "sufficiently permanent or stable to permit it to be perceived, reproduced, or otherwise communicated for a period of more than a transitory duration" (p. 363). The court therefore concluded that such a work was indeed "fixed" as defined by the 1976 Copyright Act, and the court openly refused to consider where along a time continuum—a milli-second, a second, a minute—that fixation should be said to have occurred.

A year earlier in *MAI v. Peak Computer, Inc.* (1993), the Ninth Circuit Court ruled that MAI's software license did not allow the loading of software into one of MAI's computers by Peak, a third-party computer maintenance company. The court similarly upheld a finding that the loading of copyrighted computer software from a storage medium, such as a hard disk, floppy disk, or read-only-memory into the "memory of a central processing unit (CPU) causes a copy to be made" (p. 518). The defendant, Peak Computer, contended that a copy created in RAM is not fixed, but the court insisted that there were no material facts or precedent to support such a conclusion. Instead, the court held that a "copy made in RAM is 'fixed' and qualifies as a copy under the Copyright Act" (p. 519).

The decisions reached in the courts on "the fixation issue" have found support elsewhere. In September 1995, a report issued from the Commerce Department entitled "Intellectual Property and the National Information Infrastructure" (commonly referred to as the White Paper) set forth the view of the Clinton administration that information in RAM does constitute a fixation (Stuckey, 1996). A year later, in his introductory address to the Harvard Conference on the Internet and Society, Nimmer (1996) insisted that this policy was "eminently defensible" on the grounds that 100 separate users may tap into a computer and make copies of the RAM-only text, and this overall pattern directly implicates "the copyright owner's reproduction right" (p. 11).

Despite a seemingly strong consensus of opinion, the debate over fixation is far from settled. Brandriss (1996) regarded "fixation" as a pivotal issue because of its far-reaching implications for multiple activity on the Internet. As a result, he perceives that the issues actually being debated transcend the technical questions about the stability of RAM in a computer. "The real question," wrote Brandriss, "is whether, in the digital age, the very demand of fixation as a condition of reproduction has the same meaning as it has as far as creation, or indeed, whether it has any at all" (p. 240). For Brandriss, the more significant question that follows from the current controversy over fixation is whether "the view that *browsing on-line* — accessing documents into, say, a home computer's RAM and viewing screen — could also be considered reproductive fixation and copyright infringement" (p. 252).

The status of browsing may one day be reconsidered. The court's decision reached in *Peak* and its progeny about the status of on-line browsing has generated widespread concern. Several commentators claim that the interpretation of "browsing as reproduction" seemingly amounts to a right to control reading, which was not the intention of Congress in enacting the copyright statute (Brandriss, 1996; Litman, 1994). Thus, the controversy about the treatment of RAM is a topic where digital technology may compel a legislative revamping of the copyright law and ultimately may require Congress to draw clearer boundaries between online browsing and online transmissions. This is not an issue of "market failure" per se where Congress must intervene to restore market equity as much as it is a novel problem created by the existence of communication data on various servers in cyberspace. At present, there is no such entity as a "right to browse."

2. *Fair use should be expanded in cyberspace so long as it does not damage or supplant a market where an initiating author or creator would enter.* Based on previous experience, the application of the Fair Use Doctrine to cyberspace should be a useful approach to accommodating the competing interests of owners and users of copyrighted materials. The Clinton administration's White Paper opposed applying the fair use doctrine in cyberspace where a possible licensing agreement could occur. As Samuelson (1996) observed, the White Paper's position is "neither historically accurate nor good public policy" (p. 138). The White Paper's position on fair use privileged authors and publishers and dismissed the needs of users. On the other hand, Gordon (1997) suggested that the Fair Use Doctrine is essentially a test of "reasonableness" (an equitable rule of reason), and that it draws a court into deciding the social desirability of the defendant's copying, especially where there are no formal rules on which to draw on for guidance.

The rationale for developing, and even expanding, the Fair Use Doctrine in cyberspace relies heavily on the traditional belief of promoting "reasonable" access to information. In theory, fair use has been a device designed to aid users of copyrighted materials without undermining the livelihood of creators and innovators. For users and distributors of information, including online providers, the Fair Use Doctrine represents a sensible approach to balance competing interests. The four criteria of Section 107—purpose of the use, nature of the work, amount and substantiality taken, and market effect—serve as broad lenses from which courts may view a particular contested use. Moreover, the six enumerated factors in the preface of Section 107 should permit scholars, teachers, and journalists reasonable leeway in using data from the Internet. The key factors will be the noncommercial use of the material and the lack of profit-making activities by the users. This is the central meaning of *Basic Books, Inc. v. Kinko's* (1991) and *Princeton*

University Press v. Michigan Document Services (1996).
O'Rourke (1994) viewed applying the fair use approach to
cyberspace as sound policy, especially in its applications to E-
mail and BB postings, the latter of which alternately could be
perceived as a dedication to the public domain .

Yet, two major BB cases openly reject the fair use defense.
In *Playboy Enterprises Inc. v. Frena* (1993), the U.S. District
Court for the Middle District of Florida concluded that the
operator of a BB service had violated *Playboy*'s exclusive right
to display and distribute material when a picture from the magazine, uploaded by a subscriber, was made available through
the BB. The court reached this conclusion partially because
membership on the BB was preconditioned on the payment of
a subscriber's fee. The court also found that the contested work
was entertainment, and not of a factual nature, and thereby
ruled that the future market harm could be detrimental to
Playboy if such postings became widespread.

In another BB case, *The Los Angeles Times v. Free
Republic* (2000), a district court denied the defendants a fair use
defense. In that case, *The Los Angeles Times* and *The
Washington Post* sued Free Republic, a BB whose members
used the Web site to post articles from newspapers while
adding their own commentary and remarks to the news.
Typically, Free Republic members posted the entire article
from a newspaper. At issue in the case was whether the copying
to a BB was a fair use, and whether Free Republic's postings
affected the sale of archival copies by the aggrieved newspapers.
Both the *Times* and the *Post* had a pricing structure that
allowed users to see the current edition of the newspaper for
free, but charged between $1.95 to $2.95 per page for an
archival copy. The newspapers alleged that the existence of the
BB Web site hurt their archival business. The court agreed. The
court found that the articles on the BB served as substitutes for
viewing the original newspaper article at the respective newspaper's online site. The court concluded that "the nontransforma-
tive character of the copying tips the scale in the plaintiff's
favor" (p. 1467).

Meanwhile, a year earlier, a fair use defense was upheld in
Leslie A. Kelly, et al. v. Arriba Soft Corp (1999). The defendant,
Arriba, operated a "visual search engine" on the Internet. The
search engine's distinguishing trait was that it allowed a user to
retrieve a list of thumbnail visual images, not just text, when a
search inquiry was initiated. Arriba's "ditto" crawler was

designed to catalogue and expedite access to visual images throughout the Internet. Its impressive database contained an index of approximately 2 million thumbnail images.

The plaintiff, Leslie Kelly, was a photographer who specialized in pictures of the California Gold Rush era and the works of Laura Ingalls Wilder. Kelly maintained his own Web sites with pictures, and he also offered tours and retreats in California Gold Rush country. Kelly complained that 35 of his pictures were indexed in Arriba's database and appeared on a search inquiry. But the court found that the use of the Arriba's search engine served a different purpose than Kelly's Web site: It was an indexing function that allowed a user to click on an Internet address and be forwarded to the originator's Web site. The court's conclusion was both forgiving and reluctant to impede an emerging technology. It found two factors in favor of fair use and two opposed, but it contended that "Defendant's purposes were and are inherently transformative, even if its realization of those purposes was at times imperfect. Where, as here, a new use and new technology are evolving, the broad transformative purpose of the use weighs more heavily than the inevitable flaws in its early stages of development" (p. 1121).

Like in *Arriba*, the effective application of fair use analysis to cyberspace issues will occur only if courts do not mechanically check-off the four factors of the doctrine. Rather, a greater emphasis should be placed on what the "initiating author" intended to do with the work: Was it an E-mail letter that was expected to be forwarded or was it an E-mail that should be treated similar to a regular letter? If it is the latter, then the rights to the expression in the letter still belong to the initiating author. Similarly, is the BB service open and free of charge or is there a commercial nature to the service? Does a BB perform a transformative function? In essence, there is no inherent barrier to applying fair use inquiries in cyberspace, but the analysis should be retooled to fit the nature and function of information in a digital era. A case-by-case approach will provide a slow, but sure-footed, orientation to developing an effective set of cyberspace guidelines, especially because the contours of cyberspace are still largely to be determined. The Fair Use Doctrine also carries with it another strategic advantage: It provides "American copyright law with a flexible mechanism with which to adapt to unforeseen circumstances in an era of rapid technological change" (Samuelson, 2000).

3. *Transaction costs in cyberspace may be easier to monitor than traditional materials allow.* Computer technology will aid users of copyrighted materials in obtaining works quickly and easily, but owners also will benefit from the technology. Goldstein (1994) maintained that transaction costs in cyberspace can be more easily monitored and billed, thus setting up a system that will continue to provide an incentive for individuals to produce works. Copyrighted works downloaded in the home or in a place of business will be subjected to fees. The very technology that poses challenges to a system of copyright may be used to sustain and simplify the difficult tasks of billing and fee collection. The use of passwords, pin numbers, and other identifying mechanisms will minimize the transaction costs so that a copyright system is not spending dollars to collect nickels and dimes. In this respect, the new technologies will aid authors and creators in overcoming the formidable obstacles of billing and collecting payments that existed in a pre-cyberspace era. In fact, because of the ability to monitor transaction costs, a market system in cyberspace may develop more rapidly in a digitally designed network than in earlier instances of the new technologies such as the photocopier and videotape.

4. *The private-public distinction that has strongly influenced copyright principles should be abandoned in light of the characteristics of the digital revolution.* The current copyright law places a heavy reliance on distinguishing between activities that occur within the home, and those that occur in a public place. In *Sony*, the court determined that videotaping at home constituted a fair use. In another instance, the "public display" of five consecutive hours of videotapes of ABC's popular soap opera *General Hospital* in a bar on a Saturday afternoon in Quincy, Massachusetts was a key factor in determining that copyright infringement had occurred.

   In fact, the newly emerging digital environment places a strain on this public–private distinction. The home office, which once was a typewriter, a pencil, and some file cabinets changes dramatically with the addition of a computer and a modem. It now becomes an individual's entry point to the Information Superhighway. Goldstein (1994) observed that many uses in the new digital environment "will take place in the privacy of the home, a trend that began in the mid-1960s when home audiotaping and then videotaping started to displace revenues earned in the retail marketplace of movie theaters, videocassette stores, and record outlets. But copyright has primarily been a doctrine of public places" (p. 201).

Section 106 of the 1976 Copyright Act reinforces the heavy reliance of a finding of copyright infringement on the notion of detecting a "public" use. The exclusive rights extended to the copyright owners include "public" distribution, "public" display, and "public" performance. The usage of this term in the copyright statute is premised on the ability to draw a clear and meaningful line between the public and private spheres. Yet, in the more than 27 years since the enactment of this statute, the Internet has radically changed our conception of the home office, and what constitutes the private sphere. In a digital environment, the terms *private* and *public* have become blurred and thus provide less meaning for making distinctions to guide an individual's behavior. A reassessment of the terms *private* and *public* in light of the emerging environment is warranted. The *Napster* (2001) decision, with its emphasis on the "repeated and exploitative copying of copyrighted works, even if the copies are not for sale" constitutes a first step to transcending the traditional public–private distinction.

5. *The scope and the meaning of the Digital Millennium Copyright Act (DMCA) will be clarified in the years ahead, but it will involve considerable controversy.* One of the most controversial pieces of legislation in the history of American copyright has been the DMCA of 1998. Passed by Congress and signed into law by President Clinton, the DMCA has two major sections. The first section was designed to provide immunization for Internet service providers (ISPs), such as the telephone companies, broadcasters, and equipment manufacturers if the infringing copyrighted materials are transmitted, routed, or enhanced by a connection over their system. The act provides an elaborate system of safe harbors to protect such online ISPs when transmitting transitory signals, caching information, providing storage space on a network, or facilitating links and connections to infringing materials. The act also states that an ISP does not have to affirmatively monitor its system for copyright violations in order to be eligible for the safe harbor provisions. Collectively, these provisions serve to limit the liability of ISPs. This places a heavy burden of proof on a plaintiff who wants to sue an ISP for copyright violations, although the ambiguities in the language of statute, as Yen (2000) observes, still place an ISP at some risk.

The second section of the act was designed to prohibit the development of anti-circumvention devices. The intent of this section was to discourage and penalize individuals who wrote or publicized programs or created devices to break into technically protected information, such as an encrypted digital versatile disk (DVD) movie. This provision criminalizes the act of circumvention (i.e., writing or distributing a program to allow hackers to break into protected digital files). To be found guilty, the provision does not require that an individual actually make an illegal copy of a protected file. In this respect, the anti-circumvention legislation looks more like a criminal rather than a copyright statute. As Zoellick (2002) explained, "Prohibiting circumvention is a new step in copyright law. It is a big change. It used to be perfectly legal to create products that, for example, defeated the copy protection system on floppy disks used to distribute software" (p. 29). In fact, reverse engineering and independent creation were once prized as virtues in copyright law. But the new anti-circumvention provisions discouraged this activity.

One of the first major lawsuits tried under the aegis of the DMCA was *Universal City Studios v. Reimerdes* (2000). At issue was whether encryption techniques to protect materials in digital forms from unauthorized copying violate the First Amendment and the Fair Use Doctrine. Four defendants distributed a Linux-based software program, DeCSS, that allowed them to descramble DVD video disks, including movies that were rented and purchased. Once the encryption code was descrambled, the movies could be transmitted across the Internet in a compressed video file. Eight major movie studios, including Disney, MGM, and Paramount, quickly sued the individuals who made the DeCSS program available online via *The Hacker Quarterly*. The district court held that the distribution of DeCSS violates the anti-circumvention provision of the DMCA. Moreover, the court found that there were no significant First Amendment or fair use raised by the defendants. In November 2001, the Second Circuit U.S. Court of Appeals upheld the lower court's decision. The appeals court declared that the magazine is "barred from trafficking in a decryption code that enables unauthorized access to copyrighted materials" (*Universal City v. Reimerdes*, 2001).

What is unfortunate about these decisions is that an encryption program such as the DeCSS software has substantial noninfringing uses, such as the ability to create "video clips," that could be useful for teaching, criticism, and commentary on films. If a straight fair use analysis were allowed, such an activity might be viewed as authorized and legitimate copying under Section 107 of the 1976 Copyright Act. But DMCA unambiguously criminalizes such activity. How broadly or narrowly to read the anti-circumvention provision of the 1998 DMCA, and whether there should be legitimate exceptions to these anti-circumvention rules will be issues for the courts to work out in the coming years.

CONCLUSION

The new digital technologies promise to alter the relationship between owners and users of copyrighted materials. These new technologies will compel us to reconceptualize our notion of proprietary rights in information. The relationship between owners and users of copyrighted materials increasingly will become more collaborative as the conception of an "end-user" becomes more complicated. Furthermore, as the information economy matures, the value-added activities of users will become more important, and it will place intense strains on the traditional relationship between creators and users of information.

Technological developments in cyberspace will continue the trend of making copying easier, more inexpensive, and more frequent. The combination of these trends will force a reassessment of the major components of our current copyright system, such as the fixation test, the applicability of the fair use doctrine, the changing nature of transactions costs, and the heavy reliance that has been placed on a public–private distinction in constructing copyright policy. Moreover, the scope and meaning of the provisions of the DMCA are likely to be focal points of intense controversy in the coming decade.

Unfortunately, there is no grand intellectual property scheme that can be superimposed on cyberspace at the present time. As the contours of cyberspace materialize, policymakers will acquire a better idea about the market structure and the infrastructure that support the system. In addition, policymakers will need to have a better vantage point before determining to what extent the Information Superhighway should be a "toll road" or a "freeway." The Fair Use Doctrine has never meant to be "free use," and some equitable scheme must be devised to satisfy the widely divergent needs of owners and users. In a digital environment, this balancing act will require a major reassessment of our principles of intellectual property.

Finally, there is some controversy in the intellectual property literature on how proactive policymakers should be in addressing the problems of a digital environment. Goldstein (1994) believes that Congress must act quickly because once a technology or process becomes widespread, and when its uses occur in the privacy of one's own home, it creates an attitudinal presumption against enacting legislation to regulate it—"making it virtually impossible to get Congress to prohibit its use" (p. 216). Goldstein implied that if Congress and the courts continue to hesitate about extending copyright regulations to the Internet, then the pervasiveness of the uses of the new technologies will create a standard by default and unwittingly serve as a threat to the "integrity of copyright law" (p. 30).

But several commentators advocate a "go-slow" approach. Nimmer (1996) believes that "biding our time may be the most prudent course," and he urges temporary restraint to allow some of the critical issues to simmer before seeking a legislative or private clearinghouse solution (pp. 11-12). Calvert (1998) similarly suggested a slow and deliberative public policy process in order to avoid hastily drafted and faulty legislation. Fishman (1999) maintained that "there is some wisdom in encouraging the government to pursue a minimalist agenda and thereby allow private investment and interested parties a free hand in the early stages of the development of the Internet" (p. 100). But it would be shortsighted of the public policy process to favor only entrenched interests and existing copyright holders or fail to see that private power may be coercive and subject to abuse. A more nuanced approach, therefore, is required. Given the multiple dimensions of the public policy process, allowing markets and submarkets to mature with minimal governmental regulation, a concern for the rights of copyright owners, and a recognition of the legitimate interests of information users may be the most prudent and productive course of action to follow in the coming decade.

REFERENCES

Advanced Computer Services of Michigan v. MAI Systems, 845 F. Supp. 356 (E.D., VA). (1991).

A&M Records, Inc. v. Napster, Inc., 239 F. 3d 1004. (Ninth Circuit). (2001).

American Geophysical Union v. Texaco Inc., 60 F. 3d 913 (1994).

Anderman, J. (2003, February 23). *The Boston Globe*, pp. N1, N9, N10.

Basic Books, Inc. v. Kinko's Graphic Corp., 758 F. Supp. 1522 (S.D. N.Y.). (1991).

Brandriss, I. (1996). Writing in frost on a window pane: E-mail and chatting on Ram and copyright fixation. *Journal of the Copyright Society of the USA, 43,* 237-278.

Calvert, C. (1998). Regulating cyberspace: Metaphor, rhetoric, reality and framing of legal options. *Comment, 25,* 541-566.

Campbell v. Acuff Rose, 114 S. Ct. Reporter 1170. (1994).

Carnevale, D. (2002, March 8). Supreme Court will hear copyright case affecting online resources. *The Chronicle of Higher Education*, p. A35.

Crews, K. D. (1996, May 17). What qualifies as "fair use." *The Chronicle of Higher Education*, pp. B1-2.

Eldred v. Ashcroft. (2003). U.S. LEXIS 751. Retrieved on March 4, 2003 from the World Wide Web. http://web.lexis-nexis.com/universe

Feist Publication Inc. v. Rural Telephone Service Company, 499 U.S. 340. (1991).

Fisher, W.W., III. (1992). *The growth of intellectual property: A history of the ownership of ideas in the United States.* Retrieved on January 26, 2002 from the World Wide Web: http://www.law.harvard.edu/academic_affairs/coursepages/tfisher/iphistory.html

Fisher, W.W., III. (2001). *Digital music: Problems and possibilities.* Retrieved on December 14, 2001 from the World Wide Web: http://www.law.harvard.edu/Academic_Affairs/coursepages/tfisher/music.html

Fishman, D. (1999). The promise and perils of cyberlaw: Taking communication law research to the next level. *Free Speech Yearbook, 37,* 83-106.

Gailey, E.A. (1996). Who owns digital rights? Examining the scope of copyright protection for electronically distributed works. *Communication and Law, 18,* 3-28.

Gibson, W. (1984). *Neuromancer,* New York: Berkeley.

Ginsburg, J. (1995). Putting cars on the "information superhighway": Authors, exploiters, and copyright in cyberspace. *Columbia Law Review, 95,* 1466-1499.

Goldstein, P. (1994). *Copyright's highway.* New York: Hill & Wang.

Gordon, W.J. (1982). Fair use as market failure. A structural and economic analysis of the *Betamax* case and its predecessors. *Columbia Law Review, 82,* 1600-1657.

Gordon, W.J. (1997). On the economics of copyright, restitution, and "fair use": Systemic versus case-by-case responses to market failure. *Journal of Law and Information Science, 8,* 7-45.

James, W. (1912). *Essays in radical empiricism.* London: Longmans, Green.

Katsh, M.E. (1995). *Law in a digital world.* New York: Oxford University Press.

Kaye, B.K., & Medoff, N.J. (2001). *The World Wide Web: A mass communication perspective.* Mountain View, CA: Mayfield.

Kelly v. Arriba Soft Corp. 77 F. Supp. 2d 1116. (Central District of CA). (1999).

Kravis, R. (1993). Does a song by any other name still sound as sweet?: Digital sampling and its copyright implications. *The American University Law Review, 43,* 231-276.

Lardner, J. (1987). *Fast forward.* New York: Norton.

Lessig, L. (2001). *The future of ideas: The fate of the commons in a connected world.* New York: Random House.

Levy, S. (2001, February 26). Playing fair with copyright. *Newsweek,* p. 60.

Litman, J. (1994). The exclusive right to read. *Cardozo Arts & Entertainment Law Journal, 13,* 29-54.

Litman, J. (2001). *Digital copyright.* Amherst, NY: Prometheus Books.

Los Angeles Times v. Free Republic, 54 U.S.P.Q.2d 1453. (C.D. CA). (2000).

MAI System Corp v. Peak Computer, 991 F. 2d 511. (Ninth Circuit). (1993).

Mazer v. Stein, 347 U.S. 201. (1954).

Nimmer, D. (1996). Brains and other paraphernalia of the digital age. *Harvard Journal of Law & Technology, 10*, 1-46.

O'Rourke, M. (1994). Proprietary rights in digital data. *Federal Bar News and Journal, 41*, 511-517.

Pacific & Southern Co. v. Duncan, 744 F. 2d 1490 (11th Circuit). (1984).

Playboy, Inc. v. Frena, 839 F. Supp. (M.D. FL). (1993).

Pool, I. (1983). *Technologies of freedom*. Cambridge: Belknap Press.

Princeton University Press v. Michigan Document Services, 1996 U.S. App. Lexis 29132; 1996 Federal Appeals 0357 (6th Circuit). (1996).

Rose, L. (1994). Is copyright dead on the net? *Wired*, pp. 112-113.

Samuels, E. (2000). *The illustrated story of copyright*. New York: Thomas Dunne Books of St. Martin's Press.

Samuelson, P. (1990). Digital media and the changing face of intellectual property. *Rutgers Computer and Technology Law Journal, 16*, 323-340.

Samuelson, P. (1994). Will the copyright office be obsolete in the twenty-first century. *Cardozo Arts & Entertainment Law Journal, 13*, 55-68.

Samuelson, P. (1996, January). The copyright grab. *Wired*, 135-138, 188, 190, 191.

Samuelson, P. (2000). *Economic and constitutional influences on copyright law in the United States*. Retrieved on February 20, 2002 from the World Wide Web: http://www.sims.berkeley.edu/~pam/papers/Weet&Maxwell_1.htm

Schwartz, E. (1994). The role of the copyright office in the age of information. *Cardozo Arts & Entertainment Law Journal, 13*, 69-79.

Sony Corporation of America v. Universal City Studios, 464 U.S. 414. (1984).

Straubhaar J., & LaRose, R. (2002). *Media now: Communication media in the information age*. Belmont, CA: Wadsworth.

Stuckey, K.D. (1996). *Internet online law*. New York: Law Journal Seminar Press.

Universal City Studios v. Reimerdes, 2000 U.S. Lexis 11696. (2000).

Universal City Studios v. Reimerdes, U.S. Court of Appeals, 2nd Circuit, Docket Number 00-9185. (2001). Retrieved on February 20, 2001 from the World Wide Web: http://www.law.harvard.edu/Academic_Affairs/coursepages/tfisher/2001 Reimerdes.html

Weisgrau, R. (1994). The copyright office: A proposed direction. *Cardozo Arts & Entertainment Law Journal, 13*, 81-87.

White Paper. (1995). *Information infrastructure task force, intellectual property group and the national information infrastructure: The report of the working group on intellectual property rights*. Washington, DC.

Williams & Wilkins Co. v. the United States, 487 F. 2d 1345. (1973).

Yen, A.C. (2000). Internet service provider liability for subscriber copyright infringement, enterprise liability, and the First Amendment. *Georgetown Law Review, 88*, 1833-1893.

Zoellick, B. (2002). *CyberRegs: A business guide to web property, privacy, and patents*. Boston: Addison-Wesley.

10

Music And The Internet

Some Thoughts from a Copyright Perspective

Bruce E. Colfin
Five Towns College

Jeffrey E. Jacobson
Five Towns College

Naspter, KaZaa, Gnutella, Morpheus, programs for downloading or peer to peer file sharing are known to many but the legal realities and challenges and understood by few. The issue of intellectual property rights and the downloading and copying of music retains center stage as an issue receiving attention in "cyberlaw." Bruce Colfin and Jeffrey Jacobson, attorneys practicing in this area, explore how the popularity of the Internet has stimulated creativity and commercial uses of the medium. They consider how those in the creative rights industries such as music publishers, sound recording companies, composers, writers, musicians, photographers have engaged on numerous legal fronts in seeking to protect the use of their property interests.

Just a few short years ago, prior to the proliferation of personal computers into our daily lives, the Internet was primarily an educational and research tool used by colleges and universities for storage and access of data, by some government agencies, commodities brokers, and by research analysts in the scope of their employment to seek and retrieve information for numerous purposes.

In the ensuing years, leaps in technology were made available to computer users and thus the nature of the Internet changed. The combination of easy access to numerous media resources that were not previously readily available had created a new medium that made it possible to distribute information and data worldwide. Depending on the speed of the computer being used, the data can be accessed almost instantaneously without any loss of quality. This data and information include audio, visual, news, and entertainment (such as music and video), and is reliant on intellectual property in many media formats. Programs or entities such as Napster, Gnutella, and KaZaa are examples of how music aficionados, primarily young but not necessarily so, have been able to access all sorts of recorded music by a few clicks of a computer mouse and some patience. With the inclusion of a recordable CD-ROM drive in that same computer, the music fan can make his or her own compilation of favorite tunes, from Blink 182 and Eminem to Frank Sinatra or Tchaikovsky's 1812 Overture. For the younger set, there is Bonzi Buddy, a program that says good morning to the child, engages the child in conversation, and other items, promotional and educational, through his or her session at the computer. Bonzi says goodnight or goodbye on signoff.

The popularity of the Internet for home users created a boom of creativity and commerciality. Information, data, recorded music and performances, video, and other visual images have all become available for sale, trade, and in many instances seemingly free for the taking. The industry surrounding the use of the Internet has sprung up so fast that U.S. government authorities have had a hard time determining when and if new regulations are necessary. With technology changing on a regular basis, and access to all sorts of information and intellectual property becoming increasingly easier to appropriate without authorization, it has become a challenge to figure out what is right for all the interested parties.

One view is from those users who believe in an almost nonproprietary vision of using whatever is available to them on the Internet without seeking permission from, or paying a fee to the owners of the intellectual property being used. This "wild west" concept concerning the Internet violates many of our traditional notions of intellectual property. This is a global phenomena, although for the purposes of this chapter, we focus on the U.S. perspective.

Another view is from the industries and creators that earn money from third-party use of intellectual property: music publishers, sound recording companies, literary writers and publishers, photographers, libraries, musicians, researchers, songwriters, and other creators or owners of intellectual property. To a great extent, the creative rights industries believe they have had very little time to protect themselves or to regulate the use of their property interests on the Internet. Hence, these industries believe the unfettered use of their rights by those holding the nonproprietary view adversely affects their property interests and income earning ability.

It was only natural for the music and entertainment industries to be impacted by the concerns generated by the co-mingling of new technology and communications. One party's freedom to access a multitude of information, music, or art is to be considered with another party's right to protect their proprietary rights to that information, music, or art. Along with a party's right to protect is the right to exploit and license for monetary gain, or to refrain from doing so. The Copyright Act of 1976 (effective January 1, 1978) did not anticipate the frenzy surrounding the Internet. With the Internet, a vast amount of information was suddenly available with a few keystrokes to masses of end users including those for commercial, educational, political, and artistic purposes, to name a few.

COPYRIGHT LAW

Although the Copyright Act applies to musical and artistic creative works posted or accessed on the Internet, pertinent legislation with specific regard to musical works and sound recordings was not drafted to suit the needs of the new digital medium. In the realm of music, creative artists have seen and heard their work posted or accessed legally and illegally. Recording, publishing, and media companies, some on a global scale, have an abiding economic interest in the use and access of the Internet for the exploitative use, and sometimes abuse, of intellectual property rights.

In order to firmly grasp the all-encompassing effects that the Internet has on the music industry, there must first be an examination of the provisions of the Copyright Act (17 United States Code, Sections 101, et seq).

"A work is 'created' when it is fixed in a copy or phonorecord for the first time . . . ."[1] What is commonly considered to be a piece of music may consist of two elements. One is the underlying musical composition and the other is a sound recording. The musical work is the product that is created by the writing of a composition or piece of music: the lyrics, notes, and music actually composed by the songwriter. A musical sound recording is derived from the musical work or composition being joined with musicians, instruments, and perhaps vocalists, and the resulting performance is embodied, encoded, or recorded on some physical medium that has the ability of being decoded and played back. The sound recording is the medium on which a sound can be heard when we play a compact disc (CD), cassette, or record album. When we turn on the radio and listen to a song, it is the sound recording that is being performed or broadcast on the air. The distinction between the two, one being the musical composition, the other being the sound recording of the composition, is often unrecognizable by laymen. Any person seeking to lawfully utilize another's musical sound recording would need to secure permission of the owners of both the sound recording and the musical composition that underlies or is embodied on that sound recording.

Provided that the work of an artist is original, the artist owns numerous exclusive rights to the work created. These rights are outlined in Section 106 of the Copyright Act, 17 USC §106.[2] These rights are limited by boundaries provided in 17 USC §114 for musical works and §115 for sound recordings. Additionally, the concept of fair use as an exception or defense to copyright infringement found in §107 is also relevant.

In addition to publicly performing his or her work live or via different communications media, a musical artist has the exclusive right to reproduce, distribute, display, make, and/or license new derivative works from the original. With these exclusive rights, a creative artist is free to license or assign any of the elements of the musical composition or sound recording to whomever he or she chooses.[3]

MUSIC LICENSING

It is not unusual for the owner of a copyright in a musical composition to differ from the owners of the copyright in the sound recording of that musical composition. Generally, on its creation, the owner of the copyright in a musical composition is the author (i.e., the songwriter, lyricist, and/or composer). Upon the creation of a sound recording, the author(s), and owner(s), of the copyright in the sound recording are considered to be the producer of the recording and the recording artist whose performance is embodied on the recording. Exceptions or variations to these generalities of authorship and ownership stem from the "Work for Hire" sections of the Copyright Act.[4] There are numerous situations in which the employer, contractor, or executive producer is considered the owner and author based on the specific requirements of the Copyright Act, the existence of an employer/employee relationship, and perhaps a pre-existing written document. It is typical for a "record" label to own the sound recording copyright whether it has been acquired through a transfer of rights or owned from the moment of creation as the result of a "work for hire" agreement.

It is also not uncommon for the owner of the copyright in the musical composition to be the owner of the copyright in the sound recording. In past years, a musical composition would be first written on paper and at a later date sound recordings would be created at no small expense in a recording studio. As technological advances in home recording facilities have become more affordable, many musical compositions are not completely written on paper first, but instead start as notes or ideas, which are more fully and originally expressed in a home studio sound recording. Thus, the distinction between musical composition and sound recording has been blurred into what today's masses consider to be a song.

In a commercial setting, it is much more common for a third party to become interested in acquiring permission from the owner of the musical composition to make a "cover" of the work by creating the sound recording. This third party is sometimes the producer of the new sound recording, and together with the performer, owns the copyright in the sound recording. The third party is often a recording or media company that hires the producer and performer, and also receives permission from the songwriter(s) to create the sound recording. That recording company either purchases the producer's and performer's rights in the sound recording copyright or may seek to own the recording from its creation as a "work for hire."

As recording companies do not regularly purchase all of the songwriters' rights, but instead receive permission to use the composition in the creation of sound recordings, it is not unusual for musical works as well as sound recordings to be licensed or sold to two or more different parties. It is sometimes a complicated process to discern who actually owns which parts of a song.

When a copyright owner issues licenses for the use of the work, he or she, in turn, generally receives or is entitled to compensation or consideration for the benefits bestowed on the user or licensee.[5] In order to better protect him or herself, and to maximize the ability to earn income, a songwriting artist generally will seek to license or transfer the musical compositions to a publishing company that will try to exploit the musical works, license the many uses to other third parties, register the copyright in the musical composition, monitor and collect the compensation, and royalties payable, and regulate the many uses of the musical composition.[6] Although many artists choose to seek a publisher to act on their behalf, the Copyright Act also protects unpublished works.[7] It is also not unusual for a songwriter (or for a producer and performer in regards to sound recordings) to completely assign and relinquish all of his or her rights to a purchaser in exchange for a one-time fee, or for an advance and so-called royalties, which are a series of payments based on sales or income earned.[8]

As mentioned earlier, it is typical for a producer or recording artist in a contract with a recording or media company to create sound recordings as "works for hire." Upon creation of the work, a sound recording created as a "work for hire" is owned by the employer. This arrangement is made prior to commencement of the creative process. There is no assignment of ownership to the record company. Nonetheless, the arrangement, which pre-exists the actual creation of the musical work, is also generally exchanged for a one-time fee or for contractually promised royalties.

Over the past few years, Congress has tried to keep up with technology and has updated the Copyright Act of 1976 in certain respects to adapt the law to the digital age. The enactment of the Digital Millenium Copyright Act exemplifies such an attempt. Through the Digital Millennium Copyright Act, online Internet service providers (ISPs) are now expressly covered under the regulations, consequences, and remedies of the Copyright law. Online ISPs, as well as record companies and radio stations must secure licenses of both the musical work and the sound recording in order to lawfully use musical works belonging to someone else.[9]

The ease of accessing and using a variety of Internet data of all types poses serious questions. For example, television commercials often portray children teaching their parents how to access the Internet to demonstrate the ease of Internet use. Well-known Yahoo.com commercials show characters of people from all walks of life to illustrate the impact a search engine can create. With a worldwide audience of millions of users, it is daunting for owners, licensees, or assignees to monitor what material is being posted, who is posting it, and whether they are doing so lawfully. However, it is difficult in some instances to determine the identities of the true copyright owner or owners of a composition or sound recording.

REPRODUCTION AND DISTRIBUTION OF MUSICAL COMPOSITIONS AND SOUND RECORDINGS

A copyright owner of a creative work in the form of a musical composition or sound recording holds the exclusive right to reproduce and distribute either work. In order to reproduce, manufacture, and distribute copies of the composition or sound recording, any other party who does not own the exclusive rights must seek and receive permission from the owner. Once the copyright owner of a musical composition embodied in a sound recording has commercially reproduced and distributed the work, any other party desiring to re-record the same musical composition in a new sound recording is permitted to do so provided that a compulsory license is acquired in compliance with the standards set forth in 17 USC §115.[10] This compulsory licensing scheme exists if the composition embodied in a sound recording is distributed.[11] As long as the musical composition is not substantially changed in the new recording, a compulsory license proscribes that a copyright holder cannot refuse to grant the license. The copyright owner of the musical composition must be placed on notice of the pending re-recording and they must receive payment via statutory guidelines[12] on that and every subsequent use in accordance with §115. Otherwise, one can expect to encounter a lawsuit for copyright infringement.

According to 17 USC § 114, a digital transmission must mimic its original exactly in order for it to be a copyright infringement.[13, 14] In two of the most recent high profile cases dealing with copyright infringement of music on the Internet, *UMG Recordings, Inc. v. MP3.com, Inc.* (92 F. Supp 2d 349) and *A&M Records Inc. v. Napster, Inc.*, (239 F.3d 1004) (discussed in more detail later), the defendants attempted to show, as a defense, that the digital transmission was different from the original. Napster and MP3.com both asserted that the alleged infringing songs were not in their original form and were therefore different from the tracks protected by the Copyright Act. Nonetheless, through questioning, the court discovered that these providers had every intention of offering a track so similar to the original so as to be mistaken for it.

By defining a digital sound recording delivery as a form of distribution, Congress has built a safeguard into the Copyright Act to give copyright owners recourse against potential illegal piracy. "A digital phonorecord delivery does not result from a real-time, non-interactive subscription transmission of a sound recording where no reproduction of the sound recording or the musical work embodied therein is made from the inception of the transmission through to its receipt."[15, 16] The key to licensing and rights clearances in the current digital arena seems to be whether the delivery to the consumer is interactive or not. This clause would include DXM and XM Satellite radio as lawful, but services such as Napster are considered to be unlawful. Providers of services like Napster are not entitled to the compulsory license provision of the Copyright Act of 1976. The Copyright Act prohibits any unlawful user the right to secure a compulsory license. Because providers like Napster and Morpheus are using both musical works and sound recordings for which they have not requested permission and are doing so via interactive digital communication with its subscribers and users, they are unlawfully using someone else's work without required licenses and are therefore not allowed to obtain a compulsory license.[17]

PUBLIC PERFORMANCE OF MUSICAL COMPOSITIONS AND SOUNDS RECORDING

Public performances of a musical composition or sound recording work are most performances through which people can hear the performance of the work. This includes any transmission medium, including live performances, radio, electronic, or digital transmission. In order to acquire permission to publicly perform a published musical composition, a performance rights license must be obtained from the owner of the copyright in the musical composition or from a performing rights society to which the copyright owner has granted those rights on its behalf (i.e., in the United States, ASCAP, BMI, or SESAC).[18] These major performing rights societies have developed licensing agreements, including ones for online uses, that cover all the musical compositions in their catalogues. The performing rights license agreements require payment of fees and royalties. To make the process easier, these three most important U.S. performing rights societies offer blanket licenses that allow a prospective user to pay a periodic rate in exchange for use of the society's entire catalogue of musical compositions.

Until 1995, the Copyright Act of 1976 provided no protection or recourse for owners of copyrights in sound recordings from unlawful public performances of their sound recordings. In 1995, Congress passed the Digital Performance in Sound Recording Act (DPSRA), which granted limited performance rights to copyrights of sound recordings. The DPSRA provided that digital audio interactive and on-demand transmissions (i.e., Napster, Gnutella) required a discretionary license that gave copyright owners of sound recordings discretion as to whether they would or would not grant permission.

With emerging noninteractive subscription services like DXM, and XM Satellite channel,[19] regulation within the Copyright Act creates an ambiguous dichotomy between interactive services and noninteractive services. Although not yet resolved, at this time Congress seems to be leaning toward treating the licensing of sound recordings through noninteractive providers in a similar manner to the regulations in common radio broadcast transmission. These Internet-based subscription services may find themselves subject to the necessity of acquiring a compulsory blanket-license by paying a periodic rate to the owners of sound recordings.[20] The DPSRA provides that the authority to grant a license for the public performance of a sound recording via a digital interactive medium, like Napster or Morpheus, lies with the owner of the sound recording. Although the power to grant licenses belongs to the owner of the sound recording, if the online provider of a noninteractive service complies with the provisions as set forth in Section 115 of the Copyright Act, the copyright owner "cannot refuse to grant a license nor set a different rate."[21] Blanket licenses are presently available for noninteractive digital performance of sound recordings.

The debate is ongoing as to whether radio stations that stream their broadcasts, or Internet services that provide a similar online service, should be subject to the same type of blanket licenses that traditional radio stations pay.[22] For the right to use musical compositions, radio stations currently pay licensing fees to the performing rights societies for the composer, lyricist, and publishing companies. The Copyright Arbitration Royalty Panel (CARP) proposes different rates be set for those radio stations that broadcast their music via the Internet and those Internet services that provide digital radio services.[22] The fees are to be divided between the artist and the record label. The fees are to be provided directly to the owners of sound recording copyrights rather than the publishing companies of the underlying musical compositions. This area of law is currently in tremendous flux and is the subject of serious debate. Both the Recording Industry Association of America (RIAA) and Pulver.com placed advertisements espousing their relative positions in *Billboard Magazine*. Broadcast radio stations that stream music online find this particularly unfair. They already pay a blanket license to perform those recordings via radio broadcast transmission and therefore feel this is a duplication of fees for the same rights to perform.

DEFENSES AGAINST ALLEGATIONS OF INFRINGEMENT FOR UNLICENSED USE

The Copyright Act provides various defenses to the possibility of copyright infringement lawsuits. One doctrine that has been used in rebutting allegations of copyright infringement is the Fair Use Doctrine. The Fair Use Doctrine is outlined in 17 USC § 107.[23] This section of the Copyright Act states four essential elements that courts look to as guidance when deciding whether or not a particular nonlicensed use of copyrighted material qualifies for exemption from a copyright infringement action. Courts will look to (a) the purpose and character of the use, including whether such use is of a commercial nature or is for nonprofit educational purposes; (b) the nature of the copyrighted work; (c) the amount and substantiality of the portion used in relation to the copyrighted work as a whole; and (d) the effect of the use on the potential market for or value of the copyrighted work. As the notes to this section indicate, these elements are not individually ultimate. They are used as a guideline for courts to follow when deciding whether or not the Fair Use Doctrine is applicable. No one element is determinative. The Copyright Act codifies the pre-existing case law concerning fair use, and the federal courts draw their interpretation from precedent. Fair use was asserted by both *A&M Records, Inc. v. Napster, Inc.* (239 F. 3d 1004) and *UMG Recordings v. MP3.com, Inc.* (92 F. Supp 2d 349) in their defenses to the charges brought by the various record labels against them.

In addition to the fair use defense, the Copyright Act may offer a nonlicensed user of copyrighted sound recordings protection under the First Sale

Doctrine. The Copyright Act offers the legitimate owner of a copy of a sound recording the opportunity to freely pass ownership of the sound recording to another party without the copyright owner's authority. However, if the owner of a sound recording has taken control of the sound recording without proper permission, he or she is not legally entitled to it, thereby making it illegal for him or her to pass on the copy.[24] This effectively takes the case out of the realm of the First Sale Doctrine. 17 U.S.C. § 109 (a) states, "Notwithstanding provisions of section 106 (3) the owner of a particular copy or phonorecord lawfully made under this title, or any person authorized by such owner, is entitled, without authority of copyright owner to sell or otherwise dispose of the possession of that copy."[25, 26] An owner of a copy of a sound recording must have acquired the copy lawfully. According to basic contract law, to acquire something lawfully that is not a gift, there must be sufficient consideration. If a subscriber has downloaded a sound recording that has been legitimately paid for, then consideration exists, the transaction is lawful, and ownership of the sound recording copy may be transferred to whomever. However, if this subscriber does not pay for the sound recording, it may not have been legally obtained and seemingly cannot be passed on lawfully. Additionally, if conditions are attached which permit the purchase of a download but prohibit the duplication of the sound recording, then by contract, the First Sale Doctrine may be avoided.

The recent debates on the future of the music industry and the Internet have illustrated significant differences in opinion by recording artists, record companies, and the people who use the Internet to create access to music. It is not uncommon for recording artists to be ambivalent about the possibility of earning royalties from the use of sound recordings accessible from the Internet because contractually it is typical for the payments to go to the recording companies rather than the recording artists. The income earned from Internet usage of sound recordings rarely trickle down to the recording artists unless the artists control their own sound recordings and musical compositions.

Artists with negative feelings about the Internet and the rapidly expanding world of downloadable music have experienced much media exposure. Antagonized by providers such as MyMP3.com, Napster, and others, who in their eyes do not pay any fees for allowing others access to the music, many also look suspiciously at the end users. For example, by voicing their opinions as to the piracy of their music via the Internet, Metallica became a household name to those of a younger generation who may have missed out on their music. There are numerous fan-driven Web sites and fanzines residing on the Web. Some well-known recording acts have sought to close down such unauthorized fan sites.

However, many artists, both famous and rising, enjoy the publicity that the Internet provides. Many recording artists even reach out and extend links to fan sites. The Internet reaches a larger potential fan base than any national or international publicity tour can spawn. It offers a new medium for more famous bands to beta-test their new music. For smaller, unsigned bands, it is a source of publicity unmatched by any flier posted on the bulletin board at the local high school. Relatively inexpensive, as most Internet providers offer free Web sites with the subscription fees to their services, through diligent planning and execution, bands can access a worldwide fan base. Unsigned bands may now receive income from record sales whereas 10 years ago, without a record contract, any record sale would have been virtually impossible.

Within the last 5 years, recording artists have seen the increased audience they have achieved via the Internet, but they have not yet reaped the benefits of their work. Recent retail sales figures show an actual decline in music sales for the first time in over 10 years.[27] Record companies provide large amounts of initial capital to create the music that is being both purchased and downloaded. Significant sums of money are expended in the actual recording process in addition to the packaging, marketing, and promoting of the product. In order to continue the creation of new music that keeps their newly found audience satiated, the artist and record company must receive some capital return on their investment. Recording companies expect to create a product that the consumer will purchase and enjoy. By reversing these two actions (enjoying first then possibly purchasing), potential purchasers can delay, frustrate, decrease, and possibly negate the income return that recording companies need to reinvest into the artist to create subsequent albums.

The Internet provides the perfect platform for prospective purchasers to search for their favorite song and select only that song for their recordable disc or computer download. No longer do consumers have to pay $18.99 for an entire CD by one particular artist with only two or three hit songs on it. Some consumers characterize this as tolerable. The online availability of music has heavily hit the younger generation who prior to such technological advances were responsible for significant numbers of sound recording purchases.

It was Jacobson's son who, as a preteen many years ago, taught the authors about MP3s. Colfin's son, at age 11, laments the demise of Napster and its access to thousands of songs. To the dismay of the recording industry, they believe that access to music on the Internet has kept fans, as consumers, out of record stores and kept them tied to the computer where music is free.

During the 2001 Grammy Awards, Michael Greene, former president of the National Academy of Recording Arts and Sciences, conducted a study. He asked three students to download as many songs as they could in 2 days. The students managed to grab 6,000 songs.[28] To the recording companies, those are relatively scary numbers. If each song downloaded for free is substituted for a possible in-store purchase at retail prices, the potential dollars lost, per student, is substantial.

With the lawsuits between record companies and online webcasters generating much media coverage, the publicity surrounding the newest technologies has sparked curiosity in even the most computer illiterate population. The popularity of the online services has grown both through word of mouth from teenagers and young adults as well as through the publicity engendered from the lawsuits, thereby expanding the unknowing pirate audience.[29] The publicity also demonstrates to providers how easily this can be done. Hence, the record companies are stuck in a conundrum; by pulling free music offline, they are losing their fan base via self-imposed boycott. However, by providing their catalogue online for free, record companies are losing funds to create more music and to sign more future stars. Who will win the war between the record companies and the online music providers when they both need each other in order to function?

During the 1980s, the cassette copy posed a similarly perceived threat to the record industry, but not anywhere near the scope of the perceived current problem. The copy resulting on the cassette was not of high enough quality to compete with the master quality of sound recordings. However, with the onset of digital audio transmission (DAT) devices, the record industry saw near perfect quality copies regardless of generation.[30] Initially thought to be a technology to be used primarily in the record industry, the popularity of the DAT, due to its size and sound capacity, gained popularity. Unlike cassette tapes where quality diminished after each recording, DAT technology allowed for perfect digital quality every time the product was duplicated. This opened a door to the general consumer, working contrary to the recording industry.

Within 5 years, the music industry, working with the manufacturers of these digital machines, artists, publishers and the legislature, limited the infringing and dangerous power of the DAT by enacting the At Home Recording Act (AHRA). Encompassed in 17 U.S.C. 1001, AHRA provides compensation, from both manufacturers and distributors of the digital recording devices and software, to the affected parties, being artists, record labels and copyright owners, in exchange for "immunity from copyright infringement" liability.[31] AHRA mandates that a Serial Copy Management System or similar technology protect each machine providing digital audiorecording capabilities. The mechanism recognizes whether the copy being made is a first-generation or subsequent generation. AHRA permits only first-generation recordings. If found to be generating a second-generation copy, the technology inhibits the user from making such a recording.[32]

With reasonable ease, the music industry was able to slow the progression of music piracy via DAT mechanisms through legislation after negotiation between the lobbying powers, the RIAA and the Electronic Industry Association (EIA). There is a significant difference in technology between DAT devices and the Internet, which made it easier for the companies and copyright proprietors to legislate and legitimize the DAT revolution. For example, DAT machines were and still are expensive. Furthermore, the DAT community is not as global as that of the Internet. It is a limited community of people who can afford the hardware and software of the technology. Whether or not people have home computers, they can have access to the Internet in schools, libraries, and even public "Internet cafes." The popularity of the Internet has grown so quickly and to such an extent that the entertainment industry has found it almost uncontrollable.

At first, the Internet was not considered a threat to major media industries because it was too slow. The technology had not yet developed. However, in response to public demand, technology has greatly improved. People can now get almost anything they are looking for and more within a matter of seconds. For example, www.google.com shows that complex searches will require less than 30 seconds to find matches. Searches do not require much online computer knowledge. Current Internet access, available by cable, fiber optic, and DSL lines, is fast; the future of broadband promises to be faster.

There are many systems available that have contributed to the turmoil of the music industry and the Copyright Act. Currently, various technologies are at the forefront of the online music debate. For those looking to post and download music, there is streaming, digital downloading, MP3 and peer-to-peer file sharing.[33] Streaming is a live feed of music over the Internet from site to logged on user(s). It is technologically difficult for a user to make a copy while in stream. The audio quality of a stream is generally a lower grade than that which you would expect to find on a commercially released compact disc. Products such as Pressplay utilize this method of digital transmission.

Digital downloadable files are audio files, many having CD sound quality.[33] These files may be kept and replayed once downloaded. MP3 is a faster technology that compresses signals and allows users to download CD quality music in only one tenth the time of the former technologies. MP3 files can be easily transferred or E-mailed to users or prospective listeners. The software needed to run MP3 files is available for free on the Internet. Peer-to-peer file sharing utilizes MP3 technology, allowing users to search each other's hard drives and upload the songs they are seeking. These providers, such as Napster and, more recently, KaZaa, furnish the platform or the software that, in turn, enables users to accomplish this task.[33]

The new technologies have spawned numerous lawsuits brought by record companies in efforts to keep music piracy at a minimum. One of the first cases that dealt with the liability of Internet services to record companies and artists was *UMG Recordings, Inc. v. MP3.com*.[34] In this federal district court case, MyMP3.com offered a service to subscribers that allowed listeners to hear (and copy) the music they had ostensibly formerly downloaded wherever they obtained an Internet connection. In order to provide this service, My.MP3.com purchased thousands of CDs and posted, without permission, the tracks on the site for download. The Web site first asked the user to prove his or her ownership of the music on the sound recordings by either loading the CD into their CD-ROM player or by purchasing an actual CD from a MyMP3.com affiliate.

In the *MyMP3.com* case, the court held "in actuality defendant is replaying for the subscribers converted versions of the recordings it copies, without authorization from plaintiff's copyrighted CDs."[34] My.MP3.com asserted two defenses in the Copyright action against them: (a) the available sound recordings were not identical to those available on compact disc and therefore not actionable under 17 USC 114,[35] and (b) the Fair Use Doctrine applied. Moreover, MyMP3.com also admitted "a goal of its copying to create a music file that is sonically as identical to the original CD as possible." MyMP3.com also asserted "fair use" in order to defend against causes of action for copyright infringement.

The District Court in the Southern District of New York analyzed each of the four elements to be considered when 'fair use' is asserted and denied the defendant exoneration from the infringement action under the defense of fair use. The District Court also decided that whatever differences in the sound recordings was not enough of a deviation to qualify for the exception under Section 114. In summary, the recording company plaintiffs received their desired verdict of partial summary judgment.[36]

Since the decision of *UMG Recordings, Inc. v. MP3.com* was handed down, MP3.com has settled its disputes out of court for $53.4 million. Subsequent to that time, MP3.com was acquired by Vivendi Universal. It is also significant to note that MP3.com filed suit against its lawyers in *UMG Recordings v. MP3.com* for malpractice.[37] MP3.com asserts that they relied on their law firm's strong advice that MP3.com was not committing any wrongdoing due to fair use considerations. The court found otherwise and held MP3.com liable.

One of the most infamous and ongoing cases in the entertainment industry, *A&M Records, Inc. v. Napster, Inc.* (239 F. 3d 1004), has excited the interests of thousands, from technology buffs to the basic computer user. Perhaps an example of the American dream, a 19-year-old can start an Internet company through which subscribers can share MP3 files via peer-to-peer file sharing.[38] Napster's technology provided a platform through which users could search all subscribers' MP3 files, copy the files, download the track to their hard drive, make copies of MP3 files and/or store them for future use. The software necessary (much like that which was necessary in the MyMP3.com case above) was available on the Internet for free. The District Court enjoined Napster "from engaging in, or facilitating others in, copyright, downloading, uploading, transmitting or distributing copyrighted sound recordings in accordance with this Order."[39]

Less than a year later, the U.S. Court of Appeals for the Ninth Circuit held off enforcing that injunction. The Court of Appeals for the Ninth Circuit agreed with the District Court on just about every aspect of the trial court decision but decided that the District Court decision injunction terms were "overbroad."[40] The Court of Appeals placed the burden on the plaintiffs to notify Napster as to the tracks to which it owned copyright, leaving Napster the responsibility to remove these tracks from accessibility. The Court of Appeals stated, "The mere existence of the Napster system, absent actual notice and Napster's demonstrated failure to remove the offending material, is insufficient to impose contributory liability."[40]

Judge Marilyn Hall Patel, in *A&M Records, Inc. v. Napster, Inc.* (239 F. 3d 1004), granted the record companies a 30-day cooling off period in a "halt to the case to pursue settlement talks more vigorously."[41] Although there are conflicting views as to why the record companies requested the delay, one reason cited by Judge Patel was that Napster should be able to investigate the defense of copyright misuse by the record labels. By asserting that the alleged copyright misuse of Napster was so broad and extensive it placed the record companies under scrutiny for asserting ownership over music tracks that perhaps did not belong to the labels. It is common knowledge amongst entertainment business lawyers that the big record companies are somewhat lax in their efforts to register the copyrights of sound recordings. Just as the big record companies were just getting comfortable and feeling they had secured a victory for the general industry, Federal Judge Marilyn Hall Patel startled them back into a state of anxiety.

Napster petitioned the court to allow for further discovery, calling into question the legitimacy of ownership that the record companies had been asserting throughout the life of this trial. Judge Patel ordered the record companies involved in the suit to produce documentation indicating ownership to each of the songs they had requested Napster remove.[42] This came as quite a shock to the record industry as some of its members had settled and others were in settlement talks with Napster. Facing bankruptcy, Napster has been acquired by the Bertelsmann Music Group.

After it gains permission from the other recording labels to distribute music, Napster plans to launch a subscription service. Federal Judge Marilyn Hall Patel is also concerned, from a collusion point of view, with the sudden desire for the labels to work together, pursuing the deals respectively with Pressplay and MusicNet.

Like a weed, record industries could liken the online music sharing providers to the pesky plants. Pull one out and another will grow in its place. Morpheus was once thought to be the next Napster. Morpheus is currently engaging in the addition of digital rights management to its services. It also prophesizes to be a marketing forum for independent bands worldwide. In an upgrade they gained the permissions of various independent bands to distribute their music. Steve Griffin, CEO of Morpheus owner StreamCast, says, "I think we are a distribution network and a way to create a level playing field" in the industry.[43] In an international forum, the peer-to-peer license sharing program KaZaA BV gained an important hold over music copyright organization Buma/Stemra. In the process, the Court of Appeals in Amsterdam, Netherlands stated that the users of the provider, not the provider itself, commit the acts of infringement.

The Internet is an inevitable necessity to almost every business within the entertainment and music industries. Business owners have options when it comes to the acceptance of the Internet into the marketplace. They can embrace it and work together with the online providers or they can avoid it and stick strictly to that which they have known to work in the past. The record industry has expended much of its resources to fight for what it collectively perceives as its rights. Amidst the litigation, record companies have also managed to introduce technology that gives promise to someday be able to control music piracy. Of the plausible technologies, digital rights management (DRM) seems to be the most rapidly developing MP3 control advancement. DRM systems provide a means for companies who retain Copyright interests to monitor the "encryption and capture of content; distribution and asset management" of their music.[44]

In their purest forms, these systems should protect material from unauthorized users. The systems should also monitor who is purchasing the product, how it is being purchased and how it is being used. One model by Interact involves a licensing scheme that allows a user to transfer a file to another, but the original user must first gain a license.[44] Some systems have already emerged and they continue to grow into an all inclusive information rights management system. However, the technology is still young and expensive. These newly emerging technologies are protected by the Copyright Act § 512 that makes hacking into these systems in efforts to find a means around them an illegal act.

In efforts of their own, major record labels and publishing houses are seeking ways to charge Internet consumers for the use of online music. On December 13, 2001, the RIAA and various others supported by ASCAP and BMI came to a proposed resolution regarding online subscription service which limited each download to only 30 days, and restricted the consumer from having the ability to download or copy the track.[45]

Record companies are banding together (Sony Music and Universal; AOL Time Warner and EMI) to introduce similar technologies via their PressPlay and MusicNet services.[46] These services are similarly limited in what the subscriber can do with them. For example, Pressplay launched in December 2001 allows its consumers to purchase downloads through a set pricing structure (i.e., the Basic plan $9.95 for 300 streams and 30 downloads). However, consumer downloads will only last 30 days wherein the consumer must pay again, and these downloads are not transferable to MP3 players.[47] Furthermore, since the vast catalogue was one of the most appealing qualities of projects like Napster and MP3.com, record companies are still limiting the catalogue available via the online subscription services.[46] Although Pressplay contends that they will be offering a wider range of tracks in the future, right now they are still in their experimental phase. Programs such as Pressplay and MusicNet will likely experience opposition from those Internet users who enjoyed their free downloads.

Most of the big five record companies are working on some sort of DRM that involves copy protecting and "watermarking" their CDs against file sharing via the Internet. Many record labels that have exercised such regulation have already failed at their initial attempts and are now working on a revision of the initial service. Consumers complain that they cannot play the CDs on their computer, despite warning that they will not be able to do this. Earlier this year, Universal Music Group released the soundtrack to *The Fast and The Furious* containing a warning label, "This CD purported copy protected technology which would not allow users to copy the CD."[48] The RIAA is calling this protection necessary in order to combat the downloads, which are causing a decline in record sales.[49] Virginia Senator Rick Boucher says that this copy protection technology could be in violation of the AHRA. The AHRA, he said, gives people the right to copy the CDs once they have been purchased in line with the First Sale Doctrine.

Some radio station Web sites allow listeners to log on and listen to what they are currently playing as if they had just turned on the radio. A relatively new technology has made its way onto the cyber playing field. Although still in its test phases, BitBop technology serves as a notice to legislators that any combination of things is possible. BitBop technology allows listeners to choose what song they would like to hear, then search through the Internet to find a radio station that is playing that song at that moment. The song is then sent to the computer.

The people in the record industry came out fighting when they saw a decline in sales. They were looking for someone to blame and found a global community full of the products that they had created, but for which they had yet to be paid. Rather than embracing the Internet for possibilities it could bring to their marketplace, the record industry attacked with all the assets that it had: its money. Although record companies have been slow to realize, they are finally coming around. They are looking to harness the use of the products that are rightfully theirs in order to make consumers, online providers, artists, and themselves content. This is a very precarious balance, especially taking into consideration that the consumer is accustomed to getting this product for free. However, through legislation, technology, and recent history, it seems as if these many facets of the same industry may finally operate hand in hand. As of this writing, the music industry has seen two consecutive years of at least ten percent reductions in sales income. Perhaps the publishing and recording companies will collaborate on realistic internet licensing. As recently as October 2002 a major label licensed its catalogue of sound recordings for internet downloads to another record label owned service. This may be the harbinger of a more long-term view of progress and cooperation which we hope would lead to more prosperity for all the parties involved.

ACKNOWLEDGEMENT

Bruce E. Colfin and Jeffrey E. Jacobson with the able assistance of Alyssa C. Clark, New York Law School 2004. © 2002 Jacobson & Colfin, P.C.

NOTES

1. 17 USC §101. A work is "created" when it is fixed in a copy or phonorecord for the first time; where a work is prepared over a period of time, the portion of it that has been fixed at any particular time constitutes the work as of that time, and where the work has been prepared in different versions, each version constitutes a separate work.
2. 17 USC §106. Subject to sections 107 through 120, the owner of copyright under this title has the exclusive rights to do and to authorize any of the following:
    (1) To reproduce the copyrighted work in copies or phonorecords
    (2) To distribute copies or phonorecords of the copyrighted work to the public by sale or other transfer or ownership, or by rental, lease or lending
    (5) In the case of literary, musical, dramatic and choreographic works . . . to display the copyrighted work publicly
3. 17 USC § 101. "A "transfer of copyright ownership" is an assignment, mortgage, exclusive license, or any other conveyance, alienation or hypothecation of a copyright or of any of the exclusive rights comprised in a copyright, whether or not it is limited in time or place of effect, but not including a nonexclusive license.
4. 17 USC § 101. "A Work Made for hire" is (1) a work prepared by an employee within the scope of his or her employment.
5. Hoffman, Kristine J. "Fair Use or Fair Game? The Internet MP3 and Copyright Law. 11*Alt. L. J. Sci & Tech* 153, 164.

6. I. Fred Koenigsberg, David E. Case and Stefan Mentzer, "Music, the Internet, and the Music Industry" Practicing Law Institute Intellectual Property, volume 640, p. 20.

7. 17USC 104 (a). Unpublished works. The works specified by sections 102 and 103 (17 USCS Sects 102 and 103) while unpublished, are subject to protection under this title (17 USCS).

8. Hoffman, Kristine J. "Fair Use or Fair Game? The Internet MP3 and Copyright Law." 11*Alt. L. J. Sci & Tech* 153, 163.

9. I. Fred Koenigsberg, David E. Case and Stefan Mentzer, "Music, the Internet, and the Music Industry" Practicing Law Institute Intellectual Property, volume 640, p. 20.

10. 17 USC § 115 Scope of exclusive rights in nondramatic musical works: Compulsory license for making and distributing phonorecords.

11. 17 USC §115 (c) (2) "for this purpose, a phonorecord is considered "distributed" if the person exercising the compulsory license has voluntarily and permanently parted with its possession. –11

12. William Sloan Coats, Heather D. Rafter, Vickie L. Feeman, John G. Given. "Streaming into the Future: Music and Video Online" 670 PLI/Pat 119 132, 2001.

13. Fred Koenigsberg, David E. Case and Stefan Mentzer, "Music, the Internet, and the Music Industry" (find citation), p. 22.

14. 17 USC § 114(b)(2). "The exclusive rights of the owner of copyright in a sound recording under clauses (1) and (2) of section 106 do not extend to the making or duplication of another sound recordings that consist entirely of an independent fixation of other sounds, even though such sounds imitate or simulate those in the copyrighted sound recording."

15. 17 U.S.C. 115 (d).

16. 17 U.S.C. (j) (7). "An "interactive service" is one that enables a member of the public to receive a transmission of a program specially created for the recipient, or on request a transmission of a particular sound recording, whether or not as part of a program, which is selected by or on behalf of the recipient."

17. Fred Koenigsberg, David E. Case and Stefan Mentzer, "Music, the Internet, and the Music Industry" (find citation), p. 21

18 www.ASCAP.com

19. William Sloan Coats, Heather D. Rafter, Vickie L. Feeman, John G. Given. "Streaming into the Future: Music and Video Online" 670 PLI/Pat119. 2001.

20. Hearn, Edward R. "Music The Internet: Special Problems and Emerging Solutions". 631 PLI/Pat 1285,1299.

21. William Sloan Coats, Heather D. Rafter, Vickie L. Feeman, John G. Given. "Streaming into the Future: Music and Video Online" 670 PLI/Pat119. 2001.

22. Joe D'Angelo. "Online Radio Facing Possible Extinction." SonicNet Music. 2/26/02.http://story.news,yahoo.com/news?tmpl=story &u=/020226/77/16f48.html&cid=85

23. 17 USC 107. Limitations on exclusive rights: Fair Use.

24. William Sloan Coats, Heather D. Rafter, Vickie L. Feeman, John G. Given. "Streaming into the Future: Music and Video Online" 670 PLI/Pat119. 2001.

25. 17 U.S.C. § 109 (a). "Notwithstanding provisions of section 106(3) the owner of a particular copy or phonorecord lawfully made under this title, or any person authorized by such owner, is entitled, without authority of copyright owner to sell or otherwise dispose of the possession of that copy…"

26. William Sloan Coats, Heather D. Rafter, Vickie L. Feeman, John G. Given. "Streaming into the Future: Music and Video Online" 670 PLI/Pat119. 2001 (pg?)]

27. MSNBC Staff and Wire Reports "Keys, U2, 'O Brother' Top Grammys. Retrieved from www.msnbc.com/news/717051.asp?cp1=1

28. Herman, Jan, The Associated Press and Reuters, "Keys, UZ, 'O Brother; top Grammys. "www.msnbc.com/news/717051.asp?cp1=1"

29. Bill Roberts. "An Unfinished Symphony; MP3 market waits in the wings while the recording industry whistles in the dark" Electronic Business, 10/01/01, p. 1

30. William Sloan Coats, Heather D. Rafter, Vickie L. Feeman, John G. Given. "Streaming into the Future: Music and Video Online" 670 PLI/Pat119. 2001

31. William Sloan Coats, Heather D. Rafter, Vickie L. Feeman, John G. Given. "Streaming into the Future: Music and Video Online" 670 PLI/Pat119. 2001

32. 101 Colum. L. Rev. 613. "Copyright and Control Over New Technologies of Dissemination." Jane C. Ginsburg, 2001.

33. William Sloan Coats, Heather D. Rafter, Vickie L. Feeman, John G. Given. "Streaming into the Future: Music and Video Online" 670 PLI/Pat119. 2001.

34. *UMG Recordings v. MP3.com, Inc.* (92 F. Supp 2d 349, 350).

35. 17 USC 114 (b). The exclusive rights of the owner of copyright in a sound recording under clauses (1) and (2) of section 1056 do not extend to the making or duplication of another sound recording that consists entirely of an independent fixation of other sounds, even though such sound imitate or simulate those in the copyrighted sound recording.

36. *UMG Recordings v. MP3.com, Inc.* (92 F. Supp 2d 349, 352).

37. Stephanie Francis Cahill. "Dot-Come Sues Law Firm Over Advice." ABA Journal EReport, 2/1/02. www.abanet.org/journal/ereport/flmp3.html.

38. *A&M Records, Inc. v. Napster, Inc.* (239 F. 3d 1004, 1011)

39. 2001 U.S. Dist. LEXIS 2186, 3.

40. *A&M Records, Inc. v. Napster, Inc.* (239 F. 3d 1004, 1027)

41. John Borland. "Labels Dodge Scrutiny in Napster Suit" www.msnbc.com /news/697796.asp?cp1=1.

42. Associated Press. Labels to prove Copyright Ownership. www.msnbc. com/news/720510.asp?cp1=1.

43. John Borland Morpheus seeks new role in music. www.msnbc.com/ news/723930.asp.

44. Abagial Waraker. "Internet week – Digital Rights Management.; Technology and standards are improving to guard copyright material." News Service, p. 32.

45. Bill Holland "In Hearings, Cannon Urges Labels to 'Serve' Internet Consumers" Billboard, 12/22/01, p. 1.

46. Jon Pareles. "The Many Futures of Music Maybe One of Them Real." *The New York Times*, 1/10/02

47. Jim Hu. "Pressplay comes to life after long wait." CNET News.com, 12/29/01. http://news.com.com/2100-1023-277178.html.
48. Gwendolyn Mariano. New CD protection wont play on PC's. msnbc.com/2100-1106-852952.html
49. Greg Wright. Copy-Protected CD's Face Opposition.
41. John Borland. "Labels Dodge Scrutiny in Napster Suit" www.msnbc.com/news/697796.asp?cp1=1.
42. Associated Press. Labels to prove Copyright Ownership. www.msnbc.com/news/720510.asp?cp1=1.
43. John Borland Morpheus seeks new role in music. www.msnbc.com/news/723930.asp.
44. Abagial Waraker. "Internet week – Digital Rights Management.; Technology and standards are improving to guard copyright material." News Service, p. 32.
45. Bill Holland "In Hearings, Cannon Urges Labels to 'Serve' Internet Consumers" Billboard, 12/22/01, p. 1.
46. Jon Pareles. "The Many Futures of Music Maybe One of Them Real." The New York Times, 1/10/02
47. Jim Hu. "Pressplay comes to life after long wait." CNET News.com, 12/29/01. http://news.com.com/2100-1023-277178.html.
48. Gwendolyn Mariano. New CD protection wont play on PC's. msnbc.com/2100-1106-852952.html
49. Greg Wright. Copy-Protected CD's Face Opposition.

11

Bridging the Gaps

Linking in Law, Technology, and Communication Policy

Brian M. O'Connell
Central Connecticut State University

Content accessible on the Internet is stored in thousands of linked computers and is available to and from individuals, governments, organizations from anywhere around the world. Interconnectivity may well be the defining attribute of the Internet. From virtual trespass to unfair competition in cyberspace, interconnectivity raises a myriad of novel legal issues explored by Brian O'Connell.

[I]t would be a mistake to think that these people are just *users* of computation. On the contrary, they are participating in its invention—creating user interfaces, proposing architectures, rewriting the rules on
what it is to publish, disrupting our understanding of identity.

B. Cantwell Smith (1998, p. 360)

Computing has produced a stunning array of advances within the last few
decades. Although it would be presumptuous to choose any single element
as the ultimate achievement, a compelling argument can be made that the
introduction of the World Wide Web propelled computers from the confines of scientific or technological specialization, into their current position
of centrality within society. Appropriately, the Web is technically not one
technology, but a cluster of applications and innovations that were developed to improve the existing capabilities of the nascent Internet. The thrust
of these advances centered on the interconnectivity of the individual server
components and the method by which their distributed data would be presented. This chapter concerns the legal status of this connectivity—
arguably, the defining attribute of the Internet.

By 1990, the global network had demonstrated the worth of an interconnected system of individual computers. Notwithstanding its success, the
Internet's use was hampered by distinct shortcomings, including the lack of
a graphical component for multimedia presentation and by a navigational
system that relied on hierarchical, text-based menus that often impeded the
search for, and acquisition of data residing on an increasing number of
servers. Tim Berners-Lee and associates at the Centre Europeenne pour la
Recherche Nucleaire (CERN) set out to address the deficit by implementing a design that combined text with graphics and allowed access to widely
distributed data through "hypertext"—a nonlinear format that would
seamlessly "link" users to data located within all parts of the network
through static addresses known as uniform resource locators (URLs). With
the simultaneous development of hypertext transfer protocol (HTTP),
hypertext markup language (HTML) and a browser application compatible
with personal computers, the Internet gained a new level of functionality
that encouraged nonexpert use and acceptance (Abbate, 1999).

The implementation of hypertext profoundly expanded the capabilities
of mainstream computing. Where in the past, users were largely restricted
to material that resided on their specific machines, HTTP allowed easy
access to data located within any computer that was connected to the Web,
no matter how physically distant. The ability to simply click a link without
regard to its geographic location quickly fostered the popular conception of
a unitary information network. From a technical perspective, this "seam-

less" connectivity was not mandated by digital architecture, but was achieved only by a tacit agreement among information providers. As the Web developed and proprietary interests increased, the assumption of unhindered, free access would face significant legal challenge.

Further developments, building on the work of the CERN team, resulted in the introduction of improved browsers that displayed graphical icons as links (Schatz & Hardin, 1994) and search engines that broadened access to information by allowing network-wide retrieval through the use of keywords (Rowland, 1997). Advances in processors and software allowed multiple Web sites to appear within one screen as discrete windows or "frames," whereas autonomous software agents, known as "spiders" or "robots" were developed to, among other things, gather Web site data for online catalogues and indexes (Kramer & Monahan, 2000).

As suggested by computer scientist, Brian Cantwell Smith (1998), development within his discipline is not realistically completed with the release of any device or application. Instead, evolution continues as users influence outcomes through practices, understandings, and agreements. In the early days of the Internet, the rather homogenous user group could be expected to share in Berners-Lee's goal of creating through hypertext, "a pool of human knowledge" (Berners-Lee, Loutonen et al., 1994). Today, the trajectory of the Web is negotiated by a much larger, and less cohesive group. Instead of taking place within the confines of e-mails or electronic bulletin boards, the dialogue has shifted to the courts and legislatures.

One of the results of this shift is a change in the vocabulary employed to describe issues relating to the Internet. According to White (1990), language defines community in its "shared expectations and common terms" (p. 23). This is not a static function and as terms compete for acceptance, law "works by testing one version of its language against another, one way of telling a story and thinking about it against another, and by then making a self-conscious choice between them" (p. 24). Legal issues in computing are—for reasons that include the inadequacy of technical terminology, the intimate connection with social issues, and the need to associate the "virtual" with the conventional—often presented in the language of metaphor and analogy. As the courts, legislatures, and the public work through these constructions, they are also called on to assess the quality of their terms and frequently, the efficacy of invoking the conventional laws to which they allude.

There are two metaphorical and analogical themes that dominate the current debate over Internet linking. The *physical–proprietarian* paradigm presents networked dynamics as revolving around discrete electronic spaces and analogizes this to physical notions of identifiable boundaries and zones of ownership. The primary legal model for this approach is borrowed from the law of trespass. Its primary alternative, the *information–communication* model, does not deny the fact of ownership in networks or data, but emphasizes the social, political, and economic aspects of information, normally considering the efficiency and accessibility of communication. The legal focus of this model is generally on the concept of copyright. The *physical–proprietarian* approach represents the oldest approach to these questions and, as demonstrated in the following section, is still quite popular.

THE PHYSICAL–PROPRIETARIAN MODEL

The judicial notion that charged particles are capable of trespass does not originate with computers. In *Thrifty-Tel, Inc. v. Bezenek* (1996), suit was filed against individuals who obtained free long-distance access through the unauthorized use of corporate codes. Although the action and trial verdict were premised on a claim of conversion, the Appellate Court was troubled by the fact that this cause of action traditionally requires dispossession of tangible property. Because electronic codes might not fit the definition, it modified the verdict to one of trespass to chattels. Traditionally, this also requires tangible interference, however, the panel determined that electronic activity could be likened to damaging sound and dust that other courts had found sufficiently substantial to establish trespass.

The *Thrifty-Tel* decision legitimized trespass as a digital cause of action. Within a year of its release, a trespass claim was sustained in a matter involving the mass distribution of E-mail or "spam" to an Internet service provider. In *CompuServe v. Cyber Promotions* (1997), an injunction against spamming activity was entered on the basis of trespass to chattels. Although relying on *Thrifty-Tel*, the Ohio Federal Court expanded its version of trespass beyond the scope of physical damage previously analogized to dust and sound. Instead, it reasoned that the interference caused by the electronic activity caused a degradation of value to the chattel, through the burdening of server equipment. Significantly, the court entertained the defense that connecting to the Internet constituted consent to accept all incoming messages. Although averring that some degree of acquiescence might be implied, the court noted that the terms of CompuServe's use policy expressly forbade spamming. It compared the effect of such exclusions to the conventional right of a commercial proprietor to control general invitations to enter on its premises.

Building on the broadened definitions provided by *CompuServe*, actions in trespass have become a popular method of challenging unwanted Internet contact, including that which is accomplished by linking. Attempts to restrain inter-site linking date back to 1997 when in *Ticketmaster Corp. v. Microsoft*, the plaintiff ticket seller attempted to prevent Microsoft "Sidewalk," a regional events site, from linking to pages located beyond its main point of entry. Ticketmaster claimed that the activity of "deep linking" reduced its site's value, lowered advertising revenue, and hampered visitor purchases. Microsoft countered that its linking merely took advantage of what was already freely available in the form of a public site. The matter was resolved in 1999 with Microsoft's agreement to cease deep linking and without formal judicial resolution (Tedeschi, 1999).

A claim of trespass was included by the same plaintiff when, in *Ticketmaster v. Tickets.com* (2000), it again sought to prevent deep linking by a competitor. In this situation, Tickets.com, an online dealer, would, when unable to provide tickets to specific events, directly link to the event sale site within Ticketmaster's pages. The claim for trespass was dismissed by the court, which held that prohibition to access of factual information would run contrary to the U.S. Copyright Act.[1] Furthermore, it stated (in language reminiscent of Microsoft's defense), "it is hard to see how entering a publicly available web site could be called a trespass, since all are invited to enter."[2] Although this pronouncement would seem to refute trespass as a viable cause of action, a later articulation by the court leaves no doubt that trespass theories were not discounted out of hand: "The computer is a piece of tangible personal property. . . . If the electronic impulses can do damage to the computer or to its function in a comparable way to taking a hammer to a piece of machinery, then it is no stretch to recognize that damage as trespass to chattels and provide a legal remedy for it" (2000, pp. 15-16).

Trespass theories have played determinative roles in the resolution of claims involving site access in which linking takes place by means other than conventional hypertext. In *eBay v. Bidder's Edge* (2000), the activity at issue involved the use of a software "robot," an application that automatically follows links and stores data encountered at each visited site. Bidder's Edge (BE), an auction aggregator, sent robots to a number of sites and presented the compiled data at its Web site as comparative consumer information. One of the destinations was the auction site, eBay. This destination was visited approximately 100,000 times a day, consuming an estimated 1% of computing resources (Kilbane, 2000). eBay, which had refused to renew a previous agreement with BE, allowing this activity, unsuccessfully attempted to technically block the access. In the end, it filed suit against the aggregator, claiming, among other things, infringement of intellectual rights, unjust enrichment, interference with prospective economic advantage and trespass. Significantly, when eBay requested an injunction of BE's robots' actions, it was granted solely on the trespass claim.

The *eBay* court supported its decision by finding that eBay had not established actual damage to its equipment. Rather, it held that BE's actions contained the potential for harm by encouraging others to send their robots, inevitably impairing the system. A temporary injunction was thus granted on this potentiality as well as eBay's "fundamental right to exclude others from its computer system" (*eBay v. Bidder's Edge*, 2000, p. 1067).

Although the settlement of the *eBay* matter (Saliba, 2001) precluded a
final review of the interim decision, its rationale has found acceptance in the
recent matter of *Register.com v. Verio* (2000). In this matter, Verio
employed robots to utilize the "whois"[3] feature of Register.com's server to
obtain customer information. Register.com communicated their protest
against this action to Verio and when unsuccessful, instituted suit, requesting injunctive relief on a number of grounds, including trespass. The court
granted the request. Citing *eBay*, it found no actual proof of harm, but held
that the diminishment of the system through the encouragement of other
robotic activity was sufficient to sustain the trespass claim (2000, pp. 250-
251).

Both *eBay* and *Register.com* suggest that the choice of trespass as an
analogy of Internet dynamics will have specific consequences. Particularly
apparent are the commitments of trespass to the tangible world of its origins. Rights of exclusion and access are immediately emphasized within
trespass-based Internet rulings, as are the physical components, particularly
the server. One problem with the focus is its ability to be authentically
translated into the electronic environment. O'Rourke (2001) pointed out
that the entire concept of trespass as applied to the Internet completely disregards technological reality in that the linking process does not involve
intrusion by the requesting entity. Instead, the linked-to server either
grants or denies a request for information and, if granted, then sends data to
the requesting machine, where it is then stored, assembled and displayed.
Thus, Internet systems dynamics strongly refute the easy applicability of
access and exclusion as useful terms within these situations. As suggested
by the comments made in *Tickets.com*, they also raise serious questions
about the presence of consent by the transmitting server when its software
grants another machine's request.

Likewise open to criticism are the assessments of future damage used
by the *eBay* and *Register.com* tribunals. By holding the possibilities of
damage as sufficient to establish a trespass, courts have engaged in a form of
technological guesswork that is not supported by factual evidence. Such a
subjective and deferential standard threatens to broaden rights of digital
exclusion beyond anything previously known at temporal law.

Another significant difficulty with trespass is that its emphasis on the
physical components of the Internet may blind courts to a consideration of
important communicative characteristics. Both *eBay* and *Register.com*
focused their attention on potential server damage, without considering
that the dynamic flow of information is an intrinsic aspect of the Internet.
This server-based focus disregards the fact that machines are connected to
the Internet with the expectation that they will, under normal circumstances, both take advantage of the relative free flow of data and participate
in it furthering its interchange. In withholding serious attention to the issue

of implied consent to linking,[4] trespass theories may be criticized as being unrealistically parochial and essentially inequitable when considered in the context of Internet communication norms.

THE INFORMATION–COMMUNICATION MODEL

As suggested in the trial ruling of *Tickets.com*, and elsewhere, the trespass analogy is challenged by the fact that information within the Internet is normally available to the public. Indeed, the flow of information has been intrinsic to its operation and success. The predominant theories that accentuate the informational aspect of networked communication fall under the two generally categories of those related to copyright jurisprudence and those that are directed toward the law of trademark and unfair competition.

Copyright

Like trespass, the law of copyright evolved from legal experiences in the tangible world. In contrast with trespass, copyright is not exclusively concerned with protecting possessory interests. Instead, "in the United States and elsewhere [copyright laws] begin with the principle that neither the creator of a new work of authorship nor the general public ought to be able to appropriate all the benefits that flow from the creation of a new, original work of authorship" (Littman, 2001, p. 15). In U.S. law, copyright is derived from and animated by the public policy considerations contained within the Constitution's grant of power to Congress to promote "the Progress of Science and useful Arts."[5]

According to the Copyright Act of 1976, authors of original works are given exclusive rights to duplicate, distribute, exhibit and perform their material or to designate this right to others.[6] In *MAI Systems v. Peak Computer* (1993), the Ninth Circuit Court determined that transmission to digital random access memory (RAM) constitutes copying under the statute. This judgment has not been contradicted by other courts and under its precedent, Internet postings are generally viewed as protected by copyright law.[7]

Copyright law has been employed to prevent linking under certain, although not all situations. *In Intellectual Reserve v. Utah Lighthouse Ministry* (1999), the Mormon Church petitioned for an injunction against church critics who had posted on their Web site, URLs of external sites that contained unauthorized reproductions of the copyrighted *Mormon Church Handbook of Instructions*, links to another publication that concerned the Mormon faith, portions of the *Handbook* and, instructions on how to take one's name off of church membership rosters. The Church's motion alleged direct copyright infringement as well as contributory infringement on the theory that linking would engender infringing behavior in others. Evidence considered by the court included no allegation that the defendants had any relationships with the owners of the linked sites, nor that they provided the allegedly infringing material to other sites nor had derived profit from any online publication.

The motion was granted by the court on the basis of copyright. It held that at trial, the Church would likely succeed in its claim that the material at issue were direct infringements and that the defendants' links would constitute contributory infringement. The *Handbook* portions located within the defendants' site were ordered removed as were the links to other sites.

The *Intellectual Reserve* decision presents significant implications for Internet-based linking. A primary area of concern involves its liberal definition of infringement as it relates to average computer users. Following the reasoning of *MAI Systems* (1993)—that transmission of data to RAM constitutes copying—the court held that ordinary browsing involved the same process and therefore constituted direct infringement. Consequently, by following a link, an average user could incur copyright liability. The court seemed cognizant of the massive scope of this holding by making the laconic and less-than comforting observation that damages in the case of an "innocent infringer" might be reduced. Despite this solicitude, the drastic conclusion raises questions about the ultimate utility of *MAI Systems* within networked copyright jurisprudence.[8]

Similar problems are evident in the court's characterization of linking activity as an encouragement to violate copyright. The conclusion was apparently based on the fact that URLs provide navigational assistance to sites that might otherwise be missed. This rather strained reasoning conflicts with decisions that have required some form of direct complicity in the transgressing activity. Thus, in the well known "Betamax" decision of *Sony Corp. v. Universal City Studios* (1984), a claim of contributory infringement premised on the provision of videotaping hardware was rejected on the basis that the equipment had legitimate uses that did not involve infringement.

The significance of Intellectual Reserve may lie not so much in what was considered, than what was avoided. Specifically, the court did not address the defense of fair use—a judicial doctrine and more recently, statutory law[9]—which finds no copyright violation when the activity at issue involves the use of reasonable portions of protected work for such activities as those involved in education, biography, scholarship, parody, or commentary (see Litman, 2001). Given the heated topic of the site at issue, it is difficult to understand this omission.[10]

Pope (2001) and others argued that the policy-oriented Fair Use Doctrine may have the flexibility to limit copyright sanctions in instances where its sanctions could enable "innovative uses of content in cyberspace" (Okediji, 2001, p. 146). This would require an enormous effort to investigate how digital information differs from traditional media. It might also inject greater ambiguity into the decision-making process. It would, however, have the advantage of providing realistic and more comprehensive alternatives to the constricted reasoning found in *Intellectual Reserve*.

The factors supporting the consideration of fair use also suggest an integral link to First Amendment jurisprudence. Bendotoff (2000) noted that where, as in *Intellectual Reserve*, expression is constrained before a hearing on the merits of the matter, the effects of a prior restraint must be considered. This prospect is particularly troubling in light of the court's unwillingness to conduct a fair use review. Absent these considerations, the precedential value of this decision, already limited by the preliminary nature of the ruling, is of questionable significance. Nevertheless, it retains value as an indicator of the perils of detaching copyright law from its underlying policies.

Another recent matter concerning the status of links involves the volatile issue of the Digital Millennium Copyright Act (DCMA).[11] Passed by Congress in 1998, the DCMA, with some exceptions, makes illegal, the circumvention of measures taken by copyright holders to protect their works from unauthorized access. It also prohibits the manufacture or trafficking of circumvention technologies and the dissemination of technologies that permit the copying or other subsequent use of protected digital material. Petteys (2001) pointed out that the effect of this focus is access control and not use control. The distinction involved here is that once authorized access is achieved, an individual "may legally circumvent a measure placed on the work that prevents copying without the copyright holder's permission, but that individual may not circumvent a technology preventing unauthorized access in the first place" (p. 292).

In *Universal City Studios v. Reimerdes* (2001), a complaint was filed, seeking injunctive relief and alleging that the defendants violated the DCMA by directly posting and linking to sites that contained an application known as DeCSS. This program essentially decrypts an access protection application for movies located on digital versatile disks (DVDs) known as the Content Scramble System (CSS).

DeCSS was developed by a Norwegian teenager and colleagues by reverse-engineering a DVD player, which was configured to run on a Microsoft operating system. According to the *Reimerdes* appellate decision, the apparent purpose of DeCSS was to allow the use of the DVD system within a Linux operating environment. Once the code was developed, an executable version (source code) was released on the Internet.[12] Subsequently, the defendants, who operated the print magazine, *2600: The Hacker Quarterly*, wrote an article about DeCSS and posted to its site, copies of the source and object codes as "evidence" of how the program operated.

After discovering that DeCSS had been posted to the Web, the plaintiffs requested and were granted a preliminary injunction, barring the defendants from posting the code to their site. Following the injunction, the defendants removed the code from their site, but maintained links to other sites that contained the application, in part claiming that the downloading would constitute an act of "electronic civil disobedience." No evidence was presented alleging the defendants had engaged in any movie decryption nor was it alleged that specific movies had been decrypted through the use of the Internet. After trial, a permanent injunction was granted. An appeal was made to the Second Circuit Court and the rulings of the lower court were upheld.

The Circuit Court first considered the defendants' argument that the DMCA could be interpreted as allowing DeCSS dissemination. This proposal relied on the *Sony* doctrine that technologies capable of legitimate activities, such as fair use of material, could not be made illicit. The claim was quickly rejected with the observation that the DMCA is only concerned with the "digital walls" surrounding the material and not with the material itself.

The panel went on to find that computer code, as a conveyer of information and ideas, is entitled to First Amendment protection. This characterization did not, however, end the matter. The court went on to state that the level of scrutiny that a speech-restrictive legislation receives is dependent on its association with content. Citing Supreme Court precedents, the panel noted that where content-based restrictions exist, they are permissible only when serving compelling state interests and are framed by the least restrictive measures available. Where the regulation is neutral to content, it will be upheld under an "intermediate standard" when a substantial governmental interest is served, the regulation is not related to the suppression of free speech and the regulation is narrowly tailored to substantially burden no more speech than necessary. Based on the court's functional analysis of the code, DeCSS was determined to be an access control mechanism, "like a skeleton key" (p. 453). Although the court also accepted the fact that DeCSS was also a form of communication, it tempered this characterization by noting that its ability to "accomplish unauthorized—indeed unlawful access to materials in which the Plaintiffs have intellectual property rights must inform and limit the scope of First Amendment protection" (p. 453).

The Appellate Court then upheld the neutrality, and, therefore, lessened standard of review of the DMCA-based injunction on posting as it was concerned only with a nonspeech component of DeCSS, specifically, "its capacity to instruct a computer to decrypt CSS" (p. 454). The government's interest in preventing access to copyright material was likewise judged to be substantial and narrowly served by the DMCA provision.

The injunction on linking was also upheld under the lesser, content-neutral standard. The rationale behind this decision consisted of affirming the noncommunicative function of DeCSS and favorably quoted the trial court's conclusion that the ban on linking was content-neutral because "it is justified without regard to the speech component of the hyperlink" (p. 456). Working on this characterization, the appellate panel was able to conclude that the "functional capacity" of the link was not sufficiently expressive in character, but instead, was a mere mechanism "to facilitate instantaneous unauthorized access to copyrighted materials" (p. 457).

Although not an issue on appeal, it should be noted that while easily upholding the ban on links to sites providing instantaneous downloads to DeCSS, the lower court opinion found that enjoining links to sites that contained more than the DeCSS would pose greater difficulty. Here, it stated that DMCA liability might not attach.

In the end, the appellate panel admitted that it was passing on matters that concerned the functioning of Internet communications. Significantly, it expressed the belief that it was not constructing communication policy, but was implementing the choices made by Congress. Despite this position, there is much in *Reimerdes* to suggest that the court has indeed crafted Internet policy on the foundations of its unique interpretations of network structure and purpose.

The position of the court that the DMCA regulations should be reviewed under an intermediate level of scrutiny is problematic. The justification for this lessened standard revolves around the panel's characterization of the DMCA as concerning only the "digital walls" that surround content, and not the content itself, thereby achieving neutrality. As crisp as this metaphor might first appear, it is not altogether convincing. To an extent unprecedented in history, DMCA-protected mechanisms completely control access to content for use in any of its expressive forms, including access for purposes of fair use. This can be argued to constitute a *de facto* burden on the speech of those not authorized access due to economic or other disabilities. This is a situation that would seem difficult to dismiss with ease, and yet, the "wall–content" dichotomy imposed by the panel resulted in this outcome.

The court's superficial equivocation of linking with neutral, mechanistic action is similarly problematic and suggest a lack of familiarity with common Internet practices. Most average users are well aware of a link's role as a stand-alone reference. By pointing to a remote site, it conveys information about the site's existence and perhaps, its origins, sponsors, orientation, and much more. By providing the link, the site designer is making a statement, as did the defendants in *Reimerdes* when they associated civil disobedience to the link. In this sense, a link is more like a vehicular license plate, which, while serving a neutral task of identification, also contains personal, expressive information.

Even if it were agreed that an intermediate test of review were appropriate, the standard still poses hurdles that the panel did not address. Absent the receipt of real evidence concerning economic harm, it is difficult to understand how the court found satisfaction of substantial governmental interests of protecting copyright. Originating in the computer trespass cases, the willingness of courts to simply accept unsubstantiated technical claims appears to be a growing and disturbing trend within digital jurisprudence.

Similarly, the court's position that linking to direct download sites constitutes the legal equivalent of direct facilitation of copyright violations is logically and technically incorrect. As with criticisms concerning the role of linking within infringement matters, it is simply not accurate to equate the placing of a link to the active provision of material.

At present, the information–communication model appears to have yielded decisions favoring property holders in much the same way as does its physical–proprietarian counterpart. Some hope for an eventual change may come when the full implications of copyright policy are given consideration. It is significant that the decisions described herein either ignored the public policy components of copyright, as with *Intellectual Reserve*, or attempted to cleave copyright from the discussion by setting up artificial distinctions between protective devices and content, a with *Reimerdes*. It is possible that these easy, but limited characterizations will be replaced by more comprehensive models as courts increase their understanding of the technical and social elements of computing.

One hopeful example of a more comprehensive approach is provided by the matter of *DVD Copy Control Association v. McLaughlin* (2000). This pre-*Reimerdes* case was not brought under the DMCA, but also sought the banning of DeCSS-related material. The court agreed to enjoin DeCSS posting, but denied the request as related to linking. In support of its decision, the court stated that linking was a "mainstay" of the Internet, and "indispensable" to its operation. It also declared that realistically, site operators could not be held responsible for the contents of remote sites.

Trademark And Unfair Competition

In addition to copyright-related claims, actions concerning linking have been pursued under the laws of trademark and unfair competition. Trademark may be invoked to protect names, words, symbols, or devices that identify products with particular owners.[13]

A cause of action may be maintained when an unauthorized use of a protectable trademark is likely to result in confusion. The practice of linking to remote sites has generated such allegations. In *Shetland Times v. Wills* (1996), a preliminary injunction was issued against an online paper that had linked its headlines to stories generated by another online publication. The case was settled subsequent to the injunction. Similarly, in *Washington Post v. Total News* (1997), an infringement claim was premised on the defendant's use of frames to display articles from the plaintiff's site. The complaint alleged that the defendant's presentation of its logo, advertisements and other identifying elements within separate frames created both confusion and deception. The case, which also alleged that the nonpermissive use of trademarks would dilute their uniqueness, was also settled before further proceedings.

In *Ticketmaster v. Microsoft* (1997), a trademark case was instituted against the practice of "deep linking." The defendant, which operated an entertainment site, linked to event-specific sites within the Ticketmaster page structure. Among other allegations, Ticketmaster claimed that the linking created trademark dilution. The matter was settled with an agreement to link only to the main page of the ticket seller's site. In contrast, simple linking, without more, does not appear to implicate trademark infringement. In *Playboy Enterprises v. Universal Tel-A-Talk* (1998), the inclusion of "Playboy" in a direct link to the magazine's Web site was held not to be a trademark violation.

Metatags are strings of HTML code that reside within web pages. They are used by many search engines to categorize sites within an indexing structure in order to match keywords with links. In *Playboy Enterprises v. Terri Welles* (1998), Ms. Welles, a former playmate of the month, was allowed to include the magazine's name in her unaffiliated Web site's metatags as this was considered a valid description and a fair use of the mark. In contrast, the Ninth Circuit Court of Appeals found in *Brookfield Communications v. West Coast Entertainment* (1999), that the use of a trademarked term by a nonowner for purposes of attraction to its commercial site, was likely to cause confusion between two enterprises and enjoined its inclusion. Finally, in *Bihari v. Gross* (2000), the defendants—former disgruntled clients of an interior designer—used the designer's name and marks within metatags located at sites critical of her services. The court denied a request for a preliminary injunction, stating that the employment of the marks constituted a fair use that accurately identified the character of the sites at issue.

CONCLUSION

The current lack of consistency in the jurisprudence of linking may be attributed to a number of factors. It is certainly a new issue without easy precedent. This situation forces the making of conclusions that involve both technological understanding and not a small amount of social forecasting. Although frustration may be an understandable result of this survey, it is well to remember that the passage of time may allow jurists, legislators and the public, the opportunity to understand on a firsthand basis, the dynamics of Internet and its operations. Working within the context of electronic privacy, the Supreme Court majority in *Katz v. United States* (1967) factored into their decision, the "vital role that the public telephone has come to play in private communications." A similar recognition within Internet jurisprudence will likely be hastened by an increased dialogue among legal, technical and social actors.

NOTES

1. The effect of copyright is considered in detail in the following section.
2. The original language granting the dismissal is contained within the 2000 opinion.
3. This application allows the acquisition of user information held by remote servers and is analogous to the "finger" protocol, which performs a similar function. See *Free On-Line Dictionary of Computing*, available at: www.doki.com.
4. See M. O'Rourke (1998). Fencing cyberspace: drawing borders in a virtual world. *Minn. Law Review, 82,* 609-619.
5. United States Constitution, Article I, §8, cl. 8.
6. 17 U.S.C. 102, 106.
7. But see K. Mathews (1997). Misunderstanding RAM: Digital embodiment and copyright. *Boston College Intellectual Property and Technology Forum,* http://www.bc.edu/bc_org/avp/law/st_org/iptf/articles/content/1997041501.html
8. O'Rourke (2001, p. 582) discussed many of these issues and makes the technically correct distinction between linking and copying, stating that copying does not occur through linking, but by the linked server under what might be construed as an implied license.
9. 17 U.S.C. 106.
10. See Bendotoff (2000, pp. 100-102), for a detailed analysis of the fair use issues in this matter.
11. 17 U.S.C. §§ 101, 104, 114, 512, 1201-1204.
12. In computing "object code" is language normally directly translatable to the computer. *Source code* is a term used to define programs written in higher level languages such as BASIC or Java, which have the advantage of being easi-

er to use or read. Source code is inevitably translated to object code for processing by the computer. See *Free On-Line Dictionary of Computing*, available at: www.doki.com.

13. 15 U.S.C. Chap. 22.

REFERENCES

Abbate, U. (1999). *Inventing the Internet.* Cambridge, MA : MIT Press.

Berners-Lee, T., Cailliau, A., Loutonen, A., Nielsen, H., & Secret, A. (1994). The world-wide web. *Communications of the ACM, 37*(8), 76-82.

Bendotoff, M.A. (2000). *Intellectual Reserve, Inc. v. Utah Lighthouse Ministry, Inc.:* Fair use, the First Amendment, and the freedom to link. *University of San Francisco Law Review, 33,* 83-108.

Brookfield Communications, Inc. v. West Coast Entertainment Corp., 174 F. 3d 1036 (9th Cir.). (1999).

Bihari v. Gross, 119 F. Supp. 2d 309. (2000).

CompuServe v. Cyber Promotions, 962 F. Supp. 1015 (S.D. Ohio). (1997).

DVD Copy Control Association v. McLaughlin, No. CV 786804, 2000 WL 48512 (Cal. Super. Ct.). (2000). (unpublished order).

ebay, Inc. v. Bidder's Edge, Inc., 100 F. Supp. 2d 1058 (N.D. Cal.). (2000).

Intellectual Reserve v. Utah Lighthouse Ministry, 75 F. Supp. 2d 1290 (D. Utah). (1999).

Katz v. United States, 389 U.S. 347 (1967).

Kilbane, C. (2000, November 13). Co-branding: All the rage in cyberspace. *The National Law Journal,* pp. B17-18.

Kramer, D., & Monahan, J. (2000). Panel discussion: To bot or not to bot: The implications of spidering. *Hastings Communication & Entertainment Law Journal, 22,* 241-242.

Littman, J. (2001). *Digital copyright.* New York: Prometheus Books.

MAI Systems Corp. v. Peak Computer, Inc., 991 F.2d 511 (1993), *cert. dismissed,* 510 U.S. 1033. (1994).

Okediji, R. (2001). Givers, takers, and other kinds of users: A fair use doctrine for cyberspace. *Florida Law Review, 53,* 107-146.

O'Rourke, M. (2001). Property rights and competition on the internet: In search of an appropriate analogy. *Berkeley Technology Law Journal, 16,* 561, 630.

Petteys, D. (2001). The freedom to link?: The digital millennium copyright act implicates the first amendment in *Universal City Studios, Inc. v. Reimerdes. Seattle University Law Review, 25,* 287-340.

Playboy Enterprises, Inc. v. Terri Welles, 7 F. Supp. 2d 1098 (S.D. Cal.). (1998).

Playboy Enterprises, Inc. v. Universal Tel-A-Talk, Inc., No Civ. 96-CV-6961 (E.D. Pa.). (1998).

Pope C. (2001). Missing link(s): Protecting public image and corporate profits in cyberspace. *Houston Law Review, 38,* 651-681.

Register.com, Inc. v. Verio, Inc., 126 F. Supp. 2d 238 (S.D.N.Y.). (2000).

Rowland, W. (1997). *Spirit of the web: The age of information from telegraph to internet.* Toronto: Somerville House Publishing.

Saliba, C. (2001). ebay settles suit with auction search site. *www.EcommerceTimes.com,* http://www.newsfactor.com/perl/story /7883.html (March 2, 2001).

Schatz, B., & Hardin, J. (1994). NCSA mosaic and the world-wide web: Global hypermedia protocols for the internet. *Science 265,* 895-901.

Shetland Times v. Wills and Zetnews, Ltd., F.S.R. (Ct. Sess. O.H.). (1997)

Smith, B.C. (1998). *On the origin of objects.* Cambridge, MA: MIT Press.

Sony Corp. v. Universal City Studios, 464 U.S. 417. (1984).

Thrifty-Tel, Inc. v. Bezenek, 54 Cal. Rptr. 2d 468. (1996).

Ticketmaster Corp. v. Microsoft Corp., No. 97-3055 DDP (C.D. Cal. 1997).

Ticketmaster Corp. v. Tickets.com, Inc., 2000 U.S. Dist. LEXIS 4553, at 10-11 (C.D. Cal.). (2000, March 27). (citations omitted).

Tedeschi, B. (1999). Ticketmaster and microsoft settle legal dispute. *Cybertimes,* http://www.nytimes.com/library/tech/99/02/cyber/articles/15tick.html (February 15, 1999).

Universal City Studios, Inc. v. Reimerdes, 111 F. Supp. 2d 294 (S.D.N.Y.). (2000).

Universal City Studios, Inc. v. Reimerdes, 273 F.3d 429 (2d Cir.). (2001).

Washington Post Co. v. Total News, Inc., No. 97 Civ. 1190 (PKL) (S.D.N.Y.). (1997).

White, J.B. (1990). *Justice as translation: An essay in cultural and legal criticism.* Chicago: University of Chicago Press.

12

Bad Words and Good Samaritans

Defamatory Speech in Cyberspace

Dale A. Herbeck
Boston College

Cyberspace is particularly vulnerable to charges of defamation. False statements of fact fly through cyberspace, often unchecked. The sheer number of messages, the tendency for people communicating through e-mail or electronic bulletin boards to write without considering who or how many are in the audience raise important issues with regard to liability for defamatory statements.

Hundreds of cases have now been filed leading to litigation involving diverse issues and defendants. Some cases have resulted in large awards. In this chapter Dale Herbeck focuses on one issue of liability—the question of whether Internet Service Providers (ISPs) are legally responsible for third party speech.

The unprecedented growth of the Internet has raised a variety of difficult legal questions. Although public attention has focused on efforts to regulate sexually explicit speech, more than 400 defamation suits have been filed for Internet speech since 2001 (Anschütz, 2001). Defamation actions have resulted from content available on Web sites, postings to bulletin boards (BBs), and conversations in chatrooms. A brief sampling of these suits includes filings for allegedly defamatory statements made about medical equipment (*Medphone v. DeNigris*, 1993) and direct mail (*Suarez v. Meeks*, 1994) companies, for complaints about vacations (*Bowker v. America Online*, 1995), for allegations of spousal abuse (*Blumenthal v. Drudge*, 1998), and for comments made about policemen (*Baitinger v. Fajardo*, 1997), doctors (*Morrison v. America Online*, 2001), judges (*Melvin v. Doe*, 2000), and attorneys (*PatentWizard v. Kinko's*, 2001). Although the legal burdens differ considerably, similar cases have already been brought in foreign countries (*Godfrey v. Demon Internet Ltd.*, 2001), and there have even been cases in which plaintiffs tried to reach across national boundaries to bring defamation claims (*Godfrey v. Cornell University*, 1997).

The vast majority of these claims will, undoubtedly, be settled out of court. It is worth noting, however, that a handful of Internet defamation cases have already been tried and plaintiffs have received impressive damage awards. In one of the first cases tried in January 2001, a federal jury awarded $675,000 to a prominent urologist who was defamed in a series of postings to a Yahoo! message board ("E.D. Va. Jury," 2001, p. 5). More recently, a Santa Clara County jury awarded $775,000 in damages to a California company that was defamed by two disgruntled former employees in more than 14,000 postings to 100 different message boards ("Jury Orders," 2002, p. 18). As the number of speakers in cyberspace is increasing, the number of defamation claims and jury trials will surely grow.

It would, of course, be impossible to do justice to all of the issues related to defamatory speech in cyberspace in a single chapter. Recognizing that fact, this chapter focuses on the narrow question of whether Internet service providers (ISPs) are legally responsible for third-party speech. Simply put, can a plaintiff sue an ISP like America Online (AOL) for something said by one of AOL's subscribers? In an effort to answer this question, the chapter begins by identifying two models—ISPs as distributors and ISPs as publishers—considered by the courts. In *Cubby v. CompuServe* (1991), a federal district court held that CompuServe analogized the ISP to a distributor. Because CompuServe was unaware of the content, the court ruled the ISP could not be held responsible for a defamatory posting on one of its BBs. In *Stratton Oakmont v. Prodigy* (1995a), a New York state court held that Prodigy exercised editorial control, and could therefore be held responsible for a defamatory account published on a BB it maintained. The second section of the chapter revisits this controversy in light of the U.S.

Court of Appeals for the Fourth Circuit decision in *Zeran v. America Online* (1997a, 1997b), a case involving Section 230—the so-called "Good Samaritan" clause—of the ill-fated Communications Decency Act. The final section of this chapter briefly summarizes the growing scholarly criticism of Section 230 and the *Zeran* decision. In the final pages, the chapter directly responds to this criticism, arguing the Section 230 was intended to protect immunize ISPs, and that *Zeran* was correctly decided.

DISTRIBUTOR OR PUBLISHER? *CUBBY* AND *STRATTON OAKMONT*

The first cases considering the culpability of ISPs for defamatory postings forced the courts to consider whether ISPs are properly regarded as distributors or publishers. Because distributors do not have content control, they are only liable for defamation if they know or have reason to know that they are distributing defamatory material. In contrast, publishers exercise editorial control and therefore have been held liable for the content of their publications. This distinction explains, for instance, why Random House is responsible for the content of a book that it publishes, whereas Barnes and Noble is not responsible for the contents of books on its store's shelves. ISPs, unfortunately, share qualities of both distributor and publisher, explaining the contradictory decisions in *Cubby v. CompuServe* and *Stratton Oakmont v. Prodigy*.

Cubby v. CompuServe (1991)

In *Cubby*, the court considered CompuServe's responsibility for a series of allegedly false and defamatory statements posted on its "Journalism Forum" BB. One part of the "Journalism Forum," which was managed for CompuServe by Cameron Communication, was a publication prepared by Don Fitzpatrick Associates (DFA) entitled "Rumorville, USA." Cubby's suit alleged that when it attempted to market a competing database called "Skuttlebut," postings on Rumorville defamed Cubby by characterizing the effort as a "new start-up scam" among other things.

In issuing a summary judgment for CompuServe, the court held that "First Amendment guarantees have long been recognized as protecting distribution of publications. . . . Obviously, the national distributor of hundreds of periodicals has no duty to monitor each issue of every periodical it distributes" (p. 140). Because CompuServe had no opportunity to review Rumorville's contents before DFA uploaded it to CompuServe's server, the ISP could not be "held liable on the libel claim because it neither knew nor had reason to know of the allegedly defamatory statements" (p. 139). By way of analogy, the court reasoned, "CompuServe has no more editorial control over . . . publication than does a public library, book store, or newsstand, and it would be no more feasible for CompuServe to examine every publication it carries for potentially defamatory statements than it would be for any other distributor to do so" (p. 140). To hold otherwise, the *Cubby* court concluded, "would impose an undue burden on the free flow of information" (p. 140).

Stratton Oakmont v. Prodigy (1995a, 1995b)

Early on the morning of Sunday, October 24, 1994, an anonymous message appeared on Prodigy's "Money Talk" BB. Referring to a Long Island-based broker, the posting said "THANK GOD! THE END OF STRATTON OAKMONT WILL FINALLY COME THIS WEEK!" The message continued, "This brokerage firm headed by president and soon to be proven criminal—Daniel Porush—will close this week." To document this claim, the posting offered the following circumstantial evidence: On Thursday, October 20, Stratton Oakmont had underwritten an initial public offering by the Solomon-Page Group, a recruiting and placement company. After the close of trading on Friday, October 21, Stratton Oakmont and Solomon-Page had jointly announced that Solomon-Page's biggest customer was leaving the company. The posting concluded, "THIS IS FRAUD, FRAUD, FRAUD, AND CRIMINAL!!!!!!!!" (Frankel, 1995, pp. 59-66).

The anonymous user posted additional messages over the weekend and these postings remained on "Money Talk" for 2 weeks. Although Daniel Porush was not a Prodigy subscriber, he eventually learned of the postings and he immediately brought a defamation action. Subsequent research by Prodigy revealed that the messages in question were posted on an account issued to David Lusby, a former employee of the ISP. Lusby, who had departed from Prodigy in 1991, denied authorship of the postings. Because the messages were posted anonymously through a valid account, Prodigy found itself party to one of the first legal actions brought against a provider for defamatory speech posted on a computer BB.

In an effort to expedite settlement on a $200 million claim for damages, counsel for Stratton Oakmont hastily moved for partial summary judgment on the question of whether Prodigy was a publisher, and thus liable for defamatory speech. If Prodigy was a publisher, Stratton Oakmont reasoned they would have a strong claim for damages. Conversely, if Prodigy was merely a distributor, Stratton Oakmont knew it would have a weak case because Prodigy could persuasively argue that it had no prior knowledge of the defamatory postings. Much to the surprise of many legal commentators (see, e.g., Haddad, 1995; Walker, 1995; Zitner, 1995), acting New York State Supreme Court Justice Stuart Ain decided that Prodigy was not a distributor. Because Prodigy used software to prescreen postings for obscenities and racial slurs, and because Prodigy had previously claimed to be a "family-oriented computer network," Ain held that Prodigy was exercising editorial control and could, therefore, be sued as the publisher of a defamatory posting.

In the months following Ain's ruling, Prodigy successfully negotiated a settlement with Stratton Oakmont based largely on the following public apology: "Prodigy is sorry if the offensive statements concerning Stratton and Mr. Porush, which were posted on Prodigy's Money Talk bulletin board by an unauthorized and unidentified individual, in any way caused injury to their reputation" (Lewis, 1995). As part of the settlement that produced the apology, Stratton Oakmont did not contest Prodigy's appeal of Judge Ain's earlier decision. Having settled the defamation claim, Prodigy then asked Judge Ain to reconsider his holding that Prodigy was a publisher. The judge refused, reasoning his original holding was especially compelling as "this is a developing area of the law (in which it appears that the law has thus far not kept pace with the technology) so that there is a real need for some precedent" (*Stratton Oakmont*, 1995b, p. 850).

Although the *Stratton Oakmont* case was never tried, the holding that Prodigy is a publisher raised difficult First Amendment issues. Even if the precedent was narrowly limited to New York state, "its effect could reach far beyond the Empire State. For example, if a Prodigy customer in Memphis or Phoenix writes a libelous message about a person in New York, the New Yorker could sue Prodigy, and win" (Bray, 1995, p. 51). Moreover, the precedent created the real possibility that online services might be held responsible when subscribers used their BBs to violate the rights of third parties. "By equating content control with fault," Siver (1997) explained, "*Stratton* presents online service providers with two unenviable options for avoiding defamation liability: providers must either bear the immense burden of comprehensive screening for defamation or abandon all content control efforts in order to avoid being labeled a publisher" (p. 17).

SECTION 230 AND *ZERAN V. AMERICA ONLINE*

The *Stratton Oakmont* decision was very much on legislators' minds when Congress considered adopting the Communications Decency Act (CDA) in 1996. If, as some legislators wanted, an ISP actively screened content for sexually explicit speech, future plaintiffs might claim the ISP had become a "publisher," and therefore liable for the contents of defamatory postings made by users. Fearing that this possibility would discourage ISPs from aggressively enforcing the CDA, legislators included Section 230, which stipulates that "No provider or user of an interactive computer service shall be treated as the publisher or speaker of any information provided by another information content provider" (Section 230 (c)(1)). Congress also added a second provision, the so-called "Good Samaritan" clause, which specifically exempts ISPs from liability for "any action voluntarily taken in good faith to restrict access to or availability of material that the provider or users considers to be obscene, lewd . . . or otherwise objectionable" (Section 230 (c)(2)(A)).

In *Reno v. ACLU* (1997), the U.S. Supreme Court considered the constitutionality of the CDA. This challenge was closely watched, as it was the Supreme Court's first case on free speech in cyberspace. In a landmark decision that held that the indecency provisions of the CDA were unconstitutional, the majority ruled that as a "matter of constitutional tradition . . . we presume that government regulation of the content of speech is more likely to interfere with the free exchange of ideas than to encourage it. The interest in encouraging freedom of expression in a democratic society outweighs any theoretical but unproven benefit of censorship" (p. 844). The Court did not, it is important to add, consider Section 230, nor did the Court's ruling on the indecency provisions otherwise affect this section of the law. Although the Supreme Court has yet to hear a case involving Section 230, a variety of actions involving this provision have already been argued before the lower federal courts.

Zeran v. America Online (1997a, 1997b, 1998)

The first case to rule on Section 230 was *Zeran v. America Online*, a case ultimately decided by the Court of Appeals for the Fourth Circuit. The case began on April 25, 1995, when someone anonymously, and without plaintiff Kenneth Zeran's knowledge or authority, affixed Zeran's name and telephone number to notices on AOL's electronic BB advertising "Naughty Oklahoma T-Shirts" and other items with slogans that glorified the bombing of the Alfred P. Murrah Federal Building in Oklahoma City. The slogans available included "Visit Oklahoma . . . It's a BLAST," "Putting the Kids to Bed . . . Oklahoma 1995," and "McVeigh for President 1996." To order, interested buyers were encouraged to call a Seattle phone number, ask for "Ken," and to "please call back if busy."

The ensuing public outrage was predictable, and Zeran was immediately inundated with derogatory and threatening phone calls. Because Zeran operated a small business from his home, he needed his phone and could not simply change his number or request an unlisted line. In an effort to obtain relief, Zeran notified AOL, which dutifully removed the offending messages and closed the account from which they originated. In accordance with its policy, however, AOL did not post a retraction. Despite AOL's efforts, the unknown user managed to create a new account and repost similar messages. One of the new announcements proclaimed that some items were sold out, highlighted new items with equally offensive slogans (including "Finally a day care center that keeps the kids quiet—Oklahoma 1995"), and even promised that $1 from every sale would be donated to the victims of the bombing. As with the earlier notices, the new postings also contained Zeran's name and telephone number. Once again Zeran contacted AOL, and AOL in turn, removed the anonymous postings.

If this were not bad enough, a broadcaster at radio station KRXO in Oklahoma City learned about the postings and, assuming that the postings was legitimate, actively encouraged his listeners to call "Ken" and voice their collective disgust. As a result, Zeran received death threats and violent calls from Oklahoma City residents. By April 30—5 days after the original posting—Zeran estimated that he was receiving an abusive phone call every 2 minutes. Fearing for Zeran's personal health and safety, the Seattle police placed his home under protective surveillance. Although the station subsequently discovered that the postings were part of an elaborate hoax and apologized, Zeran continued to receive abusive phone calls for several more weeks.

In 1996, Zeran brought suit "under the theory that distributors of information are liable for the distribution of material which they knew or should have known was of a defamatory character" (*Zeran*, 1997a, pp. 1128-1129). More specifically, Zeran argued that AOL was negligent in that it failed to immediately remove the defamatory postings, that AOL had not posted a retraction notifying subscribers that the postings were a hoax, and that AOL had failed to screen for future defamatory postings. AOL did not challenge Zeran's allegation of distributor liability, arguing instead that Zeran's claim was preempted by Section 230 of the CDA.

In dismissing Zeran's suit, a federal district court agreed with AOL's claim that ISPs were protected from state tort actions by the CDA. Because Zeran admitted that AOL was an interactive computer service as defined by the CDA, the case hinged on "whether a state cause of action for negligent distribution of defamatory material directly conflicts with the CDA's prohibition against treating an Internet provider as a 'publisher or speaker'" (p. 1133). To answer the question, the court needed to consider whether "distributor liability is a common law tort concept different from, and unrelated to, publisher liability" (p. 1122). Citing the Second Restatement of Torts, the court concluded that "distributor liability, or more precisely, liability for knowingly or negligently distributing defamatory material, is merely a species or type of liability for publishing defamatory material" (p. 1133). Because distributor liability is a subset of publisher liability, the court concluded, "Zeran's attempt to impose distributor liability on AOL is, in effect, an attempt to have AOL treated as the publisher of the defamatory material. This treatment is contrary to Section 230(c)(1) of the CDA and, thus, Zeran's claim for negligent distribution of the notice is preempted" (p. 1133).

When Zeran appealed, the U.S. Circuit Court of Appeals for the Fourth Circuit upheld the district court. Like the lower court, the Court of Appeals found that "Section 230 precludes courts from entertaining claims that would place a computer service provider in a publisher's role. Thus, lawsuits seeking to hold a service provider liable for its exercise of a publisher's traditional editorial functions—such as deciding whether to publish, withdraw, postpone or alter content—are barred" (*Zeran*, 1997b, p. 330). The Fourth Circuit's rationale was simple: There are millions of postings on computer BBs. If ISPs were responsible for screening all such messages, providers would have no choice but to "severely restrict the number and type of messages posted. Congress considered the weight of the speech interests implicated and chose to immunize service providers to avoid any such restrictive effect" (p. 331).

The Fourth Circuit was equally unimpressed by Zeran's effort to navigate around Section 230 by distinguishing between publisher and distributor liability. "Assuming arguendo that Zeran has satisfied the requirements for imposition of distributor liability," the court noted, "this theory of liability is merely a subset, or a species, of publisher liability, and is therefore also foreclosed by Section 230" (p. 332). Looking beyond the subset question, the court concluded, "Zeran simply attaches too much importance to the presence of the distinct notice element in distributor liability. The simple fact of notice surely cannot transform one from an original publisher to a distributor in the eyes of the law" (p. 332). The Supreme Court denied certiorari (*Zeran*, 1998).

Internet Service Providers and Beyond

Zeran provided "a clear First Amendment precedent for the view that ISPs enjoy broad immunity for such third-party material" (O'Neil, 1998, p. 628). Subsequent decisions have consistently cited this precedent to support the conclusion that Section 230 bars suit under federal or state law that might impose liability on ISPs. As these cases use similar reasoning, they can be quickly summarized as follows:

- In *Blumenthal v. Drudge* (1998), the U.S. District Court for the District of Columbia held that Congress had conferred immunity on ISPs, and hence ruled that Blumenthal could not sue AOL for a story in the *Drudge Report* alleging Blumenthal had abused his spouse. In an effort to distinguish these facts from *Zeran*, Blumenthal argued that Section 230 did not apply in this instance because Matt Drudge was not an anonymous third party using AOL's service, but rather that AOL had contracted with Drudge and paid him to provide the *Drudge Report* to AOL's subscribers. Although sympathetic to the plaintiff's claim that "AOL has certain editorial rights with respect to the content provided by Drudge and disseminated by AOL" (p. 51), the court nonetheless concluded that "Congress has made a different policy choice by providing immunity even where the interactive service provider has an active, even aggressive role in making available content prepared by others" (p. 52). This result is significant because it broadens Section 230 to include content provided by service partners like the *Drudge Report*, in addition to content provided by paying subscribers.

- In *Lunney v. Prodigy* (1999), the New York Court of Appeals held that Prodigy could not be held accountable for defamatory E-mails or postings to a BB about a local scout master made by an anonymous user who had opened a fictitious account under Lunney's name. Although the court "declined the invitation" to decide whether Section 230 could be retroactively applied to statements made before the statute was enacted (p. 543), the decision is significant as the court decided the case using common law principles. Analogizing the ISP to a common carrier, the court ruled Prodigy could not be held responsible for defamatory E-mails transmitted over its service lines. Although acknowledging that Prodigy did exercise some control over its BBs, the court nonetheless concluded that the shear quantity of posting made it impossible to hold Prodigy accountable for the contents of any given message. Although the decision in *Lunney* does not rely on Section 230, the reasoning falls neatly into the *Zeran* line in that it holds that ISPs are not responsible for their subscriber's speech.

- In *Ben Ezra, Weinstein and Company v. America Online* (2000), the Tenth Circuit Court of Appeals held that Section 230 "creates a federal immunity to any state law cause of action that would hold computer service providers liable for information originating with a third party" (pp. 984-985). In this instance, the court held this grant of immunity barred a defamation and negligence suit brought under state law alleging that inaccurate information about the plaintiff's stock price and share volume had been posted to AOL's "Quotes and Portfolio" service area. Borrowing from the language of the

Zeran decision, the court noted, "Congress enacted Section 230 to promote freedom of speech in the 'new and burgeoning Internet medium' by eliminating the 'threat [of] tort-based lawsuits' against interactive services for injury caused by 'the communication of others'" (p. 985).

- In *PatentWizard v. Kinko's* (2001), the U.S. District Court for the Southern District of South Dakota dismissed a suit against Kinko's brought by the attorney who owned and operated PatentWizard, a software package designed for inventors who want to patent their inventions. Using one of Kinko's computers, an unknown person had made disparaging comments about PatentWizard in a chatroom. Because Kinko's does not assign users a unique Internet protocol (IP) address or keep a record of who rents its computers, the plaintiff sued Kinko's for defamation and interference with a business relationship. "For now," the court noted, "Section 230 of the Communication Decency Act errs on the side of robust communication, and prevents the plaintiffs from moving forward with their claims" (p. 1072).

- In *Schneider v. Amazon.com* (2001), the Washington State Court of Appeals considered whether Amazon.com was responsible for defamatory statements about Schneider's works on taxation and asset protection posted to the book review section of Amazon.com's popular web site. When Schneider complained that some of the negative reviews of his work violated Amazon.com's own rules, the company agreed to remove the offending messages. When Amazon.com failed to make good on this promise, Schneider sought legal redress. Although Amazon is not an ISP per se, the court nonetheless analogized Amazon's web site to AOL's popular message boards for Section 230 purposes. Having drawn the parallel, the court cited *Zeran*'s holding that Section 230 "precludes courts from entertaining claims that would place a computer service provider in a publisher's role. Thus, lawsuits seeking to hold a service provider liable for its exercise of a publisher's traditional editorial functions—such as deciding whether to publish, withdraw, postpone or alter content—are barred" (p. 464).

Reviewing this entire line of cases, Patel (2002) concluded "there has not yet been a single case that has held an ISP liable for disseminating third-party defamatory statements over the Internet" (p. 661).

Beyond the defamation decisions, it is important to note that the courts have broadly defined service providers. As a result, the immunity conferred by Section 230 has been extended well beyond traditional ISPs like AOL or Prodigy. This explains why businesses like Kinko's and Amazon.com—a copy shop and a web site selling books and other goods—have successfully used Section 230 as a shield against lawsuits. In *Kathleen R. v. City of Livermore* (2001), a California city successfully argued that its public library qualified as an "interactive computer service" because "library computers enable multiple users to access the Internet" (p. 693). Given that fact, the court held the city could not be sued for its failure to install filters on the library's computers to protect minors like Kathleen R from sexually explicit content.

Although the courts have broadly construed service providers, Section 230 has also been extended to bar claims originating from third-party content involving copyright infringement, invasion of privacy, and the distribution of child pornography. In *Sotner v. eBay.com* (2000), for example, the court held that Section 230 immunized eBay against a suit alleging that eBay knew that many sound recordings being auctioned on its Web site illegally infringed on protected intellectual property. Along the same lines, in *John Does v. Franco Productions* (2000), the court held that Section 230 prevented Illinois State University football players who had been videotaped in various states of undress—without their permission—from suing ISPs that had hosted Web sites where these tapes were sold.

IN DEFENSE OF ZERAN'S INTERPRETATION OF SECTION 230

"Courts construing the CDA and the *Zeran* decision," Pantazis (1999) noted, "have come to identical conclusions even when given strikingly different fact scenarios" (p. 554; Band & Schruers, 2002, p. 301). Despite the consistency of the results, there is growing criticism (Boehm, 1998; Butler, 1999/2000; Davis, 2002; "Developments in the Law," 1999; Ehrlich, 2002; Goldstein, 2000; Hallett, 2001; Holmes, 2001; Kane, 1999; Langdon, 1999; Masur, 2000; Mirmira, 2000; Pantazis, 1999; Patel, 2002; Peterson, 2002; Sheridan, 1997; Slitt, 1998; Spencer, 2000; Waldman, 1999; Wiener, 1999) of both Section 230 and the *Zeran* interpretation in the legal literature. Although a comprehensive summary of this critique is beyond the scope of this analysis, several broad strands of argument have emerged.

Zeran and the Critics

First, critics have argued that the line of cases commencing with *Zeran* goes well beyond Congressional intent. According to this line of reasoning,

Congress only intended to exempt ISPs from publisher liability, not from distributor liability when it adopted Section 230. The significance of this point was more fully elaborated in a note appearing in the *Harvard Law Review* that thoughtfully observed:

> The legislation did not explicitly exempt ISPs from distributor liability, and its specific reference to "publisher or speaker" is evidence that Congress intended to leave distributor liability intact. Nevertheless, in the first case to test the legislation, *Zeran v. America Online, Inc.*, the Fourth Circuit held that 230 immunized defendant America Online from both publisher and distributor liability for alleged defamatory statements on its electronic bulletin boards. The court based its holding on a questionable interpretation of the word "publisher," stating that "distributor" was merely a subset of the word "publisher." ("Developments in the Law," 1999, p. 1613)

"This judicial gloss on defamation liability," Spencer (2000) continued, "shifted provider liability from the strict application in *Stratton Oakmont*, to the prerequisite standard of knew or should have known, pursuant to the CDA, and finally, the extremely generous application of no liability whatsoever in a defamation suit in which a third-party disseminates defamatory messages." By absolving ISPs of any liability, Butler (1999/2000) complained, "the current standard leaves little remedy to those individuals whose reputations have been damaged through the use of Internet communication" (p. 271).

Second, commentators have suggested that the *Zeran* interpretation of Section 230 is counterintuitive, as all agree that Congress intended to encourage ISPs to remove sexually explicit content. By interpreting Section 230 to confer blanket immunity, critics complain that the language has been construed to eliminate any incentive to remove any questionable material. "If other courts follow the path of *Zeran*," Spencer (2000) lamented, "the purpose of Section 230 of the CDA, which is to encourage self-regulation, will evaporate." Because ISPs cannot be held responsible as publishers, and because ISPs cannot be held responsible as distributors when they have knowledge of unlawful material, critics complain Section 230 might actually increase the amount of sexually explicit speech in cyberspace. "Congress was only trying to encourage service providers to take the initiative to protect children from pornography," Goldstein (2000) noted. "It did much more; it undermined defamation law and enabled service providers to escape liability even when they solicit the illegal material and actively engaged in distributing it" (p. 638).

Finally, beyond the question of what Congress intended, commentators like Butler (1999/2000) have observed "the court's current interpretation of the 'good samaritan' provisions of the CDA provide less protection than is needed for libel victims and more protection than is needed for ISPs" (pp. 271-272). By striking the balance so decidedly in favor of ISPs, *Zeran* means that many victims will never be able to recover damages. Echoing this concern, Boehm (1998) suggested, "Promoting the development of the Internet and preserving the vibrant nature of the Internet are valid policies worth protecting. They should, however, be weighed against the interests of citizens harmed by defamatory statements posted to the Internet and around the world." To prevent such an outcome, Boehm concluded "Future courts must attempt to strike a balance between regulating the Internet and providing relief to plaintiffs" (PARA. 50).

As this summary of the criticism of *Zeran* and its progeny is abstract, it may be helpful to consider a case that places these considerations in a graphic context: *Jane Doe v. America Online* (2001). Although this Florida case does not involve defamation per se, it speaks to the question of whether Section 230 should absolve ISPs of all responsibility for material that they distribute for their subscribers. In this case, Jane Doe filed suit on behalf of John Doe, her 11-year-old son. The mother claimed that Richard Lee Russell had lured her son and two other minors to engage in sexual activity with Russell and with each other. The mother further asserted that Russell had photographed and videotaped these acts and used AOL to market this material. After Russell confessed to receiving and distributing child pornography, Jane Doe filed a complaint against AOL alleging, among other things, that the ISP was negligent for allowing Russell and others like him to market child pornography. Doe further alleged that AOL had been apprised of Russell's activities and that the ISP had taken no action against Russell. In its defense, AOL argued that Section 230 of the CDA barred the complaint.

A Palm Beach court dismissed Doe's suit claiming it was barred by federal law and this ruling was upheld by the Fourth District Court of Appeals. Finding that there were legitimate concerns, the appeals court certified several issues for the state's Supreme Court. Relying heavily on *Zeran*, the Florida Supreme Court upheld the dismissal in a narrow 4–3 decision. In the words of the majority, "Section 230 expressly bars 'any actions' and we are compelled to give the language of this preemptive law its plain meaning" (p. 1018). This meant that Jane Doe had no cause of action under state or local law against AOL.

What makes this case particularly notable, however, is a vigorous dissent by Justice Lewis that echoed the themes previously identified by the critics of *Zeran*. According to the dissent, one of the primary goals of the CDA was to promote "decency" on the Internet. Given that fact, Justice Lewis wondered, "What conceivable good could a statute purporting to promote ISP self-policing efforts do if, by virtue of the courts' interpretation of that statute, an ISP which is specifically made aware of child

pornography being distributed by an identified customer through solicitation occurring on its service, may, with impunity, do absolutely nothing,
and reap the economic benefits flowing from the activity?" (pp. 1024-1025).
Reasoning that such "an absurd interpretation is totally unwarranted" (p.
1025), Lewis concluded that "the blanket immunity interpretation adopted
by the majority today thrusts Congress into the unlikely position of having
enacted legislation that encourages and protects the involvement of ISP's as
silent partners in criminal enterprises for profit" (p. 1028).

Instead of absolving AOL of all responsibility, the dissent would adopt
a more pragmatic stance and hold AOL legally responsible once it had
received formal notice. In this instance, AOL's failure to promptly respond
to Jane Doe's complaint might be used to demonstrate negligence.
Although AOL could not be held liable as a publisher, the dissent claims
that *Zeran* incorrectly extended Section 230 to preclude distributor liability. In the process, *Zeran* transformed the language "from an appropriate
shield into a sword of harm and extreme danger which places technology
buzz words and economic considerations above the safety and general welfare of our people" (p. 1020). To prevent this disastrous result, the dissent
argues that Section 230 should be interpreted to hold AOL responsible for
failing to remove Russell's messages marketing child pornography once
Jane Doe had complained about their content. Such an interpretation,
Lewis suggested, would be consistent with the narrow legislative intent of
avoiding publisher liability, while simultaneously providing recourse to
innocent victims like Jane Doe and her son.

The Case for Immunity

Contrary to the critics, a review of the legislative record suggests that the
Zeran decision reflects Congressional intent. "When Congress adopted section 230," Friedman and Buono (2000) noted, "it did not intend to split the
difference between *Cubby* and *Stratton Oakmont*, but rather sought to
replace the then-current legal regime with a clear policy of OSP [online service provider] immunity relative to third-party content, regardless of
whether the OSP was acting as a publisher or distributor of such third
party content" (p. 662). Although it might be argued that the Fourth
Circuit decision in *Zeran* is too deferential to ISPs, the floor debate that led
to the amendment that ultimately became Section 230 is far from definitive
on this point (Cannon, 1996-1997; Finn, Lahey, & Redle, 2000).

Beyond the question of legislative intent, there are compelling reasons
for broadly interpreting the immunity conferred in Section 230. Holding
ISPs accountable as distributors would have a chilling effect on the freedom
of expression. As the Court of Appeals correctly noted in *Zeran* (1997b):

> If computer service providers were subject to distributor liability, they would face potential liability each time they receive notice of a potentially defamatory statement—from any party, concerning any message. Each notification would require a careful yet rapid investigation of the circumstances surrounding the posted information, a legal judgment concerning the information's defamatory character, and an on-the-spot editorial decision whether to risk liability by allowing the continued publication of that information. (p. 333)

Under such a scheme, anyone who was displeased with a Web site or a posting to a BB could formally notify the relevant service provider and claim that the message was defamatory. Given the volume of speech and the possibility for being held responsible for not responding, most ISPs would likely suppress any controversial or otherwise objectionable speech. "Thus," the Court of Appeals concluded, "like strict liability, liability on notice has a chilling effect on the freedom of Internet speech" (p. 333).

In an effort to downplay this concern, critics of *Zeran* have attempted to minimize or even deny the significance of this chilling effect. Although some (Sheridan, 1997) have suggested that ISPs have an inherent financial incentive to protect speech, others (Butler, 1999/2000; Hallett, 2001; Holmes, 2001) have suggested that it might be possible to protect speech by creating formal notice and takedown provisions modeled after the procedure for dealing with copyright infringement set out in the Digital Millennium Copyright Act (DMCA). On closer examination, however, it is apparent that these strategies for minimizing the chilling effect are flawed. Neither incentives nor formal legal schemes afford as much protection to user's speech rights as the immunity conferred on ISPs by the *Zeran* decision. Although they discount its importance, even the critics of *Zeran* must admit that "anything but absolute immunity inevitably results in the chilling of some speech" (Sheridan, 1997, p. 178).

Consider, for example, the financial incentives argument. "News travels fast over interactive computer services," Sheridan (1997) argued, "and a service that removes members' postings without any investigation is likely to get a bad reputation in a community whose first value is the free flow of information" (pp. 176-177). Even if consumers do cherish the free flow of information, however, there is little reason to believe that they will invest the time required to gather the necessary information required to make informed decisions about the behavior of their ISP. Even if some subscribers did switch ISPs, the threat of a single defamation judgment would more than offset the loss of hundreds or even thousands of subscribers. Moreover, this entire line of reasoning assumes that the free flow of information is more important to consumers than the price of access, the quality of customer service, or the unique content provided by a particular ISP.

Along the same lines, it is doubtful that a scheme modeled after the DMCA's copyright provision would protect speech. Under the mandates of the DMCA, formal notification must include proof the party is authorized to act on behalf of the copyright owner, identification of the copyrighted work being infringed and the location of the infringing material, as well as a statement made in good faith that the complaining party believes that the use is an infringement. "Such a procedure," Butler (1999/2000) argued, "could work effectively in the context of distributor liability for defamatory statements as well. . . . Each complainer could be required to swear (under penalty of perjury) that she has made her accusation of libel in good faith, and to make a detailed factual accounting of her basis for claiming that the assertion is false and injurious to her reputation" (p. 262). By creating objective standards, Hallett (2001) suggested, "the First Amendment concerns will also be alleviated because the notice and counter notification standard takes the pressure off of the ISP" (p. 278).

Although notice and takedown procedures might provide some measure of procedural protection for speech, the analogy to copyright law is extremely tenuous. Although copyright infringement raises difficult issues, assessing copyright infringement is not nearly so complicated or as subjective as evaluating defamation claims. Along the same lines, it is difficult to imagine a corporation or a politician using copyright infringement to systematically silence its critics. The real problem with the notice and takedown solution, however, is that it offers comparatively little protection for expression (Band & Schruers, 2002). An ISP cannot be sued for removing speech on receipt of a complaint, but the ISP would become liable as a distributor if it failed to act in an expeditious manner. Given the relative risks, the prudent ISP would have little incentive to zealously defend the First Amendment rights of the subscriber.

Beyond this discussion of the chilling effect, it is important to note that holding ISPs responsible as distributors moves away from the broader principle that more speech is the best response to bad speech. "Whenever one was displeased with the speech of another party conducted over an interactive computer service," the Court of Appeals worried in *Zeran*, "the offended party could simply 'notify' the relevant service provider, claiming the information to be legally defamatory" (p. 333). Rather than encouraging a new generation of plaintiffs to seek satisfaction from ISPs and the courts, a better policy would be to encourage aggrieved parties to use the Internet to answer defamatory speech. Justice Brandeis articulated the philosophy underlying this view of the First Amendment in *Whitney v. California* (1927):

> If there be time to expose through discussion the falsehood and fallacies, to avert the evil by the processes of education, the remedy to be

applied is more speech, not enforced silence. Only an emergency can justify repression. Such must be the rule if authority is to be reconciled with freedom. Such, in my opinion, is the command of the Constitution. (p. 377)

This idea that more speech is the best solution to harmful speech holds especially true in cyberspace (Branscomb, 1995). Because of the low cost, relative ease of use, and capacity to accommodate an almost infinite number of speakers at once, the Internet provides the perfect forum for counteractive speech. In the words of Godwin (1996), "If some bozo writes 100 lines of false statement and innuendo about your self life or personal habits, you wan write 500 lines of point-by-point refutation. It's a 'day in court' that comes cheap."

All of this is not to suggest that there should be no redress for defamation on the Internet. Rather, it is to suggest that the solution is not to punish the intermediary, but rather to hold speakers who create and post unlawful material responsible for their expression. In adopting Section 230, Congress wisely decided that plaintiffs should not seek redress from ISPs, but rather from the users who actually make the defamatory statements. By renouncing both publisher and distributor liability, *Zeran v. America Online* dramatically expands the space for speech on the Internet. Given the explosive growth of the Internet, *Zeran* has the potential to become just as consequential as the Supreme Court's landmark decision in *New York Times v. Sullivan* (1964). In the words of Johnson (1997), "This case . . . will be very good for the free flow of information online. And of course it leaves liability where it belongs—in the hands of wrongdoers" (cited in Schmidt, 1997, p. 1).

REFERENCES

Anschütz, D. (2001, December). The talk of the web. www.onmagazine.com, pp. 42-44.

Baitinger v. Fajardo, No. 160034 (Cir. Ct. Va.). (1997).

Band, J., & Schruers, M. (2002). Safe harbors against the liability hurricane: The Communications Decency Act and the Digital Millennium Copyright Act. *Cardozo Arts and Entertainment Law Journal, 20*, 295-320.

Ben Ezra, Weinstein & Co. v. America Online, 206 F.3rd 980 (10th Cir.). (2000).

Blumenthal v. Drudge and America Online, 992 F. Supp. 44 (D.D.C.). (1998).

Boehm, S.B. (1998, Winter). A brave new world of free speech: Should interactive computer service providers be held liable for the material they disseminate? *Richmond Journal of Law & Technology, 5*, 7+. Available at <http://law.richmond.edu/jolt//v5i2/boehm.html>.

Bowker v. America Online, No. 95L 013509 (Cir. Ct. Cook Cty. Ill.). (1995, September).

Branscomb, A.W. (1995). Anonymity, autonomy, and accountability: Challenges to the First Amendment in cyberspaces. *Yale Law Journal, 104,* 1639-1679.

Bray, H. (1995, December 14). Prodigy loses appeal in libel case; Ruling finding firm liable for material is upheld. *Boston Globe*, p. 51.

Butler, C. (1999/2000). Plotting the return of an ancient tort to cyberspace: Towards a new federal standard of responsibility for defamation for Internet service providers. *Michigan Telecommunication and Technology Law Review, 6,* 247-272.

Cannon, R. (1996-1997). The legislative history of Senator Exon's Communications Decency Act: Regulating barbarians on the information superhighway. *Federal Communications Commission Law Journal, 49,* 51-94.

Cubby Inc. v. CompuServe, Inc., 776 F. Supp. 135 (S.D. N.Y.). (1991).

Davis, B.J. (2002). Untangling the "publisher" versus "information content provider" paradox of 47 U.S.C. Section 230: Toward a rational application of the Communications Decency Act in defamation suits against Internet service providers. *New Mexico Law Review, 32,* 75-97.

Developments in the law—The law of cyberspace: III. The long arm of cyber-reach. (1999). *Harvard Law Review, 112,* 1610-1634.

E.D. Va. Jury awards $675,000 in first Internet defamation verdict. (2001). *E-Business Insurance Legal Report, 1*(19), 5.

Ehrlich, P., III. (2002). Cyberlaw: B. Regulating conduct on the internet: Communications Decency Act Section 230. *Berkeley Technology Law Journal, 17,* 401-419.

Finn, M.K., Lahey, K., & Redle, D. (2000). Policies underlying congressional approval of criminal and civil immunity for interactive computer service providers under provisions of the Communications Decency Act of 1996— Should e-buyers beware? *University of Toledo Law Review, 31,* 347-372.

Frankel, A. (1995, October). On-line, on the hook. *American Lawyer*, pp. 59-66.

Friedman, J.A., & Buono, F.M. (2000). Limiting tort liability for online third-party content under Section 230 of the Communications Act. *Federal Communication Law Journal, 52,* 647-665.

Godfrey v. Cornell University, High Court of Justice (U.K.) (complaint filed October 1997).

Godfrey v. Demon Internet Ltd., QBD, [1999] 4 All ER 342, [2000] 3 WLR 1020; [2001] QB 201.

Godwin, M. (1996, March). Libel law: Let it die. *Wired, 4.03.* Available at <http://www.wired.com/wired/archive/4.03/letitdie.html>.

Goldstein, M.P. (2000). Service provider liability for acts committed by users: What you don't know can hurt you. *John Marshall Journal of Computer & Information Law, 18,* 591-641.

Haddad, C. (1995, May 27). Prodigy libel ruling raises questions of on-line services' responsibilities. *Atlanta Journal and Constitution*, p. 3D.

Hallett, D.E. (2001). How to destroy a reputation and get away with it—The Communication Decency Act examined: Do the policies and standards set out in the Digital Millennium Copyright Act provide a solution for a person defamed online? *IDEA: Journal of Law and Technology, 41,* 259-282.

Holmes, L.H. (2001). Making waves in statutory safe harbors: Reevaluating internet service providers' liability for third-party content and copyright infringement. *Roger Williams University Law Review, 7,* 215-245.

Jane Doe v. America Online, 783 So.2d 1010 (Fla. S. Ct.). (2001).

John Does v. Franco Productions, 2000 U.S. Dist. LEXIS 8645 (N.D. Ill.). (2000).

Jury orders former employees to pay substantial damages for Internet libel. (2002). *Computer & Internet Lawyer, 19*(3), 18.

Kane, M.J. (1999). Internet service provider liability: *Blumenthal v. Drudge. Berkeley Technology Law Journal, 14,* 483-501.

Kathleen R. v. City of Livermore, 87 Cal. App. 4th 684 (Cal. App. 1st Dist.). (2001).

Langdon, R.T. (1999). The Communication Decency Act Section 230: Make sense? Or nonsense?—A private person's inability to recover if defamed in cyberspace. *St. John's Law Review, 73,* 829-855.

Lewis, P.H. (1995, 25 October). After apology from Prodigy, firm drops suit. *The New York Times,* p. D1.

Lunney v. Prodigy, 723 N.E. 2d 539 (N.Y. Ct.). (App. 1999).

Masur, J.M. (2000). A most uncommon carrier: Online service provider immunity against defamation claims in *Blumenthal v. Drudge. Jurimetrics: The Journal of Law, Science and_Technology, 40,* 217-228.

Medphone Corp. v. DeNigris, Civil Action No. 92-3785 (D. N.J.). (1993).

Melvin v. Doe, 49 Pa. D. & C.4th 449 (Ct. of Common Pleas, Allegheny Co., Pa.). (2000).

Mirmira, S. (2000). Business law: *Lunney v. Prodigy Services Co. Berkeley Technology Law Journal, 15,* 437-458.

Morrison v. America Online, 153 F. Supp. 2d 930 (N.D. Ind.). (2001).

New York Times Co. v. Sullivan, 376 U.S. 254. (1964).

O'Neil, R.M. (1998). The *Drudge* case: A look at issues in cyberspace defamation. *Washington Law Review, 73,* 623-636.

Pantazis, A. (1999). *Zeran v. American Online, Inc.:* Insulating Internet service providers from defamation liability. *Wake Forest Law Review, 34,* 531-555.

Patel, S. (2002). Immunizing Internet service providers from third-party Internet defamation claims: How far should courts go? *Vanderbilt Law Review, 55,* 647-691.

PatentWizard, Inc. v. Kinko's, 163 F. Supp. 2d 1069 (D. S.D.). (2001).

Peterson, D.I. (2002). Child pornography on the Internet: The effect of Section 230 of the Communications Decency Act of 1996 on tort recovery for victims against internet service providers. *Hawaii Law Review, 24,* 763-795.

Reno v. ACLU, 521 U.S. 844. (1997).

Schmidt, R. (1997, November 24). Liability and libel in cyberspace. *Legal Times,* p. 1.

Schneider v. Amazon.Com, Inc., 31 P.3d 37 (Ct. of Appeals, Wash.). (2001).

Sheridan, D.R. (1997). *Zeran v. AOL* and the effects of Section 230 of the Communications Decency Act upon liability for defamation on the internet. *Albany Law Review, 61,* 147-179.

Siver, K. (1997). Good Samaritans in cyberspace. *Rutgers Computer and Technology Law Journal, 23*, 1-46.

Slitt, A.J. (1998). The anonymous publisher. Defamation on the Internet after *Reno v. American Civil Liberties Union* and *Zeran v. America Online. Connecticut Law Review, 31*, 389-421.

Sotner v. eBay.com, 56 U.S.P.Q. 1852 (Cal. Sup. Ct.). (2000).

Spencer, M.A. (2000). Defamatory e-mail and employer liability: Why razing *Zeran v. America Online* is a good thing. *Richmond Journal of Law & Technology, 6*, 25+. Available at <http://law.richmond.edu/jolt//v6i5/article4.html>.

Stratton Oakmont, Inc. and Daniel Porush, v. Prodigy Services Co., 23 Med. L. Rptr. 1795 (N.Y. Sup. Ct. May 24). (1995a).

Stratton Oakmont, Inc. v. Prodigy Services Co., No. 94-03163 (N.Y. Sup. Ct.). (1995b, December 11).

Suarez Corp. Ind. v. Meeks, No. 267513 (Ct. of Common Pleas, Cuyahoga Co., OH). (1994).

Waldman, B. J. (1999). A unified approach to cyber-libel: Defamation on the Internet, a suggested approach. *Richmond Journal of Law & Technology, 6*, 9+. Available at < http://law.richmond.edu/jolt//v6i2/note1.html>.

Walker, M. (1995, May 27). Internet rocked by US libel case. *London Guardian*, p. 3.

Whitney v. California, 274 U.S. 357. (1927).

Wiener, D. (1999). Negligent publication of statements posted on electronic bulletin boards: Is there any liability left after *Zeran? Santa Clara Law Review, 39*, 905-939.

Zeran v. America Online, 958 F. Supp. 1124 (E.D. Va.). (1997a).

Zeran v. America Online, 129 F.4d 327 (4th Cir.). (1997b).

Zeran v. America Online, 524 U.S. 937. (1998).

Zitner, A. (1995, May 26). New York judge allows ground-breaking libel suit against Prodigy. *Boston Globe*, p. 68.

13

Anonymous Defamation and Libel-by-Linking

Whom Do You Sue?

Juliet Dee
University of Delaware

The U.S. Supreme Court has ruled that anonymous speech is protected under the First Amendment. By nature, cyberspace fosters a degree of anonymity in communication. Absent the extra effort required to authenticate a source, anonymous sources may originate or retransmit defamatory statements on the Internet. Juliet Dee considers the intriguing issues raised in a cyber environment in which a person may assume a false identity, defame another and even "link" to other websites (so called libel-by-linking) which increases the potential audience and thus damage to reputation.

During the last decade, legal scholars have struggled with the question of how to apply traditional law to the Internet as lawyers scrambled to come up to speed in "cyberlaw." Anonymous speech has existed for centuries. Although the U.S. Supreme Court has clearly affirmed that anonymous speech is protected by the First Amendment (*McIntyre v. Ohio Elections Commission*, 1995), anonymous speech on the Internet raises a new set of variables. Anonymous speech is prevalent on the Internet, and it can be very difficult to learn the identity of an anonymous speaker who defames or harms others on an Internet bulletin board (BB), for example.

Anonymous speech per se is not necessarily harmful; for example, Susan Barnes (2001) explained:

> Because we do not see the electronic others in online discourse, it is easier to assume roles and play with identity. Thus, the Internet can become a playground for experimenting with concepts of self that are not bound by gender, age or physical appearance. Our true identity can remain anonymous as various online persona engage in Internet interactions. (p. 67)

But Barnes (1999) has also cautioned that because

> digital technologies enable us to separate our physical self from the communication exchange, [individuals can] assume roles, create fraudulent personas and utilize pseudonyms. Using false identities, people can write deceptive messages and behave in ways that would be socially unacceptable in traditional face-to-face situations. As a result, the presentation of self in computer-mediated communication introduces new ethical issues that do not exist in other forms of communication. . . .
>
> Anonymous individuals can make false or harmful statements about others without acknowledging responsibility for their acts. Currently, it is difficult to locate the identity of these individuals without legal intervention. How can people be protected from harmful remarks when the identity of the accuser is unknown? (pp. 371-372)

It is bad enough that one can assume a persona and then defame someone else on the Internet, but even worse, one can establish a "link"[1] from one Web site containing defamatory comments to another. This can magnify and increase the number of potential readers with access to the original libelous comments. Although courts have not issued any decisions on the specific problem of libel-by-linking, the recent case of *Universal City Studios, Inc. et al. V. Corley and 2600 Enterprises, Inc.* (2001) addresses the problem of linking with regard to copyright infringement. Thus, the discussion here concludes with a look at how *Universal City Studios* (2001) may affect future court rulings on the dilemma of libel-by-linking.

IMMUNITY FROM LIABILITY FOR DEFAMATION GRANTED TO INTERNET SERVICE PROVIDERS

When the Fourth Circuit affirmed *Zeran v. America Online, Inc.* (1997), it interpreted the Communications Decency Act (CDA), which was part of the Telecommunications Act of 1996, as granting total immunity to Internet service providers (ISPs) such as America Online (AOL) in cases in which they were sued for content originating with a third party. Congress thus treated them as common carriers just as telephone companies have (nearly always) enjoyed the legal status of common carriers (Dee, 1994). *Zeran* set a precedent that made it difficult and in some cases impossible for anyone defamed on an Internet BB or Web site to prevail in a libel suit when the defendant was anonymous.

To complicate matters, in some cases, victims of defamation have found that injuries to their reputations were magnified through Internet "links" to other Web sites. In one case, *Curzon-Brown and Wall v. City College of San Francisco and Lathouwers* (2000), two plaintiffs brought suit against a community college that had a link to a BB on which one of the plaintiffs was falsely described as a rapist, child molester, and a murderer. In contrast, there are four cases, *HealthSouth Corp. v. Krum* (1998), *Attkisson v. John Doe* (1999), *Graham v. Oppenheimer* (2000), and *Sabbato v. Hardy and Rudy* (2000), in which the plaintiffs have prevailed in suits against an initially anonymous detractor. In *HealthSouth, Attkisson, Graham,* and *Sabbato,* the plaintiffs' attorneys sued *John Doe* in order to win the right to engage in discovery to learn real identities of the John Does. The following discussion examines the effects of the *Zeran* decision on subsequent attempts to sue anonymous defendants for defamation on Internet BBs.

Surprisingly, the Supreme Court of Florida has even relied on *Zeran* to grant immunity to AOL for knowingly permitting advertising of videos of child pornography (*Doe v. America Online, Inc.,* 2001). Although this discussion focuses primarily on the problem of anonymous Internet defamation, it briefly considers the implications of applying *Zeran* to other types of cases such as those involving child pornography.

CYBERSLAPP SUITS

This discussion focuses on the problem of one individual defaming another individual. It does *not* focus on the problem of an anonymous individual criticizing a corporation and then suddenly becoming the defendant in a "cyberSLAPP" lawsuit, although a brief explanation of the issue of cyberSLAPP suits is provided here. In a cyberSLAPP suit, a corporation files a frivolous suit and issues a subpoena in bad faith, simply to discover the identity of its anonymous online critics in order to silence them. (SLAPP is an acronym for Strategic Lawsuits Against Public Participation.) Of course, courts must find a way to balance the conflict between a company's right to be free from defamatory harm and an Internet user's First Amendment right to anonymously criticize a company online. Unlike traditional defamation cases in which an individual sues a media defendant, a traditional cybersmear lawsuit pits corporate plaintiffs against individuals with little or no resources to hire legal representation (Lidsky, 2000).

Judges also need guidelines on when to issue a subpoena. At present, the Electronic Communications Privacy Act (ECPA), as amended in 1994, is the only federal statute that provides a specific set of guidelines for judges to issue subpoenas for law enforcement agencies that seek to discover the identity of an Internet user in a criminal case (18 U.S.C. S 2703 [c] [1] [C] 1994). Legal scholar Wade Davis (2002) observed, however, that "Unfortunately, the [ECPA] is virtually silent when it comes to subpoena requests in a civil action" (p. 14). Indeed, "the [ECPA] merely notes that an ISP may disclose a record or other information pertaining to a subscriber . . . to any person other than a governmental entity" (18 U.S.C. S 2703 [c] [1] [A] 1994). Davis explained that at present there is "no coherent statutory or common law national standard determining when a court should issue a subpoena requiring an ISP to disclose identifying information on its users in a civil action" (p. 14). Davis argued: "The ECPA's failure to establish any standard to protect anonymous Internet users against civil suits . . . has resulted in a situation where Internet users' privacy and free speech rights are threatened" (pp. 14-15).

In addition to the problem that judges have no guidelines for issuing subpoenas, there is also the problem that, at present, there is also no legal requirement that ISPs notify their customers before complying with such subpoenas even though many cyberSLAPP suits are frivolous and have no chance of prevailing in court. In 2002, a coalition of the American Civil Liberties Union (ACLU), the Center for Democracy and Technology (CDT), the Electronic Frontier Foundation (EFF), the Electronic Privacy Information Center (EPIC), and Public Citizen asked more than 100 ISPs to include in their privacy policies a promise that they would notify any subscribers whose personal information or identities are subpoenaed. Three major online service providers (OPSs), Yahoo!, Earthlink, and AOL,[2] already notify their customers when they receive subpoenas for identifying information, but many others do not ("Privacy Groups," 2002).

The ISPs that do notify their subscribers before disclosing individual identities in response to a subpoena may have been encouraged to do so as a result of a case in which the company AnswerThink Consulting Group, Inc. issued subpoenas in order to learn the identities of 12 anonymous defendants whom AnswerThink claimed had defamed it ("John Doe," 2000). One of these 12 defendants was identified as Aquacool_2000; he had described AnswerThink's management team as follows: "One of them is an arrested adolescent whose favorite word is 'turd.' One is so dull that a 5-watt bulb gives him a run for the money. And the third believes that the faster you go in your car, the smarter you get" (*Aquacool_2000 v. Inc.,* 2000, Complaint, 8). Anyone familiar with the law of defamation would immediately recognize that "Aquacool's" comments, although derogatory, would not constitute defamation because they are statements of opinion rather than fact and were thus not actionable. Nonetheless, Yahoo! released the identities of the 12 defendants in response to the subpoenas, and AnswerThink immediately fired Aquacool_2000, who subsequently filed suit against Yahoo! for violation of privacy, breach of contract, negligent misrepresentation, and false advertising (*Aquacool_2000 v. Inc.,* 2000, Complaint, 1). Aquacool's attorney, Megan Gray, charged that "With sensitive egos and money to burn, such companies [as AnswerThink] often file a lawsuit merely in order to obtain the right to subpoena for members' information so that the company's curiosity and desire to silence the member [of the message board] can be satiated" (*Aquacool_2000 v. Inc.,* 2000, Complaint, 6).

Although Yahoo!'s Privacy Policy cautions that "We respond to subpoenas, court orders, or legal process" (Privacy Policy, 2002), "Aquacool" charged that "Yahoo! does not inform or in any way notify a member when Yahoo! receives a subpoena for the member's private information" (*Aquacool_2000 v. Inc.,* 2000, Complaint, 5). Aquacool's case against Yahoo! was eventually settled out of court with the terms of the settlement under seal ("Cybersmears and Message Boards," 2002).

The case of *Aquacool_2000* is merely one example of what can occur when a corporation uses a subpoena to unmask its critics. The larger question of the problem posed when corporations use all of their legal resources to silence critics in cyberSLAPP suits is beyond the scope of the current discussion, however. Various legal scholars (Davis, 2002; "Cybersmears and Message Boards," 2002; Lidsky, 2000) have provided invaluable analyses of the issue of cyberSLAPP suits, and readers are encouraged to pursue this question elsewhere.

As mentioned earlier, the current discussion focuses instead on cases in which there is at least ostensibly a more level playing field. In other words, this discussion covers situations in which one anonymous individual is defaming another individual as opposed to criticizing a corporation, and there is no underlying motive such as an attempt to manipulate stock prices, for example.

SETTING PRECEDENTS: SECTION 230 PROTECTS ISPS FROM LIABILITY

In the cases of Zeran (1997), Lunney (1998), and Doe (2001), the plaintiffs were victims of cruel practical jokes (Zeran; Lunney) or child pornography (Doe). Although the plaintiffs pleaded with AOL or Prodigy to help them stop the virtual torture from Internet postings, all three plaintiffs lost their cases due to the protections for ISPs granted in Section 230 of the Communications Decency Act (CDA).

Zeran v. America Online (1997)

On April 19, 1995, Timothy McVeigh killed 168 people when he bombed the Alfred P. Murrah Federal Building in Oklahoma City. Six days later, on April 25, 1995, an unidentified person posted a message on an AOL BB advertising T-shirts featuring offensive and vulgar slogans glorifying the bombing, such as "Finally, a daycare that keeps its kids quiet." The posting instructed anyone wanting to buy the T-shirts to call "Ken" at Kenneth Zeran's home phone number in Seattle, Washington. Zeran himself was utterly unaware of the AOL posting, but he immediately received angry and abusive telephone calls about every 2 minutes, and some of the callers made death threats against him. Zeran lived at home so that he could look after his elderly parents, and he was very concerned that they might be harmed because the AOL posting had included his address. After Oklahoma City radio station KRXO urged its listeners to call Zeran and denounce him for the offensive postings, the death threats increased, and Zeran had to receive police protection for several months. Zeran called AOL repeatedly and asked them to take down the posting, but AOL simply stone-walled Zeran. AOL kept promising Zeran that it would close the account of the anonymous and vicious prankster, but the vicious postings identifying Zeran as the seller of the T-shirts continued for several months after April 1995.

Zeran wanted to sue the anonymous party who posted the messages, but AOL made no effort whatsoever to assist him in learning the identity of the vicious prankster. AOL claimed that it had been running a promotion in which anyone who received its "sign-on" disk in the mail could sign on for several days without letting AOL know his/her true identity. Thus, AOL claimed that the vicious prankster had availed himself of this promotion but that AOL could not tell Zeran his actual identity because it did not know. Although AOL's excuses sound both irresponsible and disingenuous, Zeran had to explain in court that AOL made it impossible to identify the original party by failing to maintain adequate records of its users. When AOL refused to identify the vicious prankster who had posted the messages in Zeran's name, Zeran felt that he had no option other than to sue AOL for negligence. He argued that AOL had (a) failed to remove the postings for several months, (b) refused to post retractions of the postings, and (c) failed to screen for similar postings thereafter.

AOL argued that the CDA of 1996 (47 U.S.C. § 230) barred Zeran's claims because Section 230 grants immunity from liability to ISPs like AOL when defamatory content originates with third parties. AOL prevailed in the federal district court, and the U.S. Court of Appeals for the Fourth Circuit affirmed the district court decision. *Zeran* thus provided the first opportunity for the judiciary to interpret the CDA in a case that involved not obscenity, the statute's target, but defamation, which Congress had not overtly contemplated during its deliberations regarding the CDA.

In deciding *Zeran*, the Fourth Circuit reasoned that if ISPs such as AOL were subject to "distributor liability," they would face potential liability "each time they receive notice of a potentially defamatory statement. . . . Although this might be feasible for the traditional print publisher, the sheer number of postings on interactive computer services would create an impossible burden in the Internet context" (*Zeran v. American Online, Inc.,* 1997, p. 333).

The Fourth Circuit further argued that

> notice-based liability for interactive computer service providers would provide third parties with a no-cost means to create the basis for future lawsuits. Whenever one was displeased with the speech of another party conducted over an interactive computer service, the offended party could simply "notify" the relevant service provider, claiming the information to be legally defamatory. In light of the vast amount of speech communicated through interactive computer services, these notices could produce an impossible burden for service providers, who would be faced with ceaseless choices of suppressing controversial speech or sustaining prohibitive liability. Because the probable effects of distributor liability on the vigor of Internet speech and on service provider self-regulation are directly contrary to § 230's statutory

purposes, we will not assume that Congress intended to leave liability
on notice intact. (*Zeran v. America Online*, Inc., 1997, p. 333)

The Fourth Circuit thus interpreted Section 230 as conferring immunity on
AOL, finding that AOL could not be held liable for carrying the defamatory postings. Furthermore, it could not be held liable for failing to remove
the postings even when Zeran had pleaded repeatedly with AOL to do so.
Zeran himself was left with legal bills, the lingering fear that the anonymous prankster could strike again, and the knowledge that if the prankster
should strike again, there was absolutely nothing Zeran could do to protect
himself. How fair was that?

Following *Zeran*, there were numerous law review articles whose
authors questioned the *Zeran* court's interpretation of Section 230 of the
CDA. Sheridan (1997) observed that after *Zeran*,

> Legal treatment of defamatory material in electronic letters to the
> editor and postings on electronic bulletin boards . . . differs dramatical-
> ly from that of printed letters to the editor. . . . Under *Zeran*, the
> publisher of a print newspaper could face liability for printing a defam-
> atory letter to the editor, while the publisher of an electronic newspa-
> per would be immune from liability for carrying . . . the same text. . . .
> A newspaper that published the same letter in its print and electronic
> version could face defamation liability for the paper version, but not
> the electronic version.
>
> These differences in legal treatment are difficult to justify by any
> differences in the technology involved. Further, to the extent that the
> immunity from liability from in *Zeran* is mandated by the CDA, it
> exceeds any that is required to implement the CDA's goals. (Sheridan,
> 1997, pp. 149-150)

Sheridan concluded that "construing Section 230 to immunize interactive [Internet] services from distributor liability creates an asymmetry
between electronic and print media that is difficult to justify" (p. 179).

Slitt (1998) described Section 230 of the CDA as "a loophole in a law
that . . . protects the First Amendment integrity of cyberspace communications, but . . . does so at the expense of the libel victim" (p. 389). Slitt continued: "Unfortunately, the CDA still leaves an unresolved paradox—the
anonymous publisher . . . Defamed plaintiffs may be left with no redress
when their reputations are damaged or they are otherwise harassed by a
defendant whose identity is unknown and undiscoverable" (p. 391). Lidsky
(2000) likewise questioned *Zeran*, noting that "The poisonous atmosphere
of the easy lie can infect a whole society" (p. 857).

Lunney v. Prodigy Services Company (1998)

Zeran became the precedent for denying distributor liability in subsequent cases such as *Lunney v. Prodigy Services Company* (1998). In September 1994, a "foul-mouthed teenager" usurped the identity of 15-year-old prospective Eagle Scout Alex Lunney and sent a vulgar E-mail message via Prodigy to Lunney's Boy Scout leader in which he threatened to sodomize the scout leader's sons and made other threats as well. The Boy Scout leader immediately reported the threats to the police and to Alex Lunney's scout master, who confronted Lunney and his mother and demanded an explanation. Lunney, of course, knew nothing about the threatening E-mail messages, and explained that he had never subscribed to Prodigy. The scout master apparently believed Lunney.

Lunney, however, was so distressed at learning that someone was sending vicious threats in his name that he filed suit against Prodigy for libel, negligence, and harassment. The libel suit against Prodigy was based on an internal electronic bookkeeping entry made by a Prodigy agent describing Lunney as "a non-paying disconnect subscriber 143 days delinquent" and also a handwritten internal memo stating that "Alex Lunney has been terminated for credit card fraud as well as obscene material" (*Lunney v. Prodigy Services Company*, 1998, p. 559). In a letter dated October 27, 1994, however, a representative of Prodigy apologized to Lunney and advised him that several fictitious accounts that had been opened under his name had been terminated.

Despite Prodigy's apology, however, Lunney did not withdraw his suit. The Supreme Court of New York, citing *Zeran* and Section 230 of the CDA, granted Prodigy's motion for summary judgment. Just as AOL claimed that it did not know who the vicious prankster was in *Zeran*, Prodigy did not provide Lunney with the identity of the person who was threatening the Boy Scout leader in Lunney's name; thus, Lunney could not pursue a defamation action against the person who was actually harming his reputation.

Doe v. America Online, Inc. (2001)

As mentioned earlier, the focus of this discussion is on lawsuits involving anonymous Internet defamation, but I briefly digress because in *Doe v. America Online, Inc.* (2001), the Supreme Court of Florida relied on *Zeran* in its ruling that AOL was immune from an action involving advertising of child pornography. This case began when Richard Lee Russell lured 11-year-old "John Doe" and two other boys to engage in sexual activity with Russell, who photographed and videotaped their encounter and used

AOL's chatrooms to market this child pornography. Russell used AOL to distribute an advertisement with "a visual depiction of sexual conduct involving John Doe." Despite repeated notices from John Doe's mother, AOL neither warned Russell to stop advertising the obscene and unlawful images of John Doe, nor did AOL suspend Russell's service.

John Doe's mother sued AOL for negligence after it made no attempt to stop Russell from advertising child pornography, but AOL moved to dismiss, arguing that "John Doe's" claims were barred by Section 230 of the CDA. The trial court granted AOL's motion to dismiss, the Fourth District Court of Appeal affirmed the trial court, and the Supreme Court of Florida likewise affirmed, ruling that Section 230 did indeed guarantee AOL immunity, even for carrying advertisements for child pornography.

The Supreme Court of Florida's decision was not unanimous, however; it was a 4–3 decision with three justices dissenting. Justice Lewis, who authored the dissent, questioned the interpretation of the Section 230 in *Zeran*:

> Contrary to the majority's view, [Section 230] . . . does not reflect an intent to totally exonerate and insulate an ISP (Internet Service Provider) from responsibility where, as here, it is alleged that an ISP has acted as a knowing distributor of material leading to the purchase, sale, expansion and advancement of child pornography, after having been given actual notice of the particular activity, by taking absolutely no steps to curtail continued dissemination of [the ad] . . . when it had the right and power to do so. . . . Through the majority's interpretation, the so-called "Decency Act" has, contrary to well-established legal principles, been transformed from an appropriate shield into a sword of harm and extreme danger which places technology buzz words and economic considerations above the safety and general welfare of our people. . . . By interpreting the statute to provide this carte blanche immunity for wrongful conduct plainly not intended by Congress, the majority view ignores . . . the statute's legislative history. (*Doe v. America Online, Inc.*, 2001, p. 1019)

Justice Lewis continued, arguing that "the fatal flaw in Zeran's logic—and thus, in the majority view—is its erroneous conclusion that, under Section 577 of the Restatement of Torts (Second), distributors are merely an internal category of publishers" (p. 1021). Justice Lewis explained that Section 577(2) of the Restatement recognizes potential liability for a proprietor's failure to remove defamatory material on his/her land of which he or she is aware (p. 1021).

Justice Lewis asked:

> What conceivable good could [Section 230], a statute purporting to promote ISP self-policing efforts, do if, by virtue of the courts' interpretation of that statute, an ISP which is specifically made aware of child pornography being distributed to an identified customer through solicitation occurring on its service, may, with impunity, do absolutely nothing, and reap the economic benefits flowing from the activity? Such an absurd interpretation is totally unwarranted. . . . As one legal commentator has observed, . . . Congress intended to leave distributor liability intact. (pp. 1024-1025)

> . . . Congress never intended for such a broad immunity to apply. In cutting a wide swath of immunity from the cloth of the purposefully narrow language, the analysis contained in *Zeran* (and approved by the majority here) turns on its head the very goal of the Communications Decency Act . . . most particularly where such alleged speech is an invitation to purchase child pornography. (pp. 1026-1027)

Justice Lewis thus questions the Fourth Circuit's ruling in *Zeran*, especially in light of AOL's cavalier attitude in permitting advertising of child pornography. At present, however, *Zeran* appears to be the controlling case with regard to granting immunity to Internet service providers. Thus, we will return to an examination of cases involving anonymous Internet defamation in the discussion below.

BRANDISHING THE SUBPOENA TO UNMASK THE "JOHN DOES"

Despite the plaintiffs' failures to obtain court rulings preventing further victimization of themselves in *Zeran, Lunney,* and *Doe,* a chief executive officer (CEO) (*Healthsouth,* 1998), a stockbroker (*Attkisson,* 1999), and a urologist (*Graham,* 2000) actually prevailed when their attorneys were successful in issuing subpoenas to the ISPs in order to learn the identities of those who were defaming them on Internet BBs.

Healthsouth Corp. v. Krum (1998)

In 1997, Richard Scrushy, CEO of HealthSouth Corporation, learned that a person who identified himself as "Dirk Diggler" (a reference to a porn star in the 1997 movie *Boogie Nights*) was posting messages on a Yahoo! Finance message board; the messages suggested that "Dirk Diggler" was having an affair with Scrushy's wife, Leslie, and discussed the affair in salacious detail. "Dirk Diggler" also accused Richard Scrushy of fraud, claiming that Scrushy was "bilking . . . Medicare reimbursement." Scrushy and HealthSouth Corporation sued John Doe, which permitted them to proceed to discovery. They later learned that "John Doe" was in fact Peter Krum, an embittered and malicious former employee of HealthSouth. Krum was now a food service worker at Penn State University, which fired Krum when it learned of his defamatory activities.

Attkisson v. John Doe (1999)

As in *HealthSouth, Zeran,* and *Lunney, Attkisson v. John Doe* (1999) involved a defamation case in which an anonymous prankster assumed the identity of Atlanta stockbroker Ronald Attkisson and then posted threats against Attkisson's clients at Applied Cellular Technology. In December 1998, the prankster called for a "death sentence" on the CEO of Applied Cellular Technology. This message, along with many "false, profane and offensive statements" about Attkisson's clients, were posted on Applied Cellular Technology's electronic BB on Yahoo! (Croft, 1999, p. 1B).

Ronald Attkisson wanted to sue the anonymous prankster for libel, but Yahoo! identifies its subscribers only if compelled by subpoena. But a subpoena is generally served after a lawsuit has been filed naming a defendant, putting Attkisson in a catch-22. Attkisson's attorney, Phillip McKinney, filed a suit against "John Doe" and then served Yahoo! with a subpoena. In response to the subpoena, Yahoo! reported that the vicious prankster who had assumed Attkisson's name was in fact Scott Gerstein of Atlanta, Georgia. Gerstein was a former employee of Attkisson's stock brokerage firm.

Attkisson and McKinney thus succeeded where Kenneth Zeran and Alex Lunney had failed, suggesting that victims of anonymous defamation on the Internet can successfully sue those who defame them if they serve the ISPs with a subpoena in order to force disclosure of the anonymous prankster's identity.

Graham v. Oppenheimer (2000)

A year after *Attkisson*, urologist Dr. Sam D. Graham, Jr. came across a posting on a Yahoo! message board from someone who called himself "fbi-informant" accusing Graham of taking kickbacks from Urocor, a medical testing company. The posting also said that Dr. Graham had been forced to resign as chair of the Urology Department at Emory University School of Medicine after colleagues discovered that he had taken the kickbacks:

Sam Graham, M.D., used to be the Department Chair of Urology at Emory Clinic in Atlanta. Urocor decided to underbid the Emory Pathology Department for pathology services and give Graham a cut of the money it got from doing the pathology. This worked well until the poor SOB got caught with his hand in the cookie jar. Poor guy had to resign his prestigious position. (Plaintiff's Exhibit 40, Plaintiff's Trial Memorandum, *Graham v. Oppenheimer,* filed October 23, 2000)

In fact, the posting was utterly fabricated; Graham had never taken kickbacks, and he had led the Urology Department at Emory from probationary status to having a reputation as one of the top 20 urology departments in the country. It had been Graham's own decision to resign from Emory so that he could go into private practice in Richmond, Virginia.

Graham retained attorneys Alan Rudlin and J. Burke McCormick, who filed a defamation suit against John Doe so that he could issue subpoenas to Yahoo! As it turned out, however, it was not Yahoo! but another ISP that was the ISP for "fbiinformant." After many, many hours of searching, attorneys Rudlin and McCormick learned of litigation between Urocor and pathologist Dr. Jonathan Oppenheimer. They subpoenaed the records in that case, including a deposition wherein Dr. Oppenheimer admitted that he and "fbiinformant" were the same person. Oppenheimer had never even met Graham; Oppenheimer's motive in defaming Graham was apparently an attempt to discredit Urocor in order to draw more customers to his own company, Prost-Data, Inc.

The case went to trial in the U.S. District Court for the Eastern District of Virginia, and the jury ruled that Oppenheimer and his company Prost-Data, Inc. had to pay Dr. Graham $325,000 in compensatory damages and $350,000 in punitive damages. Oppenheimer filed an appeal with the U.S. Court of Appeals for the Fourth Circuit, but the case was settled before it actually went to the Fourth Circuit.

DOES A WEBMASTER HAVE IMMUNITY FROM LIABILITY JUST AS AN ISP DOES?

In the following two cases, *Curzon-Brown and Wall* (2000) and *Sabbato* (2000), a crucial question is whether or not Section 230 of the CDA provides immunity from liability to a webmaster for a third party's defamatory comments. *Curzon-Brown* (2000) also deals with the question of libel-by-linking.

Curzon-Brown and Wall v.
San Francisco Community College District,
Ryan Lathouwers, Associated Students and
Doe's 1-25 (2000): Libel-by-Linking

Two professors at the City College of San Francisco were less fortunate than Ronald Attkisson and Dr. Sam Graham when they found themselves defamed on the Web site teacherreview.com. In October 1997, City College of San Francisco alumnus Ryan Lathouwers set up an Internet Web site, teacherreview.com, in which he encouraged students to post comments about their professors in order to identify "the good, the bad, and the incompetent" instructors.

Physics professor Jesse David Wall, who received very few reviews during the Web site's first 18 months, became a target of anonymous derogatory comments immediately following his public announcement regarding how easy it was to put phony reviews on the Web site. Wall suspected (and alleged in his complaint for defamation) that webmaster Ryan Lathouwers himself wrote the following false statements about Professor Wall:

> Never, in the history of my education, have I had a teacher as incompetent as this. . . . The demonstrations Wall gives rarely prove anything except that he knows a few magic tricks. . . . His book is expensive and outdated. Mr. Wall seems to have an attitude that it doesn't matter how bad of a teacher he is because he is tenured . . . 75% of the class has dropped. (First Cause of Action, Defamation, *Curzon-Brown and Wall v. San Francisco Community College District, Ryan Lathouwers, Associated Students and Does 1-100*, 2000, p. 4)

Whereas the comments about Wall were at first loosely confined to his classroom performance, after the case was widely publicized, Wall's reviews became increasingly obscene, even accusing him of committing crimes in the classroom. Even before Wall was targeted, English Professor Daniel Curzon-Brown, who is openly gay, had become a target of extremely vicious and obscene lies by anonymous persons who may or may not have ever been students at City College of San Francisco.[3] Curzon-Brown attributes very few of these reviews to his actual students, seeing them as cyber grafitti following his media appearances and proving that the Web site allowed and encouraged egregious fraud (Curzon-Brown, 2002b).

There were also anonymous comments that could possibly be interpreted as threats, such as "I know where Curzon lives," and "Mr. Wall, how's your daughter?" (First Cause of Action, Defamation, *Curzon-*

Brown and Wall v. City College of San Francisco, Ryan Lathowers,
Associated Students and Does 1-100, 2000, p. 8).

Curzon-Brown and Wall filed suit against webmaster Ryan
Lathouwers, charging the following:

> Lathowers deletes positive reviews of those [professors] he wishes to
> punish, particularly those who . . . have exercised their right of free
> speech by criticizing "Teacher Review," and by deleting negative
> reviews of those he wishes to reward, particularly those [professors]
> who support "Teacher Review." In the case of [Jesse David Wall and
> his wife Ellen Wall, an English professor], deletions of positive reviews
> occurred within days after [the Walls] had criticized "Teacher Review"
> at a City College Board meeting, causing substantial reductions in class
> sizes and the cancellation of at least one class. In the case of Curzon-
> Brown, multiple negative reviews are posted by the same few people.
> (First Case of Action, Defamation, *Curzon-Brown and Wall v. City*
> *College of San Francisco, Ryan Lathouwers, Associated Students, and*
> *Does 1-100,* 2000, pp. 6-7)

Adding insult to injury, the Associated Students Organization of City
College of San Francisco maintained a link from its Web site to teacherre-
view.com, making it falsely appear to be an official Web site of Associated
Students and San Francisco City College. Curzon-Brown and Wall sued
Associated Students, arguing that their link to teacherreview.com constituted republication of the original defamatory comments. (According to the
law of defamation, the re-publisher of a defamatory comment is liable just
as the original speaker is liable.) City College of San Francisco paid for an
attorney for Associated Students, who argued that their link to teacherre-
view.com did not constitute republication; furthermore, any litigation
against Associated Students was barred by Section 230 of the CDA.

Ryan Lathouwers turned to the ACLU to defend him. The ACLU
argued that Professors Wall and Curzon-Brown had no cause of action
because the anonymous comments about them were merely opinions that
could not be proven true or false; furthermore, expression of opinion is
protected by the First Amendment. The ACLU also argued that Wall and
Curzon-Brown were public figures and would have to prove actual malice
on the part of those who had posted the anonymous comments.

The ACLU also accused both Wall and Curzon-Brown of attempting
to sabotage teacherreview.com by posting "hundreds of falsified or irrelevant reviews" themselves:

> Wall even went so far as to post on his Website for public use an
> elaborate computer program that generates and posts to Teacher

Review "random" falsified anonymous . . . reviews of various
instructors, dozens at a time. (Memorandum of Points and
Authorities in Support of Demurrer and Special Motion to Strike of
Defendant Ryan Lathouwers, *Curzon-Brown and Wall v. San
Francisco Community College District, Ryan Lathouwers,
Associated Students and Does 1-100*, filed September 22, 2000, p. 6)

The ACLU thus argued that Wall and Curzon-Brown's suit should be
barred because they were suing with "unclean hands" (citing *Buchanan
Home & Auto Supply Co. v. Firestone Tire & Rubber Co.*, 1981, in which
plaintiff was denied relief for "unclean hands" when its submission of falsified documents along with legitimate ones "hopelessly [obscured] any possibility of accurately resolving the question" of which documents were
legitimate).

In response to the ACLU's "unclean hands" argument, Curzon-Brown
explained that neither he nor Wall had ever used a computer program to
generate false reviews; in fact, it was a math professor who had set up a
computer program that fed positive reviews to the Web site. Jesse David
Wall never posted "hundreds of falsified or irrelevant reviews" as the
ACLU had charged; in fact, he sent in about 40 false (positive) reviews one
by one, merely to demonstrate to all of the City College community how
easy it was to post false reviews. Wall had also posted the false positive
reviews in order to see how long they remained posted. At a public Board
of Trustees meeting, Wall reported that 20 were still in place, but 20 more
that praised professors that Ryan Lathouwers disliked had been quickly
removed (Curzon-Brown, 2002b).

Although Wall and Curzon-Brown strongly suspected that Ryan
Lathouwers himself (or his cronies) had written the statements so critical of
Wall, Lathouwers denied this. But Wall and Curzon-Brown believe that
Lathouwers, besides removing some reviews and deleting others by guess-
ing which were real ones and which were not, added editorial comments
above certain reviews, especially Curzon-Brown's, attempting to turn other
students' opinions against Curzon-Brown.

In Lathouwers' defense, the ACLU cited *Zeran*, arguing that Curzon-
Brown and Wall's claims were barred by Section 230 of the CDA.
According to the ACLU, as webmaster of teacherreview.com, Lathouwers
was a statutorily protected "provider" of an "interactive computer service."
Thus, Lathouwers could not be held liable for the comments of anonymous
third parties (Memorandum of Points and Authorities in Support of
Demurrer and Special Motion to Strike of Defendant Ryan Lathouwers,
*Curzon-Brown and Wall v. City College of San Francisco, Ryan
Lathouwers, Associated Students and Does 1-100*, filed September 22, 2000,
p. 9).

Wall and Curzon-Brown's attorney Paul Kleven ultimately sought to remove City College and the Associated Students from the amended complaint. With assistance from a member of the Board of Trustees, Kleven succeeded in removing City College and the Associated Students from the pleadings, leaving only Ryan Lathouwers and a number of John Does. But Judge David Garcia of the Superior Court of the City and County of San Francisco strongly suggested at a hearing that Wall and Curzon-Brown should seek to settle the case. If they declined to settle, Judge Garcia hinted strongly that he was inclined to rule in favor of the ACLU and Lathouwers and award court costs of more than $100,000 (Curzon-Brown, 2002b).

But Wall and Curzon-Brown filed a motion to engage in discovery under California's Code of Civil Procedure Section 425.16(g) with Ryan Lathouwers in order to determine the identities of those who had posted the anonymous comments. Judge David Garcia of the Superior Court of the City and County of San Francisco held that Curzon-Brown and Wall's claims against Lathouwers were barred by Section 230 of the CDA. As "webmaster" of teacherreview.com, Lathouwers was a "provider" of an "interactive computer service" within the meaning of Section 230. "Section 230(c)(1) provides an absolute immunity to Defendant Lathouwers for state-law claims such as Plaintiffs' based on statements posted on the Web site by third parties" (Order Sustaining Demurrer, Granting Special Motion to Strike, Denying Motion to Conduct Discovery and Dismissing Action with Prejudice, *Curzon-Brown and Wall v. City College of San Francisco, Ryan Lathouwers, Associated Students and Does 1-25*, filed October 20, 2000, p. 5).

Judge David Garcia thus denied Curzon-Brown and Wall the opportunity to engage in discovery, and Wall and Curzon-Brown were required to pay $10,000 to the ACLU to cover its legal fees. Curzon-Brown subsequently declared bankruptcy.

Even now, more than 7 years after Lathouwers set up teacherreview.com in 1997, Curzon-Brown has noticed that search engines such as MSN still bring one to teacherreview.com. Curzon-Brown has contacted MSN and asked that all links be disconnected from his name (Curzon-Brown, 2002a).

Sabbato v. Hardy and Rudy (2000)

Whereas Judge David Garcia of the California Superior Court held that a webmaster enjoyed the same immunity from liability for libel by a third party that an ISP such as AOL enjoyed in *Zeran*, an appellate court in Ohio declined to grant a webmaster immunity when an anonymous third party defamed a woman on his Web site. In *Sabbato v. Hardy and Rudy*

(2000), the following messages were posted anonymously on a Web site and addressed to Lori Sabbato:

> I miss you, Lori.
>
> I know who you are, Lori.
>
> I thought you were going to reveal yourself to me last night, but it would have violated public decency laws.
>
> I took an oath to stomp out ignorance, and you are ignorant.
>
> Lori Sabbato is a cocaine dealer.

Although the first four comments range from ploddingly dull to disturbing, the fifth comment accusing Lori Sabbato of dealing cocaine constitutes libel per se. Lori Sabbato retained attorney Craig Conley and filed suit against University of Akron chemistry professor James K. Hardy, the webmaster of the Web site "CBJT" (Citizens for a Better Jackson Township) on which she was defamed. Conley also filed suit against John Doe in order to serve Hardy with a subpoena to engage in discovery in order to learn the identity of the person who was defaming Lori Sabbato.

Hardy filed a motion to dismiss, arguing that, as webmaster, he was a "provider" of an "interactive computer service" just like AOL, and the trial judge of the Court of Common Pleas in Stark County, Ohio, agreed and dismissed the suit.

Craig Conley appealed to the Fifth Appellate Division of the Ohio Court of Appeals. Conley argued that Hardy was *not* an ISP like AOL. In contrast, Hardy was a "referee" because he often participated in the threads of "conversations" on his Web site, and he could exacerbate or mitigate the tone of disagreements; for example, if an argument on the Web site became heated, Hardy could say, "Now, boys and girls, let's move on to a new topic." Conley further argued that the immunity guaranteed by Section 230 of the CDA is predicated on good faith, but Hardy had demonstrated "bad faith" in editing comments on his Web site (leaving comments that he liked up for a long time but deleting comments he disliked after a few hours).

In the meantime, Conley had figured out that the person who had defamed Lori Sabbato was Jackson Township Police Lieutenant Christopher Rudy, who had developed a dislike of Sabbato when she had exposed him for the lazy and incompetent officer that he was in a previous incident. Sabbato had discovered that someone had embezzled a great deal of money from a Little League baseball team, and she had tried to get Lieutenant Rudy to investigate, but he was apparently too lazy to do so. Sabbato finally went to a prosecutor, who charged and won several felony convictions against the embezzler. But Lieutenant Rudy was apparently resentful that Sabbato had finally given up on getting him to take any action in the case, and resorted to anonymous attacks on her on Hardy's Web site.

When Conley, Sabbato's attorney, discovered Rudy's identity, Rudy paid a confidential amount of money in damages to Sabbato, and the case was settled. What is significant about this case, of course, is not the fact that the victim of anonymous defamation ultimately prevailed, however. What is significant is that this is a ground-breaking case in that it constitutes the first time that a court has ruled that a webmaster is *not* guaranteed immunity from a defamation action as an ISP would be.

UNIVERSAL CITY STUDIOS, INC., v. ERIC CORLEY AND 2600 ENTERPRISES INC. (2001): LINKING AND COPYRIGHT INFRINGEMENT

Whereas the California Superior Court in *Curzon-Brown* dismissed Wall and Curzon-Brown's case against City College of San Francisco and the Associated Students for the link they maintained to teacherreview.com, in effect finding that a link to another Web site did not constitute republication of a defamatory comment, the U.S. Court of Appeals for the Second Circuit has taken a far less sanguine approach to linking when it involved copyright infringement. In *Universal City Studios,* the Second Circuit held that Eric Corley could not post on his Web site a computer program that decrypts the encryption code limiting access to DVD movies. Furthermore, Eric Corley could not provide links to other Web sites containing the same decryption program. Corley and his company, 2600 Enterprises, Inc., were charged with violating the Digital Millennium Copyright Act (DMCA), 17 U.S.C. § 512 (1998).

More recently, the U.S. Court of Appeals for the district of Columbia Circuit upheld Verizon's refusal to disclose the names of its subscribers when subpoenaed by the Recording Industry Association of America (RIAA), despite the fact that the RIAA was attempting to pursue Verizon subscribers suspected of copyright infringement (trading large numbers of .mp3 files of copyrighted music) (*Recording Industry Association of America, Inc., Appellee v. Verizon Internet Services, Inc., Appellant,* No. 03-7053, U.S. Court of Appeals for the District of Columbia Circuit, filed December 19, 2003).

Despite the setback for the RIAA, Judge Susan Illston of the federal district court in San Francisco recently followed the *Universal City Studios v. Corley* (2001) precedent in *321 Studios v. Metro Goldwyn Mayer Studio, Inc. et al.* (No. C 02-1955 SI, Order Granting Defendants' Motion for Partial Summary Judgment and Resolving Related Motions, filed February 19, 2004). Judge Illston ruled that 321 Studios must stop making software that allows users to copy digital video discs (DVDs) Judge Illston thus handed Hollywood's movie studios a major victory in their ongoing battle against copyright pirates. However, the St. Louis-based 321 Studios said that it would appeal the ruling.

DISCUSSION

If the purpose of American jurisprudence in general is to protect "the little guy" in addition to protecting the interests of large corporations, we certainly need to be wary of cyberSLAPP suits in which corporations try to use subpoenas as weapons for harassment or for unmasking anonymous critics. Davis (2002), Lidsky (2000), and other legal scholars have cautioned against the dangers that cyberSLAPP suits pose to freedom of speech. At the same time, Davis (2002) provided practical suggestions for guidelines on when a subpoena is justifiable versus when a subpoena is a thinly veiled attempt to learn an anonymous critic's identity, even when no defamation exists. In those cases in which one individual maliciously harms the reputation of another individual, however, it seems clear that issuing a subpoena to learn the source of the defamation is justifiable.

It is perhaps worth noting that courts are apparently unconcerned with libel-by-linking involving damage to the reputations of a couple of college professors, but when Hollywood studios would lose millions of dollars as a result of the general public's access to the decryption computer program DeCSS, which permitted unauthorized access to view and copy motion pictures, the Second Circuit quickly upheld an injunction against copyright-infringement-by-linking. Should we conclude that our judicial system places greater weight on protecting the property rights of large corporations such as Hollywood studios than on protecting the reputations of those who suffer anonymous defamation?

Although Section 230 of the CDA appears to provide an impenetrable shield that protects ISPs from lawsuits filed in the United States, it is unlikely that it will protect ISPs from lawsuits filed in other countries. British law, for example, treats OSPs as if they were newspapers; it does not protect ISPs who simply act as distributors of a defamatory message that has been posted on the Internet by a third party. Demon Internet, an ISP in England, agreed to pay $25,000 in damages plus several hundred thousand dollars in court costs to British physicist Laurence Godfrey for distributing allegedly defamatory comments carried by Demon's news servers. If Demon had been in the United States, Godfrey's case would have been dismissed. But the British government has not given ISPs immunity from libel actions, even when they merely act as distributors of the material (Lyall, 2000).

The Fourth Circuit's decision in *Zeran* raises other questions as well. For example, if someone receives obscene telephone calls, telephone companies will assist the victim of the obscene calls by tracing them to determine the identity of the person placing the calls. Telephone companies are common carriers just as AOL, Yahoo!, and other ISPs are, but they appear to be more willing to assist victims of obscene phone calls than AOL was in *Zeran* when Kenneth Zeran received hundreds of hate phone calls as a result of the vicious posting on an AOL BB.

One also cannot help wondering whether the outcome in *Zeran* would have been the same if the FBI had served AOL with a subpoena in order to determine who was victimizing Kenneth Zeran, the small businessman in Seattle who lived with his parents and was terrified that they would be harmed when his name and address were posted, identifying Zeran as the seller of the T-shirts glorifying the Oklahoma City bombing.

The Bill of Rights in our Constitution has sometimes been said to protect "the little guy," and during the last two centuries, courts have indeed interpreted the Bill of Rights to do just that. But the courts' interpretation of Section 230 in *Zeran* clearly failed to protect "the little guys" Kenneth Zeran, John Doe (the 11-year-old who was lured by a child pornographer), or Professors Jesse David Wall and Daniel Curzon-Brown. We could, of course, turn to cliches such as "Life is not fair," shrug such cases off and try to forget about them. In the meantime, however, some are working to persuade Congress to clarify Section 230 of the CDA with an amendment so that AOL would not be immune when notified that it is carrying ads for child pornography. Others are hoping that the Supreme Court will overrule *Zeran* if another U.S. Court of Appeals takes a case and declines to follow the precedent set by *Zeran*. Then, perhaps the capricious world of Internet BBs will be just a bit safer for "the little guys."

NOTES

1. A link or hyperlink is "a cross-reference (in a distinctive font or color) appearing on one web page that, when activated by the point-and-click of a mouse, brings onto the computer screen another web page. . . . With a hyperlink on a web page, the linked Web site is just one click away" (*Universal City Studios, Inc. et al. V. Corley and 2600 Enterprises Inc.*, 273 F.3d 429, 2001).
2. In its "Privacy Policy," America Online promises: "America Online, Inc. (AOL) is strongly committed to protecting the privacy of consumers of its interactive products and services. . . . We do not use or disclose information about your individual visits to AOL Anywhere or information that you may give us on AOL Anywhere, such as your name, address, E-mail address or telephone number, to any outside companies. AOL Anywhere may share such

information in response to legal process, such as a court order or subpoena. . . ."
(AOL Anywhere, 2002).

3.   A few of the anonymous comments are as follows: "[Brown] is emotionally unbalanced and mentally ill, engaging in violent mood swings, irrational personal attacks on students, and insane progressions in thought."

1.   Hi, I'm Curzon-Brown and hot for some dick right now . . . [more obscenities]

2.   That's to teach you a lesson, Curzon-Brown, you fucking piece of shit fag . . . you really do pick up boys on Broad Street. . . . Ohhh yesss, Mr. Brown, I love the way you fuck me so hard up the ass, please harder, harder, mooooo, quack, quack, oink, oink, bark, bark. Farm animal fucker!!!!

3.   [Brown's' #1 student was probably a hot-looking stud who refused to get rammed up the ass by Brown . . . I wish yo [sic] kill yourself. There's no need for faggots in this world. They are an abomination.

4.   I took [Brown's] butt-fucking class, and he raped me in front of the whole class. It was embarrassing . . . But he did rape my friend's 3-year-old brother . . . [more obscenity]

5.   I do not understand what he thought he was doing when he killed that student last year for not handing in his assignment. He routinely keeps the pretty girls after class for "extra credit" assignments, and they come out screaming a few minutes later.

6.   Hey, when is Brown Curzon going to stop mucking up here. . . . ?

7.   [Brown] whipped out his cock and tried to shove it down my throat in the middle of class! I sit in the very front and he always was making passes at me, that faggot. Several times he invited me to the bathroom because he wanted to suck my dick but I told him to get the fuck away and he grabbed onto my balls so tight. . . . Then his grip gave out and I decked that boy-fucking queer.

8.   I got failed and he told me he was gonna kill me if I told anyone here he tried to rape me. He was always making fun of us girls and he was always trying to grope me.

9.   I seen [Curzon-Brown] tooling for ass on Polk Street.

10.   In fact, my English 1A teacher . . . warned our whole class against taking [Curzon-Brown's] class . . . (First Cause of Action, Defamation, *Curzon-Brown and Wall v. San Francisco Community College District, Ryan Lathouwers, Associated Students and Does 1-100*, 2000, pp. 3-4).

REFERENCES

AOL Anywhere. (2002). Privacy policy. http://www.aol.com/info/privacy.html (Site visited July 22, 2002).

Aquacool_2000 v. Inc. CV 00-04993 (C.D. Cal. 2000). Complaint (filed May 11, 2000). Available at http://epic.org/privacy/anonymity/## (Site visited July 23, 2002).

Barnes, S.B. (1999). Ethical issues for a virtual self. In S. J. Drucker & G. Gumpert (Eds.), *Real law @ virtual space: Regulation in cyberspace.* Cresskill, NJ: Hampton Press.

Attkisson v. John Doe, No. 99VS148988A, State Court, Fulton County, Georgia, filed January 28, 1999. (1999).

Attkisson v. Gerstein, No. 1999CV06397, Superior Court Fulton County, Georgia, filed March 18, 1999; dismissed June 19, 2000. (2000).

Barnes, S.B. (2001). *Online connections: Internet interpersonal relationships.* Cresskill, NJ: Hampton Press.

Buchanan Home & Auto Supply Co. v. Firestone Tire & Rubber Co., 554 F. Supp. 242 (D.S.C.). (1981).

Croft, J. (1999, April 5). Lawsuit alleges cyberlibel: A Fulton court will struggle with the question of how free speech applies to the Internet. *The Atlanta Journal and Constitution,* p. 1B.

Curzon-Brown and Wall v. San Francisco Community College District, Ryan Lathouwers, Associated Students and Does 1-25, No. 307335 (California Superior Court, City and County of San Francisco, filed October 20, 2000). (2000).

Curzon-Brown, D. (2002a, February 8). E-mail message.

Curzon-Brown, D. (2002b, December 2). E-mail message.

Cybersmears and message boards. (2002). R.R. Donelly and Sons Co. http://www.realcorporatelawyer.com/msgboards.html (Site visited July 26, 2002).

Davis, W. (2002, November). *Defending "John Doe:" Establishing a standard to protect anonymous Internet speech.* Paper accepted for presentation by the Freedom of Expression Commission for the 2002 National Communication Association Convention, New Orleans, LA.

Dee, J. (1994, March). "To avoid charges of indecency, please hang up now:" An analysis of legislation and litigation involving dial-a-porn. *Communications and the Law, 16(1),* 3-28.

Doe v. America Online, Inc., 783 So. 2d 1010 (Supreme Court of Florida). (2001).

Graham v. Oppenheimer, No. 3:00CV57 (E.D. Va., filed October 23, 2000). (2000).

HealthSouth Corp. v. Krum, No. 98-2812 (Pa. C.P. Centre County, filed October 28, 1998). (1998).

John Doe fights back by suing for privacy infringement. (2000, May 11). Electronic Privacy Information Center. http://www.epic.org/privacy /anonymity/aquacool_release.html (Site visited July 22, 2002).

Lidsky, L.B. (2000, February). Silencing John Doe: Defamation & discourse in cyberspace. *Duke Law Journal, 49,* 855.

Lunney v. Prodigy Services Company, 683 N.Y.S.2d 557 (Supreme Court of New York, Appellate Division, Second Department). (1998).

Lyall, S. (2000, April 1). British Internet provider to pay physicist who says e-bulletin board libeled him. *The New York Times,* p. A5.

McIntyre v. Ohio Elections Commission, 514 U.S. 334. (1995).

Privacy groups demand protection of users' anonymity online. (2002, July 11).
    http://www.aclu.org/news/2002/n071102a.html. Site visited July 14, 2002.

*Recording Industry Association of America, Inc., Appellee v. Verizon Internet
    Services, Inc., Appellant*, (No. 03-7015; 03-7053 U.S. Court of Appeals for the
    District of Columbia Circuit, filed December 19, 2003). (2003).

Sabbato v. Hardy and Rudy, 1999 CV 02909; 2000 CA 00136 (Court of Appeals,
    Fifth Appellate Division, Stark County, OH). (2000).

Sheridan, D.R. (1997). *Zeran v. AOL* and the effect of Section 230 of the
    Communications Decency Act on liability for defamation on the Internet.
    Albany Law Review, 61, 147.

Slitt, A.J. (1998). The anonymous publisher: Defamation on the Internet after *Reno
    v. American Civil Liberties Union* and *Zeran v. America Online, Conn. L. Rev,
    31, 389. 321 Studios v. Metro Goldwyn Mayer Studio, Inc. et al.* (No. C 02-
    1955 SI, Order Granting Defendants' Motion for Partial Summary Judgment
    and Resolving Related Motions, filed February 19, 2004). (2004).

*Universal City Studios, Inc., Paramount Pictures Corporation, Metro-Goldwyn
    Mayer Studios, Inc., Tristar Pictures, Inc., Columbia Pictures Industries, Inc.,
    Time Warner Entertainment Company, L.P., Disney Enterprises, Inc., and
    Twentieth Century Fox Film Corporation v. Eric Corley and 2600 Enterprises,
    Inc.* (U.S. Court of Appeals for Second Circuit). (2001).

Yahoo! Privacy Policy. (2002). http://privacy.Yahoo.com/privacy/us/ (Site visited
    July 24, 2002).

Zeran v. America Online, Inc., 958 F. Supp. 1124 (U.S.D. Eastern District of
    Virginia, 1997); 129 F.3d 327 (U.S. Court of Appeals for the Fourth Circuit,
    1997).

14

Electronic Privacy and the Ability to Leap Tall Firewalls in a Single Bound

Susan J. Drucker
Hofstra University

Gary Gumpert
Communication Landscapers

The onslaught of e-mail, Internet access, chat rooms, intranet and web sites generate new legal and ethical issues as the technology of communications challenge developments in applicable laws governing privacy.. In an age of increased concern for security, the authors ask: Is this electronic space private? Can one assume e-mail correspondence is private? Do employees have privacy right in their e-mail communications? Can one choose to remain anonymous in their computer-mediated environment? Susan Drucker and Gary Gumpert argue that the while the 20th century saw the ascendancy of the value placed upon privacy and control, the post September 11th era ushered in greater acceptance of incursions into privacy rights in the name of security and the war on terrorism. This chapter outlines the parameters of privacy in cyberspace and provides an overview of the technological, contractual, administrative and legislated limits on privacy in cyberspace.

The warnings appear at an ever-increasing pace:

> The Web is one place where it actually may be a good idea to be para-
> noid, because "they" may really be watching you. Many people surf
> around unaware that they might be leaving a trail of information about
> themselves scattered across the Net. Most folks are also unaware of
> how vulnerable their E-mails are to snoops and hackers. Every time
> you visit a site, it's possible that you're leaving a trail of personal data.
> When you surf the Web, send E-mail or post to newsgroups, be sure to
> protect your privacy. (The FreeSite.com Anonymous Freebies, 2003)

The consumer is offered options. "StealthMessage.com" offers a secure
messaging system that encrypts private messages and stores messages
anonymously. For $29.95 "Anonymizer.com" offers "Private Surfing.com"
but for $99.95 a customer can get "Total Net Shield for maximum protec-
tion" (Anonymizer.com). "SurfinGuard Pro" protects PC users from new,
unknown Internet threats by monitoring and containing the behavior of
downloaded programs and active content (SurfinGuard Internet Tools,
2003). "Sneakemail" is a free service that lets the user create disposable
E-mail addresses. The Electronic Privacy Information Center (EPIC) lists
privacy protection products under the following headings: "Snoop Proof
Email, Anonymous Remailers, Surf Anonymously, HTML Filters, Cookie
Busters, Voice Privacy, E-mail and File Privacy, Secure Instant Messaging,
Web Encryption, Telnet Encryption, Disk Encryption, Disk File Erasing
Programs, Privacy Policy Generators, Password Security, Firewalls, and
other resources" (EPIC Online Guide to Practical Privacy Tools, 2003). All
are needed to counter the growing industry in information and data avail-
able to data-miners in both the private and public sectors.

For a $11.95 *Info-revolution* in Lawrenceville, Georgia offers the
following in its advertisement:

> We give you addresses to hundreds of sites that will supply you with
> DMV records, credit profiles, medical and criminal records, most any-
> thing you would want to know . . . with this information you can track
> down phone numbers, social security information, E-mail addresses,
> surnames, birth, marriage, divorce and death records. Look up a long
> lost relative with sites like Parent-Finders and Birth-Quest, look for
> biological parents!". . . You can know EVERYTHING about EVERY-
> BODY with this information!!!" (www.Searcher@finder.com, 2003)

Consumer, medical, and workplace privacy have entered the realm of
Internet privacy as interaction and information migrate to cyberspace. As
private surveillance capabilities and practices, with few restrictions grow,

government surveillance increases fueled by the "war on terrorism." The USA Patriot Act, The Total Information Awareness Program, and the Homeland Security Act sanction and encourage government surveillance in an atmosphere of relaxed restrictions. Although some privacy watchdog groups continue to emerge and civil liberties organizations lament "the September 11 attacks have led some to embrace the fallacy that weakening the Constitution will strengthen America" (Stanley & Steinhardt, 2003).

For law enforcement officers, debt collectors, voyeurs, and the just plain curious, the Internet, and its variations, offers a plethora of surveillance tools—nothing should be assumed to be private. The Center for Democracy and Technology (CDT) notes:

> [P]rivacy is the number one concern of Internet users; it is also the top reason why non-users still avoid the Internet. Survey after survey indicates mounting concern. While privacy faces threats from both private and government intrusions, the existing motley patchwork of privacy laws and practices fails to provide comprehensive protection. Instead, it causes confusion that fuels a sense of distrust and skepticism, limiting realization of the Internet's potential. (CDT's Guide to Online Privacy, 2003)

Providing a seamless web of privacy protection to data as it flows through this international network requires a careful reconsideration of the business community's interest in promoting commerce, the government's interests in fostering economic growth and protecting its citizens, and the self-interest of individuals in protecting themselves from the overreaching of the government and the private sector. It requires the use all of all possible tools to protect the right of privacy of Internet users which include international agreements, legislation, self-regulation, public education, and the technology itself.

Since the 1970s, there has been a consistent increase in not only the value placed on privacy but also on threats to personal privacy (Regan, 1995). It is understandable that privacy and security are important issues in the developing world of computer-mediated communication (CMC).

The vast amount of potential data and the increasing quest for privacy and simultaneous control sets up a complex and perplexing balancing game. Privacy is often conceptualized as "the right of the individual" to decide for him or herself how much he or she wishes to share with others in terms of personal thoughts, feelings, and facts. Privacy rights have been conceived of as the right to be left alone, therefore encompassing the protection of individual dignity and integrity by preventing the loss of individual freedom and independence (Hixson, 1987). During the past several decades, public opinion polls have indicated the importance that Americans place on privacy. In 1990, 79% of respondents felt that privacy should be added to "life, liberty, and the pursuit of happiness" as a fundamental right (Louis Harris and Associates and Westin, 1990). Asked the question: "How concerned are you about threats to your personal privacy in America today?" responses indicated that the percentage of those *somewhat* concerned increased from 64% in 1978 to 79% in 1990 (Harris-Equifax Consumer Privacy Survey, 1992).[1] An American Civil Liberties Union (ACLU) survey addressed a broad range of privacy issues ranging from employer monitoring, to secondary use of information, to gay and lesbian rights[2] with respondents generally indicating a high level of concern (Regan, 1995). In 2002, surveys indicated concern was on the rise, with 81% of respondents reporting that the right to privacy was "essential" (Paulson, 2002). In a February 2002 Harris Poll, 63% of respondents thought current laws were inadequate to protect privacy. The solution to this perceived problem was revealed in a June 2001 Gallup poll that indicated that two thirds of respondents favored new federal legislation to protect privacy online. A report from Pew Internet & American Life showed that 94% of Internet users thought that privacy violators should be disciplined (EPIC Public Opinion on Privacy, 2003) but in the immediate aftermath of the September 11th terrorist attacks, with Americans feeling threatened, respondents indicated they were willing to give up some personal freedoms. In 2003, the EPIC continued to report that "public opinion polls consistently find strong support among Americans for privacy rights in law to protect their personal information from government and commercial entities" (Public Opinion on Privacy, EPIC, 2003). Although continuing to profess great concern for privacy rights, particularly in an age of cyberspace, some Americans are conflicted. We are reminded that "fear can short-circuit freedom" (Paulson, 2002).

At the dawn of cyberlaw, perhaps one of the stickiest values to be addressed is that of privacy, which has long been the subject of heated debate and inconsistent rulings as well as occupying the status of penumbra right, not enunciated, but recognized, in the U.S. Constitution. Although the value placed on personal privacy has changed over time, so have the media technologies that may protect or invade that privacy.

Privacy has long been seen as crucial to individual liberties. Westin's (1967) seminal works on privacy rests on the significance of privacy in the individual's relationship to society. He argued that privacy in a democratic system is a critical element in one's relationship to government, noting for instance, the importance of privacy with regard to supporting limits on police power, electoral system integrity, and religious tolerance. But more recently, Regan, (1995) in *Legislating Privacy: Technology, Social Values and Public Policy,* argued that this individualistic concept of privacy is insufficient, requiring the reconceptualization of privacy as having broader social and collective purposes. In distinguishing informational privacy,[3] communication privacy, and psychological privacy, Regan made the case for the social importance of privacy:

> This social importance derives from the fact that privacy is a common value in that it is shared by individuals, a public vale in that it has value to the democratic political system, and a collective value in that technology and market forces make it increasingly difficult for any one person to have privacy unless everyone has a similar minimum level of privacy. (p. xvi)

Regan's approach, when combined with the individual liberties conceptualization of privacy, supports the re-evaluation of privacy at a time in history when there is some reconsideration of the value placed on public and private relationships.

Privacy rights and communication freedoms are among those areas particularly intertwined in societal valuation of individual rights. Diverse laws around the world reflect competing and often conflicting liberties. Given the global nature of cyberspace, any discussion of privacy and personal control must take these value differences into account when evaluating the expectation of privacy at points of transmission and reception as well as at all nodes through which information passes. Therefore, privacy rights may well invoke culturally divergent conceptualization and protection for CMC. Privacy rights also invoke psychological and functional anticipation in using that given medium or instrument.

In one of the early and more comprehensive works on the developments in cyberlaw, *Internet and Online Law*, Stuckey (1996) identified principles that have formed the basis of most privacy protection in the United States and Canada as well as Europe. He isolated the following principles based on fair informational practice principles:

1. Personal data record-keeping practices should not be kept secret.
2. An individual should have the ability to find out what information about him or her is on record and how it is disclosed, and should have the ability to correct it.
3. An individual should have the ability to correct or amend a record of identifiable information about him or her.
4. An individual should have the ability to limit the disclosure of information about her or him that was obtained for one purpose from being disclosed for other unrelated purposes.
5. An organization creating, maintaining, using, or disseminating records of identifiable personal data must guarantee the relia-

bility of the data for their intended use and must take precautions to prevent misuse of the data. (Stuckey, 1996, § 5.01)

In considering these issues, practices, both nongovernmental and governmental, warrant consideration.

NONGOVERNMENTAL ASSOCIATED CONCERNS WITH PRIVACY

Rich commercial opportunities and innovative management practices abound in cyberspace, bringing with them thorny privacy issues. A myriad of online practices portend serious privacy consequences. There is a large market for detailed personal profiles on the Internet.

Challenges to Online Privacy

Internet Cookies: Cookies are unique, small text files that Web sites write directly onto a hard drive. They enable sites to surreptitiously collect information about users' online activities by collecting such data as log-in or registration information, user preferences, and online buying patterns. Information stored in a cookie can range from a random number to identify repeat visitors (anonymous profile) to a code identifying a specific customer in the web site's database. Designed for the "benign purpose" of enabling Web sites to recognize a repeat visitor, "cookies were quickly adopted to facilitate the tracking of specific individuals' activities in order to customize content and advertisement" (cookiecentral.com, 2003). Cookies are saved to a simple text file that can be deleted. Both Internet Explorer and Netscape allow some level of cookie verification with a menu option to accept all, some, or none of the incoming cookies.

Web Bugs: Cyberspace activities may also be monitored by "web bugs" and other hardware and software information-gathering techniques. A web bug is a graphic on a Web page or in an E-mail message that is designed to monitor who is reading the Web page or the E-mail message. Web bugs are often invisible, thereby disguising the fact that monitoring is taking place. These bugs (named to signify their eavesdropping function) are typically a hypertext markup language (HTML) that specifies an inline image via an IMG tag (which defines an image), and are only 1-x-1 pixel in size. Web bugs have been used by *Quicken, FedEx,* and even the *Metamucil* and *Oil of Olay* sites as a way to add information to a profile of Web sites a person is visiting and as a means of gathering figures on Web browser usage.

Online Profiling: Clickstream data is a potentially rich source of information. Data collected by a Web site can include personal information such as the type of computer used, the Internet protocol (IP) address, the browser used, and specific Web sites visited. Clickstream data can be captured at various points in the network and available for reuse and disclosure (CDT's Guide to Online Privacy, 2003). Web site log files contain a user's IP address, time, pages and images downloaded, the Referrer (last page where the user clicked a link to the current page), data entered by the user, and Internet cookies. A user's Web browser sends most of this information in the browser "header." "Click-through" responses required online in order to complete desired tasks may leave a trail of unintended information. These click-through responses may be captured by advertising networks or "profiling companies." With the permission of the Web site, but without user knowledge or permission, these companies place a tag or identifier on a computer that enables the organization to track the user's Web activities. Lists of data can be collected, and some companies compile a profile with "inferential" or "psychographic" data the company infers based on surfing habits (CDTs Guide to Online Privacy, 2003). Online tracking is seen has having great commercial potential with good exactitude for one-to-one targeted marketing, and direct or personalized marketing.

DoubleClick is one of the companies most associated with this type of controversial service, particularly in light of the FCC investigation into its business practices. DoubleClick provides Internet advertising technology and services and posts banner advertising on web pages. In June 1999, DoubleClick purchased Abacus, a company that distributes catalogues through the mail. In January 2000, it was revealed that DoubleClick was going to merge online information with offline information. The Federal Trade Commission's (FTC) Bureau of Consumer Protection investigated the company's collection and distribution of personally identifiable information (PII) and sought to determine if they were engaged in any unfair or deceptive acts or practices. In January 2001, after much mainstream media coverage, the FTC staff concluded "DoubleClick never used or disclosed consumers' PII for purposes other than those disclosed in its privacy policy." DoubleClick currently retains information in the chronological "log file" of the advertisements with these log files purged on a 2-year schedule. For more detailed information about DoubleClick policy see http://www.doubleclick.com/us/corporate/privacy/privacy/policies.asp?as p_object_1=&.

The type of browser capabilities, screen resolution, and so on, can generally be obtained by using Java, JavaScript, and VB Script. This information is then used to provide customized content formatted to users' capabilities. Web sites often gather personal data by a Web-based input form provided by the visitor. Two methods by which information is obtained are the "Get" method contained in the URL and the "Post" that transfers the data "behind the scenes" without having it appear as part of the URL. Web sites track responses to E-mail campaigns by having consumers respond to a specific URL and then a tracking system detects a user's E-mail so that an E-mail ad (i.e., Spam) can be forwarded. A related privacy issue receiving increased scrutiny has been the effort to regulate unsolicited unwanted, E-mail that invades privacy in that it forces unwanted and objectionable materials into electronic mailboxes. Drafting a legislative solution to the problem of unsolicited commercial E-mail is difficult because it requires accommodating the expressive rights of communicators.

Online Seal Programs: One nongovernmental approach to the problem of online privacy has been offered by online seal programs. *Online seal programs* have become the primary form of industry self-regulation. One of the best known of these programs is TRUSTe, a nonprofit organization known for its privacy certification and seal program. TRUSTe allows companies to attempt to build consumer confidence through certification and validation of adherence to privacy principles of fair information practices approved by the U.S. Department of Commerce, FTC Fair Information Practices, and industry organizations. There is periodic auditing and monitoring to ensure compliance. The TRUSTe "trustmark," is an online seal displayed by member Web sites and awarded to sites found to adhere to established privacy principles. Web sites displaying the TRUSTe Privacy Seal warrant that they are "committed to abiding by a privacy policy that gives users notice, choice, access, security, and redress with regard to their personal information" (TRUSTE, 2003). The principles include the following:

- Adoption and implementation of a privacy policy that takes into account consumer anxiety over sharing personal information online.
- Notice and disclosure of information collection and use practices.
- Choice and consent, giving users the opportunity to exercise control over their information.
- Data security and quality and access measures to help protect the security and accuracy of personally identifiable information. (TRUSTe, 2003)

In addition, TRUSTe has a children's program for children under the age of 13. A Web site displaying the TRUSTe children's seal is committed to obtaining prior verifiable parental consent when and if information will be collected, as well as giving parental notice of how that information will be used. These online seal programs have grown in popularity since first introduced. In addition to TRUSTe, BBBOnLine Privacy Seal and CPA WebTrust, are other programs that independently verifies and tests e-commerce sites for compliance.

Workplace Mechanisms and Rights

It is a widely recognized that individuals have less privacy in their workplace activities than in their private lives. Although these workplace mechanisms may be disliked by employees, they are, perhaps, more likely to be tolerated, when the common perception of the workplace is of an environment where an individual's privacy is likely to be significantly reduced, and this reduction is a price not unreasonably paid for by the benefits of employment. To date, most case law reflects the fact that an individual has little or no expectation of privacy in the workplace, but that attempts by employers to obtain information about, or assert control over, aspects of an employee's life pertaining to life and activities outside the workplace should be subject to much greater legal scrutiny and control (Charlesworth, 2003).

On the federal level, the prime statutory law in this area is the Electronic Communications Privacy Act of 1986 (ECPA), which generally protects E-mail from illegal monitoring and makes it a federal crime, punishable by imprisonment for up to five years or a fine of up to $250,000 for an individual and $500,000 for an organization (18 USC 2510)[4,5] to intercept and disclose electronic communications. The ECPA addresses the problem of unauthorized access or access by persons exceeding their authorization for items such as personal and business correspondence, which were intended to be kept confidential. The ECPA includes a stored communication provision (18 U.S.C. § 2701) that prohibits the unauthorized access to or use of stored electronic communication including voice mail and E-mail and prohibits providers of electronic communication services from disclosing the contents of stored communication. The rules against disclosure apply only to E-mail systems offered to the public (Stuckey, 1996). The law makes it a crime and also creates a civil cause of action against any party committing a "knowing or intentional" violation of the provisions (18 U.S.C. § 2707).[6]

Issues that are addressed by the ECPA become more complex when raised in the university or business setting. Employers often monitor employee's job performance but should employers have access to their employee's E-mail? Employers say yes and claim they do this for reasons ranging from system maintenance, message routing, trouble-shooting, protection of trade secrets, and quality control (Kelly 1994).[7] Do employees have a privacy right in their electronic mail communications? Under what circumstances can managers lawfully monitor employees' E-mail? Is consent by employees necessary? What facts are necessary to show consent? Answers? The ECPA does not protect privacy of messages sent on internal company E-mail systems. The law treats such messages as interoffice memos that can be read by authorized employees, supervisors, or systems managers—without violating the law. The prime exceptions to the ECPA allow employers broad rights to monitor employees if monitoring occurs in the ordinary course of business or with the employee's implied consent. One party to the communication must consent to the monitoring, but employees' consent can be implied from the circumstances of employment. Employees claim this violates their privacy rights, particularly if the intercepted communication is of a personal nature, but to date, the courts have not found a right of privacy in the context of employee E-mail monitored for legitimate business reasons. Under the Fourth Amendment, courts have even upheld an employer's right to engage in workplace surveillance for legitimate business reasons (O'Connor v. Ortega, 1987). The ECPA contains a "business exclusion exemption"[8] that excepts interceptions that are made by equipment furnished to the subscriber or users by a communications carrier in the ordinary course of its business and that are being used by the subscriber or user in the ordinary course of its business. Under this exception, an employer may monitor phone calls in an employer-supplied telephone system by attaching a device supplied by the employer.[9] At this point, unless legislation or judicial decisions recognize a new employee privacy right, employers have the right to monitor and read workers' E-mail correspondence. It is interesting that in the age of telecommuting with employees potentially doing a great deal of work online at home, the blurring between work and home suggests it is not altogether clear what the expectation of privacy is with regard to work-related E-mail sent to a home computer.

Given the lack of protection afforded by the ECPA and state action, many employees are seeking recourse under common law rights action typically for invasions of privacy but most often the cases are decided on the key condition of "reasonable expectation of privacy" which courts across the country are finding with great frequency that there is such reasonable expectation with regard to employee mail (Smith v. The Pillsbury Company, 1996).[10]

Ad hoc business policies are being developed regarding employee expectations of privacy. These policies seem to reflect the position that privacy is not a reasonable expectation in regard to company files and business correspondence generated by employees during work time and while using company equipment. This extends from physical files to E-mail and computer files. Increasingly, businesses and universities are dealing with the controversies generated by E-mail privacy by formulating and disseminating E-mail policies as a means of clarifying expectations and averting possible legal action. In formulating these policies, the organizational culture is generally addressed along with issues such as whether any messages are considered private, under what circumstances E-mail is monitored and by whom, and whether personal communication will be permitted (and kept private).

A limited common law tort of invasion of privacy has been judicially recognized, a right generally left to each state. This tort is based on distinct categories of intrusion, false light, and appropriation.[11]

Technological and Legal Solutions

Both technology and the legal system have been looked to for solutions to privacy problems. In June 2000, major Internet companies introduced a new generation of Web-browsing software designed to give users more control over their personal information online. The new products are based on the Platform for Privacy Preferences Project (P3P), a set of software-writing guidelines developed by the World Wide Web Consortium (W3C), the standard-setting body for the Web. P3P is designed to provide Internet users with a clear understanding of how personal information will be used by a particular Web site. Web site operators are able to use the P3P language to explain their privacy practices to visitors. The main goals are (a) to inform a user agent of a site's data collection and privacy practices; (b) allow a user agent and service to automatically negotiate and to come to an agreement satisfactory to both parties; alternatively, for the user agent to notify the user and take instruction concerning proposed data exchanges from the user; and (c) exchange data when such exchange is authorized by the user and consistent with a user's preferences and any outstanding agreement (Cookiecentral.com). Many ISPs and free E-mail services now provide spam filtering. Although filters are not perfect, they can reduce tremendously the amount of spam a user receives. Firewalls and proxies are barriers between a computer and the Internet restricting communications or blocking communications. "Anonymizer" services are proxies that allow a user to browse the Internet using an intermediary to prevent unauthorized parties from gathering personal information. The proxy computer can be set up to block communications such as cookies, junk E-mail, Java, ad banners—the types of communications used by intruders attempting to hack into computers. Several software products allow users to set up personal firewalls that depend on user preferences so that "rules" can be set up to block all cookies from a certain domain or reject communications from a specified E-mail server.

The Opt-In Approach: Another approach to online privacy concerns has been the opt-in/opt-out approach. Notice and consent is key to this approach. In the opt-out approach, the assumption or default is that information will be used for any number of purposes unless the individual says "no." Opt-in plans are associated with a key issue, which is the manner in which an individual (e.g., consumer) has a choice with regard to secondary users of information. "Secondary use," is the sharing of date to a third party or organization (Regan, 2003). Secondary use runs counter to the fair information principle that information should be used only for the purpose for which it is collected. Some businesses now offer consumers incentives to agree to information-sharing. Incentives include discounts, coons, or download of additional digital content (Lawler, 2003). Priscilla Regan (2003) noted:

> The way the "market" in personal information is currently constructed; the individual who wishes to control or restrict her flow of personal information bears the burden and cost. Privacy decisions are generally hidden transaction costs associated with a consumer or communication transaction. For example, one purchases a product online or visits a website and a record of that purchase or that visit is recorded as transactional information. That information might then be further used by the organization or resold. From the individual's perspective, however, the primary activity engaged in is the transaction, not the recording of the transaction. But it is the recording of the transaction that triggers the need or opportunity to make a decision about privacy. (p. 25)

With opt-out approaches, most consumer advocates (and bills) seek clear notice, conspicuous and understandable, but more consumer advocates prefer opt-in regimes. The opt-in approach, the principle that a company should obtain an individual's affirmative consent before collecting or sharing data, is popular with consumers. A March 2000 BusinessWeek/Harris Poll showed that 86% of users want a Web site to obtain opt-in consent before even collecting users' names, addresses, phone numbers, or financial information. The same poll showed that 88% of users support opt-in as the standard before a Web site shares personal information with others (Public Opinion on Privacy, EPIC, 2003).

Encryption: Encryption is one of the principal technical means of attaining Internet security, but public policy has long been a controversial issue, particularly within the United States. Encryption is based on the use of mathematical procedures to scramble data so that it is difficult, if not impossible, for unauthorized recipients to recover the original text. Cryptographic techniques allow information to be stored on insecure computers or transmitted across insecure networks while protecting files from theft, unauthorized access, or interception, and guarantees that the contents have not been altered. It is frequently argued that encryption is essential for promoting e-commerce by providing message integrity by preventing alteration and by providing for authentication of documents by establishing parties to an electronic message. Only parties with the correct decryption "key" (or keys) are able to recover the information. In the 1990s, the U.S. Department of Justice investigated Phil Zimmerman for possible violations of Arms Control Regulations after Pretty Good Privacy (PGP) software the first user-friendly encryption software was posted to Usenet news-groups and distributed worldwide via the Internet.[12] At that time, the administration went so far as to classify encryption software under the category of munitions. Three other cases challenged the legality of the encryption export regulations on the grounds that regulations constituted an unconstitutional prior restrain on speech protected by the First Amendment. It was also argued that such restrictions violated rights to due process under the Fifth Amendment.[13] In Junger v. Daley (2000), the Sixth Circuit Court found that encryption source code is speech protected by the First Amendment.

Strong encryption makes information secure from unwanted eaves-dropping, interception, and theft, simultaneously making it increasingly more difficult for law enforcement to conduct certain types of electronic surveillance of CMC. Under the Clinton administration, after several years of efforts to limit the sale and exportation of encryption software, a new policy was announced in January 2000 easing restrictions. After September 11, 2001, new efforts to limit encryption were launched in the name of fighting terrorism. Under one proposed regime, government officials could get access to keys for encryption products built in America or imported into the country "under a strict structure which is legal and judicially controlled."[14] Attorney General John Ashcroft has pushed to include anti-encryption laws into the Domestic Security Enhancement Act of 2003, which has not yet been officially proposed. The plan would make the use of encryption to conceal a federal crime or an attempted federal crime an offense punishable by 5 to 10 years in prison (in addition to the sentence imposed for the crime itself; Vamosi, 2003).

Associational Privacy

Among the many privacy issues concerning CMC are data confidentiality, law enforcement eavesdropping and/or surveillance, unrestricted access to erotic and pornographic text and images, message encryption, the ability to have secured transactions, source anonymity, and associational privacy. The first significant dimension of interpersonal electronic privacy is the degree to which a message can be directed and shared with only the intended recipient(s). Is the nearly instantaneous means of delivering written messages and documents via electronic mail E-mail a private transaction? Can one assume that no unseen intruder could open E-mail? E-mail conjures up images of letters in sealed envelopes, but "mail messages being routed from computer system to computer system on their journey through the Internet [for example] are more like postcards than letters" (Netsurfer Focus, 1995). The nature of E-mail may also lead to behavior in which disclosure of information is fostered. It has been noted that "E-mail is a very informal medium. It is far closer to speech than written communication, and . . . the care given to a written communication. It has evolved into a hybrid of speech and writing by the use of emoticons, those shorthand signs which explain the tones of the E-mail" (Aftab, 1996, p. S2).

Private service providers including Prodigy, CompuServe and AOL, under contract with customers to deliver service, claim the right to monitor not only publicly posted BB messages, but person-to-person messages. For example, dating back as early as 1995, the AOL, stipulated:

> AOL Inc. may elect to electronically monitor the public areas (e.g., chat rooms and public message boards) for adherence to the TOS Agreement and the Rules of the Road and may disclose any content or records to satisfy any law, regulation or other governmental request or to properly operate the AOL Service and protect its members. AOL Inc. reserves the right at its sole discretion to review, edit, or refuse to post any material or information submitted for display or posted on the AOL Service. Notwithstanding the foregoing, AOL will not intentionally monitor or disclose any private E-mail message unless permitted or required by law. (America Online Service Membership, 1995)[15]

Despite the assurance of E-mail privacy, in the Fall 1995, AOL gave law enforcement agents access to the private electronic mailboxes of an unknown number of subscribers leading to the arrest of a dozen people suspected of being among the most active traders of online child pornography. The Justice Department indicated more arrests were planned (Lewis, 1995). In another case, AOL recently blocked all E-mail messages sent from five domains (Internet addresses), including three used by CyberPromotions that sent unsolicited E-mail or spam. AOL argues that spamming violates the Electronic Privacy Act and the Computer Fraud and Abuse Act.[16] Inherent in this case is not only the right of AOL to monitor but to also block transmissions implicating the rights of not only those who would send the messages but limiting what subscribers receive.[17] AOL maintains that it is a private, proprietary system and the spammers are not "leafleting the public square" (Leibowitz, 1996a). Lawyers for Cyber Promotions claimed a First Amendment right to send junk E-mail to AOL users despite the ISP's objections, noting that messages were sent over the public Internet rather than the private AOL pipeline.[18] This distinction, they argued, leads to applying laws of privately owned public places like the shopping mall by analogy.[19] The Electronic Communication Privacy Act and similar state statues prohibit ISPs from reviewing transmitted communications. ISPs have no editorial control, acting like a bookseller or newsvendor in the analogy used to determine liability and responsibility (Stuckey, 1994). But several ISPs have attempted to exercise editorial control over the content of their services as was the case of Prodigy, which censors messages that directly attack other subscribers and uses what it calls "George Carlin" software, which searches and deletes messages containing objectionable words (Lewis, 1994).

In the United States, privacy rights have developed in the form of a patchwork of industry-specific statutes. Legislation designed to protect the right to privacy from private and government sector infringement includes the following:

- Privacy of communications (the 1986 Electronic Communications Privacy Act and the Telephone Consumer Protection Act of 1991).
- Privacy of financial information (the 1970 Fair Credit Reporting Act).
- Privacy of government collections (the Privacy Act of 1974).
- Privacy of medical records (the Health Insurance Portability and Accountability Act of 1996.

Various U.S. agencies have been involved in this concern for privacy of consumers. In April 1995, the FTC staff held its first public workshop on Internet privacy. Since then, the FTC has held numerous additional hearings and workshops, and has issued a number of surveys, studies, and reports (CDT Guide to Online Privacy, 2003). In October 1999, the FTC released its Final Rule, which operationalzed the Child Online Protection Act (COPA; 16 C.F.R. PART 312) effective April 21, 2000. The Children's Online Privacy Protection Rule requires Web sites targeted to children 12 and under to obtain parental consent before collecting personal information. COPA gives the FTC authority to regulate companies that collect information from minors without "verifiable parental consent."

The FTC examined online profiling, in November 1999. In July 2000, the FTC voted to seek a preliminary injunction against Toysmart.com, which planed to sell customer data as it searched for a buyer for the business, despite a guarantee not share the information. Later that month, FTC announced a settlement that forbade the sale of Toysmart.com's customer database except under very limited circumstances to a "Qualified Buyer"

("FTC Announces Settlement," 2000). On May 23, 2000, after several years of relying on a self-regulatory approach, the FTC issued a report to Congress asking for the authority to regulate online privacy. Although the report noted that an increasing number of Web sites now post privacy policies, it also noted that only 20% meet the FTC's fair information practices ("Privacy Online," 2000). The FTC unanimously recommended the Network Advertising Initiative (NAI), a self-regulatory proposal that seeks to implement fair information practices for the major Internet advertisers' collection of online consumer data. By July 2000, however, the report also asked Congress to enact baseline legislation to protect consumer privacy.

Under the Clinton administration, the Office of Management and Budget (OMB) created the office of the Chief Counselor for Privacy to coordinate the federal government's response to privacy issues. In 1999, Peter P. Swire, a professor of law at Ohio State University and internationally recognized expert on privacy issues, was appointed Chief Counselor for Privacy. This position in the OMB's Office of Information and Regulatory Affairs was charged with coordinating a wide range of federal government agencies in their efforts to shape privacy issues. However, under the Bush administration it was announced that the position of privacy adviser expired and there were no plans to replace Swire. The administration asserted it did not need the guidance of a privacy czar (Matthews, 2001).

Another key question concerning legislation is whether federal legislation should pre-empt state law restrictions on spam. Although more than 30 states have enacted anti-spam laws, there has been concern over their ineffectiveness given the global nature of the medium. Limitations found in some on the ability for individuals to bring suit have also brought state legislation under criticism. Federal regulators and lawmakers are trying to find ways to keep computers from being inundated with spam E-mails, which are estimated to account for between one third and one half of E-mail traffic ("California Senate Okays," 2003). Anti-spam action on Capitol Hill is mounting, with bills being introduced in every congressional session since 1998. By the Spring 2003 several new proposals looked promising. The House of Representatives considered the "Reduction in Distribution of Spam Act," sponsored by Representative Richard Burr, (R-NC). This bill focused on the worst bulk E-mailers by providing for prison terms and millions of dollars in fines. The most recent legislation proposes that no one may send "any commercial electronic mail message" unless it permits the recipient to unsubscribe, includes valid return E-mail and street addresses, and makes it obvious that the message is an advertisement or solicitation. An ISP could sue for damages of $10 for each E-mail sent to someone who had "opted out," up to a maximum of $500,000. False or misleading header information would be banned. Inclusion of "sexually oriented material" in any commercial E-mail message would become a federal crime, unless the sender follows regulations to be devised by the FTC. Violators of the rule would be punished by up to 2 years in a federal prison. Other bills take different approaches. Representative Zoe Lofgren (D-Calif.) introduced a bill requiring unsolicited commercial E-mail to be labeled as "ADV" in the subject line. Failure to comply with the "ADV" requirement could lead to a lawsuit brought by the FTC. A Senate bill would make it a federal crime to use a false address when sending unsolicited commercial E-mail (McCullagh & Hu, 2003). Simultaneously, the FTC held a 3-day workshop on spam.

Stuckey (1996, §5.02) identified a dozen key privacy laws in the United States governing personal privacy related to issues arising in cyberspace. Most of these laws concern the relationship between government and the individual. For example, in the United States, the Fourth Amendment, which guarantees the right of the people to be secure in their persons, houses, papers, and effects against unreasonable searches and seizures, has been recognized as "creating a zone of privacy which courts have interpreted to mean limits government surveillance, data collection and intrusion. The U.S. Supreme Court has relied on the analysis of 'reasonable expectations of privacy' and have found that there is no reasonable expectation of privacy in numbers dialed on the telephone" (*Smith v. Maryland*, 1979), bank records (*United States v. Miller*, 1976), and even in secured areas such as the curtilage (area around) a home (*California v. Ciraolo*, 1986).[20]

The Fifth Amendment of the U.S. Constitution, which protects a person from being compelled to bear witness against themselves in a criminal case, limits how the government may gather incriminating information from an individual so that government may be limited in using business records and encrypted records.[21] "It is unclear that compelling a person to furnish the key to encrypted electronic records or communications is a means available to the government for collecting evidence of a crime" (Stuckey, 1996, §5.02[2]). Law enforcement agents with a warrant may decrypt encrypted file themselves but it is unclear whether the government can coerce a person to provide the code for decrypting the file. Stuckey noted the mail privacy statute that prohibits the opening of mail without a search warrant or addressee consent (39 U.S.C. §3623)[22] and federal wiretap statutes (18 U.S.C. §§ 2510 *et seq.*), which prohibit the use of eavesdropping technology and the interception of radio communications, data transmission, and telephone calls without consent of at least one party to the communication. The Computer Fraud and Abuse Act (18 U.S. C. §1030) focuses on computer crime and security. The act address six offenses designed to protect the federal interest in computers, and protect private computers connected to an interstate network. Personal information protected is a "by-product" of the protection of the system (Stuckey, 1996, §5.02[6]).[23]

The Privacy Act (5 U.S.C. §552a) protects the privacy of personally identifiable information held by the federal government and applies primarily to records maintained in an agency's "system of records" (Stuckey, 1996, §5.02[9]). The act restricts federal agencies from disclosing personal data and requires agencies to publish detailed notices of records kept on the system and procedures for individuals to obtain access to records about themselves. The Fair Credit Reporting Act (15 U.S.C. §§ 1681 *et seq.)* regulates the collection and use of personal data by credit reporting agencies and prohibits agency reports on people from disclosing information about an individual without consent. But beyond the governmental setting, many privacy issues emerge.

GOVERNMENT ACTION AND PRIVACY

United States Perspectives on Privacy

Immediately after the September 11, 2001 terrorist attacks, polls showed that Americans were willing to accept more invasive police surveillance technologies. The exchange of security bartered for at the expense of individual liberties, including personal privacy, is not new.[24] The effort to prevent further terrorist attacks and wage the war on terrorism brings with it the recognition and acceptance of the need for the government to improve intelligence gathering and analytic capability. Civil libertarians note with concern that "As long as this deterioration in personal sense of safety and security exists, we're in some jeopardy about the erosion of our civil liberties" (Lester, 2002). Simultaneously, in the days following the domestic attacks, many Americans reported greater trust in government.

USA Patriot Act

On October 26, 2001, barely 1 month after the attacks on the Twin Towers and the Pentagon, President George W. Bush, signed into law the USA Patriot Act of 2001, otherwise known as "Uniting and Strengthening America by Providing Appropriate Tools Required to Intercept and Obstruct Terrorism Act of 2001" (Weekly Compilation of Presidential Documents, 2001). The USA Patriot Act emphasizes the importance of communication technology as instruments of potential espionage and design, particularly in light of terrorism's global nature and the convergent nature of recent communication technology in which one medium is intimately integrated into another. At the same time, the USA Patriot Act represents the application and growing sophistication of the U.S. government in using and applying communication technology to invade the privacy of its citizens in its attempt to deter and apprehend those deemed to be enemies of the state (McCullagh, 2001b). Although the act was not an unexpected response to the attacks of September 11th, the implications of governmental action and legislation requires carefully scrutiny.

The short title of the USA Patriot Act (2001) states that the purpose of the legislation is "too deter and punish terrorist acts in the United States and around the world, to enhance law enforcement investigatory tools, and for other purposes." The Patriot Act amended more than 15 federal statutes, including the laws governing criminal procedure, computer fraud and abuse, foreign intelligence, wiretapping, immigration, and the privacy of student records. These amendments expanded the authority of the FBI and law enforcement to gain access to business, medical, educational, and library records, including stored electronic data and communications. It also expanded the laws governing wiretaps and "trap and trace" phone devices to Internet and electronic communications. These enhanced surveillance procedures pose the greatest challenge to privacy and confidentiality in the library. At this writing, much is left to conjecture. To provide a taste of the implications of the changing legal and psychological environment, however, consider the following as noted by Declan McCullagh in *Wired Magazine* (2001b).

- Police will have the permanent ability to conduct Internet surveillance *without a court order* in some circumstances, secretly search homes and offices without notifying the owner, and share confidential grand jury information with the CIA.
- Any U.S. attorney or state attorney general can order the installation of the FBI's Carnivore surveillance system and record addresses of Web pages visited and E-mail correspondents — without going to a judge. Previously, there were stiffer legal restrictions on Carnivore and other Internet surveillance techniques. (Section 216).
- Expands records that can be sought under the Electronic Communications Privacy Act (ECPA) without a court order to include records of session times and durations, means and source of payments including any credit card or bank account number (Section 210).

A key to understanding the scope of the act is the recognition that most of its powers are not limited to terrorism but also apply to any *criminal investigations*. Governmental authority already permitted courts to order a telephone company to turn over a list of the numbers being dialed to and from a particular telephone, on a standard less than probable cause, if the government certifies that the information sought is "relevant to an ongoing criminal investigation." This has now been extended to "dialing, routing, and signaling information" in connection with computers. This tool provides information on context (i.e., E-mail addresses, Web sites visited) rather than content. Although the Department of Justice promises to limit observation to avoid content, there is no way (to date) to oversee whether this promise is kept. Furthermore, public access computers, such as those in public libraries and cybercafes, can subject unsuspecting "nontarget" citizens who are using those computers to government surveillance. So-called "roving wiretaps" are authorized. These extend wiretapping activities by permitting such activity to apply to a person rather than to a designated telephone number. All forms of communication become searchable without the designated person's awareness, including mobile telephones, cell phones, and online communication means. In many instances, the act requires the Department of the Treasury ("Treasury") or other departments or agencies to enact certain rules and regulations to implement the act's various requirements. Many of the rules required by the act have already been proposed. Some of the rules are currently in effect or are expected to be in effect soon. The act is constantly evolving, with new requirements and compliance procedures being added periodically (Polek, 2002).

Section 215 of the act refers to Access to Records Under Foreign Intelligence Security Act (FISA). The act allows an FBI agent to obtain a search warrant for "any tangible thing," which can include books, records, papers, floppy disks, data tapes, and computers with hard drives. It permits the FBI to compel production of library circulation records, Internet use records, and registration information stored in any medium. FISA standards do not require that probable cause be demonstrated to support the existence of specific facts related to the commission of a crime. Instead, the agent only needs to claim that the belief that the records sought may be related to an ongoing investigation related to terrorism or intelligence activities—a very low legal standard. Libraries or librarians served with a search warrant issued under FISA rules may not disclose, under of penalty of law, the existence of the warrant or the fact that records were produced as a result of the warrant. A patron cannot be told that his or her records were given to the FBI or that he or she is the subject of an FBI investigation. As a result of this provision and the FBI's broad new powers to check borrower records, Internet use and other materials that could help track client reading histories in libraries, bookstores, and medical records, the FBI has been forcing these entities to reveal patron information without notifying the client that their information has been subject of investigation. By February 2002, it was estimated that hundreds of librarians had been asked for information and were under orders not to reveal this information. To date the ACLU is seeking a test case to challenge this law (Piore, 2002).

Section 505 of the PATRIOT Act similarly expanded the government's power to obtain telephone and E-mail transactional records, credit reports, and financial data with the use of a document called the National Security Letter (NSL), which is issued by FBI officials without judicial approval. Sections 507 and 508 granted authority to the attorney general or his designee to obtain a court record for disclosure of educational records. There is not a great deal of information on how the USA Patriot Act has been used. Legislators who approved the bill note that the most controversial surveillance sections will expire in 2005. But exempt from the expiration date are investigations underway by December 2005, and any future investigations of crimes that took place before that date. On May 30, 2002, Attorney General John Ashcroft issued revised guidelines for FBI investigations with several provisions significantly expanding surveillance and use of data mining. When conducting terrorism investigations, the FBI is subject to two sets of guidelines, one classified set for foreign intelligence and international terrorism and the second an unclassified set focusing on general crimes, racketeering, and domestic terrorism. The foreign guidelines are applicable to investigations inside the United States of foreign powers and international terrorism organizations (like al Qaeda or Hamas) that originate abroad, but carry out their actions within the United States. These foreign guidelines have been much more relaxed than the old domestic guidelines that govern investigations of groups that operate or originate in the United States. The guideline changes that contained serious implications for online privacy pertain to the attorney general's announced changes to the domestic guidelines, leading civil libertarians to question whether they were really related to conducting the war on terrorism associated with foreign organizations (Johnson, 2002).

Among the guidelines changed were online surfing provisions, which relate not only to terrorism cases, but to all other investigations — drugs, white-collar crime, public corruption, and copyright infringement. The FBI has never been prohibited from surfing the Internet or using *commercial data-mining services* if the search had to be related to some investigation. Under pre-existing guidelines, the FBI could maintain a *preliminary inquiry* for 90 days using investigatory techniques including data mining, whenever it had "information or an allegation whose responsible handling required some further scrutiny."[25] The FBI could even begin a preliminary inquiry for the purpose of data mining, while at the same time criminal conduct. Under the revised guidelines, data mining can be used as the basis for generating the suspicion of criminal conduct in the first place. Critics argue this is a form of data-fishing expedition making use of commercial services associated with direct digital marketing and spam E-mail. These enhanced preliminary inquiries permit the FBI to conduct investigations even when there is no reasonable indication of criminal activity for one year without approval of headquarters, whereas under the old guidelines, if 90 days of investigation turned up no indication of criminal activity, the investigation could be continued only with Headquarter's approval. Under the heading "Enhancing Information Analysis at FBI Headquarters," the new Ashcroft guidelines authorize the FBI to "participate in . . . information systems . . . [that] draw on and retain pertinent information from any source . . . including . . . publicly available information, whether obtained directly or through services or resources (whether nonprofit or commercial) that compile or analyze such information." Therefore, the FBI can subscribe to any commercial profiling and data-mining service. Some data-mining services routinely profile people by race and religion. Another clause in the same new section permits acceptance and retention of information "voluntarily provided by private entities," which harkens back to the days of private intelligence gathering by right-wing groups (The Attorney General's Guidelines, 2001).

In another area that blurs foreign and domestic surveillance, under the USA Patriot Act, the FISA was specifically amended to eliminate the requirement that *foreign* intelligence gathering be "the primary purpose of the monitoring." There is a difference between the domestic jurisdiction of the FBI and the Department of Justice in domestic criminal cases, and surveillance conducted for intelligence purposes. The FISA has dealt with the authorization of search and surveillance warrants for foreign intelligence targets, which could be obtained by meeting a much lower threshold than warrants for warrants related to a domestic criminal investigation. Under Department of Justice guidelines approved in March 2002 by Ashcroft, prosecutors would be permitted to "advise intelligence officials on the initiation, operation, continuation, or expansion of FISA searches or surveillance." In May 2002, a FISA court unanimously ruled that such extensive collaboration would amount to law enforcement "directing FISA surveillances and searches from start to finish," which it considers illegal and an erosion of the distinction between law enforcement and intelligence work. However, in November 2002, a secret three-judge Foreign Intelligence Surveillance Court of Review[26] granted the government permission to fully involve prosecutors and FBI agents in foreign intelligence surveillance operations, giving the Justice Department broad discretion in the use of wiretaps and other surveillance techniques to track suspected terrorists and spies and overruling a unanimous decision issued in May by seven trial judges of a lower surveillance court that was highly critical of the government's approach. The Homeland Security Act—legislation to create the new Department of Homeland Security (DHS)—was enacted in November 2002, giving the new department considerable authority for data collection and analysis and at the same time, raising numerous privacy concerns. Although the law includes provisions for the protection of privacy, including the creation of a Privacy Office, privacy advocates have voiced great concern (CDT, 2003). "Powerful intelligence agencies require powerful checks and balances," said CDT Director Jerry Berman. "This new department is part of a trend that involves more surveillance and sweeps of data about innocent people. Neither the President nor the Congress have answered any of the fundamental questions, including how this is going to work, what are the checks and balances" (CDT, 2003).

Further confusion and concern with regard to privacy has arisen as result of the creation of a new U.S. government department announced in President George W. Bush's State of the Union address in January 2003. At that time, the president indicated this new government department would compile information, from government and private sources, on people deemed possible terrorist threats. Few details about the plan to create the agency, dubbed the Terrorist Threat Integration Center (TTIC), have been made public (CDT, 2003).

Even before September 11th, the FBI designed and developed a diagnostic tool, called Carnivore. Carnivore is a device that allows the FBI to intercept and collect electronic communication with a precise or "surgical" ability, while ignoring those communications that they are not authorized to intercept. It was argued that this tool was necessary to meet stringent requirements of the federal wiretapping statutes. The Carnivore device works much like commercial "sniffers" and other network diagnostic tools used by ISPs. The device provides law enforcement agents the ability to

> distinguish between communications which may be lawfully intercepted and those that may not. For example, if a court order provides for the lawful interception of one type of communication (e.g., E-mail), but excludes all other communications (e.g., online shopping) the Carnivore tool can be configured to intercept only those E-mails being transmitted either to or from the named subject. (Internet and Data Interception Capabilities Developed by the FBI, 2003)

The system generated a great tempest when its existence became known in 2000. The relaxation of restrictions on Carnivore's use authorized by the USA Patriot Act have come with a new reporting provision that requires reports for the years 2002 and 2003 on details, including the number of times Carnivore is used, both to collect transactional data and to intercept the content of communications, and the number of persons whose communications are intercepted. The reporting requirement became law in Section 305 of the 21st Century Department of Justice Appropriations Authorization Act, Pub. L. No. 107-273, signed by the president on November 2, 2002.

The Total Information Awareness (TIA) program became public knowledge during the Summer of 2002. TIA, which is within the Defense Department under the Defense Advanced Research Project Agency, and headed by John Poindexter, was designed to jump start new methods of knowledge gathering, integration, and prediction. TIA's 5-year goal is the "total reinvention of technologies for storing and accessing information . . . although database size will no longer be measured in the traditional sense, the amounts of data that will need to be stored and accessed will be unprecedented, measured in petabytes" (Information Awareness Office, 2003).[27] Defense Agency (DARPA) hopes to predict terrorist attacks by detecting patterns of behavior in electronic records in a still to be developed computer system that would give access to government and commercial records from around the world that could fill the Library of Congress more than 50 times (Sniffen, 2003a). It is one high-tech answer to the terrorist menace, however widespread criticism in mainstream media has proclaimed concern for privacy. The Electronic Frontier Foundation's newsletter announced this program was a lesson in "how to build a police state." By November, the TIA program, with its ominous looking logo (an "all-seeing eye," the Masonic symbol found on a $1 bill) caught the attention of thousands on Web sites. Newspapers, including *The New York Times*, called it a "snooper's dream," laying down "a vast electronic dragnet" ("A Snooper's Dream," 2002). Not only was the program controversial but also the choice of John Poindexter, who had previously been embroiled in the Reagan era Iran-Contra scandal as its director, drew fire.[28] In February 2003, Congress voiced its displeasure with the implications of such a surveillance-rich program under the Defense Department, putting the Pentagon on notice that it would not tolerate the surveillance of U.S. citizens. The program was renamed, becoming the Terrorism Information Awareness program within the Information Awareness Office (IAO), and the director resigned (Sniffen, 2003). DARPA argues that TIA searches do not actually amount to data mining, at least not data mining as it is practiced by marketers and other commercial entities. DARPA officials acknowledge that they can seek evidence of possible terrorist preparations by scanning billions of everyday transactions, potentially including a vast array of information about the personal lives of Americans, such as medical information, travel records, and credit card and financial data. DARPA notes that because the United States has no comprehensive privacy law for commercial data, a great deal of information is available for purchase by law enforcement and intelligence agencies from private-sector data aggregators. DARPA officials point to new powers under the USA Patriot Act which sanction government data mining.[29]

Privacy concerns are being addressed with a proactive policy. In testimony given before Congress, the Department of Defense promised to use only legally collected personal data. But a coalition of groups with privacy concerns is not satisfied. Democratic Senator Ron Wyden noted that "most Americans don't know that laws that protect consumer privacy fail to apply to governmental efforts to obtain data including medical records, financial and credit card data and information about travel" ("Wyden Calls for Congressional Oversight," 2003).

In April 2003, the Air Force Research Laboratory Information Directorate awarded a 42-month, $3.5 million contract to a Palo Alto research center to begin the TIA project. The contract includes a focus on "creating privacy filters, 'aliasing' methods and automated data expunging agents to protect the privacy of U.S. citizens and people not involved with foreign terrorists" (Caterinicchia, 2003).

In January 2003, a draft copy of legislation being drafted by the Department of Justice designed as a sequel to the USA Patriot Act became available. The draft legislation, which has been dubbed "Patriot Act 2," would grant sweeping powers to the government, eliminating or weakening many of the checks and balances that remained on government surveillance, wiretapping, detention and criminal prosecution even after passage of the USA Patriot Act ("How 'Patriot Act 2' Would Further Erode," 2003).

Public Opinion and Post-September 11th

As time has passed, public support of invasive government initiatives in the name of security has waned. Immediately after the September 11th attacks, a Harris Poll found that 68% of Americans supported a national identification system. By March 2002, the Gartner Group found that only 26% of Americans favored a national identification program, and that 41% opposed the idea. Popular support for other surveillance technologies has declined as well (Public Agenda and the National Constitution Center, 2002).

The NPR/Kaiser/Kennedy School National Survey on Civil Liberties conducted a survey in October 2001 and November 2001. When asked, "In order to curb terrorism in this country, do you think it will be necessary for the average person to give up some rights and liberties, or do you think we can curb terrorism without the average person giving up rights and liberties?" Fifty-one % of respondents answered that it would be necessary for the average person to give up some civil liberties. Fifty-eight percent indicated they thought they would have to give up some of their own rights and liberties in order to curb terrorism. With regard to anti-terrorist measures, 72% indicated they would support giving law enforcement broader authority to intercept E-mail and 82% reported support for examination of Internet activity. However, 68% believed law enforcement officers should still be required to obtain a court order before conducting these activities. Sixty-five percent did indicated they were concerned that if law enforcement were granted wider authority it would be used against innocent people. But only 38% indicated they were very concerned (NPR/Kaiser/Kennedy School Poll on Civil Liberties, 2001). Results from a follow-up survey conducted in August 2002 by the same group revealed the nation was "evenly divided on the question of tradeoffs between civil liberties and security" (NPR/Kaiser/Kennedy School Poll on Civil Liberties, 2002). It was reported that "a small but statistically significant number of Americans have shifted toward the civil liberties side of the issue since last year, although majorities still support some government actions that could be seen as curtailing such liberties" (NPR/Kaiser/Kennedy School Poll on Civil Liberties, 2002). Asked whether "it's more important to ensure people's constitutional rights, even if it means that some suspected terrorists are never found," or "it's more important to find every potential terrorist, even if some innocent people are seriously hurt," 44% saw the need to ensure people's constitutional rights as more important, whereas 47% indicated it is more important to find every potential terrorist. Whereas only 21% reported they felt that they had personally given up some rights and liberties, 56% of Americans believed that many others have had to give up some rights and liberties in order to curb terrorism. The survey indicated that American's trust in the government was decreasing with regard to the war on terrorism. Although 65% said they are satisfied with the way the government's anti-terrorism program is progressing, only 20% said they are very satisfied. Forty-four percent said they have a great deal of confidence in the government's ability to protect them from future terrorist attacks, down from 58% in November 2001 (NPR/Kaiser/Kennedy School Civil Liberties Update Americans More Concerned with Liberties, Back War on Terrorism, 2002). An August 2002 First Amendment Center study found that 60% of respondents thought that the government possessed too much personal information about individuals (Public Opinion on Privacy, EPIC, 2003).

A special Foreign Intelligence Surveillance Court of Review ruled on November 18, 2002, that the USA Patriot Act gave the Justice Department the authority to use in criminal cases the special and in some ways looser rules created for foreign intelligence investigations. The court, which rejected arguments made by the CDT, ACLU, and others in a friend of the court brief, nevertheless emphasized that the law still required a finding of probable cause to believe that the target of the surveillance was an agent of a foreign power and was engaged in terrorism or activities in preparation therefore. But oversight is difficult, as many targets are never told they were the subjects of surveillance.[30]

Amitai Etzioni (2000) stated that "without privacy no society can long remain free" (p. 1). But sentiments today also reflect another Etzioni assertion—that our communities also have other goals that sometimes must override the privacy imperative. Whereas the surveillance/privacy relationship formerly distinguished between attitudes associated with risk in the physical versus mediated environments, post-September 11th reactions seem to have minimized the distinction with regard to privacy. Physical and mediated spaces have been merged, differences have become transparent as the threats in one environment are fueled by activities in the other.

European Perspectives on Privacy and the United States

The European Union (EU) Privacy Directive, officially known as the Directive 95/46/EC of the European Parliament and of the Council of 24 October 1995 on the protection of individuals with regard to the processing of personal data and on the free movement of such data (EU Data Protection Directive), took effect on October 25, 1998. Article 1 of the directive recognizes privacy as a fundamental human right by requiring member states to protect the "fundamental rights and freedoms of natural persons, and in particular their right to privacy with respect to the processing of personal data." All EU member states were required to enact comprehensive privacy legislation requiring organizations to implement personal data policies to include transparency in order to process data fairly; limited purpose for use so that data can only be collected and possessed for specified, legitimate purposes; and keeping data no longer than necessary to fulfill the stated purpose. The data transfer policy restricts authorized users of personal information from transferring that information to third parties without the permission of the individual providing the data, or data subject. In the case of data transfers across national boundaries, the directive prohibits data transfers outright to any country lacking an "adequate level of protection," as determined by the EU. The special protection policy requires restrictions on, and special government scrutiny of, data collection and processing activities of information identifying "racial or ethnic origin, political opinions, religious or philosophical beliefs . . . [or] concerning health or sex life." Each EU member state must create an independent public authority to supervise personal data protection. The EU will oversee the directive's implementation. Individuals are guaranteed the right to access and correct data collected about them.

The EU directive has great significance beyond the borders of the EU because under the terms of the directive, not only must all EU member states comply but *any nonmember state doing business in the EU* is required to follow "minimum standards" with respect to safeguarding personal data. Article 25 of the EU directive forbids any transfer of personal data outside the EU to countries that do not guarantee or do not have in place adequate safeguards for such data. For countries like the United States, where privacy laws may not conform to the EU's privacy standards, the directive could result in penalties or even the denial of access to the EU market for companies that fail to protect the privacy of EU citizens. It is expected that financial services and health care companies would be most greatly affected. The directive has been criticized on the grounds that it is too highly centralized, rigidly bureaucratic, and too expensive to implement. Congress has expressed concern that the EU directive could become a global standard. It might also be a nontariff barrier to free trade and an impediment to law enforcement. The directive caused a good deal of conflict between the United States and the EU, and some disruption of commerce because the United States does not have consumer data protection laws that would satisfy the EU data protection requirement. Some U.S. companies report they have been denied or have had delayed human resources or customer data from their own facilities located in EU countries. For a protracted period of time, the U.S. Department of Commerce and the European Commission engaged in negotiations, finally agreeing on a safe harbor policy by which U.S. companies could comply with the EU data protection directive. A safe harbor agreement was reached in the Summer of 2000. The compromise, which was meant to bridge the U.S. and EU's different privacy approaches and provide streamlined means for U.S. organizations, would be shielded from the directive. The safe harbor agreement went into effect on November 1, 2000. The Clinton administration negotiated the safe harbor agreement to allow the self-regulatory nature of U.S. privacy protections to co-exist with the EU's regulatory culture. U.S. companies who signed up promised to follow fair information practices in e-commerce enforced by the FTC in return for which the EU would not prosecute U.S. firms or cut-off European data from them. Few firms actually signed up to follow this agreement. The Department of Commerce, in conjunction with TRUSTe and Oracle Corporation, have looked into the issue of compliance with EU data protection requirements

By early 2001, under the new Bush administration, critics of the safe harbor agreement gained ground. The argument was made that U.S. financial institutions are putting in place privacy protections under the Gramm-Leach-Bliley Act that modernized the banking system sufficiently. This act (P.L. 106-102), passed in late 1999, requires financial institutions to disclose privacy policies once a year, and to give customers the opportunity to "opt-out" and block information sharing with unaffiliated third parties. The support for the safe harbor agreement within the Bush Department of Commerce is unclear.

The EU has not been immune to the shock of September 11th. Under the guise of tackling "terrorism," the EU's Justice and Home Affairs minister decided on September 20, 2001, that the law enforcement agencies needed to have access to all traffic data (phone calls, mobile calls, E-mails, faxes, and Internet usage) for the purpose of criminal investigations in general. What stood in the way was the 1997 directive on privacy in telecommunications. This was the follow-up to the directive on data protection. The 1997 directive stated that the only purpose for which traffic data could be retained was for billing (i.e., for the benefit of customers) and then it had to be erased. Law enforcement agencies could get access to the traffic data with a judicial order for a specific person or group (EU Considering New Internet, 2002).

CONCLUSIONS

Privacy is a historical reality, which different societies have construed in different ways. The division of human activity between public and private spheres is subject to change—its history is first of all the history of definition (Prost & Vincent, 1991) and has long been the subject of heated debate and inconsistent rulings (Regan, 1995). The computer offers conflicting opportunities for connection and privacy. As technology has expanded the ability to protect privacy, there has been a psychological shift from an expectation of privacy to near paranoia about loss of privacy. Simultaneously, social interaction has moved from the public realm into protected and controlled homes, offices, and laptops. Control of the communication environment is at the heart of the incongruous public/private nature of our use of computer technology and forays into cyberspace but the legal protections of those rights remain at a developmental stage.

NOTES

1. Public opinion polls have measured different domains of privacy revealing that concern about privacy is very context specific. For example, The ACLU Foundation's survey (Regan, 1995) and Harris-Equifax (1993) surveys broke down issues of privacy with respect to employment contexts ranging from employer collection of information to the monitoring of employees such as telephone monitoring with regard to job performance and monitoring of employees' out-of-work activities. Concern for secondary uses of personal information such as credit card information, insurance company information, telephone records, and even video rental records were considered significant in the ACLU Foundation survey of 1994 (Cantril & Cantril, 1994; Regan, 1995).
2. Opinion polls reveal that concerns for personal privacy appear to be situation-specific. Cantril and Cantril (1994), having worked on the ACLU Foundation's survey, concluded that there is little consistency in concern for privacy from one domain of privacy to another.

3. Regan (1995) dealt with information privacy associated with computerized data, communication privacy related to interpersonal communication, eavesdropping and bugging devices and privacy in telephonic communication in particular and psychological privacy, which she related to what individuals are thinking, and honesty, which she associated with "mental wire-tapping" and polygraph testing.

4. Individuals who show communications have been intercepted or used in violation of said statute can claim actual and punitive damages of up to $100 per day of violation (18 USC 2510).

5. THE ECPA is an amendment to Title III of the Omnibus Crime Control and Safe Streets Act of 1968, commonly known as the "wiretap law." This law was originally created to govern third-party interceptions of electronic communications, rather than to address concerns of employee rights.

6. The Stored Communications Provisions of the Electronic Communication Privacy Act prohibits an entity form obtaining access to, altering, or preventing access to an electronic communication while it is in storage. There are exceptions in §2701 of the act including Subsection (c)(1) which excuses conduct authorized by the provider of the service. This is not thought to be authorized as a system operator to monitor the contents of E-mail messages between subscribers. The ECPA prohibits service providers from disclosing the content of a communication whether it is in storage or transmission. Disclosures of content pursuant to a third-party subpoena in civil litigation are also prohibited (§2702). But the act does not prohibit the collection, disclosure, or use of transnational information such as E-mail addresses and billing information that can provide a good deal of information about subscribers (Stuckey, §5.03[1]).

7. According to Joel P. Kelly (1994), writing in *Employment Law Strategist*, "The tremendous rise in the number of employees who now use this technology, and the increasing ability of management to monitor such use, raise novel legal and ethical issues."

8. Most of these cases, which developed under the ECPA, have involved criminal justice and investigatory wiretaps of telephone and E-mail communication. In the civil application of ECPA, most of the case law has focused on telephone communication monitoring (Aftab, 1996).

9. There has been legislative activity in this realm recently. Senator Paul Simon introduced legislation in Congress that would require advance notification to both employees and customers of electronic monitoring. On the federal level, this bill, known as "The Privacy for Consumers and Workers Act," would prohibit undisclosed monitoring of restroom, dressing room, and locker room facilities unless an employer suspects illegal activities. The bill never passed and similar legislation on the state level has been unsuccessful in overruling the employer's right to monitor workplace actions or to intercept communications (Aftab, 1996, p. S10).

10. Two cases in which no reasonable expectation of privacy was found was the case of *Smith v. The Pillsbury Company* (1996), and a case involving Epson America and the California based subsidiary of Nissan.

11. William Prosser (1971), formerly dean of the University of California at Berkeley Law School, has been influential in characterizing privacy. The three distinct tort actions outlined by Prosser are each applicable to cyberspace transmissions and interactions. The private facts tort is defined in the *Restatement of Torts (1977)*, as a publication of private information that "(a) would be highly offensive to a reasonable person and (b) is not of legitimate concern to the public" (1977), which covers disclosure of embarrassing facts of a personal nature not justified by newsworthiness. Appropriation or commercialization involves the unauthorized commercial use of another's name or picture in an advertisement, promotion, or other commercial context, in which case the injury suffered is either the humiliation similar to the tort of private facts or a commercial property harm. A false light invasion of privacy tort is the knowing dissemination of highly offensive false publicity. The injury is to the plaintiff's peace of mind. The right to publicity involving celebrity plaintiffs suing defendants for damaging their right to control the commercialization of their names and likenesses. In 1994, talk radio "shock jock" Howard Stern was involved in such an action when, after announcing his candidacy for the governor of New York, Delphi Internet Services Corporation established a bulletin board about the candidacy and Stern sued Delphi for using his name and image without permission in an ad for its Internet service. In that case, the court ruled that Delphi was entitled to advertise its service related to news dissemination (*Stern v. Delphi Internet Services Corp.*, 1995).

12· After a 3-year investigation, the Department of Justice announced that it would not seek an indictment of Zimmerman (Lynch, 1996).

13· The three cases were *Karn v. United States Dep't of State* (1996), *Bernstein v. United States Dep't of State* (D.C.Cir. 1997, 1999), and *Junger v. Daley*(2000).
   It was also argued that restrictions on the export of encryption software was not authorized by the International Emergency Economic Powers Act (IEEPA), which the president invoked by Executive Order to extend the Export Administration Regulations after the Export Administration Act expired in 1994 (Encryption Litigation, 2003).

14. Senator Judd Gregg (R-N.H.) called for a new encryption regime that would give the law enforcement and intelligence communities the capabilities needed to monitor terrorist communications. Under his proposal. government officials could get access to keys for encryption products built in America or imported into the country "under a strict structure which is legal and judicially controlled" (McCullagh, 2001a).

15. The AOL service agreement (Section 4.1) reserves the right to remove "any content that it deems in its sole discretion to be unacceptable, undesirable or in violation of the Rules of the Road. AOL Inc. May terminate immediately any Member who misuses or fails to abide by the applicable AOL rules. AOL Inc. May terminate without notice Member's access to and use of the AOL Service and America Online Software on a breach of the AOL rules, including without limitation, misuse of the software libraries, discussion boards, E-mail, or public conference areas" (AOL Service Agreement, 1995).

16. The 1991 Telephone Consumer Protection Act bars the transmission of unsolicited commercial faxes and prerecorded telephone calls, but does not directly address unsolicited E-mail (Leibowitz, 1996b).

17. On September 5, 1996 a U.S. District Court judge in Philadelphia issued a temporary injunction prohibiting AOL from blocking the messages sent by Cyber Promotions with a trial date set for November to expedite the case (Leibowitz, 1996a).

18. The argument set forth by Cyber Promotions argues from analogy stating that sending unsolicited E-mail messages through the Internet is not over AOL's private pipeline and the Internet has governmental origins thereby placing such messages under the protections of the First Amendment (Leibowitz, 1996).

19. Cyber Promotions relied on *Marsh v. Alabama* (1946) and *PruneYard Shopping Center v. Robins* (1980), in which the Supreme Court permitted distribution of leaflets in a private shopping mall.

20. Some states have provided greater protections against government searches and seizures for banking records and telephone numbers.

21. If a document is made voluntarily, such as a *personal record*, there is no compulsion present to trigger the Fifth Amendment right.

22. There is a good deal of information that can be gotten via "mail covers," an investigatory technique of recording information from the outside of an envelop that does not require a warrant (39 C.F.R. § 233.3).

23. The Computer Fraud and Abuse Act articulates three felonies and three misdemeanor offenses. So it is a felony to fraudulently obtain anything of value by accessing a federal interest computer without authorization or by exceeding authorization.

24. Harvard researchers Robert Blendon and John Benson noted that the trade-off of civil liberties for personal security is nothing new in a time of conflict. They noted that although civil liberties have broad public support, the public will support substantial limits on those freedoms when there are serious threats, either at home or from overseas. In the post-Pearl Harbor period and during the Cold War, civil liberties took a backseat. Yet they note that by 2002, polls reported that about two thirds of respondents said they were at least somewhat concerned about losing civil liberties (Lester, 2002).

25· The Department of Justice claimed that under the old guidelines, preliminary inquiries could not serve as the basis for broader intelligence investigations. Yet the old guidelines clearly stated, "If, on the basis of information discovered in the course of a preliminary inquiry, an investigation is warranted, it may be conducted as a general crimes investigation, or a criminal intelligence investigation, or both." See http://www.usdoj.gov/ag/readingroom/general-crimea.htm#general.

26. The intelligence court was created as part of the FISA in 1978, and is charged with overseeing sensitive law enforcement surveillance by the U.S. government. Under the 1978 law, U.S. Supreme Court Justice William H. Rehnquist has appointed all the trial and appellate judges of the Foreign Intelligence Surveillance Act Court. (There are now 11 trial judges as a result of a new provision in the USA Patriot Act) (Wise, 2002). The Foreign Intelligence

Surveillance Court of Review had not in its nearly 25 years of existence, has actually reviewed anything until it was called on to review the Ashcroft Guideline changes announced in May 2002 (Blum, 2002).

27. In May 2003, the director of the Defense Advanced Research Projects Agency, Tony Tether, testified before Congress in an effort to clarify misconceptions about how DARPA's Total Information Awareness (TIA) program works. He indicated that TIA takes a hypothesis of an attack scenario, creates a pattern of behavior, and then checks that pattern against databases. The system focuses on information collected from government intelligence agencies and seeks what other information could assist in counterterrorism efforts, such as transportation information and transactions (Michael, 2003).

28. Poindexter was well known for his role in the Iran-Contra scandal when he admitted to a 1986 committee investigating the administration's activities that as President Reagan's national security adviser he destroyed evidence in connection with the Iran-Contra affair. Specifically, he tore up the only signed copy of a document called a "presidential finding" that retroactively authorized shipment of arms to Iran in return for the release of American hostages in Lebanon. He testified that he did this to avoid embarrassment to Mr. Reagan. Poindexter, like Oliver North who reported to him, was convicted in federal district court of lying to Congress and of obstruction. The conviction was overturned on technical grounds by an appeals court majority of two Reagan-appointed judges (Schorr, 2002).

29. Data-mining technology refers to searches of large databases looking for data that fit patterns. Within the realm of governmental activities, such data mining seeks out potential terrorist activity.

30. The failure of the federal government to enact an overarching law to deal with privacy issues has led to piecemeal federal and state laws that address portions of privacy concerns in different sectors. If this were not complicated enough, especially when it comes to corporate privacy compliance, now municipal governments are getting into the game. San Francisco is the latest municipal government to enact its own privacy legislation. Commencing in 2004, financial institutions that have customers or do business in San Francisco will be required to obtain consent and provide hard copy and electronic notice prior to disclosing personally identifiable financial information to affiliates or third parties. This move by San Francisco comes not only on the heels of the federal government's failure so far to tackle privacy issues in a comprehensive way, but also follows California's inability to pass financial privacy legislation in 2003. Privacy legislation similar to that enacted for San Francisco has passed in other municipalities, such as San Mateo County and Contra Costa County in California. Privacy is important. Still, confusion may reign, or at least significant sums will be spent by companies seeking to obey the privacy commands of different federal, state, and municipal laws, if a comprehensive privacy law is not put in place by the federal government. That time has come. It will not be easy to achieve consensus on what that law should require, but in the long run, it should be better than the patchwork of differing privacy laws under one U.S. roof.

REFERENCES

Aftab, P. (1996, September 30). Monitoring communication on the Internet. *The National Law Journal*, pp. S2, S10.

America Online Service Membership. (1995). Site visited November 19, 1995. www.aol.com

The Attorney General's Guidelines Regarding the Use of Confidential Informants. (2002). Site visited October 22, 2002. http://www.usdog.gov/olp/doiguidelines.pdf.

Bernstein v. United States Dep't of State, 176 F.3d 1132 (9th Cir.). (1999).

Blum, V. (2002, September 9). Spy court steps onto foreign soil. *Legal Times*.

California Senate Okays Antispam Bill. (2003, May 22). http://news.com.com /2100-1028-1009411.html?tag=nl.

California v. Ciraolo, 476 U.S. 207. (1986).

Cantril, A.H., & Cantril, S.D. (1994). *Live and let live: American public opinion about privacy at home and at work*. New York: American Civil Liberties Union Foundation.

Caterinicchia, D. (2003, April 28). DARPA funds TIA privacy study. *Federal Computer Week*. Site visited May 12, 2003. http://www.fcw.com/fcw/articles/2003/0428/web-afrl-04-28-03.asp.

Center for Democracy and Technology, (2003). Site visited February 12, 2003. http://www.cdt.org/crypto/litigation/.

CDT's Guide to Online Privacy. (2003). Site visited May 12, 2003. http:// www.cdt.org/privacy/guide/basic/.

Charlesworth, A.J. (2003). Opinion. Privacy, personal information and employment. *Surveillance & Society*, *1*(2), 217-222 Site visited May 12, 2003. http://www.surveillance-and-society.org.

Cookiecentral.com. (2003). Site visited June 2, 2003. www.cookiecentral.com.

Encryption Litigation, Center for Democracy and Technology. (2003). Site visited June 2, 2003. http://www.cdt.org/crypto/litigation/.

EPIC Online Guide to Practical Privacy Tools. (2003). Site visited May 2, 2003. http://www.epic.org/privacy/tools.html.

Etzioni, A. (2000). *The limits of privacy*. New York: Basic Books.

EU Considering New Internet Surveillance Requirements. (2002). Site visited May 22, 2003. http://www.privacyinternational.org/parts/index.html.

Free Site.com Anonymous Freebies. (2003). Site visited May 12, 2003. http://www.thefreesite.com/Anonymous_Freebies/.

FTC Announces Settlement With Bankrupt Website, Toysmart.com, Regarding Alleged Privacy Policy Violations. (2000, July 21). Site visited February 14, 2003. http://www.ftc.gov/opa/2000/07/toysmart2.htm.

Harris, L. & Associates, & Westin, A.F. (1990). *The Equifax Report on Consumers in the Information Age*. Atlanta, GA: Equifax, Inc.

Harris, L. & Associates, & Westin, A.F. (1992). *Harris-Equifax Consumer Privacy Survey*. Atlanta, GA: Equifax, Inc.

Harris, L. & Associates, & Westin, A.F. (1993). *Workplace Health and Privacy Issues: Survey of Private Sector Employees and Leaders*. Commissioned by

Educational Film Center. New York: Louis Harris & Associates. Site visited May 10, 2000. http://www.privacyexchange.org/iss/surveys/work health.html.

Hixson, R.F. (1987). *Privacy in a public society: Human rights in conflict.* New York: Oxford University Press.

How "Patriot Act 2" Would Further Erode, The Basic Checks on Government Power That Keep America Safe and Free. (2003, March 20). Site visited May 12, 2003. ACLU. http://www.cdt.org/security/patriot2/030320aclu.pdf.

Information Awareness Office. (2003). Site visited June 3, 2003 http://www.darpa.mil/iao/.

Internet and Data Interception Capabilities Developed by the FBI. (2003). Site visited May 22, 2003. http://www.cdt.org/security/carnivore/000724fbi.shtml.

Johnson, M.J. (2002, June 5). *ACLU Analysis of changes to attorney general guidelines.* http://archive.aclu.org/congress/l060602c.html.

Junger v. Daley, 209 F.3d 481. (6th Cir.). (2000).

Karn v. United States Dep't of State, 107 F.3d 923 (D.C.Cir.). (1997).

Kelly, J.P. (1994). Whose e-mail is it anyway? In E.M. Kirsh, L. Rose, & S. Steele (Eds.), *Business and legal aspects of the Internet and online services* (pp. 831-834). New York: Law Journal Seminars-Press.

Lawler, B. (2003). The opt-in approach to choice. Site visited May 21, 2003, www.hp.com/country/us/eng/p[rivacy.htm.

Lewis, P. (1994, June 29). No more "anything goes": Cyberspace gets censors. *The New York Times,* p. A1.

Lewis, P. (1995, September 15). Company says electronic mail was opened to find pornography. *The New York Times.* p. A 16.

Leibowitz, W. L. (1996a, September 3). Geography isn't destiny: High tech is reshaping legal basics. *The National Law Journal,* pp. A1 & A16.

Leibowitz, W.L. (1996b, August 5). Technology and the law meet online commerce: "Digital signature" guidelines and an upgraded U.C.C. will ease Internet transactions. An L.A. court tries it out. *The National Law Journal,* pp. B1 & B2.

Lester, W. (2002, May 19). *Nation: Americans historically trade liberties for security pollsters say.* AP Online. http:// seclists.org/lists/politech/ 2002/May/0088.html.

Lynch, C. (1996). Zimmerman investigation closed. Site visited February 11, 2000. http://www.unt.edu/UNT/departments/CC/Benchmarks/aprmay96/pgp.htm.

McCullagh, D. (2001a, September 13). Congress mulls stiff crypto laws. *Wired News.* Site visited October 8, 2001. http://www.wired.com/news/politics/0,1283,46816,00.html.

McCullagh, D. (2001b, October 26). Terror act has lasting effects. *Wired.* Site visited November 13, 2001. http://www.wired.com/news/privacy/0,1848,47901,00.html.

McCullagh, D., & Hu, J. (2003, May 23). *Antispam measure gains steam in House.* Site visited June 3, 2003. http://news.com.com/2100-1025-1009467.html?tag=nl.

Marsh v. Alabama, 326 U.S. 501. (1946).

Matthews, W. (2001, April 6). Bush won't have privacy czar. *Federal Computer Week.* Site visited February 14. 2003www.fcw.com/fcw/articles/2001/0402/ web-swire-04-06-01.asp.

Michael, S. (2003, May 7). DARPA trying to soothe TIA fears. *Federal Computer Week*. Site visited June 2, 2003. http://www.fcw.com/fcw/articles/2003/0505/web-tia-05-07-03.asp.

Netsurfer Focus: On Cryptography and Privacy. (1995, August 21). Postcards from Cyberspace. Vol. 01, Issue 03. Site visited November 12, 2001. http://www.net-surf.com/nsf/v01/03/nsf.01.03html#sc3.

NPR/Kaiser/Kennedy School Civil Liberties Update. (2002, September 9). *Americans more concerned with liberties, back war on terrorism*. Site visited Dec. 23, 2002. http://www.npr.org/news/specials/civillibertiespoll2/index.html.

NPR/Kaiser/Kennedy School Poll on Civil Liberties. (2001, November 30). Site visited May 12, 2002 http://www.npr.org/programs/specials/poll/civil_liberties.

Paulson, K.A. (2002). *The state of the first amendment 2002* (TennFreedom Forum). Nashville, TN.

Piore, A. (2002, October 28). Librarians keep quiet. *Newsweek*, p. 12.

Polek, F. (2002). *Keeping step with the USA Patriot Act*. Site visited November 5, 2002. http://www.smrh.com/publications/pubview.cfm?pubID=176.

Privacy Online: Fair Information Practices in the Electronic Marketplace. (2000). Site visited May 12, 2002. www.ftc.gov/reports/privacy2000/privacy2000.pdf.

Prosser, W.L. (1971). *Handbook of the law of torts* (4th ed.). St. Paul, MN: West Publishing.

Prost, A., & Vincent, G. (Eds.). (1991). *A history of private life: Riddles of identity in modern times*. Cambridge, MA: The Belknap Press.

Pruneyard Shopping Center v. Robins, 447 U.S. 74. (1980).

Public Agenda and the National Constitution Center. (2002, September 17). Site visited May 23, 2003. http://www.epic.org/privacy/survey/.

Public Opinion on Privacy, Electronic Privacy Information Center. (2003). Site visited May 12, 2003. http//www.epic.org/privacy/survey/default.html.

O'Connor v. Ortega, 480 U.S. 709. (1987).

Regan, P. (2003). *The role of consent in information privacy protection*. Site visited May 12, 2003. http://www.cdt.org/privacy/ccp/consentchoice2.pdf.

Regan, P.M. (1995). *Legislating privacy: Technology, social values, and public policy*. Chapel Hill: The University of North Carolina Press.

Schorr, D. (2002, November 29). Poindexter redux. *The Christian Science Monitor*. Site visited March 3, 2003. http://www.csmonitor.com/2002/1129/p11s01-coop.html.

Searcher@finder.com. (1996, December 27). Site visited March 3, 2003.

Smith v. Maryland, 442 U.S. 735. (1979).

Smith v. The Pillsbury Company, No. 95-5712. (e.D. Pa.). (1996).

Sniffen, M. (2003a, May 21). *TIA get pentagon makeover*. News.com.au. Site visited June 3, 2003. http://www.news.com.au/common/story_page/0,4057,6469949%255E15306,00.html.

Sniffen, M. (2003, May 20). *TIA would access 50 more data than Library of Congress*. WashingtonPost.com. Site visited June 4, 2003. http://www.washing-tonpost.com/wp-dyn/articles/A13528-2003May20.html.

A Snooper's Dream. (2003, Nov. 18). [Editorial] *The New York Times*. p. 18.

Stanley, J., & Steinhardt, B. (2003, January). Bigger monster, weaker chains: The growth of an American surveillance society. Site visited March 17, 2003. http:www.aclu.org/Files/OpenFile.cfm?id=11572.

Stern v. Delphi Internet Services Corp. 626 N.Y.S. 2d 694, (N.Y. Sup.). (1995).

Stuckey, K. (1996). *Internet and online law.* New York: Law Journal Seminars-Press.

SurfinGuard, Internet Tools. (2003). Site visited, May 11, 2003. http://www.rdacustomsoftware.com/services/systemsintegration/tools-hostIDS.pdf.

United States v. Miller 425 U.S. 435. (1976).

TRUSTe. (2003). Site visited June 3, 2003. www.truste.org.

Vamosi, R. (2003, February 24). Why we must stop the plot to ban encryption. *CNET/ZDNet Reviews.* Site visited June 2, 2003. http://techupdate.zdnet.com/anchordesk/stories/story/0,10738,2911336,00.html.

Weekly Compilation of Presidential Documents 2001. Remarks on Signing the USA Patriot Act. (2001, October 26). Site visited October 22, 2002. http://frwebgate.access.gpo.gov/cgi-bin/getdoc.cgi?dbname=2001_presidential_documents&docid=pd29oc01_txt-26.

Westin, A.F. (1967). *Privacy and freedom.* New York: Atheneum.

Wise, D. (2002, November 21). Critics eye surveillance ruling. *New York Law Journal.*

Wyden Calls for Congressional Oversight, Accountability of Total Information Awareness Office. (2003, January 15). Site visited May 22, 2003. http://www.senate.gov/-wyden/media/speeches/2003/01152003_tia_statement.htm.

15

Cybercrime, Felonies, and Misdemeanors and New Legal Frontiers

Susan J. Drucker
Hofstra University

Cyberspace has provided a new environment in which to conduct old criminal behavior and has also introduced new injuries and new crimes. What is the status of the law on criminal behavior and punishment when liability or guilt is found to exist? In this chapter Susan Drucker considers the nature of criminal behavior in cyberspace and explores sources of criminal law emerging today. She considers U.S. federal and state law as well as European law and international conventions that have emerged in response to a new environment in which the crime rate is rising.

Fydor Dostoyevsky meets Woody Allen—a thought-provoking image that came to mind in seeking to explore the nature of cybercrime—a portrait of amorality and ingenuity. From garden variety crimes like fraud and credit card theft facilitated by new technology to "cyber attacks" (e.g., viruses and worms that attack hard drives), the incidents and variations of cybercrime are on the rise. The addition of "cyber" to "crime" has both stimulated traditional crime and added new variations. The implications of September 11th and America's involvement in Iraq has provided a new sphere of cybercriminality. America's most wanted transnational terrorist, Osama bin Laden, uses laptops with satellite uplinks and heavily encrypted messages to liaise across national borders with his global underground network. There is no shortage of terrorist recipes on the Internet, step-by-step cookbooks for hackers and crackers (criminal hackers) and cyberterrorists. The USA Patriot Act, passed in response to the September 11th attacks, allows increased surveillance in criminal investigations, including surveillance of the Internet (see chapter 14).

Attorney General John Ashcroft (2001) has noted, "Although there are no exact figures on the costs of cybercrime in America, estimates run into the billions of dollars each year. And unlike more traditional crimes, cybercrime is especially difficult to investigate" In his address at the First Annual Computer Privacy, Policy & Security Institute on May 22, 2001, Ashcroft noted the unique challenge of cybercrime. He assured the audience that cybercrime was an area of criminal behavior of great concern. He stated:

> First, the Internet can provide anonymity. On the Internet, it is easy for a criminal to create a fictitious identity to perpetrate frauds, extortions, and other crimes. Since many computer crimes —such as trading pirated software or child pornography—can be committed entirely on-line, this anonymity can significantly complicate an investigation.
>
> Second, compounding these difficulties is the Internet's borderless nature. A criminal anywhere in the world armed with nothing more than a personal computer connected to a modem can victimize individuals and businesses worldwide.
>
> Third, the tremendous power of today's computers makes it possible for a single cybercriminal to do a staggering amount of damage—damage far beyond what a single person could typically do in the traditional criminal world. For example, a sophisticated cybercriminal can release a virus or launch a denial of service attack affecting hundreds of thousands of computer users or critical infrastructures like power grids. (Ashcroft, 2001)

There is nothing new in the reality that technologies of communication challenge developments in applicable laws. Both substantive and procedural areas of criminal law are strained when confronted by cyber perpetrators (cyber-perp). But more than other technological developments that create new means and ways for criminal conduct, cyberspace is not a clearly defined medium through which crime may be committed and criminals chased. In order to understand the nature and developments in cybercrime, the convergent nature of cyberspace must be considered. Convergence transforms the medium of the Internet into a transmitter of media, resulting in a system of media supervision and regulation that has become increasingly complex, rapidly more globalized from both a technological and market-oriented perspective.

From a regulatory perspective, the Internet is an infrastructure of nodes, routers, gateways, paths, and so on, that is distinguishable from cyberspace. It is the nature of the Internet, consisting of definable elements, that makes Internet cybercrime *more regulable* than cyberspace (Drucker & Gumpert, 2000b).

This chapter places the area of cybercrime into the larger regulatory framework of cyberspace today, considers the two major forces of (marketplace and security) guiding initiatives both domestic and internationally, and suggests the phases of development in the area of cybercrime and punishment.

DEFINITIONS

Cybercrime takes many forms and has many definitions from computer network break-ins, to industrial espionage, software piracy, child pornography, fraud, forgery, illegal gambling, hacking, copyright infringement, theft, E-mail bombings, password sniffers, and even cyberstalking (Jones Encyclopedia—Media & Information Technology, 2003). There is much concern, many anecdotes, and different law enforcement fronts on which the pursuit of the cyber-perp is being conducted. But perhaps the first step is the need to define cybercrime, but that definition is still being debated, and in some cases, assumed.

In 2000, Gary Gumpert and I developed a taxonomy or an organizational structure that could be used to predict the regulatory framework that could govern acceptable behavior and criminal activities (Drucker & Gumpert, 2000a). Given the overwhelming number of ways crimes may be committed, punishments meted out, and tacks criminals and law enforcement officials could take in cyberspace, this taxonomy of cybercrimes sought to conceptualize the nexus of criminal law and CMC. Four major types of cybercrimes were identified.

1. Crime committed using E-mail and the Internet as an instrument or agency: Electronic connection serves as the means by which the violation is actualized, but these crimes are not indigenous to a computer environment (e.g., breaking and entering, fraud, online gambling).
2. Virtual crimes (mediated felonies, misdemeanors, and violations committed in cyberspace): Resembles and characterized by the existence of the crime in "actual" nonmediated circumstances, but indigenous to a computer environment (e.g., cyberstalking and cyberharassment).
3. Violation of regulations governing E-mail, the Internet, or a regulated medium administered by a regulatory agency[ies] transmitted via the Internet: Governmentally regulated electronic medium and/or regulation by virtue of interconnection between regulated medium and computer (e.g., The Children's Online Privacy Protection Act [COPPA], anti-spam rules, Children's Internet Protection Act [CHIPA] providing for public library filters).
4. Ethical violation of cybercodes of conduct: No law is violated, but ethical impropriety does occur (e.g., Internet service provider's [ISP] terms of service agreements).

The regulatory approach used needs to distinguish both prior law and medium. It would be too easy to fall into the metaphorical approach to regulation that applies prior law to present behavior, regardless of medium. When criminal behavior meets cyberspace, there is a collision between material and virtual worlds. The taxonomy of cybercrime is rooted in the differences between materiality and virtuality, between the "real" and the fabricated that results in interaction of a more transient, detached nature or interaction without obligation. The impact, the harm, is determined by the nature of the experience. Some behavior facilitated by cyberspace produces tangible effects in the material sense, as when a crime is committed using E-mail or the Internet as an agency for the crime (e.g., Internet fraud), that is to say, Cybercrime 1. A violation of regulations governing Internet usage such as a violation of the COPA would be a violation of federal law or violation of a state online gambling law, that is to say, Cybercrime 3 would also constitute criminal behavior facilitated by cyberspace. More problematic is the behavior that produces effects that can be characterized along the psychological criteria of "verisimilitude" in which there is the appearance or semblance of reality as the experience is simulated (i.e., Cybercrime 2). These virtual crimes create a harm in cyberspace such as hacking (Drucker & Gumpert, 2000a).[1]

Although the cases raise tantalizing issues themselves, it is ultimately the question of jurisdiction that is at the heart of the current confusion and future initiatives. In August 1999, President Clinton established an interagency Working Group on Unlawful Conduct on the Internet ("Working Group") (Executive Order 13133, 1999). Executive Order 13133 directed the Working Group, under the leadership of the attorney general, to address the issue of unlawful conduct involving the use of the Internet and to prepare a report with recommendations focusing on the following:

- The extent to which existing federal laws provide a sufficient basis for effective investigation and prosecution of unlawful conduct that involves the use of the Internet, such as the illegal sale of guns, explosives, controlled substances, and prescription drugs, as well as fraud and child pornography.
- The extent to which new technology tools, capabilities, or legal authorities may be required for effective investigation and prosecution of unlawful conduct that involves the use of the Internet.
- The potential for new or existing tools and capabilities to educate and empower parents, teachers, and others to prevent or to minimize the risks from unlawful conduct that involves the use of the Internet.

The Working Group sought to determine whether *new* laws were needed and in so doing utilized four general principles to guide its analysis in examining any Internet-specific issues of criminal law: The principles stressed the following:

1. Online–offline consistency: The first step in any analysis of unlawful conduct involving the use of the Internet is to examine how the law treats the same conduct in the offline world. The Internet should not become a safe haven for unlawful activities.
2. Appropriate investigatory tools should be used: To enforce substantive laws that apply to online conduct, law enforcement authorities need appropriate tools for detecting and investigating unlawful conduct involving the Internet. New technologies may justify new forms of investigative authority.
3. Technology neutrality: To the extent specific regulation of online activity may be necessary any such regulation should be drafted in a technology-neutral way. Regulation tied to a particular technology may quickly become obsolete and may require further amendment.

4. Consideration of other societal interests: Any government regulation of conduct involving the use of the Internet requires a
   careful consideration of different societal interests. Internet-
   specific laws and policies that operate by analogy to those
   designed for telephone communications or the press may not
   fit the new medium. The Internet also presents new issues relating to online expectations of privacy and confidentiality that
   may or may not have analogs in the offline world. Accordingly,
   rules and regulations designed to protect the safety and security
   of Internet users should be carefully tailored to accomplish
   their objectives without unintended consequences, such as sti-
   fling the growth of the Internet or chilling its use as a free and
   open communication medium.

The policy guiding the Working Group was to encourage the growth of the
Internet and to support the enormous potential economic and social benefits of the medium. Consistent with the administration's overall e-commerce policy, the private sector had a critical role to play in ensuring a safe
and secure online environment (A Report of the President's Working
Group on Unlawful Conduct on the Internet, 2000). Almost all of the
Fortune 500 corporations have been penetrated electronically by cybercriminals. The FBI estimates that electronic crimes are running at about $10
billion a year.[2] The goal of domestic security, while protecting Internet
growth for commercial needs, is a thread that will become increasingly pro-
nounced in the development of cyberlaw. The significance of commercial
interests and the security needed for e-commerce to grow has been a driving force in the area of cybercrime. Not surprisingly, this is reflected not
only in U.S. policy but in European Union (EU) policy as well. Given that
the United States and EU are the major forces today shaping cyberlaw in
general, this trend in the criminal realm is significant.

DIVERSE SOURCES OF LAW

An uncoordinated mélange of governments, organizations, corporations,
educational institutions, and others have sought to agree on set standards
and protocols. The focus, however, has remained technical rather than
behavioral and there is no clear sense of cyber "law enforcement," no
"cybersherriff" waiting to zap potential offenders with a radar gun (Jones
Encyclopedia—Media & Information Technology, 2003) or search for
weapons of virtual mass destruction. "By almost all accounts, this lack of
'law enforcement' leaves net users to regulate each other according to the

reigning norms of the moment" (Jones Encyclopedia—Media & Information Technology, 2003). Yet there have been diverse sources of law enforcement emerging on an ad hoc basis. Certainly, the complexity of cybercrime, diverse interested parties, and the breadth, or potential breadth of its impact, are part of the reason for this.

The question of jurisdiction, the power to legislate or administer justice, leaps immediately to mind when considering a medium able to leap borders in a single bound. Yet, geographically based governments, from local to national, continue to enter the fray of legal complexities that include competing law enforcement, national security, privacy, and commercial interests.

States

If a state asserts criminal jurisdiction over online activities, the question of *situs* arises. Where "is" a cyberspace located? The nature of *situs* becomes problematic in its application to cyberspace because the borders of cyberspace may or may not eradicate traditional delineations of "state." Nevertheless, in the United States, states have a specific spatial orientation—the 50 territorially based states. Twenty-six states have enacted some type of computer law according to the National Security Institute's Security Resource Net (Cybercrimes, Dayton School of Law, 2001).[3] According to Sean Thornton, (1997) writing on state criminal laws in cyberspace, from a policy perspective, competing interests exist between free development of cyberspace and the needs for effective law enforcement—at the state level. But state attorneys general make the common assertion that state laws apply to out-of-state proprietors of online services. Any other policy would seriously undermine the states' legitimate interest in maintaining order within its territory. Under the doctrine of constructive presence, online activities have been subject to the laws of jurisdictions wherein their effects are felt. Even if the defendant's actions are perfectly legal in the state where they are acting, American courts have long held that punishment in any state where the effects of actions violate local laws is possible. International law also recognizes the doctrine of constructive presence,[4] so a foreign proprietor online could be accountable. One of the most common examples of this type of case has been online gambling (for a full discussion, see pages 334-335 in this chapter). For example, Minnesota's Granite Gate case in which the Granite Gate, a Nevada corporation, planned to establish an online casino where users could enter a credit card number to bet on casino-style games. Such gambling is legal in Nevada but not in Minnesota, where authorities sought to criminally prosecute proprietors of online services accessible from within Minnesota. In this case, ultimately the Minnesota attorney general took a milder approach, asserting civil rather than criminal jurisdiction under a federal statute. From the criminal prosecution prospective, this is a "hot" issue. Anti-gambling laws, framed as consumer-protection laws, raise serious questions of how the criminal laws of some jurisdictions will affect the online activities carried out elsewhere.

The state computer crime statutes are characterized by their very limited scope, generally focusing on Cybercrime types 1 and 2 (Crime committed using E-mail and the Internet as an instrument or agency or virtual crimes). Examples of state computer crime statutes include: New York's Computer Tampering/Theft law; the addition to California's Penal Code Part 1, Title 13 of Crimes Against Property, Chapter 5 Larceny and California Penal Codes Section 502; Georgia state law includes the Computer System Protection Act (focusing on white-color crime), and Chapter 9, Title 16 of its Penal Code relating to crimes involving forgery and fraudulent practices (Georgia Computer Systems Protection Act, 1991). Minnesota was the first state to address computer viruses by passing the Computer Virus Crime Bill providing for up to 10 years in prison and a $50,000 fine for crimes that result in more than $2,500 worth of damages. West Virginia and Maryland have followed suit with similar anti-virus laws. As part of its "fraud in obtaining telecommunication services law," Washington has a computer trespass law (Title 9A of the Washington Criminal Code) that makes it a class C felony to gain access to a governmental database and a gross misdemeanor to gain access to other types of databases. For a thorough listing of state actions on cybercrime see "Cybercriminals Most Wanted" list at http://www.ccmostwanted.com/stateagencies.htm.

It is estimated that approximately 200,000 people stalk someone each year. Dramatic cases have received much attention, such as the case of a South Carolina woman who was stalked for several years via E-mail by an unknown person. The stalker threatened the woman's life and threatened to rape her daughter. The stalker posted the woman's home address on E-mail, making it openly available to anyone with access to the Internet. California was the first state to pass a stalking law and seven states have passed statutes that include stalking by computer. Cyberstalking legislation has been passed by 33 states with several other state laws pending. One such effort pending would amend Title 18 of the U.S. Code to expand the prohibition on stalking, and for other purposes (S.2991 proposed before the 106th Congress).

Although there continues to be much activity on the state level, conflict of laws remains a major issue. Laws remain limited and much regulatory activity is taking place at the national and international levels.

Federal Government

There has been much activity on the federal level.[5] In March 2000, the Department of Justice launched a Web site devoted exclusively to cybercrime (www.cybercrime.gov., 2000).[6] Each agency associated with some category of cybercrime is listed. Some federal law enforcement agencies that investigate domestic crime on the Internet include the FBI, the U.S. Secret Service, the U.S. Customs Service, the U.S. Postal Inspection Service, and the Bureau of Alcohol, Tobacco and Firearms (ATF). The FBI generally investigates violations of federal criminal law but certain specific law enforcement agencies focus on particular kinds of crimes. Other federal agencies with investigative authority are the Federal Trade Commission (FTC) and the U.S. Securities and Exchange Commission.

Furthermore, the Web site provides a table to determine which federal investigative law enforcement agency may be appropriate for reporting certain kinds of crime (see Table 15.1).

TABLE 15.1 Variations of Cybercrimes

Type of Crime	Appropriate Federal Investigative Law Enforcement Agencies
Computer intrusion (i.e., hacking)	FBI local office; NIPC (202-323-3205); U.S. Secret Service local office
Password trafficking	FBI local office; NIPC (202-323-3205); U.S. Secret Service local office
Copyright (software, movie, sound recording) piracy	FBI local office; if imported, U.S. Customs Service local office (800-BE-ALERT, or 800-232-2538)
Theft of trade secrets	FBI local office
Trademark counterfeiting	FBI local office; if imported, U.S. Customs Service local office (800-BE-ALERT, or 800-232-2538)
Counterfeiting of currency	U.S. Secret Service local office; FBI local office
Child pornography or exploitation	FBI local office; if imported, U.S. Customs Service local office (800-BE-ALERT, or 800-232-2538)

TABLE 15.1 Variations of Cybercrimes *(Continued)*

Type of Crime	Appropriate Federal Investigative Law Enforcement Agencies
Child exploitation and Internet fraud matters that have a mail nexus	U.S. Postal Inspection local office
Internet fraud	The Internet Fraud Complaint Center; FBI local office; U.S. Secret Service local office; FTC; if securities fraud, Securities and Exchange Commission
Internet harassment	FBI local office
Internet bomb threats	FBI local office; ATF local office
Trafficking in explosive or incendiary devices or firearms over the Internet	FBI local office; ATF local office

From the Computer Crime and Intellectual Property Section of the Department of Justice (2001).

In 1995, the Department of Justice created the Computer and Telecommunication Crime (CTC) coordinator program to protect businesses and citizens from the rising tide of computer crime. The CTC program has now grown to include 137 attorneys. The CTC includes the Computer Crime and Intellectual Property Section (CCIPS) attorney staff, which consists of about 24 lawyers who focus exclusively on the issues raised by computer and intellectual property crime (Computer Crime and Intellectual Property Section, 2001). The CTC program prosecuted David Smith, the creator of the Melissa virus, which caused damages in excess of $80 million. CCIPS is also a key component in enforcing the "Economic Espionage Act," enacted in 1996 to deter and punish the theft of valuable trade secrets. The CTC has been responsible for the prosecution of computer crimes across the country, including the prosecution of the notorious hacker, Kevin Mitnick, in Los Angeles.

The Department of Justice has been particularly active in its initiatives in the area of cybercrime. The FBI has created computer crime squads in 16 metropolitan areas around the country specifically to investigate cybercrime. The FBI's National Infrastructure Protection Center acts as a clearinghouse for information and expertise relating to cybercrime. And each federal judicial district has at least one assistant U.S. attorney, who is a

CTC coordinator, who has received special training in how to investigate and prosecute cybercrime.[7]

Ashcroft noted "we at the federal level need effective partnerships with our law enforcement colleagues at the federal, state and local levels, as well as overseas." It is the concept of *partnering* that marks the discourse of cyberlaw. Almost as if by partnering, the more fundamental question of whether there can be international law enforcement in cyberspace can be avoided. Partnering is looked to as a means of steering clear of the difficulties associated with incompatible or parallel laws. The border-hopping nature of cybercrime showed that the need for international law enforcement cooperation "has never been greater." All of this represents the law prior to September 11th.

National Initiatives/Foreign Governments

Individual governments have different agendas and a few nations have independently drafted cybercrime laws that conflict with other nation's laws and could hamper the possible prosecution of criminals committing cybercrimes. Germany, for example, prohibits distributing Nazi propaganda, yet in the United States, free speech laws allow for such dissemination. What if Germany issues international warrants to German Internet users who access a non-German Web site that distributes Nazi propaganda? Should a teenager researching World War II for a high school project be served with an arrest warrant?

Child pornography is illegal in almost every industrialized nation but recently, Italian investigators sought international warrants against almost 1,600 individuals worldwide suspected of participating in online child pornography—indicating the degree to which some governments are willing to pursue cybercrime.[8] The Web site that generated this manhunt is "Childlovers" which, although clearly pornographic, may have led unsuspecting surfers anywhere else on the planet to innocently click on the site, only to discover an outstanding Italian warrant has been issued against them.

Those creating and disseminating computer viruses may be subject to laws of nation-states. For example, a Swedish law has been applied to a Swedish citizen who confessed to creating and spreading a virus, known as a worm. The person faces a 2-year prison sentence and fines for creating and spreading the worm that was contained in an E-mail attachment detected in at least 40 countries ("Spreader of Multinational Virus," 2003).

Clearly, cybercrime and/or electronic criminal activity is an issue of global proportions that by its very nature necessitates the willing participation of every nation to arrive at some sort of blanket International treaty. The treaty should provide for the prosecution of those who commit crimes causing damage, and should detail retribution methods that victims could pursue. Yet, what kind of a watering down effect might this globalized approach have on individual rights and the rights of criminals?

International

The call for international cooperation and coordination is a recurring theme. Cases of informal cooperation abound, but reflect the limitations and problems of this approach. For example, in May 2000 a cyberhacker used the "I Love You" virus to cripple E-mail systems worldwide, leading to a joint U.S.–Philippine collaborative hunt. (This worm caused an estimated $10 billion in damages and even infiltrated the Pentagon computers. Onel De Guzman was ultimately charged with the crime, Zetter, 2000).[9]

More than 100 countries lack laws dealing with computer-related crime, thereby undercutting the efforts of law enforcement to cope with what is perceived to be a "growing threat." According to Edgar Adamson of the U.S. Customs Service, 60% of INTERPOL members lack legislation to deal with Internet/computer-related crime.[10] Recent cases involving international cooperation include "hacker" attacks that have led to prosecution in Israel, Canada, Britain, and the Philippines ("U.S. Wants More Cybercrime," 2000).

One of the early international efforts to coordinate international cyber penal law came in the form of the *United Nations Manual on the Prevention and Control of Computer-Related Crime* which includes fraud, forgery, computer sabotage, unauthorized access, and copying of computer programs as examples of computer crimes.

Multilateral agreements have been relied on in the past for assistance in international cybercrime cases. The United States is party to more than 20 bilateral mutual legal assistance treaties (MLATs). Where there is no MLAT in force, international legal assistance is governed by domestic MLAT laws and practices that include the letters of rogatory process (i.e., a letter requesting assistance form one country's judicial authority eg. US 28 USC Section 1782).[11] The United States has entered into more than 100 bilateral treaties with other countries, so if one country does not yet criminalize a computer-mediated crime, this existing approach may be ineffective.[12]

The Council of Europe developed the "Convention on Cybercrime,"[13] intended to be the first ever international treaty to address criminal law and procedural aspects of various types of criminal behavior directed against computer systems, networks, or data and other types of similar misuse. The convention is the product of 4 years of work by Council of Europe experts along with assistance from the United States, Canada, Japan, and other countries, which are not members of the organization. The treaty was pro-

posed by the Council of Europe. The U.S. Department of Justice was a primary architect and used this foreign forum to create an international law
enforcement regime that makes it much easier to get evidence from abroad
and to extradite and prosecute foreign nationals for certain types of crimes.
On September 19, 2001, the Council of Europe Ministers' Deputies
approved the convention, which was then presented for formal adoption to
Foreign Affairs Ministers meeting in Strasbourg on November 8 and was
signed by the representatives of 26 nations at an international conference in
Budapest at the end of November 2001.[14] The United States, as a partici-
pant in the drafting of the treaty, has been invited to ratify. The convention
requires signing countries to adopt similar criminal laws on hacking,
infringements of copyright, computer-related fraud, and child pornography. It also contains a series of powers and procedures, such as the search
of computer networks and interception. In January 2003, 11 member states
of the Council of Europe signed the Additional Protocol to the Convention
on Cybercrime, concerning the criminalization of acts of a racist and xenophobic nature, committed through the use of computer systems (The
Convention on Cybercrime, 2003).

The main objective of the convention, set out in the preamble, is to
pursue a common criminal policy aimed at the protection of society against
cybercrime, especially by adopting appropriate legislation and fostering
international cooperation. It will be supplemented by an additional protocol making any publication of racist and xenophobic propaganda via computer networks a criminal offense. The treaty has a threefold aim: (a) to lay
down common definitions of certain criminal offenses relating to the use of
the new technologies, (b) to define methods for criminal investigations and
prosecution, and (c) to define methods for international communication.
The criminal offenses concerned include:

- Offenses committed against the confidentiality, integrity and
  availability of computer data or systems (such as the spreading
  o   f
  viruses).
- Computer-related offenses (such as virtual fraud and forgery).
- Content-related offenses (such as the possession and intentional
  distribution of child pornography).
- Offenses related to infringements of intellectual property and
  related rights (The Convention on Cybercrime, 2003).

Another objective is to facilitate the conduct of criminal investigations in
cyberspace, thanks to a number of procedural powers, such as the powers to
preserve data, search and seize, collect traffic data, and intercept communications (Information Related to Cybercrime Policy Making Process, 2001).

The Group of Eight (G-8; the seven major industrial nations plus Russia) has been discussing cybercrime at the ministerial level. Specifically, a subgroup on high-tech crime has been focusing on ways to enhance the abilities of law enforcement agencies to investigate and prosecute computer- and Internet-facilitated crimes. The subgroup is working on establishing a global network of high-tech crime experts and developing capabilities to locate and identify those who use the Internet to commit crimes. In May 1998, President Clinton and his G-8 counterparts adopted a set of principles and an action plan, developed by the subgroup for fighting computer crime (Department of Justice Web site, 2000).

The question of jurisdiction and international cooperation raises questions of power and punishment. What system of punishment is available for a virtual crime?

TYPES OF CASES

Although there are diverse and vivid cases falling within all four categories of cybercrime identified earlier (Drucker & Gumpert, 2000a), among the areas of greatest activity to date are online gambling, fraud, and piracy.

Online Gambling

One of the areas of regulated behavior that has received the greatest attention in the realm of cyberspace has been online gambling, which has fallen under both federal and state jurisdiction. The federal government regulates gambling through the Commerce Clause of the Constitution, meaning that federal laws regulate gambling only as information relating to gambling (e.g., bets) pass through interstate or foreign commerce. There are three federal laws aimed at regulating gambling: The *Wire Act, 18 U.S.C. 1084 (1994)*; The *Travel Act, 18 U.S.C. 1952 (1994)*; and The *Organized Crime Control Act of 1970, 18 U.S.C. 1955 (1994)*. Because the current legal status of Internet gambling in the United States remains unclear, Congress considered specific Internet Gambling Prohibition legislation in 2000 but has not yet taken action, although it continues to appear on the Congressional agenda.[15] The Leach Bill aims to stop online gambling through making the use of financial instruments for gambling illegal. In March 2003, Representative John Conyers, Jr. introduced legislation to create a commission to make recommendations as to how the states might regulate Internet gambling. His proposal takes a somewhat different approach because it accepts online gambling as a given and seeks to find ways to regulate it. Conyers noted:

> Instead of a prohibition that will drive gambling underground and into the hands of unscrupulous merchants, Congress should examine the feasibility of strictly licensing and regulating the online gaming industry. State regulation will ensure that gaming companies play fair and drive out dishonest operators. It also provides potential tax revenue for financially-strapped States. . . . That is why today I am introducing legislation to create an Internet Gambling Licensing and Regulation Study Commission to evaluate how to regulate online gambling to protect consumers, provide badly needed tax revenue, and prevent criminal elements from penetrating this industry. (Internet Gambling, 2003)

In order to avoid federalism concerns, some experts have proposed a state enforcement mechanism. Others have suggested that First Amendment and Commerce Clause concerns can be avoided by turning online gambling over to state-based regulations. The main objectives in moving into state law is that allowing states to make their own laws in this area, online gambling site operators could be regulated (reducing fraud) and tax revenue could be increased. Several states have taken action. For example, Illinois, Louisiana, Michigan, South Dakota, and Nevada have passed legislation specifically relating to Internet gambling. Although the scope and intent of the laws vary, the Illinois statute is particularly noteworthy because it not only prohibits Internet gambling but, specifically declares it unlawful to advertise any gambling activity not sanctioned by the state. Neither the Michigan, Nevada, nor South Dakota laws make any direct reference to Internet gambling advertising, but outlaw Internet gambling activities (including the "solicitation" of gambling, in the case of Michigan) not sanctioned by their respective states. Other states, including New York and Montana, have all-encompassing laws that make all gambling illegal unless authorized by the state. The legality of Internet gambling gets even murkier when it involves Indian online services crossing state lines. Tribes contend that they are sovereign entities, thus generally independent of laws made by a particular state ("Internet Gambling," 2003).

Missouri Attorney General Jay Nixon sued the Coeur d'Alene tribe of Idaho in 1997, claiming the tribe's online lottery violated Missouri laws that prohibit offering betting services to state citizens. The tribe countered that its operations were legal under the Indian Gaming Regulatory Act of 1988—a law that made at least Class II gaming (sports betting, bingo, and lotteries) exempt from all federal gambling statutes. The matter is still tied up in courts.

Fraud

Fraud on the Internet tripled in 2002 compared to 2001, according to the FBI. The agency's Internet Fraud Complaint Center (IFCC) registered more than 48,000 complaints to federal, state, and local law enforcement authorities. The top types of fraud on the Internet were online auctions, nondelivery of merchandise, credit card fraud, and fake investments (IFCC, 2003). IFCC, which is co-managed by the National White Collar Crime Center and the FBI, found that California, New York, Florida, Texas, and Illinois were the top five states for victims of Internet crime.[16] According to Internet Fraud Watch (2003), 90% of online fraud cases involved online auctions, 5% were related to general merchandise, and 4% were associated with the so-called "Nigerian money scam." Other studies corroborate the trend that online auction fraud remains the most prevalent form of cyber-crime (Saliba, 2001).

An FBI report said one persistent type of fraud involved the "Nigerian letter scam." It starts with a letter, fax, or E-mail that requests help in getting millions of dollars out of the African country. In return, the receiver is supposed to get a percentage of the total. In March 2002, two men were sentenced to prison terms in Ontario for operating the "Nigerian letter scam" (Finney, 2003; Nigeria—the 410 Coalition Web site, 2003). Federal and state fraud fighters are cracking down on Internet auction scams that fleeced thousands of consumers out of money and merchandise.

E-mail messages that refer recipients to Web sites that masquerade as legitimate e-commerce sites have targeted customers of PayPal, eBay, Wells Fargo Bank, and others. To illustrate, Best Buy, a Minneapolis-based electronics and consumer goods chain was used in a scam in which an E-mail is sent stating that an order was made on the BestBuy.com Web site using the person's credit card information. The E-mail recipient is told to follow a link to the company's page for its fraud department but the link goes to a masquerade Web site that requests credit card information and other personal information (Lemos, 2003).

A form of fraud that has received a good deal of media coverage is identity theft. This theft of one's identity involves the criminal uses of someone else's identity. The cyberimpersonator can steal unlimited funds in the victim's name without the victim's knowledge for extended periods of time. Examples include fraudulently stealing money from the victim's bank accounts, establishing accounts with utility companies, renting apartments, using the victim's credit card number, and obtaining credit by using the victim's name. In a report for the Department of Justice entitled "Identity Theft: The Crime of the New Millennium" issued in March 2001, Sean B. Hoar (2001) reported it "is estimated that identity theft has become the fastest-growing financial crime in America and perhaps the fastest-growing crime of any kind in our society." This report identified federal and state laws applicable to identity theft. Some of these laws may be used for prosecution of identity-theft offenses, and some of which exist to assist victims in repairing their credit history. The primary identity-theft statute is 18 U.S.C. § 1028(a)(7) and was enacted on October 30, 1998 as part of the Identity Theft and Assumption Deterrence Act (Identity Theft Act). The Identity Theft Act criminalizes fraud in connection with the unlawful theft and misuse of personal identifying information, regardless of whether the information appears or is used in documents.

In 2003, the FTC and 33 states and local law enforcement agencies announced they were joining to target auction con artists with 57 actions ranging from prosecutions to warning letters. "Real-world law enforcement will not let you get away with virtual fraud," Howard Beales, chief of the FTC's Bureau of Consumer Protection, said at a news conference ("33 States," 2003). Business is the prime target—but public authorities and even individuals are vulnerable, too. A survey of U.S. business firms showed that 85% of those covered had at some time been targeted by hackers. In the United States, the Pentagon's systems alone were attacked more than 22,000 times in 1 year. And the FBI has identified 5,000 systems as being "highly vulnerable" to cybercrime, which has, according to Ronald L. Dick, the FBI's director, the capacity "to destabilise a country's whole economy" ("Cybercrime," 2003).

Piracy

One of the most controversial areas of cybercrime is piracy. Although much litigation, legislation, and negotiation has surrounded the myriad copyright issues (see Chapters 9 and 10). Some action has been taken within the realm of criminal law as well. According to estimates by the U.S. Software and Information Industry Association (SIIA), as much as $7.5 billion of American software may be illegally copied and distributed annually worldwide (SIIA, 2003). In June 2003, a new House Intellectual Property Promotion and Piracy Prevention Caucus was created in the U.S. House of Representatives. The caucus was formed to address issues surrounding copyrights, trademarks, and patents in an era of escalating technological advance ("SIIA Applauds," 2003). Internet piracy, frequently referred to as the "warez scene," has been targeted by Ashcroft. In December 2001, Ashcroft he announced that in three separate federal law enforcement actions federal agents executed approximately 100 search warrants worldwide. The three operations, codenamed "Buccaneer," "Bandwidth," and "Digital Piratez," struck at all aspects of the illegal software, game, and movie trade. The U.S. Department of Justice has an active CCIPS (2003).

Rampant video game piracy has been one area of great concern. In June 2003, Japanese video game maker, Nintendo Co. Ltd., won an anti-piracy judgment against a Hong Kong firm that sold devices capable of copying its games and posting them to the Internet for downloading. A Hong Kong judge ordered Lik Sang International to pay an interim amount of US $641,000 in damages. Nintendo characterized the judgment as one of its "most significant anti-piracy judgments ever" (Young, 2003).

Crimes Against Persons

Many of these cases can be classified as virtual crimes (mediated felonies, misdemeanors, and violations committed in cyberspace). They are offenses such as cyberharassment, cyberstalking, E-mail threats, E-mail bombs, "nuking," unwanted "talk" requests in chatrooms, forged source E-mail addresses, postings about one, and obscene materials. One such crime, cyberstalking, refers to sending harassing or threatening E-mail to others and includes E-mail threats, E-mail bombs, "nuking," sending unwanted messages or files, inappropriate requests in chatrooms, forged E-mail source addresses, and inappropriate postings on message boards. Cyberstalkers have been known to make death threats, to publicize the victim's home address and telephone number, and worse. It has been estimated that approximately 200,000 people stalk someone each year.

CONCLUSIONS

"In the marriage of new technology and dynamic social change, history instructs that we must anticipate the rise of criminal activity" (Clarke, 1996, p. 203) So it has not been a surprise to find ourselves attempting to make sense of cybercrime. Cyberspace in general, the development of cyber penal law in particular, has gone through distinct phases of development. The first phase can be characterized as a process of "metaphor mapping" or seeking the "best fit" with existing laws. Because no perfect fit was found, there were two distinct directions taken to either ignore the unique nature of virtual environments in which crimes were committed or through which they were facilitated, treating them like any other offense, or determine that government could not regulate cyberspace, that cyberspace was essentially a lawless frontier. Today, we find ourselves in the second generation or next phase of conceptualizing laws in cyberspace. According to Stanford Law Professor Lawrence Lessig (2000), this phase of evolution sees control of the Internet as possible with regulation emerging from an alliance of *commerce* and *government.*

As cybercrimes are increasingly defined, it is this commercially driven set of legal wrongs that emerge as offenses first to be addressed: Internet fraud, hacking, copyright infringement, white-collar crime, forgery. Although other crimes are not being ignored, the crimes that could retard the growth of e-commerce, those that raise the spectre of risk online and within computerized databases, are the significant shared concerns of government and business.

In October 2001, Congress was urged to create a nonprofit body to set up an expert "cybercourt" to oversee investigation of cybercrime and to encourage academic research in the area. Virginia Governor James Gilmore testified before the House Science Committee forcefully arguing for the United States to step up efforts to thwart computer-based attacks (McCullagh, 2001). It would appear that Lessig is on the right track.

The potential cybercrimes receiving greatest concern are crimes of terrorists who challenge security by nontraditional threats. The criminals being pursued will include international criminals and terrorists who, we are told, search for new ways to attack by exploiting new technologies and the world's increasing openness. Security is no longer defined by armed forces standing between the aggressor and the homeland. Two directions in which developments in cybercrime can be expected to develop are areas concerned with money and security—two very basic human needs. Appeals to fear can be expected in the debates to come over the nature and response to cyber felonies and misdemeanors in the future.

NOTES

1. At that time we considered cases using CMC as the instrumentality of criminal activity ranging from white-collar misdemeanors to violent felonies, from fraud to homicide. In a survey conducted by C. T. Clarke (1996), published in the *Oregon Law Review,* entitled "Policing the Evolving Criminal Mens Rea on the Internet," lawyers around the United States asked to define criminals on the Internet overwhelmingly associated them as being the same as those off the Internet. Crimes against persons including behavior leading to homicides, use of the Internet by pedophiles, harassment and cyberstalking by using the Internet to threaten imminent bodily harm and cause emotional distress by postings, were considered activities well suited to electronic communication. Other crimes include those against property (i.e., hacking and trespass). These cases continue to be reported. One example occurred on October 23, 2001, in which Microsoft told Reuters it was looking into its legal options regarding an unidentified hacker who breached its anti-piracy technology the previous week, enabling users to distribute songs without restrictions. But how to narrow those legal options is still a mystery, even to the mighty lawyers representing still mighty Microsoft. Several prosecutions have since focused on online gambling and "digital forgery" and there have even been attempts to consider "virtual rape" cases marking a move into crimes with no physical world referent.
2. But only 17% of the companies victimized report these intrusions to law enforcement agencies. Their main concern is protecting consumer confidence

and shareholder value. They say that reporting cyberrobberies exposes them to leaks and that there is no substitute for constantly enhancing their own defensive electronic security.

3. Of the more than 26 states that have some sort of cybercrime law are the following: Alabama, Alaska, Arizona, California, Colorado, Connecticut, Delaware, Florida, Georgia, Hawaii, Idaho, Illinois, Indiana, Iowa, Maryland, Minnesota, New Jersey, New Mexico, New York, North Carolina, Oregon, Texas, Virginia, Washington, West Virginia, and Wisconsin (State Agency, 2003).

4. The U.S. Supreme Court articulated the doctrine of constructive presence in 1911 in *Strassheim v. Daily*. A Michigan court convicted an Illinois man for bribery and for defrauding the state. The court found that acts outside a jurisdiction, but intended to produce and producing detrimental effects within it, justify a state in punishing the cause of the harm (Thornton, 1997).

5. According to the Michael Chertoff, assistant attorney general, Criminal Division of the U.S. Department of Justice (in testifying before the House Subcommittee on Crime) (June 12, 2001), the Department of Justice believes "cybercrime" can be divided into two categories: the migration of "traditional" crimes from the physical to the online world (including threats, child pornography, fraud, gambling, extortion, and theft of intellectual property) and spawned an entirely new set of criminal activity that targets computer networks themselves. Included in this category are such crimes as hacking, releasing viruses, and shutting down computers by flooding them with unwanted information (so-called "denial of service" attacks). Chertoff warned that "simply put, criminals are migrating online because they can reach more victims quickly, can collaborate with other criminals, can disguise their identities, and can use the global nature of the Internet to remain anonymous."

6. The Web site includes a wide variety of materials, including press releases, speeches by Justice Department officials including the attorney general, Congressional testimony, letters and Justice Department reports. In addition, there is material to help the general public and law enforcement, including information on how to report Internet-related cybercrime. Because cybercrime is of special interest to children and parents, the site also provides a direct link to the "Internet Do's and Don'ts" section of the Department of Justice's kids' page.

    Materials on WWW.CYBERCRIME.GOV are organized by subject in 12 "channels." The channels span a broad range of issues related to computers and crime, including information on prosecuting computer hacking, intellectual property piracy and counterfeiting, legal issues related to electronic commerce, freedom of speech, searching and seizing computers, encryption, privacy, and international aspects of cybercrime (Justice Department Launches Web Site to Address Cybercrime "WWW.CYBERCRIME.GOV" Provides Information On DOJ's Efforts to Stop High-Tech Crime, March 2000, http://www.usdoj.gov/opa/pr/2000/March/119crm.htm).

7. Through the FBI, the DOJ has sponsored the InfraGard program, a partnership between the Department of Justice, businesses, academic institutions, and state and local law enforcement agencies, dedicated to increasing the security of

the U.S. critical infrastructures. Ashcroft (2001) has also reported that "we are putting cybercriminals in jail. The arrest and guilty plea of both the author of the Melissa virus in the United States and 'MafiaBoy' in Canada demonstrate our ability to solve cybercrime—even when it occurs on a massive scale or comes from outside our borders."

8. The Italian government intends to seek an additional 1,030 international warrants pending the completed investigations of the Italian police. Those additional 1,030 international warrants are to be granted as soon as Internet users who entered a Web site named "Childlovers" are identified.

9. Vatsis told a U.S. subcommittee on government management that the lack of substantive laws that specifically criminalize computer crimes in many countries undercuts investigations.

10. For instance, senior police from Israel, Sweden, Germany, the Philippines, and Latvia each testified that computer-related crime was a mounting danger requiring stepped–up law enforcement coordination.

11. Dual criminality is often required to issue a subpoena, interview witnesses, produce documents or conduct searches and seizures. This means that in order to obtain permission to search, the activity must be considered a crime in both the requesting and requested countries and is punishable by at least 1 year in prison. In some cases, assistance is only permitted if dual criminality exists and the offense is extraditable as is the case with the mutual assistance laws of Germany.

12. As multilateral efforts for more formal mechanisms for cooperation are being developed, law enforcement agencies in the United States and other countries are cooperating informally and undertaking joint cyber-investigations. For example, a 24/7 high-tech point-of-contact network established among the G-8 countries and others is continuing to expand to more countries. Multilateral efforts are a more important path to follow given the nature of the Internet, which is available in more than 200 countries. Criminals can route communication through any of these countries requiring greater multilateral opportunities for cooperation in law enforcement.

13. In 1997, the Council of Europe's Committee of Ministers asked a committee of experts to "draft a binding legal instrument" examining the issues of offenses, substantive criminal law, the use of coercive powers—including at the international level—and the problem of jurisdiction over computer crimes.

14. Ministers or their representatives from the 26 following member states signed the treaty: Albania, Armenia, Austria, Belgium, Bulgaria, Croatia, Cyprus, Estonia, Finland, France, Germany, Greece, Hungary, Italy, Moldova, the Netherlands, Norway, Poland, Portugal, Romania, Spain, Sweden, Switzerland, the Former Yugoslav Republic of Macedonia, Ukraine and the United Kingdom. Canada, Japan, South Africa and the United States, who took part in the drafting, also signed the treaty. Other nonmember states may also be invited by the Committee of Ministers to sign this treaty at a later date.

15. Commonly referred to as the Kyl Bill initially proposed by Senator Jon Kyl (R-AZ), the basic purpose was to update the Wire Wager Act so that Internet gambling would addressed. Initially, the act aimed at the activities of individual who placed bets, or for parties engaged in the business of betting or wagering

to do so via the Internet or a nonclosed circuit interactive computer service in any state. In 2000, Senator Kyl reintroduced the bill with some significant changes. The provision that targeted the individual bettor was abandoned. In addition, exceptions were inserted for intrastate networks, fantasy sports, pari-mutual totes, news reporting and odds, state lotteries, and horse racing bets. These added exceptions could prevent criticism based on the Commerce Clause.

16. In cases where the perpetrator had been identified, nearly four in five were male and more than half resided in California, New York, Florida, Texas, Illinois, and Pennsylvania.

REFERENCES

Ashcroft, J. (2001) Department of Justice press release. Site visited November 12, 2001. http://www.cybercrime.gov/AGCPPSI.htm.

California Penal codes Section 502. http://nsi.org/Library/Compsec/computer-law/Californ.txt.

Clarke C.T. (1996). CrinINet to cyber-perp: Toward an inclusive approach to policing the evolving criminal mens rea on the Internet. *Oregon Law Review*, p. 75.

Computer Crime and Intellectual Property Section of the Department of Justice. (2001). http://www.cybercrime.gov/reporting.htm.

The Convention on Cybercrime. (2003). Council of Europe. Site visited May 22, 2003. http://www.coe.int/T/E/Legal_affairs/Legal_co-operation/Combating_economic_crime/Cybercrime/Convention/default.asp#TopOfPage.

Cybercrime, The Targets It Hits, the Damage It Does. (2003). Site visited May 23, 2003. http://www.coe.int/T/E/Communication_and_Research/Press/Theme_Files/Cybercrime/e_cybercrime.asp.

Cybercrimes, Dayton School of Law. (2001). Site visited November 16, 2001, www.cybercrimes.net/state.

Department of Justice Web site. (2000). Site visited November 12, 2002. www.cybercrime.gov.

Drucker, S., & Gumpert, G. (2000a). Cybercrime and punishment. *Critical Studies in Media Communication, 17*(2), pp. N133-N158.

Drucker, S. & Gumpert, G. (2000b). The emergence of convergence: Technologies, industries, and regulations. *The Public*, 37-54.

Executive Order 13133. (1999, August 6). Site visited November 12, 2001. http://www.usdoj.gov/criminal/cybercrime/execord.htm.

Finney, M. (2003, April 9). Old Nigerian letter scam. *San Francisco Examiner*. Site visited May 22, 2003. http://www.examiner.com/news/default.jsp?story=n.finney.0409w.

Georgia Computer Systems Protection Act. Section 1, Article 6. (1991). http://nsi.org/Library/Compsec/computerlaw/Georgia.txt

Hoar, S. (2001). Identity theft: The Crime of the New Millennium. Site visited May 22, 2003. http://www.usdoj.gov/criminal/cybercrime/usamarch2001_ 3.htm.

IFCC Report. (2002). Site visited May 12, 2003. http://www1.ifccfbi.gov/strategy/2002_IFCCReport.pdf.

Information Related to Cybercrime Policy Making Process within the Council of Europe, European Union, G8, and the United Nations. (2001). *Cyber-Rights & Cyber-Liberties (UK)*. Site visited May 14, 2003. http://www.cyber-rights.org/cybercrime/.

Internet Fraud Watch. (2003). Site visited May 22, 2003. http://www.fraud.org/internet/ intset.htm.

Internet Gambling Regulation Study Commission Bill. (2003). Site visited May 22, 2003. http://www.onlinegamblingtimes.com/pr/gambling_pr_mar015_03.html.

Internet Gambling: Regulation, Prohibition or Let 'em Play?? (2003). Site visited May 22, 2003. http://www.law.wayne.edu/weinberg/law cyberspace/Internet %20Gambling.htm.

Justice Department Launches Web site to Address Cybercrime. (2000, March). Site visited March 3, 2000. http://www.usdoj.gov/opa/pr/2000/March/119crm.htm).

Jones Encyclopedia—Media & Information Technology. (2003). Site visited May 2, 2003. www.digitalcentury.com.

Lemos, R. (2003, June 19). E-mail scam makes Best Buy scramble. *CNET News.com*. Site visited June 20, 2003 http://news.com.com/2100-1002_3-1019192.html.

Lessig, L. (2000). *Code and other laws of cyberspace*. New York: Basic Books.

McCullagh, D. (2001, October 18). Governor calls for "cyber-court." Site visited February 12, 2003. http://www.wired.com/news/conflict/0,2100,47676,00.html.

Minnesota Computer Virus Crime Bill. http://nsi.org/Library/Compsec/computerlaw/Minnesot.txt.

Nigeria—the 410 Coalition Web site. (2003). Site visited May 22, 2003. http://home.rica.net/alphae/419coal/.

A report of the President's Working Group on unlawful conduct on the internet Department of Justice: The electronic frontier: The challenge of unlawful conduct involving the use of the Internet. (2000, March). Site visited November 12, 2001. http://www.usdoj.gov/criminal/cybercrime/unlawful.htm.

Revised Code of Washington Annotated, *Title 9A.52 http://nsi.org/Library/Compsec/computerlaw/Washingt.txt.*

Saliba, C. (2001, January 10). Study: *Auction fraud still top cybercrime*. E-Commerce Times News Site. Site visited May 22, 2003. http://www.ecommercetimes.com/perl/story/6590.html.

SIIA Applauds New Congressional Anti-piracy Coalition. (2003). Site visited May 24, 2003. http://www.siia.net/.

Software and Information Industry Association. (2003). Site visited May 24, 2003. http://www.siia.net/.

Spreader of Multinational Virus Faces Fines, Prison. (2003, April 21). *Cybercrime Law Report*, 3(8), Site visited May 12, 2003. http://www.pf.com/pdf/cybercrime.pdf.

State Agency Lists. (2003). Site visited June 2, 2003. http://www.ccmost wanted.com/stateagencies.htm.

Thornton, S. (1997). State criminal laws in cyberspace: Reconciling freedom for users with effective law enforcement. *Richmond Journal of Law and Technology,* Winter. Volume IV, Issue 2, Site visited November 12, 2001. http://www.richmond.edu/~jolt/v4i2/thornton.html.

The U.S. Department of Justice has an active Computer Crime and Intellectual Property Section (CCIPS). (2003). Site visited May 22, 2003. http://www.usdoj.gov/criminal/cybercrime/ip.html#VIIIc.

U.S. wants more cybercrime laws. (2000, July 26). *Wired News.* Site visited November 12, 2001. http://www.wired.com/news/politics/0,1283, 37809,00.html.

West Virginia State Law. http://nsi.org/Library/Compsec/computerlaw /Westvirg.txt.

The Wire Act, 18 U.S.C. 1084. (1994).

Young, D. (2003, June 19). Nintendo wins piracy case against Hong Kong firm. *Yahoo Asia News.* Site visited June 20, 2003. http://asia.news. yahoo.com/030619/3/znaj.html.

Zetter, K. (2000, November 13). When love came to town: A virus investigation. *PC World.com.* Site visited November 12, 2001.http://www.pcworld.com/news/ article/0,aid,33392,00.asp.

33 states and FTC go after Internet auction scams. (2003, May 1). Seattle pi.com. Site visited May 22, 2003. http://seattlepi.nwsource.com/business/ 119993_netscams01.html.

16

Debating Community or Code

Case Studies in Alternative Internet Regulation

Thomas Flynn
Slippery Rock University

Mark Chase
Slippery Rock University

Taking a divergent path from previous authors, Thomas Flynn and Mark Chase seek regulation of cyberspace from non-governmental sources. They consider whether cyberspace is best suited for a form of "community-based" self-regulation. Noting the difficulties posed when attempting to apply traditional laws and legal institutions to cyberspace, they explore the virtues of community self-regulation versus regulation through code (software) technological regulation.

Creation of the Internet provided not only a new communication media; it created social space. To many, the social significance of this new social space resided in the promise of a renewed sense of community, and in some cases, new forms of community. Early enthusiasts envisioned a place where individuals shaped their own communities by choosing the communities based on common interest (Rheingold, 1993). Others anticipated a democratization of communication media (Brand, 1988). Mediated awareness of deviance online, however, brought about political pressure to enact legislation to regulate the Internet. In response, concern was expressed that misguided attempts by Congress to regulate online activity (i.e., the Communications Decency Act [CDA] would not only chill online access to a vast array of information, but would inexorably skew the growth and development of the new medium. Against this backdrop, a scholarly debate emerged concerning how best to regulate online behavior.

Legal experts recognize that the Internet poses particular challenges to the ability of traditional legal approaches to regulate online behavior. Some legal theorists, such as McCullagh and Johnson and Post, argue that the Internet is capable of self-regulation. Referred to variously as "polycentric law" (Hayek 1973), "decentralized emergent law" (Post, 1997), or "community-based" regulation (O'Connell, 1997), collective self-regulation may well be capable of generating responsible self-regulation that provides reasonable protection to activities occurring on the global net. Lessig (1996b, 2001) responded, however, that although the social norms that provide the basis of collective self-regulation do provide real constraint in cyberspace, software code, not social norms will provide the most efficient means of regulating online behavior. This chapter examines this debate by reviewing briefly the perceived challenges to traditional legal constraint posed by the Internet, and outlining the perceived merits of community self-regulation and technological regulation as articulated by Johnson and Post (1996a, 1996b), and Lessig (1996, 2001), alternatively. The chapter then explores the merits of these arguments by presenting two brief case studies in the regulation of online behavior. In the first case study, that of an adult-oriented discussion forum, we witness the failure of community-based regulation and find support for Lessig's vision of code-based regulation. In the second, the evolution of the feedback ratings employed in eBay online auctions indicates that community-based self-regulation may not be a viable means of regulating online behavior without some code-based mechanisms.

CHALLENGES TO TRADITIONAL LEGAL CONSTRAINT

All societies produce value systems or ideologies that act not only to interpret and reflect social reality, but to construct a preferred vision of society by establishing normative premises as well. These norms outline the parameters of what is considered to be acceptable and unacceptable. A variety of social institutions, such as legislatures, judiciaries, and government bureaucracies act to construct, disseminate, and transmit this value system through a varied body of laws, rules, and social practices. Because of rapid technological innovation and its dynamic influence on human interaction, however, the medium poses a number of difficulties to the imposition of traditional legal protocols.

First, traditional Anglo-American jurisprudence is built on the notion of precedent, relying on the existence of prior decisions from which courts may derive rules to apply to future situations requiring adjudication. Without clear historical precedent to guide the judiciary, legislators will be compelled to create new laws to regulate the Internet, or will need to devise analogies between new and old media. Both solutions will require an understanding of the dynamics of the Internet to do so effectively. Moreover, if we grant for a moment that political bodies are capable of acquiring the technical/theoretical understanding necessary to draft meaningful, effective legislation regulating Internet use and content, would they be able to demonstrate the political discipline to pass that legislation into law? Overly aggressive regulation, such as the ill-considered CDA, could threaten to drive commercial operations offshore. Moreover, any laws developed nationally are unlikely to have universal, long-term impact. International codes of law or international institutions to govern the Internet would be slower than the development of any national body of law, and might be quickly rendered obsolete by the rapid development of new technologies.

Second, the biggest obstacle seems to be the basic design of the Internet itself, which was created during the Cold War to allow uninterrupted routing of data traffic even in the event of a nuclear war. At that time, the Internet was composed of only a handful of computers, and if one computer failed, the data packets would automatically detour around it. The Internet is now composed of millions of "host" computers, all but a few of them privately maintained. Tens of millions of personal computer users tap into this vast ocean of data on any given day. It is as easy to retrieve data files from halfway around the world as it is to get a file from the computer on the next desk, and the data path may snake through dozens of cities and countries along the way. Trying to keep certain types of information from entering a jurisdiction would be as difficult as keeping air pollution generated in one state from entering the air space of another.

Third, we have taken for granted, until now, a world in which geographical borders were of primary importance in establishing legal sovereignty. Territorial boundaries constitute areas within which different systems of law and sets of legal rules apply. Cyberspace, however, challenges the ability of physical location to determine legal authority. First, the cost and speed of message transmission on the Internet is entirely independent of physical location. The Internet enables simultaneous transactions between large numbers of people who do not know the physical location of the other party. Moreover, the effects of the information posted on the Internet are experienced in all jurisdictions simultaneously. The question is raised, therefore, as to who has primary claim to make the law governing the content of the site (Post, 1996). Second, cyberspace radically undermines the relationship between legally significant online activity and physical location by destroying the link between geographical location and (a) the ability of governments to assert control over online behavior, (b) the legitimacy of the efforts of a local government to establish rules to be applied to applicable to global activity, and (c) the ability of physical location to give notice of which sets of rules apply. The Internet, therefore, radically subverts a system of rule-making based on borders between physical spaces, at least with respect to the claim that cyberspace should naturally be governed by territorially defined rules (Johnson & Post, 1996b).

COMMUNITY-BASED REGULATION

Clearly, there are serious problems in attempting to regulate the Internet in terms of the traditional means of centralized authority. Are we left with a choice between unregulated chaos or imperfect, inefficient regulation that may well preempt the growth of this new efficient and empowering medium? Theorists respond with an emphatic "No!" Johnson and Post and Lessig agree that cyberspace is not a place of anarchy. Where they disagree is what form the regulation of cyberspace should take.

The Internet may be capable of being governed by a decentralized form of law based on the voluntary acceptance of standards and user consensus on working code. Post and Johnson (1996b) argued that "the technical protocols" of the Internet have "created a complex adaptive system" that produces social order independent of traditional legal means. They contended that the same "decentralized decision making that created the net at a technical level," may be able to create a workable form of order at a higher level: "the realm of rules applicable to the collective social evaluation and governance of human behavior" (p. 5). There are operational and theoretical arguments to support this contention.

Internet as Operating System

First, one must consider what makes the Internet work. The Internet itself solves the "immensely difficult collective action problem: how to get large numbers of individual computer networks, running diverse operating systems, to communicate with one another for the common good" (Johnson & Post, 1996b, p. 8). The Internet accomplishes this through a voluntary set of standards regarding message transmission, routing, and reception. Consensus, not law, established TCP/IP as the necessary means to communicate electronically on the global net. Again, consensus established that HTTP was required to communicate on the World Wide Web. Communicators are free to decline to use any standard or obey any protocol. By doing so, however, they limit their ability to communicate to only those who share an alternative standard or protocol. Communicators who conform to standard usage can connect with and be heard by all other users who conform to that standard. Most Internet users are interested in accurate routing of messages. They will want to connect to the standards and protocols that most other people use. Because people look to reliable sources for their information, good data drives out the potential for a "balkanized" Internet. Therefore, although it is physically possible and currently lawful for system operators to create a mess by adapting incompatible standards and protocols, such problems have been avoided through collective self-interest (Johnson & Post, 1996b). Similarly, they argued, decentralized regulation emerges from the "complex interplay of individual decisions" made by: (a) domain name and Internet Protocol (IP) address registries, regarding what conditions to impose on possession of an online address; (b) by system operators, regarding what local rules to adopt, what filters to install, what users to allow to sign on, and with which other systems to connect; and (c) users, regarding which personal filters to install and which systems to patronize (Johnson & Post, 1996b). Johnson and Post concluded that there is reason to believe that as domain name registries impose rules as condition to access to the Internet, there will emerge consensus as to what constitutes wrongdoing on the net. Similarly, the competitive act of selecting one online venue over another by Internet users will serve to keep such regulation from becoming either too oppressive or too lax. Johnson and Post concluded: "No matter what your policy goal, acting through the filtering power of sysops and users is much more likely to produce rapid and effective results than lobbying for the enactment of some rule by a new transnational legislative body" (pp. 15-16). The Internet does not exist simply as a technologically based system existing within the confines of traditional society. The human interaction mediated by this system produces a form of social space presenting ethical characteristics similar to those residing in a more traditional social system. The dominant metaphor employed describing that social space has been that of "community" (Johnson & Post, 1996b).

Emergence of Social Norms

The study of the uses and effects of computer-mediated communication (CMC) systems has drawn the attention of scholars in a variety of disciplines. While the early emphasis of much of this research concerned technological questions, focus has shifted to the interactive nature of the medium. The modes of interaction available to the Internet user have achieved overwhelming popularity among diverse groups of people in a short period of time. O'Connell (1997) contended that this accomplishment was due, not to the technological features of computers, but to the "plasticity by which networked communications have allowed users to build their own environments" (p. 6). Scholars associate the symbolic connections constituted in CMC with the emergence of a new form of social space, the "virtual" community (Harasim, 1993; Jones, 1995; Rheingold, 1993; Van Gelder, 1991). Virtual communities are characterized as "incontrovertibly spaces in which people still meet face-to-face, but under new definitions of both 'meet' and 'face' . . . [Virtual] communities [are] passage points for collections of common beliefs and practices that unite people who are physically separated" (Stone, 1991). The space of cyberspace is predicated not only in terms of the knowledge and information transmitted, but in the common beliefs and practices of a society abstracted from physical space (Jones, 1995). Virtual community, in short, represents a coming into being of a type of public life a form of mediated human interaction that draws persons together in common interest.

Early CMC research indicates this form of networked interaction takes place in a social milieu structured by social norms and rules (Newby, 1993). At present, much of the work done in the field has studied asynchronous computer use in laboratory settings (i.e., bulletin boards [BBs] or E-mail; Mundorf, Westin, Dhaka, & Brownell, 1992; Poole, Holmes, Watson, & DeSanctos, 1993; Walther, 1994; Walther & Burgoon, 1995), or in asynchronous task-oriented use in organizational settings (Goodman & Sproull, 1990; Kiesler & Sproull, 1992; Schmitz & Fulk, 1991). Studies focusing on nonprofessional asynchronous use outside laboratory settings were few (Chesebro & Bonsall, 1989; Rice & Love, 1987). Studies of synchronous (real-time chat) computer use have been rare as well (Rheingold, 1993; Walther, 1994). Results of these early studies support the contention that, to communicate effectively, virtual communities develop social conventions or norms to determine what communication behaviors are acceptable and appropriate.

Closer examination of the following studies helps underscore the reasons why social norms emerge to regulate online behavior, and how those norms function to influence behavior. Myers' (1987) ethnography of an electronic bulletin board system (BBs) found that BBS users created social context through the development of online identities, leadership roles, and social norms. Myers reported that participants believed themselves to be engaging in an ideal social context. Social norms were established to preserve this ideal space from more negative behaviors acted out by "crashers" and "psychos"—those antisocial individuals who violate the principles of an open communication system. Different systems develop different means to enforce norms. On moderated systems, such as Prodigy, inappropriate messages can be edited or deleted entirely. In Usenet's unmoderated groups, group members themselves must develop the means to influence behavior. Baym's (1995) study of Usenet groups suggests such groups create social context, in part through the creation of social norms. The norms that develop serve to establish standards of behavior and methods of sanctioning inappropriate behavior, functioning to maintain a safe environment for free and open discussion. Fox and Roberts (2000) performed a cyber-ethnography of a virtual community operated by general practitioners (doctors). They reported the existence of a distinct social order and identified a range of strategies that functioned to establish and maintain this order in a text-based environment. Williams' (2000) examination of virtual deviance indicates that language based strategies function as forms of surveillance, regulation, and mediation in virtual community practice.

CODE AS LAW

Lessig (1996b) concurred on the futility of the application of traditional legal constraints in cyberspace: "the architecture of cyberspace compels a different kind of regulation" (p. 1403-1411). The efforts of government to control what exists on servers will "be defeated by this structural plasticity." He disagreed with the argument, however, that cyberspace should be immune from regulation. It will be regulated to the degree to that it affects real space, an impact which he predicted would be dramatic. Lessig contended that cyberlaw will evolve to the extent to which it is easier to develop this separate common law than to resolve the endless series of conflicts that cross-border existences create. Cyberlaw will emerge as the simpler means to resolve the inevitable conflicts cyberspace raises.

The Internet As It Is

The flaw, Lessig insisted, is that Johnson and Post based their arguments on a vision of the Internet as it exists now and how it existed in the past. He wrote: "I think Johnson and Post are most ambitious, one might say romantic" in constructing a vision of "a democracy in cyberspace-a world of cybercitizens deciding on the laws that apply to them" (Lessig, 1996b, p. 1407). At the present, he noted, cyberspace is a place of relative freedom, fairly crude technologies of constraint, and what controls do exist are exercised through the creation and enforcement of social norms. Lessig (1996b) admitted that

> how this [form of regulation] happens is an amazing question-how people who need never meet can establish and enforce a rich set of social norms is a question that will push theories of social norm development for years. But no one who has spent any part of her life in this space as it is just now can doubt that this is a space filled with community. (p. 1407)

Constraint of behavior in cyberspace, however, operates much in the same way as it does in real space. Laws are passed to induce people to internalize norms. Ultimately, however, it is the individual who decides whether or not to conform.

Technological Regulation

Regulation in cyberspace, Lessig argued, can and will be different. Although regulation in real space relies on the cooperation of the individuals who live under regulation, regulation in cyberspace can enforce its control directly. If one seeks to induce a certain behavior, one does not need to induce conformity through coercion. One only needs to change the code—the software that defines the terms by which people gain access to the system or use assets provided by the system. In short, Lessig (1996b) argued, law will be inscribed increasingly in code. Such code is an "efficient means of regulation," according to Lessig, in that it is obeyed because one can do nothing else. "There is no choice about whether to yield to the demand for a password; one complies if one wants to enter the system" (p. 1408). He contended that "Law as Code" is the beginning of a "perfect technology of justice, one that allows policy makers to select a social end, and then assure compliance by individuals to that end. Code as software becomes a means to that end" (p. 900).

Lessig (1996b) conceded that the current architecture of the Internet does not currently exist to support this "Code as Law" function, but as cyberspace evolves, he believes a form of virtual zoning is possible. *Zoning* is the practice of multiplying the dimensions of discrimination possible within a system, and setting access based on those dimensions. As the number of dimensions of discrimination increases, these dimensions of discrimination will make it possible to control a wide range of behavior.

CASE STUDY 1: THE "PIC-POSTING FORUM"

Pornography on the Internet is available in different formats, ranging from pictures and short animated movies, to sound files and stories. Most forms of pornography are available on the World Wide Web. The Internet also makes it possible to discuss sex, see live sex acts, and arrange sexual activities from computer screens. There are also sex-related discussions on the Internet Relay Chat (IRC) channels where users in small groups or in private channels exchange messages and files. Like the Usenet discussion groups, a small fraction of the IRC channels are dedicated to sex. There are more than 14,000 Usenet discussion groups, but only 200 are sex-related, and some of these relate to serious and legitimate discussions, such as homosexuality and sexual abuse. These Web sites and newsgroups are accessible through the Internet by any online user. Although many sites are free to access, an increasing number of Web sites, such as those operated by Playboy or Hustler, require proof of age and payment by credit card to access their materials.

The "Pic-Posting Forum" was a Web site dedicated to the exploration, identification, sharing, and discussion of cyberporn. It was the visually oriented component of a broader range of adult-oriented web sites, referred to as "shacklets," that comprise "Bianca's Smut Shack," one of many virtual community forums housed on the Web domain Bianca.com. Message postings to this site were observed daily for 8 months from July 1997 until its precipitous closing by its systems operator in February 1998. On a typical day, 200 to 300 postings were made to the forum by regular members. An individual would post a link to a picture and write a commentary as to why they found that particular image worthy of note. The nature and range of the images and reasons provided for posting messages were limitless. Participants who viewed the images could then respond with their own comments and discussions would ensue. Observers could access all images posted and commentaries provided by poster and respondents.

Because this study focused on the establishment and maintenance of the social boundaries of virtual communities, messages were identified, examined, and downloaded that served to enunciate or uphold the established social norms of the forum, and conversely, those message postings that violated the group norms. Violations were often identified by the manner, tone, and number of responses made by forum participants. Some 240 of these forum message postings were downloaded and analyzed. Space considerations preclude a detailed exposition of the analysis in this chapter, but a brief description of the communicative practices of forum participants sheds light on the efficacy of community self-regulation versus code-based regulation (Flynn, 2001).

Forum Interaction

Analysis indicates that the primary purpose of the participation in the forum is related to the finding and sharing of cyberporn. Other purposes emerge from the examination of the group's interaction. An important finding was that this forum, and others like it, provided participants the sole means to discuss sexuality with other like-minded individuals. Pictures evoking particular fantasies, fetishes, and proclivities provided the grist for discussions that participants repeatedly indicated they could not share in real space due to social norms and superficial sexual conformity. Participants indicated that the collaborative and discussive elements of forum participation enhanced their interest in and understanding of sexual issues. Individuals also vied to outdo others in terms of technical ability and creative uses of the forum technical capabilities. For example, one trend saw individuals crafting stories that would be illustrated by multiple links to images on the Web.

Collaboration also involved sharing individual perspectives on a range of other issues toward which participants were concerned as well. Discussion concerning the growth of and future direction of the Internet were common, particularly as this related to concerns about governmental regulation and censorship. Discussions of and instruction regarding the development of technical skills were prominent as well. Many individuals learned to write hypertext markup language (HTML) code through online instruction at the forum, shifting their perspectives from observer to active participants by posting links to pictures. Status was established and maintained through technical expertise and through their knowledge of where to find requested material. Through the exchange of personal talk over time, friendships were established and maintained. People would watch for postings by their friends and would exchange greetings, often commenting on any noticeable absence (Flynn, 2001).

Forum Rules and Social Norms

Observation of messages posted by regular participants leads to these conclusions in regards to the emergent social norms of the Forum: (a) The primary purpose was the finding and sharing of different forms of cyberporn, with an emphasis on sharing. Visitors seeking to buy, sell, or trade images were told repeatedly: "we share here." (b) Information on the Internet, cyberporn in particular, should be free. Participants expressed increasing concern over the commercialization of the Internet and disdain for commercial pornographic Web sites. (c) Technology is power, therefore, development of technical skills and knowledge of the Internet were perceived to give participants greater influence over other users of the Internet. (d) Interest in sexually graphic materials were considered part of a healthy interest in human sexuality. Participants were nonjudgmental of other's sexual interests as expressed in picture postings, requests, and discussions. The only observable exception to this tolerance regarded child pornography, which was perceived to be outside the realm of acceptable sexual interest.

Regular participants employed an informal set of ethical and principles and cultural norms that acted to constrain the actions of the visitors to the site. Regulars sought first to instruct those who violated the norms of the group. Severe violations would be met with messages seeking to shame them into altering their behavior, or into leaving the site. Violations of forum norms prompted other members of the Forum to take retaliatory action. Some of these violations ranged from being merely impolite to more antisocial behavior, such as the misappropriation of a regular member's pseudonym, to multiple postings, to continuous flames. Responses to these behaviors ranged from sternly worded retorts to the use of flames as well. Regular participants did report and comment on the precipitous decline in the civility of discourse in the weeks preceding the closing of the Forum. Analysis reveals, however, that the Forum was faced with two persisting problems that violated the norms of the group: spam and child pornography.

"Spam"

Spam stands for Spontaneously Produced Advertising Message. Spam usually refers to unsolicited bulk commercial e-mail, but has taken on a much broader meaning and usage. At the "Pic-Posting Forum," spam takes the form of links posted by alleged participants to commercial pornographic sites. Advertisers pay site operators to post ads and banners on their Web sites. Payment is based on the amount of traffic a site operator can generate. Therefore, site operators would post links to their Web sites, not to particular images, in order to boost revenue. Such activity was perceived to be a severe violation of the norms of the Forum. All regular participants saw themselves as the "spam police," and would quickly identify and label any such posts. One or two respondents labeling a post spam would be sufficient to keep others from clicking on the posted link, and elicit howls of protest from the individual who had posted the message.

Child Pornography

As bothersome as persistent spamming was to Forum regulars, the issue of child pornography presented a much more serious threat to the functioning of the Forum, both legally and morally. Although the site was dedicated to pornography, Forum rules and emergent social norms clearly established the message that child pornography was not tolerated at the site. As with spam, regular members kept a sharp look out for links posted to sites that apparently contained these materials, and would alert system operators, who would delete the posting. Message postings requesting this sort of material would be met with flames. Despite the efforts of regulars and system operators at the "Pic-Posting Forum," early in the Winter of 1998, members expressed increasing concern that pedophiles were exploiting the Forum. Apparent persistent interest in child pornography expressed by visitors to the forum appears to have played a central role in the demise of this virtual community.

On February 23, members and visitors to the "Pic-Posting Forum" found a message posted by the sites' systems operator: "Closed. Sorry it's just not fun anymore." The operator closed the Forum for these reasons:

> I have no desire to watch the forum degenerate any farther. Ever since the last of November the spam, flames and abusive behavior has been on a steady increase. It s time to quit when I have to remove 10%-30% of the posts 2 or 3 times a day. I want The PIC Posting Forum to be remembered as a fun place. I dont want to finally call it quits when all the posters that are left are the abusive ones. I am no longer having any fun with it. Fun was the only thing I wanted from the forum and I am burned out from removing posts. I dreaded to check the forum. It s time for me to explore the net again.
>
> Spammers are making money off of mine and your efforts. Too many people wanting child porn. These people need help. I tried to remove every one of their posts. Good riddance. Some webmasters complained to me that they were experiencing bandwidth theft. And that I was making money! Never once did I claim I owned any images posted. And I sure never made any money.
>
> I will be contacting other PIC forums to see if they want a link posted here. This will give you a place to go to. I would never post a link without asking them first because Im sure they don't want the abusive posters. I hope the other 80% of you find a good home!
>
> Thanks to all the posters. Especially the ones who came back day after day even though they got flamed or impersonated. It killed me to remove the forum.
>
> You may find The PIC Posting Forum on another server one day. But a login will be required. Any abuse and you loose your login.

Analysis

In examining the failure of community self-regulation in this instance, it is necessary to consider an antecedent question: What mechanisms exist by which such a behavioral influence/control/sanction could be implemented? Who can make and enforce the rules in cyberspace, whatever the substantive content of those rules might be? Ellickson's (1991) framework for behavioral controls is a useful starting point for a discussion of the various forces governing individual behavior in electronic networks. Ellickson identified five controllers that can provide substantive rules governing an individual's behavior:

1. The actor him or herself.
2. Other individuals being acted upon.
3. Nonhierarchically organized social forces.
4. Hierarchically organized nongovernmental organizations.
5. Governments (i.e., hierarchical organizations widely regarded as having the legitimate authority to employ coercive force within its geographically defined jurisdiction).

Community self-regulation can be said to occur at the first three levels, consisting in this case study of the rules and governing mechanisms created by the site operators and the community members. Self-regulation begins with individual self-restraint from which emerges a set of shared and observed ethical norms. It does require, however, a variety of enforcement mechanisms to deal with visitors who do share these norms or refuse to exercise self-restraint. The primary enforcement means employed at the "Pic-Posting Forum" were language-based, in short, attempts to cajole, persuade, shame, and so on. Failure of these efforts were to be addressed by the system operator. As participation in the site grew, fewer participants shared the vision and norms of the original members who built the site. Increasingly, participants refused to exercise self-restraint and ignored peer pressure. As problems mounted at the site, the operator became overwhelmed in his or her efforts to regulate material and pulled the plug.

In this case study, we witnessed the failure of a virtual community to engage in effective self-regulation through the development and communication of forum rules, social norms, and enforcement mechanisms. Support is given to the position that regulation will rely increasingly on technological forms (i.e., the use of passwords and logins to control access to forums). The question remains, however, whether community-based law is a viable means of regulating online behavior. The failure of this form of behavioral constraint in this case does not signal its failure in all instances.

CASE STUDY 2: eBAY

Since the 1980s, there has been a dramatic change in the nature of the international economy. Longstanding multinational corporations are being challenged by emerging firms. New companies are being created by entrepreneurs or being spun out of existing companies, providing Internet-based services and products to customers, new opportunities to managers and investors, and new vitality to the national economy. The Internet has had a significant impact on the conduct of business; standard practices have undergone major transformations to capitalize on it commercialization. Firms and entrepreneurs are using the Internet to offer unique services, reach new markets, increase customer convenience, and improve transaction efficiency. Particularly, the emergence and recognition of the significance of virtual communities is affecting the traditional approaches for designing and producing products and services, pricing advertising, and managing the distribution to end users (Foreman, 1999; Gray, 1999; Hawkins, Mansell, & Skinmueller, 1999; & Sanchez, 2000).

Virtual e-commerce communities have matured to a level that self-regulation is a commonly accepted practice (Etzioni, 2000; Munir, 2000). The concept of feedback ratings maintained by a third party, such as those employed in eBay online auctions, have developed as a reliable indicator of entrepreneurial credibility in a business environment that can often be hostile or even predatory. The models developed by these online organizations are having an impact not only on their own business constructs, but on other Internet e-commerce and traditional forms of business transactions.

Auctions on eBay

Virtual communities are filled with members who have no identity beyond a screen name. These faceless Web users have become common within chatrooms, BBs, and trading communities. Members of each of these groups interact, conduct business, and exchange goods and services from behind a digital facade. However for most participants, a user ID alone is not enough information to base a financial transaction of any significance. Do members really want to send a check for $500 to someone with the user ID "Clown Killer"? Perhaps if there is sufficient documentation to validate the credibility and trustworthiness of the user, forwarding payments for unseen goods to an unknown person is a safe process for conducting e-commerce.

The Internet company eBay provides a forum for Internet auctions for a variety of goods from cars to collectibles. Begun on Labor Day 1995, eBay has become the world's largest personal online trading community

(About-eBay, 2000). On any given day, more than 4 million items are up for sale in this interactive auction environment. Registered users can post items for sale or bid on items currently posted. Each item listed is given a specific time limit by the seller (3, 5, 7, or 10 days) for the auction to take place. During this time, registered users can bid on posted items. Users indicated their maximum bid, and eBay executes the bids through a proxy process. In proxy bidding, the host computer completes the incremental raises of the bid to indicated maximum as other competing bids are posted. When the time limit expires, the user with the highest bid is declared the winner. eBay does not get involved directly in the transaction other than to provide the seller and winning bidder an E-mail detailing the closing information along with E-mail addresses of the other party. The buyer and seller are responsible for contacting each other and completing the transaction. eBay charges a fee to the seller for listing the item and collects an additional fee based on the final selling price.

Feedback Ratings as Behavioral Constraint

The measurement of a user's credibility is done through feedback ratings. On the completion of a transaction, buyer and seller can exchange comments that are publicly posted for review. These comments are prefaced by one of three feedback indications: positive, neutral, or negative. By leaving a user positive feedback, their rating incremented by 1 point. By leaving a user a negative feedback, their rating will be decreased by 1 point. Neutral feedback is posted as part of a feedback history but has no impact on a user's numerical rating.

In the first few years, any registered user could leave any type of feedback for any other registered user. eBay was forced to review these policies after several abusive strategies were developed by unscrupulous users. For instance, users could leave negative feedback for a user with whom they had never conducted a transaction. If a user had a competitor who they wanted to discredit, they could leave negative feedback for that person. A poster might risk retaliatory negative feedback, however, this risk could be eliminated by creating multiple "dummy" accounts. Using these dummy accounts, negative feedback could then "bomb" a person's account. eBay later revised this system to only permit negative feedback that was tied directly to a transaction. To post negative feedback, a registered user would need to submit the unique transaction number that is given to each auction along with their registered ID. The system checked that both parties were involved with the transaction before the posting of negative feedback was permitted (eBay: The Feedback Forum, 2000). Users also found ways to manipulate the system by using secondary user IDs to artificially raise the level of their own feedback. Because positive feedback could be posted without a transaction number, users could inflate their own rating or collaborate with friends to boost their positive numbers. eBay has more recently changed its policy to require a transaction number for any feedback postings.

Other reported abuses of feedback rating include feedback extortion. A user might bid on an item and be the highest bidder, but the item may have a reserve. If a reserve is included at the time of the posting, the seller is not required to sell the item. However, the bidder might threaten to leave negative feedback if the user doesn't lower the reserve or sell the item at the bid price. Although this might seem like an empty threat, users may take years to build spotless ratings. Users building rating in the hundreds or thousands without a single negative feedback are not uncommon. Does that seller want to risk losing perfect rating that took years to amass? eBay has a strict policy that it will only remove Feedback if there is an exceptional circumstance (eBay—Leave Feedback, 2000). These circumstances include court orders, libelous or slanderous material, offensive language, or few other narrowly defined categories (eBay Help, 2000). A warning screen before the final placement of negative feedback warns the users that these comments cannot be retracted. eBay also suggests contacting the second party by telephone and provide an avenue to receive additional information about a user.

Other offenses noted by eBay personnel include feedback solicitation. This includes offering to sell feedback, trade feedback undeservedly, or buy feedback (eBay Safe Harbor, 2000a). The recent implementation requiring all feedback to be related to transactions will make this type of activity much more difficult to execute. Disciplinary actions taken by the organization range from a formal warning, up to indefinite suspension of a user's account. Normally, the first two offenses are provided warnings. The third offense results in a 30-day suspension, and a fourth offense results in permanent removal (eBay Safe Harbor, 2000a).

eBay is not immune from "psychos" or "crashers" despite an evolving regulation mechanism. Accounts can be created and manipulated with only minimal information and no verification. An account can be created and used to place winning bids on numerous items without intending to complete the transactions. Once the bidding closes on these items, negative feedback can be left to taint the ratings of credible sellers. The process to reverse this malicious behavior is difficult to initiate and time consuming to document.

Analysis

The evolution of eBay policy illustrates the maturation of a virtual community that initially relied on a community-based regulation model. Early adopters were able to provide feedback freely on other users in an attempt to bolster their credibility or to warn about unscrupulous actions. As the community grew, so did the associated problems and dysfunctional behaviors. Members' disruptive behavior forced eBay to implement increasing levels of restriction through policy changes that were implemented by additional software code. The pure community-based model threatened to alienate legitimate customers. A model reflecting Lessig's concept of virtual zoning was implemented, allowing different users to participate at different levels (i.e., lurking, bidding, providing feedback). Increased forms of behavioral controls based in code will undoubtedly be on the horizon for eBay users as the company continues to thwart the efforts of "crashers" and "psychos."

IMPLICATIONS

As the world becomes increasingly "wired," and millions more people use the Internet, governments, businesses, and system operators will be asking how to establish and enforce rules of conduct to facilitate reliable communications, and identify and punish online activity, which violate social norms. Although some of these issues reflect questions of technology, others raise fundamental ethical questions, which might be best addressed by looking to a primary source of ethics as well as law: the values and dynamics of community. In this case study, we witness the particular success of a virtual community that has evolved from a self-regulated environment to a hybrid approach of self-regulation with necessary constraints of code added to insure credibility and the viability of the economic community. This study, therefore, supports a position that community-based self-regulation in its purest form may not be a viable means of regulating online behavior without the addition of some technological or coding restraints.

The Internet operates within a global environment where regulations developed within one country may not conform to the legal principles of another. The Internet raises questions of the uniformity of law, reciprocity of enforcement, and carries the potential for generating numerous international conflicts of law. The current situation presents society with a seldom-experienced opportunity to formulate laws and policy that will be responsive to the needs of Internet users, instead of forcing the medium to conform to traditional forms of regulation. Virtual e-commerce communities have matured beyond the level of self-regulation as a commonly accepted practice. The concept of feedback rating maintained by a third party, such as those employed in eBay online auctions, have developed as reliable indicator of entrepreneurial credibility when properly regulated and maintained. The models developed by these online organizations will have an impact not only on Internet e-commerce, but on other forms of human interaction as well. The evolutionary process that we have witnessed may only be in its infancy, and the virtual community models will continue to grow in diversity, complexity, and efficiency.

REFERENCES

About-eBay: Company Overview. (2000).

Baym, N. (1995). The emergence of community in computer-mediated communication. In S. Jones (Ed.), *CyberSociety: Computer-mediated-communication and community* (pp. 138-161). Thousand Oaks, CA: Sage.

Brand, S. (1988). *The media lab: Inventing the future at M.I.T.* New York: Penguin Books.

Chesebro, J., & Bonsall, D. (1989). *Computer-mediated communication human relationships in a computerized world.* Tuscaloosa: University of Alabama Press.

eBay: The Feedback Forum. (2000, April). <http://pages.ebay.com/services/forum /feedback.html>

eBay Help: Community Standards: Polices and Conduct. (2000, April 25). <http://pages.ebay.com/help/community/fbremove.html>

eBay—Leave Feedback about and eBay User. (2000, April 25). <http://pages.ebay. com/services/forum/feedback-old.html>

eBay: Safe Harbor. (2000a, April 25) <http://pages.ebay.com/help/community /npb.html>

eBay Sage Harbor: Investigations. (2000b, April 25) <http://pages.ebay.com/help/ community/investigates.html>.

Ellickson, R. (1991). *Order without law: How neighbors settle disputes.* Boston, MA: Harvard University Press.

Etzioni, A. (2000, February 10). E-Communities build new ties, but ties that bind. *The New York Times*, p. G7.

Flynn, T.R. (2001, July). *Ethics, law and technology: A case study in computer-mediated communication.* In International Symposium on Technology and Society, Sponsored by The IEEE Society on Social Implications of Technology (SSIT) & IEEE Computer Society, Los Alamitos, CA.

Foreman, S. K. (1999, Fall). Marketing organizations and virtual communities. *Manager Update*, 11-21.

Fox, N., & Roberts, C. (1999). GP's in cyberspace: The sociology of a "virtual community." *The Sociological Review, 47*, 643-671.

Goodman, P., & Sproull, L. (1990). *Technology and organizations.* San Francisco, CA: Jossey-Bass.

Gray, A. (1999). Threats and opportunities. *Information World Review, 149*, 22-24.

Harasim, L. (1993). Global networks: An introduction. In L. Harasim (Ed.), *Global networks: Computers and international communication.* Cambridge, MA: MIT Press.

Hawkins, R., Mansell, R., & Steinmueller, E. (1999). Toward digital intermediation in the information society. *Journal of Economic Issues, 33*, 383-392.

Hayek, F. A. (1973). *Law, legislation and liberty, Vol. I: Rules and order.* Chicago: University of Chicago Press.

Johnson, D., & Post, D. (1996a). And how shall the net be governed: A meditation on the relative virtues of decentralized, emergent law. *Internet Document*, pp. 1-16.

Johnson, D., & Post, D. (1996b, May). Law and borders—The rise of law in cyberspace. *Stanford Law Review*, pp. 1-20.

Jones, S. (1995). Understanding community in the information age. In S. Jones, (Ed.), *Cybersociety: Computer-mediated communication and community* (pp. 10-35). Thousand Oaks, CA: Sage.

Kiesler, S., & Sproull, L. (1992). Group decision making and communication technology. *Organizational Behavior and Human Decision Processes, 52*, 96-123.

Lessig, L. (1996 a). Reading the Constitution in cyberspace. *Emory Law Journal, 45*, 869-910.

Lessig, L. (1996b). The zones of cyberspace. *Stanford Law Review, 48*, 1403-1411.

Lessig, L. (2001). *The future of ideas: The fate of the commons in a connected world.* New York: Random House.

Mundorf, N., Westin, S., Dholakia, N., & Brownell, W. (1992). Reevaluating gender differences in new communication technologies. *Communication Research Reports, 45*, 869-910.

Munir, K. (2000). Net gain: Expanding markets through virtual communities. *Technology Analysis & Strategic Management, 12*, 303-305.

Myers, D. (1987). Anonymity is part of the magic: Individual manipulation of computer-mediated communication contexts. *Qualitative Sociology, 10*(3), 257-266.

Newby, G. (1993). The maturation of norms for computer-mediated communication. *Internet Research, 3*, 30.

O'Connell, B. (1997). Law, ethics and the internet: Finding solid ground in virtual space. *The Australian Computer Journal, 9*(1), 6-11.

Poole, M., Holmes, M., Watson, R., & DeSanctus, G. (1993). Group decisions support systems and group communication: A comparison of decision making in computer-supported and non-supported groups. *Communication Research, 20*, 176-213.

Post, D. (1996, October). How shall the net be governed? *Plugging In*, 1-3.

Post, D. (1997, Fall). Governing cyberspace. *Wayne Law Review*, 1-11.

Rheingold, H. (1993). A slice of life in my virtual community. In L. Harasim (Ed.), *Global networks: Computers and international communication.* Cambridge, MA: MIT Press.

Rice, R., & Love, G. (1987). Electronic emotion: Socioemotional content in a computer-mediated communication network. *Communication Research, 14*(1), 85-108.

Sanchez, S. (2000). E-commerce profile: Farmbid.com: Creating a one-stop shop. *Agri Marketing, 38*, 70.

Schmitz, J., & Fulk, J. (1991). Organizational colleagues, media richness, and electronic mail. *Communication Research, 18*, 487-523.

Stone, A. (1991). Will the real body please stand up? Boundary stories about virtual cultures. In M. Benedikt (Ed.), *Cyberspace* (pp. 181-118). Cambridge, MA: MIT Press.

Van Gelder, L. (1991). The strange case of the electronic lover. In C. Dunlop & R. Kling (Eds.), *Computerization and controversy: Value conflicts and social choices.* New York: Academic Press.

Walther, J. (1994). Anticipated ongoing interaction versus channel effects on relational communication in computer-mediated interaction. *Human Communication Research, 20,* 473-501.

Walther, J., & Burgoon, J. (1992). Relational communication in computer-mediated interaction. *Human Communication Research, 19,* 50-88.

Williams, M. (2000, March). Virtually criminal: Discourse, deviance and anxiety within virtual communities. *International Review of Law, Computers, and Technology, 14,* 95-102.

Author Index

A

Abbate, U., 224, *237*
Abrams, F., 99(*n*18), *110*
Aftab, P., 292(*n*9), 296, *316*
Albiniak, P., 29, *37*
Alexander, L., 98(*n*4), *108*
American Civil Liberties Union, 144, *165*
American Library Association, 77, *80*
Anderman, J., 188, *198*
Ang, P.H., 11, *20*
Anschütz, D., 240, *255*
Aragón, A.R., 12, 13, *20*
Ashcroft, J., 322, *342*

B

Band, J., 249, *255*
Barnes, S.B., 260, *281*
Bastian, J., 153, *166*
Baym, N., 351, *362*
Beach, S., 117, *140*
Becker, L., 45, *61*
Bendotoff, M.A., 231, *237*
Berman, J., 53, *61*, 101, *112*
Berners-Lee, T., 225, *237*
Bertelsmann Foundation, 143, *166*
Bertot, J., 153, *166*
BeVier, L., 98(*n*8), *108*
Blackman, C., 12, *20*
Blankenship, J., 40, *61*
Blomley, N.K., 9(*n*7), *20*

Bloomberg News, 143, *166*
Blum, V., 304(*n*26), 315, *316*
Boas, T. C., 11, *21*
Boehm, S.B., 249, *255*
Bonsall, D., 350, *362*
Borrus, A., 129, *139*
Bosmajian, H., 40, *61*
Brand, S., 346, *362*
Brandriss, I., 177, 190, *198*
Branscomb, A.W., 255, *256*
Bray, H., 243, *256*
Braybrooke, D., 25, *37*
Brickley, P., 133, *139*
Brownell, W., 350, *363*
Buono, F.M., 252, *257*
Burgoon, J., 350, *364*
Butler, C., 249, 250, 253, *256*

C

Cailliau, A., 225, *237*
Calvert, C., 198, *198*
Cannon, R., 252, *256*
Cantril, A.H., 311(*n*1), *316*
Cantril, S.D., 311(*n*1), *316*
Carlson, D.K., 129, *139*
Carnevale, D., 181, *199*
Caterinicchia, D., 307, *316*
Charlesworth, A.J., 291, *316*
Chesebro, J., 350, *362*
Clarke, C.T., 324(*n*1), 338, *342*

Case Index

Subject Index

Printed in the United States
25698LVS00002BB/1-3